Chef's Manual of
Kitchen Management

Chef's Manual of

Kitchen Management

John Fuller

B. T. BATSFORD LTD   LONDON

© John Fuller 1962

First Published 1962

MADE AND PRINTED IN GREAT BRITAIN BY
WILLIAM CLOWES AND SONS, LIMITED, LONDON AND BECCLES
FOR THE PUBLISHERS
B. T. BATSFORD LTD
4 FITZHARDINGE STREET, PORTMAN SQUARE, LONDON W.I

To my wife
Pamela Honor Fuller

Preface

Many books on food and cookery have appeared in recent years and are likely to continue to do so. Fewer contributions seem to have been made in the way of books about the general operation of a professional kitchen.

This manual is an attempt both to assemble background information about the evolution of modern kitchen organisation through the partie system and also to provide information for the chef and caterer about the many aspects of kitchen work which are an integral part, together with cookery, in producing meals.

The hotel and catering industry comprises so many widely differing components that it is not always easy to relate, for example, the activities of a school meals kitchen with those of a high-class commercial restaurant or what goes on in a hospital catering service with the procedure in a hotel kitchen.

The various committees set up under the old Catering Trades Education Committee, its successor the National Council for Hotel and Catering Education and today the Education Committee of the Hotel and Catering Institute have, however, unfailingly been assured by representatives from all sections of the hotel and catering industry that an initial training to the highest culinary standards involving at least some acquaintanceship with French cuisine and the partie system is desirable.

The cookery and catering examinations of the City and Guilds of London Institute reflect this attitude and their examination qualifications are recognised in the different sections of catering including welfare catering like schools, hospitals and catering for industry as well as by hotels, restaurants and other catering establishments.

It was thus considered essential to base this manual on the highest common denominator, as it were, of kitchen organisation and practice; for it is assumed that it is far easier to adapt downwards and to simplify the application of the partie system than to attempt to organise and practise good kitchen procedures in ignorance of their origins and traditions.

The manual is intended to furnish information for the experienced and practising chef and caterer and particularly the entrant to the industry. It is hoped that the book will meet the requirements of cookery apprentices or those who are undergoing full or part-time courses of instruction in hotel schools and the hotel and catering departments of technical institutions up and down the country. For this reason an attempt has been made to cover the requirements of the examinations in cookery and catering of the City and Guilds of London Institute in regard to facets of kitchen practice and catering other than actual cookery and also of relevant parts of the National Diploma in Hotel Keeping and Catering and the examination for Associate Membership of the Hotel and Catering Institute.

JOHN FULLER

Glasgow,
1961

Contents

Contents xi

List of Tables

List of Diagrams

Acknowledgment

Because this manual ranges over many aspects of kitchen practice and organisation, advice and assistance has been sought from many people. I gratefully acknowledge help so readily given and in particular indebtedness to the following individuals and organisations who have assisted especially with the chapters indicated.

For advice and assistance with the chapters on 'Kitchen Layout and Facilities' and 'Equipment and Fuel in the Kitchen Plan':

Mr R. W. Coombes, F.H.C.I.; Mr J. C. Morris, Managing Director, Messrs Benham & Sons Ltd; The Catering Equipment Department, the Falkirk Iron Co. Ltd (Allied Ironfounders Ltd), and in particular their Consultant Dietician, Miss M. E. Furnivall; The British Colour Council; The Electrical Development Association, and in particular to Mr E. M. Ackery, Senior Technical Adviser (permission to quote from the E.D.A. Handbook is also acknowledged with gratitude); The South of Scotland Electricity Board; The Gas Council, for general assistance and for permission to make use of their Catering Handbook; The North Thames Gas Board, and in particular to Mr A. S. Williams, Senior Catering Representative; Mr R. H. Rowse, Technical Director, Smith and Welstead Ltd.

Also to Mr S. O. J. Willer, F.H.C.I., for illustrating the chapters on 'The Cookery Craftsman's Tools' and 'Batterie de Cuisine', and for substantial assistance in preparing the text for that section of the book; to Mr R. Kotas, B.Com., A.C.I.S., for comments on 'Kitchen Records and Control'; to the National Joint Apprenticeship Council of the Hotel and Catering Industry for permission to make use of information on apprenticeship training; and to Mrs A. Fisher for her patient work in deciphering rough drafts and in preparing the MS.

I am grateful for the help of my colleagues and staff of the Scottish Hotel School and in particular to Mr J. Walker Graham, B.Com., Dip. Com., for advice on the chapter on 'Kitchen Management and Foremanship'; Mrs C. G. Kent, B.Sc.(Nut.), for assistance in the chapters on 'Hygiene for the Kitchen' and 'Food Values in Cooking and

Menu-Making'; and to Mr J. S. McKee for checking and test weighing meat cuts in the 'Buying' chapter.

In expressing gratitude for the help of the foregoing, I would stress that the responsibility for any errors or omissions is mine alone and that those whose advice and aid I have sought do not necessarily concur with conclusions reached by me.

Finally, I wish to acknowledge the encouragement and help of my wife who has unsparingly given major assistance in research, in assembling information and in generally collaborating in compiling this manual.

I Chefs and the development of professional cookery

Chefs, although they are artistic, pride themselves on being essentially practical people. They tend, therefore, to place manipulative skills and culinary techniques higher on the list of desirable acquisites for the kitchen craftsman than book learning or theory. There may be some chefs, therefore, who would question the desirability of concerning themselves with any historical information about the evolution of their craft or the great figures in it. Yet if the great figures of kitchen history are considered to set an example, it is noteworthy that the most eminent chefs of the Western world in the past have not only left evidence of their practical abilities but even stronger evidence of their knowledge of the evolution and traditions of their calling.

The great men of the kitchen were not boorish manual workers who had somehow acquired superlative skills, they were men of sensibility who quickly realised that the understanding of the history of their trade and the performance of their predecessors could give them special understanding of, and sympathy for, their work. This helped awaken them into full consciousness of their culinary heritage. Such knowledge and such consciousness was not something merely to give a veneer of kitchen culture but the development of mood, instinct and the desire to take part in and urge forward the whole process of a fascinating and artistic craft.

Today it is significant that leaders of the hotel world and of the professional cuisine are more concerned than ever before that the young craftsman should not merely learn vocational skills and accompanying cookery theory but should also interest himself in the general background of his craft. The examples of the master chefs of the past, the way in which the classical, culinary repertoire has been built up, the development of kitchen tools and equipment are all matters to which the older chef is urged to direct the attention of the apprentice. A place has been found in the syllabuses in professional cookery and catering of major examining bodies, such as the City and Guilds of London Institute, to refer to this background knowledge. This they do because of the conviction that awareness of the past can enormously help in achieving an intelligent and adventurous approach into the future.

Alien influences

In a catalogue of *Antiquities, manuscripts, books and engravings treating of cookery, eating and drinking* which was published just before the Second World War when the book and cookery ephemera collection of Robert Viel, the famous Paris restaurateur, was for sale, were listed Babylonian tablets of baked clay. These tablets were inscribed in cuneiform characters listing foodstuffs and relating to catering. They dated from 2500 B.C. and from them and through the centuries can be traced the steady growth of the art of cookery. This vast subject reflecting, and no doubt affecting, civilisations and empires as they flowered and faded is beyond the scope of this present manual. The vast literature which has both recorded and moulded cookery trends does, however, tend to support the belief that just as the cooking of food may be regarded as one of the first, if not the first, distinctions civilised man has to distinguish himself from the animal, so is the art of the table a continuing sign and adornment of the richness and perfection of society. In this work the full story of the growth of cookery cannot be followed through Greek and Roman times. Only a fleeting thought can be spared for the influence of Eastern and exotic kingdoms on Western dishes through the ages; yet it must be apparent to the most casual student that the craft of cookery in any country (however bleak its culinary inheritance may seem) is one which has kinship with that of other folk and other regions. Cookery in Britain, as in the rest of the Western world, has borrowed and lent and will continue to borrow and lend from the kitchen lore of other lands.

Norman Conquest

Just as 1066 remains one of the few dates immovably fixed in the mind of every British schoolboy so the significance of the Norman Conquest becomes apparent to the student of cookery as being the first but by no means the last mark of French influence on our table. From that time onward the blunt Anglo-Saxon approach to food came under the influence of Gallic civilisation. It is significant that whilst some of the Anglo-Saxon words for animals remained attached to the cheaper and coarser parts of meat like ox tail and pigs' feet, that more delicate expressions of French derivation such as veal (from veau), beef (from bœuf) and pork (from porc) masked, for table purposes, the brasher designations: calf, ox and pig.

In the little leather-bound volumes of the Middle Ages ragouts and fricassés, blancmanges and other French processes which followed in the train of William the Conqueror began to give to cookery in this country some of the finer dishes that had already been developed on the Continent. These more refined plats exploited to the full by the French had, nevertheless, been born in turn through other influences in which, for example, the achievements of Italian kitchen craftsmen had their part.

The history of our islands remains interwoven with that of France from the time of the Norman Conquest through to the Edwardian days of the Entente Cordiale and to the present time. The interweaving of our histories has not always been evidence of peaceful co-existence; but even during the years when France was our traditional enemy, discriminating diners in the United Kingdom have enjoyed her wine and extolled her cooks, exploiting both of them at our island tables.

Despite, in more recent times, a somewhat melancholy reputation for cookery the British, particularly in the great days of the Empire, achieved distinction as patrons of food and as organisers of their own comfort. Long before the days of hotels as they exist today, the English country house set high standards of gentle living. By Victorian times, English gentlemen who sought social pleasures and relaxation outside their own houses had created the club, and this institution flourished not only in London but in other capitals of Europe. In the distinctively British club the great French master cooks of modern times came out of the relative obscurity of private houses to become public figures of note and distinction. Three Frenchmen in the long years of Victoria's reign were the first to become culinary celebrities on a national scale so far as this country was concerned. Louis Eustace Ude of the St James's Club, Alexis Soyer at the Reform and Francatelli at Crockford's constitute a triumvirate of names which heralded a period of distinction of professional cookery in London and which helped to usher in the hotel era—an era whose beginnings were almost exactly matched by the days of Queen Victoria's heir as the worldly Prince of Wales and later as the monarch.

Carême and Regency cookery

The fame of these three chefs and their contemporaries and successors was, however, largely made possible by their fellow-countryman, Antonin Carême, who, though he worked only a short time in England, was chef to the Prince Regent and profoundly affected professional cookery in Britain as he did in France and the rest of the Continent where high society gathered.

Carême, who died in 1833 in his fiftieth year, had in a relatively short life firmly established his place in culinary history as the great fore-runner of modern professional cookery in the French manner.

Humbly born as the sixteenth child of a workman, Carême had few advantages as a child. At about ten years of age he left an impoverished household and found work as a kitchen boy and general factotum in a lowly catering establishment in Montparnasse. After half a dozen years of drudgery in a period when France was undergoing the upheaval of the Reign of Terror and its consequences, young Carême managed to secure employment as an apprentice to Bailly, fashionable pâtissier in the more select environment of the Right Bank. In Bailly the young chef-to-be had a kind and encouraging master. During the days of his apprenticeship, the young Carême taught himself to read and write and he also applied himself to learning something of the elements of architecture. This latter interest is of special significance for the work of the pâtissier, at the time Carême was learning it, was very much a monumental art. Socles and pediments, figures and columns were forged and fashioned in the kitchens of those times with the dedication to art of a sculptor, of a monumental mason, of a master builder. It is said that Carême's father was a wandering stonemason and the boy certainly learned to deal with food as if with building materials; and gum and pastillage came to his hand for reinforcement to give an almost stone-like solidity to the works of art of otherwise fleeting permanence that he learned to erect.

The birth pangs of the French Revolution and the troubled times that followed it can hardly have been ideal years for the development of cookery and the production of chefs, but such an era must have thrown into sharper silhouette the capabilities and the ambitions of young Carême as he emerged from his apprenticeship. By 1803 he had secured employment as chef pâtissier to Talleyrand and under Talleyrand's chef, Boucher, he rounded off his knowledge of other sections of kitchen work to become the leading chef de cuisine of his time. As France's Foreign Minister the Prince de Talleyrand gave splendid hospitality and consequently offered enormous scope for the efforts of his master chef. The Minister was himself a great gastronome and indeed described himself as 'the sanctuary of modern cookery'.

In the year before the Battle of Waterloo, Carême took charge of the kitchens of Czar Alexander on the occasion of the Russian monarch's visit to France but resisted persuasion to return with him to take charge of his cooking in St Petersburg. Some two years later, however, despite his deep attachment to Paris, Carême did succumb to an invitation to go to England as maître chef to the Prince Regent.

At Carlton House, the Prince Regent's London residence, and at Brighton which the Prince made fashionable, Carême not only enhanced his own reputation but began to set the standards for fine cooking which has given inspiration, impetus and drive to subsequent generations of cooks in this country. The worldly Prince Regent was not slow to appreciate Carême's qualities and one anecdote which has survived and is often repeated refers to an occasion when the Prince complained that the great chef's dishes were so appetising that he could not help over-eating. Carême's supreme confidence and facility for the mot juste is typified by his quiet reply: 'Sir, my duty is to tempt your appetite; your's to control it.'

Despite his appreciative English patron, Carême returned to his beloved France after barely two years in Britain. But his influence endured and persisted, even after his death, through the media of his published works. This boy from the Paris slums who painfully tutored himself to read and write left behind a selection of classic works on the art of the pâtissier, the maître d'hôtel and the chef de cuisine. Amongst the best known of his publications are *Le Maître d'Hôtel Française*, *Le Cuisinier Parisienne* and *Le Pâtissier Royale*. Several of these were translated into English which enabled Carême's influence to reach the ordinary British cook. It is, however, said that even this great figure of the kitchen learnt something himself in England for it is generally considered that he was responsible for taking back to France the English practice of positioning the fish course immediately following the soup instead of this being interspersed at various times throughout the meal.

As a true Frenchman, however, Carême asserted that this service à l'Anglaise was only being reintroduced into France. He contended that England acquired the form of service originally from France and that the revolution had caused its decay in its alleged country of origin as it had caused the decay of so many other things. Dishes composed by Carême during his days in England still survive in the classical cookery repertoire where they are styled à la Regence.

It is said that Carême like many dedicated artists was opinionated and conceited. His books certainly breathe the flavour of a self-confidence as massive as the architectural cookery monuments to which he was addicted.

Though one may gently poke fun at the grandeur of Carême's pâtisserie pieces it is evident that he was by no means an indiscriminate supporter of grandiose and vulgar display. On the contrary he, like other great chefs, undoubtedly appreciated the perfection of simplicity and simple perfection. He even expressed a preference for fish, birds and joints of delicate size. Whilst we may find amongst his recipes items like Tour Gothique (Gothic tower), Pavillon Indienne (Indian pavilion) and Rotund Rustique (rustic rotunda) which suggest the landscape gardeners' catalogue rather than the cookery book and whilst modes of making a 'Ruin of Athens', 'a Small Chinese Ship' and a

'Venetian Gondola' now seem impossibly fanciful, many of his methods of treating savoury items and simpler sweets would likely still be agreeable to the sophisticated palates of today.

In the last resort, however, it is difficult to resist the conclusion that Carême's power and influence is not only due to his undoubted skills as a pâtissier, a cuisinier, an innovater and a simplifier but due also to his character and personality. His whole life and manner asserted a new standing and new prestige for the chef de cuisine. The art of gastronomy was a common interest between him and Talleyrand, between him and the Prince Regent. Royalty and statesmen admired him for his craft and he, in turn, found a pride in his craft which enabled him to speak like a man of standing to notabilities and to the world. His art and his character paved the way for the developments that were to follow later in the century in which he died.

Chefs of Victorian times

The passing of the gay days of the Regency did not mean the passing of the cult of gastronomy in Britain so far as the better-off sections of society were concerned. By the Victorian era several Frenchmen had gained or were gaining high repute for carrying forward the Carême tradition. Jules Gouffé (*Royal Cookery Book* (Le Livre de Cuisine) and the *Royal Book of Pastry and Confectionery* (Le Livre de Pâtisserie)) came to fame as chef de cuisine of the Paris Jockey Club but his works were translated into English by his brother, Alphonse, who was chef to Queen Victoria for well over a quarter of a century. Gouffé acknowledged as one of his instructors, advisors and friends, Antoine Carême, with whom he began to work as a lad of sixteen.

But Gouffé was only one of a firmament of culinary stars of that period. Another was Louis Eustace Ude, who after gaining a reputation as a chef to English noblemen, took charge of the catering at Crockford's Club and the St James's Club.

Ude's activities spanned the years between the departure of Carême and the blossoming of Soyer. He, too, was a literate man as well as a practical one and left his little testament in the form of *The French Cook; a system of fashionable, practical and economical cookery.* Just as Carême had studied architecture, Ude, too, had early artistic associations for he worked, after trying printing and ladies' hairdressing, as a jeweller and engraver (on stone as well as metal) and gained several prizes in the National School of Design in Paris. Like Carême, Ude was by no means modest for he admits 'exhibiting considerable intelligence in these varied trades'. He was compelled to abandon them, however, 'to learn in a hurry the art of cookery' in order to succeed his father in the latter's situation at the French court.

Ude firmly adhered to the French tradition in the kitchen. He entreated the reader of his work to 'familiarise himself with the technical names, which will shorten explanation and assist him in making his bill of fare, which, by a good cook, either in France or England, is always written in French. The practitioner must not disdain to learn the words indispensable to his trade.' He deplored the fact that 'cooks in this country have not the opportunity of instructing their pupils that we have, in France'. But Ude did much by his exhortations to remedy this deficiency.

By 1841, *The French Cook* had run into fourteen editions and the forthright opinions that Ude expressed must not only have instructed, but encouraged, other chefs. He directed attention particularly to the sauces which he described as the 'soul of cookery'. He criticised sternly 'ridiculous names' for dishes and stated with conviction that 'cookery cannot be done like pharmacy'. He bolstered the confidence of cooks by counselling disdain for any disrespect displayed 'by some young noblemen, who affected to depreciate cookery because they are positively ashamed of their ignorance in the subject'. For such as they, 'unable to judge anything in cookery beyond boiled chicken and parsley and butter', he said 'never mind. Do as I have done. Do not be frightened by their repulsive manners.'

It is not surprising that Ude was greatly taken by the young Alexis Soyer whose culinary patron to some extent he became, for Soyer, although he may have made gentle fun of the older and irascible chef, had charming manners as well as considerable dash and aplomb in the kitchen.

Born in 1809, Soyer lived almost exactly as long as the great Carême, and though he had not quite reached fifty when he died he had achieved fame not previously equalled, and hardly surpassed since, by any French chef working in England.

Alexis Soyer had a modest beginning as one of three sons of French shopkeepers. Initially he gained free instruction as chorister at a cathedral school and was earmarked by his parents for the priesthood. But at sixteen already giving evidence of the high spirits that characterised his later career, Soyer entered the kitchens. Despite a momentary deviation to conduct a flirtation with the theatrical profession, young Soyer showed marked kitchen promise and quickly achieved comfortable posts as a chef while still a young man. It was only, however, after his arrival in England that Soyer began to build his great reputation on the basis of some skill and craftsmanship but also on the foundation of an artistic temperament, supreme self-confidence, inventiveness and a remarkable flair for publicity.

Soyer's greatest days were as chef at the Reform Club but he also gained, what was for a chef, tremendous fame and acclaim by being invited to go to the Crimea where, to some extent, he did for British military cooking what Florence Nightingale did for nursing. His strictly culinary fame rests on Côtelette d'Agneau à la Reforme and other sound, classic productions at the Reform Club but also, and to a greater extent, because of his writings and his knack of commanding attention through ventures as varied as a luxury restaurant during the Great Exhibition, a soup kitchen and a shilling cookery book for the poorer classes. He invented a military cooking stove which was still widely used in the Second World War and may still be encountered here and there today and a host of less practical things both culinary and non-culinary. (One of his more bizarre contraptions was a suit capable of being turned into evening dress at the pulling of a string.) One of his principal works was entitled *The Gastronomic Regenerator* and he claimed that such a title could only be sustained by virtue of 'an entire change from the system of any other publication on the art of cookery'. But this claim can hardly be supported by the cookery methods it contained and which are largely conventional. Even gadgets such as his 'new tendon separator' described in this book hardly make for the regeneration of cookery. It was, in fact, Soyer himself who was the regenerator. He is a supreme example of the value to an aspiring profession of an ebullient, go-ahead leader figure. He could hold his own amongst men of the world and as much by his own personal qualities as by his craft skills helped to stake for chefs a place in the sun.

It is not surprising that he rather overshadowed a worthy contemporary who outlived him by nearly twenty years though he was actually born four years before him. This was Charles Elmé Francatelli who was proud to describe himself in his published works as 'pupil to the celebrated Carême'. Indeed, Francatelli gave this qualification before the description 'late maître d'hôtel and chief cook to Her Majesty the Queen'. Before obtaining this supreme appointment he had catered at Crockford's Club and after the royal assignment occupied for some seven years the post at the Reform Club which Soyer had abandoned. One has only to compare the portraits of the two men to detect the difference in temperament and qualities. Soyer, a man of many faces, was often portrayed in weird hats, strange costumes and even, on one occasion at least, in distorting caricature.

Francatelli, on the other hand, is delineated sober-suited and bewhiskered giving every sign of being the soul of discretion expected from a royal chef. Yet despite the whiskers which had something of the Dundreary look, Francatelli was no dreary. He unhesitatingly put forward the view that 'simplicity is as essential an element in cookery as it is in other arts' and this was by no means unadventurous thinking in the era of the Victorian cult of the elaborate. He may also be credited with a movement to reduce the number of sub-divisions of courses at a dinner. He also observed that 'the French, too, regard the dessert as a mere délassement after dinner, intended rather to propitiate than to thwart digestion'. He pioneered a movement towards service à la Russe involving the placing of the dessert straight away on the table 'while the whole of the dinner is served from the side-table'.

His most important published works include the *Modern Cook* which ran into many editions and the *Royal Confectioner* which achieved a lesser popularity. Like Soyer he wrote, too, a cheaper book for the poorer classes. Although lacking Soyer's appeal and without having made quite the dynamic contribution to culinary history in Britain, Francatelli has his significance in being a direct link with Carême. By surviving until 1876, Francatelli brought this phase of modern French classical cookery to the threshold of the present time. The men who later carried on the work of advancing French classical cookery in Britain did so worthily and well but with the passing of Francatelli no name was to be remembered with quite the same respect until Escoffier began to make his mark at the beginning of the hotel era.

By 1885 the art of cookery was thus beginning to be respected in London as it had long been in Paris. The work and personality of men like Carême, Ude, Soyer, Gouffé and Francatelli had given self-confidence and respect to the chefs in Britain's capital city and who were still led by Frenchmen. It was in that year that a group of them under the leadership of Eugène Pouard, who had been born just ten years before Alexis Soyer died, met together to organise an exhibition of professional cookery; the first time that anything of this kind had ever before been attempted on an important scale.

This was still a period when hotels were by no means in the lead as far as luxury cooking was concerned for the great establishments had yet to be created. The best cookery was still to be found in gentlemen's clubs, military messes and in the private houses of the great. Pouard like the eminent chefs who had preceded him in the nineteenth century had made his mark after leaving France in the familiar way with, perhaps, rather more emphasis on catering in officers' messes. This had led him eventually to the position of 'caterer to Queen Victoria's bodyguard', a post of sufficient eminence for other chefs of the time to

give him the support necessary to make this first cookery exhibition a
success.

The Edwardian era in the kitchen

From this beginning has grown the famous Salon Culinaire Internationale de Londres which is now an integral part of the equally
famous Hotelympia which is held every two years in London. But this
first step of Pouard's and his aides was so encouraging that it prompted
them to form a culinary society which after a change of names became
later known as the Universal Cookery and Food Association and which
from that time until the outbreak of the Second World War played a
leading and vigorous part in the advancement of cookery and in promoting the good name of chefs in this country. Yet the name of the
man with whom the most important work of this association will
always be linked was not its actual founder but Charles Herman Senn.
Senn devoted himself to culinary writing and to the work of this chefs'
association during the early part of the twentieth century so that though
he, himself, did not rank amongst the greatest chefs he certainly earned
a lasting place in culinary literature and amongst the leaders who helped
to promote the good name and standing of the cookery profession. The
New Century Cookery Book, The Menu Book and many other volumes
are still widely used and will no doubt last for many more years as a
monument to the indefatigable little Swiss who died (undoubtedly as
he would have wished) at work at his desk in the offices of the cookery
association he did so much to build and which, after his passing unfortunately lost much of its drive and influence.

Senn the writer, the organiser, the association man was, however,
quite overshadowed as a cookery practitioner by the immense figure of
Escoffier. Overshadowed not in stature, for Escoffier also was physically
a little man, but in repute and prestige as a chef. The first quarter of the
twentieth century was undoubtedly the Escoffier era not only in the top
kitchens in this country but of the entire Western world.

Born two years before Senn in 1846, Escoffier lived till his ninetieth
year, dying just four years before the outbreak of the Second World
War, in France where he had been living in retirement. He was a man
whose talents opportunely dovetailed into the trends of the times and
who was fortunate enough to be linked with a man who was perhaps
the greatest hotelier of all times, César Ritz. In those momentous days
as the nineteenth century emerged into the twentieth (a period marked
by the passing of Victoria and the accession of Edward VII) economic
and social forces were changing the dining and wining habits of society.
The great hotels of London (and of the rest of the world) began to be

created. The Ritz, the Carlton, the Savoy, the Cecil and the Langham were built and lived in the period—the period of the big hotels as big hotels are still familiar to us today. Ritz, whose name was to become synonymous with luxury and high life, was a born hotelier and a great creator of hotels. Brought together in Monte Carlo, Ritz found in Escoffier the perfect complement to his genius; for Escoffier, like Ritz, perfectly sensed the need of the times and was prepared not merely to go with the trend but to anticipate it. Ritz, who played the leading part in creating the Savoy and the Ritz Hotel, brought Escoffier to London and there this great man of the kitchen placed his imprint on cookery. His talent was able to attract fashionable ladies who had to be lured into taking part in the more open social activities such as public dining in hotels. He refined and simplified the classic cuisine and not only did he create dishes which have become part of the classic repertory for all time (dishes like Filet de Sole Waleska, Pêche Melba, Salad Réjane and many more) but was a supreme organiser. He is, for example, considered to have been the man who did most to perfect and exploit to the full the partie system.

César Ritz regarded him as the premier cook in the world and Lucius Beebe, the famous American hotelier, voiced a similar opinion in more recent times. The opinion has been echoed by hotelmen and other chefs ever since.

For a picture of Escoffier in his hey-day at the turn of the century we may turn to Lt-Col. Newnham Davis, a celebrated gastronomic writer of his day, who wrote of him as the commanding personality at the Carlton: the chef who, he said, 'had he been a man of the pen and not a man of the spoon, would have been a poet'. Newnham Davis recorded in his *Gourmet's Guide to London* that: 'M. Escoffier is a little below middle height, grey-haired, and grey of moustache. His face is the face of an artist, or a statesman, and the quick eye tells of his capacity for command. The quiet little man who, amidst all the clangour of the great white-tiled kitchen below the restaurant of the Carlton, seems to have nothing to do except occasionally glance at the dishes before they leave his realm or to give a word of counsel when some very delicate entremet is in the making, to taste a sauce or give a final touch to the arrangement of some elaborate cold entrée, has organised his brigade of vociferous cooks of all nations as thoroughly as Crawford organised the Light Division of Peninsular fame. There is never any difficulty, for every difficulty has been foreseen. Only a man who has climbed the ladder from its lowest rung possesses such knowledge and such authority.'

Pierre Hamp in his *Kitchen Prelude* does not give much description of the chef's actual culinary work, as distinct from his organisation, which he regarded as harsh but he does pay tribute to the wax flowers which Escoffier made to perfection and with which he garnished both meat and confectionery.

It is not, however, decoration that is principally linked with the Escoffier tradition. Escoffier was a pioneer in the movement towards exquisite simplicity. Socles and pedestals so beloved by Alexis Soyer and by his forerunner, Carême, were under Escoffier's influence, fast becoming unfashionable. We may now smile at the notion that Carême should have studied architecture as part of his cook's training, for to modern taste the elaborate edifices he produced for the table are as ugly as some Victorian Gothic villas. Yet the need to study underlying artistic principles must always remain a feature of a cook's training. What was doomed to go was only the extravagant forms which dishes took, the artistry run wild. Escoffier believed in the simple concept that food should look like food and, what is more important, should taste like food. Intricate sauces and disguise for the flavour and appearance of the principal ingredient was not in the Escoffier tradition. A basic feature of his art was the use of the fumet or essence culled from the main foodstuff featured as the basis of an accompanying and garnishing sauce. Contrasts of flavour were not taboo but they were delicate where those of the former masters had been, perhaps, more blatant. The obvious wisdom and the obvious artistry of such principles explain why Escoffier's *Guide to Modern Cookery* is still the most esteemed textbook of the professional cook in Britain.

A heretical view is today beginning to be voiced that some of the precepts of Escoffier's book are already out of date, but it is true to say that so far nothing has yet appeared which can satisfactorily take the *Guide*'s place. All the great names in culinary history have left their mark and have in turn been replaced. The work of Carême, Ude, Soyer and Escoffier does not disappear but blends, like the flavours they used themselves, into the whole art of cookery which, as a living one, continues always to develop. There will be, it is inevitable, further developments leading, perhaps, still farther from Escoffier's school. The features of simplicity may be even further emphasised; as much as from necessity due to economic and social causes as from any other. Whatever developments may take place, however, there is no doubt that Escoffier's name and reputation is assured for as long as kitchen history is recorded.

The second half of the twentieth century

At the present time there are still happily some men of stature in the kitchens of this country and the French influence and French tradition is still happily not entirely lost. Marius Dutrey, who, like so many chefs, has interests in art and letters as well as in the kitchen, made an illustrious name at the Savoy, at the Langham and is still adding to his reputation at the Westbury. Henri Malet, who occupied Soyer's sanctum at the Reform Club as well as controlling the kitchens of great hotels, is in retirement but still, in the wings, helps and guides the rising generation. Men like Toulemon at the Connaught, Perrin at the Park Lane and Lebegue at Grosvenor House, both by their positions and by their abilities show the cuisiniers of today the opportunities and the success that can accompany talent in the professional kitchen. To the French, the Swiss and Italian masters, cookery in this country owes a tremendous debt and it must continue to draw support and nourishment from the Continental tradition and the Continental craftsmen for some time to come. But the great work of the masters has not been without its effect in awakening our own countrymen to the possibilities, if not of fame and fortune in every case, at least of a rewarding and satisfying career as a culinary craftsman.

This country, then, still shares its professional culinary inheritance with those from France and other countries who have helped to fashion it. But, happily, today gives signs of a tomorrow in which the British themselves can take over and carry forward their own kitchen reputation. Teams of British chefs have, in the post-war years, gained satisfying successes at international culinary exhibitions and young student and apprentice cooks have also shown great promise in contests against their counterparts from the Continent. British cooks have, in fact, shown themselves capable of mastering the skills and developing the flair and finesse needed in the kitchen, and it is hoped that they will prove worthy of the kitchen tradition which it seems certain they will ultimately fully inherit. If hotel and professional cookery in this country comes more and more into British hands it is to be hoped that there will be no abandonment of the French classical tradition which has become fully integrated into our craft here in this country. Rather is it to be hoped that British dishes themselves will be refined and improved as a result of these continuing influences and that ultimately some of our own native creations may be increasingly adopted on international hotel menus. Insularity, xenophobia should have no place in the kitchen craft however much we may want our own rising generation to show themselves capable of taking over successfully the largest cuisines. Rather must we remember the need to keep cookery great by the process of borrowing as from one nation to another and the cross fertilisation from land to land of talents and ideas.

2

The chef's professional standing

In the quarter of a century that has passed since the death of Escoffier in 1935, there has been no generally accepted leader of the culinary profession of his stature. Many of his pupils and disciples have had distinguished careers and have ornamented the kitchen tradition, but it nevertheless appears that the passing of Escoffier has to some extent been the passing of an era of dominant master figures of the professional kitchen. These figures, of whom Escoffier was the last, by their stature imparted a nobility and importance to the calling of chef which their disappearance from the scene may to some extent have diminished.

Put quite simply the leading men of the kitchen in recent years have not been, perhaps, quite the large size either in repute or achievement of the older masters. Thus the top-most peaks of the profession may not seem to have towered with quite their former grandeur. The standing of the leading chef de cuisine has been, too, somewhat reduced in the years following the Second World War by an ultra-conservatism and sterile traditionalism which has sometimes caused chefs to follow rather than to lead the culinary trends which modern developments in processing, equipment and staff training have rendered possible.

Fortunately, the influence of some of the older, traditional chefs de cuisine has not been the only force at work in promoting the standing of the professional kitchen during the last quarter of a century. Other factors have helped to counteract the slight loss of prestige undergone by the top men. The most important cause of a general improvement in the status of the ordinary chef de cuisine or chef de partie has been the strong development of training in Great Britain and the emergence of bodies other than chef associations which have made significant contributions to advancing the prestige of cookery and those who practise it.

Factors aiding the prestige of cookery and the chef

Factors which have aided culinary advancement have been:

1. The work of the technical colleges offering cookery training in their hotel and catering departments.
2. The establishment of a National Joint Apprenticeship Council of the Hotel and Catering Industry which launched as its first scheme one for apprentice cooks.

3. The establishment of a national three-year training scheme for cooks.
4. The work of the Hotel and Catering Institute and its forerunners, the National Council for Hotel and Catering Education and the Catering Trades' Education Committee.
5. The establishment of craft cookery examinations of national currency by the City and Guilds of London Institute.

All these (and they have not necessarily been mentioned in order of importance) have exerted powerful influences for the benefit of the industry at large; and for the cookery profession in particular they have more than made good the somewhat neglectful and laissez-faire attitude of some of the older generation of chefs de cuisine, caterers and cookery societies.

Because of these factors and particularly because of hotel school and technical college training, a national apprenticeship system and the propaganda work of the Hotel and Catering Institute, the chef of British nationality is beginning to enjoy a standing in society which is certainly not less than that of skilled craftsmen from other industries.

Other influences have also helped to enhance the standing of the skilled cookery practitioner. These influences include the increasing economic importance of the hotel and catering industry as part of a top, foreign-currency-earning tourist trade and the spread of catering within the welfare field such as in catering for industry, hospitals and schools.

There is, too, every indication that the shift in economic and industrial emphasis in this country (for example the new impetus in the growth of the tourist trade) will cause the hotel and catering industry further to advance in importance, and the chef, like other key men and women within it, will continue to gain in standing.

Personal attributes of the chef

It has already been noted that the chef de cuisine is not only something of an artist and certainly a craftsman but an executive with managerial responsibilities within his own department. He must organise and direct the activities of other people, watch costs and kitchen percentages, plan and compile menus, order commodities and superintend and undertake many more administrative chores connected with his kitchen.

His duties involve tact and understanding not only in controlling his own subordinates but in collaborating with the manager, proprietor and/or directors of the hotel or restaurant. Moreover, it should be his constant aim to foster good relations with the maître d'hôtel so that kitchen staff and restaurant staff work together smoothly and efficiently.

His duties demand certain obvious qualifications and qualities other than cookery skill and even managerial ability. Amongst the requisites desirable could be included:

1. *Integrity and honesty.* The character of the chef and his ethical standards should be those of the best type of professional man.

2. *Temperance.* The avoidance of excess in drinking, smoking (and, indeed, in eating) and the consequent setting of high personal standards to his staff is of great importance. It has to be remembered that this is of particular significance in an industry of the type of hotelkeeping and catering where special precautions against over-indulgence on the part of lower level staff are often necessary.

3. *Cultivation of quiet temperament.* The tantrums of the prima donna were sometimes, in the past, almost expected of the 'artistic' chef. It is obvious that a calm, logical approach to problems, to crises and to staff is essential to kitchen efficiency.

4. *Immaculate appearance.* Regard for hygiene is of top importance in the kitchen and there is hardly a better beginning than with the chef's own person. His white clothing, check trousers and shoes should be impeccable and his hands, attention to shaving, haircut and other details should set the standard for others to aim at.

5. *Knowledge of French, current affairs, commodities and tools of his trade.* The chef will do well to harness his vocational interest in French and, for example, those commodities needed for his duties to wider cultural interests related to them. He must be a 'man of the world' and of some culture if he is to make his menus, his dishes and his style of cookery appealing, topical and apposite.

Creative aspects

Many famous chefs de cuisine of the past have revealed skills, taste, judgment and imagination enabling them to create dishes which the discerning have recognised as works of art—impermanent though such works might be. It may, however, always be a matter of controversy whether chefs may generally claim to be artists. That they must be highly skilled craftsmen if they are successfully to fulfil their role there can be no disputing.

Craftsmanship for the best chefs must be akin to artistry because they normally have to create for a public which may include, at any time, a demanding clientele wishing to see preserved a traditional grace in dining coupled with progressive and imaginative treatment of food. The greatest of chefs will tend to be judged by artistic standards and the humblest of cooks must learn in turn to be measured against sound and decent standards of craftsmanship.

The creative aspect of cookery depending upon personal taste and manipulative skill is so dominant in the chef's vocation that it must not obscure or overshadow other important factors such as organising ability, personal standards of integrity, regard for cleanliness and, not least, commercial understanding.

The chef (and the would-be chef) must, therefore, have a creative urge linked with an interest in food and cookery sufficient to make him patient and painstaking in mastering its complex processes and in acquiring manual dexterity.

This strong and genuine interest in food and cookery is a key which will ultimately unlock, for the aspiring chef, most of the doors into skills and techniques. The same interest is also a powerful factor in insuring the development of taste and judgment. Certainly, without genuine interest in the craft of cookery the man with technical ability and craft skills at the stove is still unlikely wholly to succeed and reach the pinnacles of the profession.

Sense of service and responsibility

The chef's skill is bound up with personal service to the public which demands, too, a consciousness of such service and a sense of satisfaction from performing it well. Not only must food be delightful to look at, smell and taste, but it should be wholesome and safe. It must, that is to say, be nutritious and clean as well as appealing. Thus the best type of chef must have a sense of vocation. The production of nutritious dishes depends greatly on a conscientious sense of service on the part of the cook because much damage nutritionally can be caused invisibly by such negligent processes as cooking too far in advance. Similarly the observance of the laws of hygiene cannot be merely a matter of rule of thumb, but must be based on a sense of duty, craft pride and a desire to serve his public well.

Such feelings as the urge to create and a sense of responsibility in regard to nutrition and hygiene is inevitably cultivated most success-fully where there is native intelligence and reasonable education. Any idea that cookery may be entrusted to the least alert and the worst educated must inevitably result in a low standard of national cuisine. Apart, too, from purely craft skills in the manual sense, the chef needs to use and understand recipes and to calculate quantities both to order his stores and to adapt his recipes to varying numbers. Frequently, also, his calculations will involve estimates and comparisons of cost.

Meeting the demands of the job

Though working conditions in the kitchen have greatly improved in recent years and though total hours of work do not compare unfavourably with many industries, it is likely that for many chefs there will always be a need to work hours different from the majority of men who are involved in a straight day of 9 a.m.–5 p.m. or thereabouts. The chef, or the would-be chef, must, therefore, have a sufficient interest in his task, a sufficient sense of vocation, to cope happily with a career which may involve at least some periods when his hours of work will differ from those of many of his friends and which may cause him to give more than usual thought to the organisation of his leisure as well as to his working time.

Advising would-be chefs

In counselling those who are entering or thinking of entering the craft of cookery such aspects have all to be remembered. Yet it is not always easy to reduce the needs of the job into simple principles on the one hand and on the other to express the human qualities needed and to assess them in such a way as to make them add up with mathematical inevitability to a conclusion that the owner of such qualities was destined to be a chef.

Amongst the qualities and characteristics of the good chef already summarised one must try to recognise from the would-be entrant that he has at least the following:

1. Capacity for and willingness to undertake hard work, including hard work in the physical as well as the mental sense.
2. Honesty.
3. Sufficient education and intelligence to cope, for example, with the calculation of recipe commodities, for orders and costs and to appreciate and understand the demands of hygiene and nutrition.
4. Good personal standards, both physical and moral so that a sense of responsibility and citizenship can be developed in relation to the job, sufficient to ensure that social demands, like hygiene and nutrition, are met fully as well as aesthetic ones.

To detect a promise of these potentials in a craft entrant is not necessarily difficult. Evidence of aptitudes is often found in such simple facts as that a boy has enjoyed cooking in scout camps or at home; or if he has never cooked, has a curiosity and interest in food and has gained enjoyment from other forms of handicraft at school or in his hobbies. Honesty, intelligence, educational level and sense of responsibility are all factors about which evidence may be gained not only from personal interview but more importantly from the school. It should, however, always be remembered that many who are inept handymen in every other activity may become skilled chefs simply because they want to.

The chef's dress

Although the chef de cuisine works behind the scenes his dress is one that is perfectly familiar to the man in the street. His high, white, starched cap or toque, white double-breasted jacket topped with white neckerchief, his blue and white check cotton trousers protected by the white apron into the string of which is tucked the 'rubber' or kitchen cloth, is a costume which would be readily identified by even the least hotel-conscious person.

Evolution of chef's dress

Yet this dress is not really of great antiquity but is the outcome rather of gradual evolution. It appears to have been completely standardised only during the full blossoming of the hotel industry in this century.

Cooks in mediaeval kitchens appeared to work in a variety of costumes of which some sort of apron would seem to be the only common denominator. By Victorian times, certainly, chefs in old prints are portrayed in white clothing and ordinary cuisiners and chefs de partie generally are shown wearing white caps but these resemble much more closely either cotton night caps or the flat caps which are today seen in the bakery rather than the kitchen. Alfred Suzanne in his *La Cuisine Anglaise* (1894) gives 1840 as the year when the toque began to replace 'le classique bonnet de coton' (the classic cotton bonnet or beret-type cap).

Carême is, in fact, credited with having introduced to Britain the starched, high hat to take the place of the 'night cap' type during the time he was chef to the Prince Regent.

The chef's skull cap

The great Alexis Soyer even when in 'whites' did not wear the high bonnet, the toque, the chef's tall hat but a somewhat flamboyant creation which approximated to a tasselled beret in black velvet. Even after Soyer's day the white hat was by no means de rigeur amongst all chefs and in the last ten years of the nineteenth century there were many instances of chefs like M. Claudius, the specialist confectioner and glacier at Laborde's, who (Hamp tells us in his *Kitchen Prelude*) wore a headgear something like a librarian's black skull cap. Indeed, in a cookery book published in 1919 there is a photograph of Victor Hirtzler who was chef of the Hotel St Francis, San Francisco, wearing a dark skull cap very much of this pattern. He is dressed otherwise in the chef's costume familiar today.

In this country, a similar black skull cap is still worn by the master cook (the equivalent of the maître chefs des cuisines) at the famous English-style restaurant, Simpson's in the Strand. It has accordingly been inferred that this is specifically an English cook's distinctive insignia but as has already been noted there is pictorial evidence that chefs of other nationalities have, in relatively recent times, sported a head-dress not dissimilar.

Nevertheless, there is something particularly agreeable to the traditionally minded British in the fact that this trait has persisted and become adopted as a mark of the English master cook. No one, surely, would cavil at any factor, such as this, which might help to contribute to native pride of craftsmanship.

One observation that might be made, however, is that the darker, closer-fitting cap whilst possibly a suitable mark of rank for the top man is less likely to be cool and comfortable in wear for the working chef at the stove.

Conferring distinction

There is no doubt that working dress (apart from its functional purpose) plays an important part in establishing morale and in heightening or diminishing job prestige. There may have been a time when the chef's uniform was not one which greatly interested the Britisher, but there is every reason to think that this is by no means so today and that the working costume of the chef de cuisine is one regarded as conferring some distinction. If it is, in fact, to add to the prestige and status of its wearer the chef's dress must be worn with pride and maintained with care. Because of the nature of the work he has to do it is equally important that it is worn with intelligent regard for its purpose, which includes, importantly, the maintenance of hygiene and the aiding of cool working.

From seeing many hundreds of youngsters putting on chef's clothing for the first time it has been noticeable to the author how some have the happy knack of wearing it immediately as to the manner born; whilst others take some time to acquire the little knacks of adjusting neckcloth and apron, for example, to achieve the right touch of smartness and ease.

Bearing in mind the aims of hygiene and comfort, here are some points regarding clothing and its wear and maintenance:

Provision of clothing

It is the custom in some hotels and catering establishments for young apprentices to be provided with their working dress and for laundering to be undertaken for them. At others they may be required to provide their own clothing but laundry facilities may still be offered. Some laundry service may also be offered to commis and to chefs themselves but this is entirely a matter of establishment policy. When the responsibility for providing and laundering rests with the employee it is important and in his own interests that he has sufficient of each item to ensure frequent changes. Allowing for laundering delays, it is thought that the following is by no means over-generous:

4 Chef's caps.
4 Chef's white double-breasted jackets.
6 Chef's white neckerchiefs.
6 White aprons.
6 Plain (white or unbleached) linen kitchen cloths ('rubbers').
3 Pairs kitchen trousers—blue and white check (small).

In addition to the outward and visible garments, a word should be said about underclothing and socks. It should be remembered that in some sections of the kitchen the work not only involves physical activity but physical activity in warm surroundings and will be accompanied by the inevitable tendency to perspire. There should, therefore, be an equally sensible and generous provision of underclothing. The exact type of garment is largely a matter of choice but a singlet vest of absorbent type with short underpants of similar material are the most suitable. Proper undergarments should always be worn with chef's dress and should be changed and laundered daily. Socks similarly should be changed daily. Incidentally, it is equally important to wear sound shoes in a good state of repair. Quite apart from foot hygiene, the bad practice of wearing old, split shoes does not, as was commonly supposed, aid comfort or efficiency and certainly has a depressing effect on kitchen morale and prestige.

As far as the items of uniform are concerned the following points may be noted:

The chef's cap. The cap should be laundered regularly irrespective of whether it is obviously dirty or not. Tell-tale marks such as perspiration staining round the band must be particularly avoided.

The neck cloth. There are many modes of tying and wearing the neck cloth. The original purpose of this appendage namely to remove or trap facial perspiration is almost lost sight of today for there is a growing tendency to wear this part of the dress as a close-fitting, neatly knotted cravat. No doubt this trend is because working conditions and heat are somewhat less rigorous than in former days when open fires and overheated kitchens were much more common.

The jacket. The accepted chef jacket is a double-breasted or cross-over style and the type with cloth buttons is generally favoured for appearance.

No true chef wears the sleeves of this garment rolled up but simply turns back the cuffs which are adapted with a slit especially for this purpose. The sleeves are kept long, turned back only at the wrist in order to protect the arms from splashing from hot liquids and fats and from contact with the hot oven doors, saucepans, etc.

The trousers. The chef trousers are made of blue and white check cotton material and it is, of course, significant that this is a washable garment. The lower part of the leg, for example, can relatively quickly become splashed and soiled and it is important that they are washed frequently.

The apron. The white apron which these days is seldom of the bib type except perhaps in the case of first-year apprentices takes the worst of the workaday soiling and will almost certainly need at least daily changing (reversing the apron once is a permissible device). Whilst some length-ening of usage time may be accomplished by adjusting the number of folds at the waist, the practice of folding to camouflage staining to such an extent as to make the apron ludicrously short cannot be too strongly deplored.

The 'rubber'. The 'rubber' which the chef, commis or cook apprentice wears tucked into his apron string usually at the rear left, quickly be-comes an instinctively used attachment. It has, of course, an infinite number of uses but most of them are concerned with the protection of the hands when moving objects around stoves and in the ovens (though the kitchen cloth should not be regarded as a substitute for the thick oven cloth). The kitchen cloth should be used and not abused and it is not a floor swab, duster, etc. As it is *worn* as well as used every effort should be made to keep it clean and sweet smelling during the day.

Personal hygiene

More than ordinary standards of personal hygiene are required from a chef or would-be chef true to his pride of craft and with a due sense of his own status and his own responsibilities. Reference should be made to the chapter on hygiene for special factors to be borne in mind in regard to personal standards of hygiene (see page 193). Dress and hygiene combined should result in a craftsman well turned out, well groomed with due attention to regular hair cutting; neatly trimmed and clean nails; freshly laundered dress, a close daily shave as well as general neatness.

It is from such signs linked with businesslike deportment and the competent handling of tools that the real craftsman chef is distinguished. It is an utter fallacy to believe that dirty, dishevelled dress is evidence of the hard worker. It is invariably the sign of the careless and disorderly minded cook. Pride in appearance, in fact, makes a strong contribution to pride of craft and consequent efficiency.

Sense of vocation

Personal qualities, of character and outward appearance, are important in the chef because, as has been noted, his work impinges so much on the well-being and happiness of others. His work may truly be described as one for which a sense of vocation is essential if it is to be well done. The sense of vocation once the career of chef is adopted will be expressed in ways both large and small—from complete integrity in business matters to punctilious regard for cleanliness and appearance. In short, for the true chef de cuisine good character and good characteristics are both essential.

3   Development of the partie system

As the task of the professional kitchen has become greater, its organisation has inevitably become more complex. To provide meals in the large modern hotel this kitchen organisation has reached its culminating point. In such establishments there are many customers to be served in many different ways. For example, there are usually different menus or forms of service in a table d'hôte restaurant, à la carte restaurant, grill room or buttery and for banqueting and floor service. Moreover, the menus, dishes and presentation can be highly elaborate and certainly even when relatively simple, will usually involve high skills.

Basic divisions of kitchen work

Yet even in earliest times and in the simplest kitchens catering for social groups larger than individual families there has been an obvious tendency to divide the work of preparing and cooking so that the most efficient results can be obtained from the minimum of effort. The broad features of a kitchen organisation soon began to emerge in divisions such as:

(*a*) The storage of commodities both perishable and non-perishable.
(*b*) The preparation of meat, fish and poultry, etc. (larder work).
(*c*) The preparation and cooking of pastry and desserts (the pastry).
(*d*) The preparation of vegetables.
(*e*) The general stove section at which prepared foods were assembled and cooked.

In small kitchens even this basic arrangement can, to some extent, be contracted and simplified and on the other hand as kitchens increase in size and volume of work the basic arrangement can be expanded by varying degrees.

There is sound reason for asserting that despite the antiquity of kitchen work the modern pattern now followed in hotel restaurants began to emerge in the kitchens of the large clubs of London (emulated and taken as a pattern throughout the Western world) and which provided to a large extent both the staff and the organisational model for the hotels which began to develop in their modern form at the beginning of the end of the nineteenth century.

It is the misfortune of professional cookery that the great chefs of the past have tended to write, when they have written at all, with the domestic cook of the private house in view. Some have been generous in revealing their cookery secrets but few have left behind in enduring form much information of how they organised their work on a large scale.

Club kitchen of Victorian times

Happily the greatest chef of the Victorian era, Alexis Soyer, did include some indication of his approach to these problems in *The Gastronomic Regenerator* written and published in the middle of the nineteenth century when the author was at the height of his fame at the Reform Club. Indeed, *The Gastronomic Regenerator*, sub-titled a 'Simplified and Entirely New System of Cookery' indicated that within its pages were included 'correct and minute plans how kitchens of every size, from the kitchen of a royal palace to that of the humble cottage, are to be constructed and furnished'.

Soyer's kitchen plan provided for a larder department adjoining his own office and which included three sub-sections:

La boucherie. 'In which all joints are trimmed for cooking'—the meat and game larder, the cold meat and sauce larder. The pastry and confectionery adjoined the larder and the chef's office was but of modest size, indeed, rather less than half of the size of Soyer's sanctum.

The kitchen was L-shaped. In the long narrow section a roasting kitchen was at one end with a vegetable kitchen at the other and against these two at the roasting kitchen end and somewhat divided by fitments was the principal kitchen.

In addition to these two main departments, there were, of course, ancillary sections including scouring scullery, butler's pantry, fish slab within a passage, kitchen maids' dining room and the like.

Soyer was not only an articulate and literate chef but a highly inventive one. The various sections were well equipped and considerable thought had been given to problems of storage. His ventilated storage boxes, for example, have not been greatly improved upon to this day but on the other hand, far-sighted though his plans and inventions were, a close study of his plant in modern times can be of historical interest only because open-fire roasting, non-refrigerated storage, charcoal stoves, solid fuel vegetable boilers and the widespread use of cast-iron are inevitably out-moded. Yet many consider that Soyer was amongst professional chefs the most significant figure between Carême's baroque cookery of Regency days and Escoffier's 'new look' cookery of subtle simplicity. Soyer bridged, as it were, the era of Carême who was the last and greatest of the chefs to royal houses and noble families (but basically, a private chef) and Escoffier the first and so far the greatest of the chefs who engaged their talents in cooking for the wider custom of the great modern hotel.

Significance of Escoffier

There are many, indeed, who consider that the true significance of Escoffier lies in his organising ability.

It was clear to this generation of the kitchen that the problem of getting beautifully cooked food of wide variety to a large number without delay was a challenge as much to organising genius as culinary artistry. The partie (or 'corner' as it is known in many British establishments) system as perfected by Escoffier was the result of studying the food and cookery work behind the recipes and allocating tasks to different specialists so as to help produce the most complex dishes regularly, efficiently and swiftly. This meant breaking down processes and allocating different tasks, even in one dish, to different sections so that a veal escalope, for example, might be cut from the cushion by the butcher, flattened and panéed (breadcrumbed) by the larder cook, sautéed (shallow fried) in butter by the sauce cook and assembled by him using appropriate garnishes which in turn might well have come from other corners of the kitchen.

In the kind of kitchen that Escoffier and his colleagues organised, the partie system reached the height of complexity because the end products had to be of the highest finish and yet be completed to order in rapid sequence for a substantial number of customers.

Factors causing change

There are, however, several factors which can cause the amendment and simplification of the partie system and some of them are already at work in many establishments. They include:

1. The introduction of machinery to do the work previously done by men.
2. Changing public taste which seeks simpler menus and meals.
3. Economic factors which both encourage the reduction of expensive labour and the simplification of recipes and service.
4. The processing of food by freezing, canning and dehydration which may eliminate much basic preparation work.

Already, therefore, the partie system perfected from early in the twentieth century and reaching its heights just before the Second World War, is undergoing change and will undergo still more change as automation, method study and work simplification is increasingly applied within the kitchen.

The fact remains, however, that a knowledge of the partie system is still vital to understanding both good cookery itself and good service. It is clear, too, that improvements are more likely to be effected by those who have a thorough appreciation of the partie system; for the advance will be, surely, evolutionary rather than destructive.

The partie system summarised

The essence of the partie system is the division of work into sections, each section or partie being controlled by a chef de partie who might be regarded as the section foreman as well as a craft specialist. All the parties come under the control of the chef de cuisine aided by one or more sous chefs who, in large establishments have no partie or section duties although in smaller establishments an important chef de partie such as the chef saucier or, even, the chef garde manger may act as sous chef. The chain of responsibility and the organisation of a large kitchen under the partie system is illustrated in diagram (I), p. 28.

In the largest hotels and restaurants there will be ordinarily about a dozen principal parties under the chef de cuisine assisted by his sous chefs. The team of cooks and their assistants under the partie system is commonly called the 'Brigade'.

Adaptation of the partie system

It is clear that only a few of the top luxury hotels still carry a brigade of cooks divided into parties which include each and every section referred to in the next chapter. As hotels and restaurants have more modest commitments either in the scope of meals or in the number of clients catered for, there have been and continue to be widespread and varied adaptations of the partie system.

Common variations include some of the following:

1. The garde manger undertaking with a small staff or single-handed, much of the work of the butcher, fishmonger, poulterer and charcutier other than that which is done by suppliers before arrival in the kitchen.

2. One or two main kitchen parties may be joined together. For example, the roast cook taking charge of grilling with the aid of a commis or the entremettier's task being combined with that of the potager or other combinations of duty convenient to the house.

3. Finally, the small establishments with the working chef de cuisine where there is so much fusion of the functions of the partie system

KITCHEN BRIGADE

(I) Possible Arrangement of Larger Kitchen Brigade

Maître Chef des Cuisines

Sous Chefs (Under Chefs, i.e., assistants to the Master Chef)

Chef Garde Manger (Larder Cook)

Commis (Assistants)
Aides (Apprentices/Trainees)
— Boucher (Butcher)
— Poissonier (Fishmonger)
— Volailleur (Poultryman)
— Hors d'Œuvrier (Hors d'Œuvre Cook)
— Saladier (Salad maker)
— Charcutier (Pork Butcher/Sausage maker)
— Cold Room Man

Chef de Nuit (Night Duty Cook)

Commis

Chef Potager (Soup Cook)

Commis
Aides

Chef Saucier (Sauce Cook)

Commis
Aides

Chef Communar (Staff Cook)

Commis
Aides

Chef Entremetier (Vegetable Cook)

Commis
Aides
Kitchen (Vegetable) Hands

Breakfast Cook
Assistants

Chef Rôtisseur (Roast Cook)

Commis
Aides
Grillardin (Grill Cook)
Savourier (Savoury Cook)

Chef Poissonier (Fish Cook)

Commis
Aides

Chef de Banquets (Banquet Chef) and Subsidiary Banqueting Brigade

Chef Pâtissier (Pastry Chef)

Commis
Aides
Glacier (Ice Cream Chef)
Boulanger (Baker)

Foreman Porter, Kitchen Porters, Plongeur (Pot Washer)

Administrative
Secretaire de Cuisine (Kitchen Clerk)
Aboyeurs (Announcer, i.e. the clerk who calls the orders at the servery)
L'Econome (Storekeeper)

KITCHEN BRIGADE

(II)   Possible Adaptation for Medium-sized Establishment

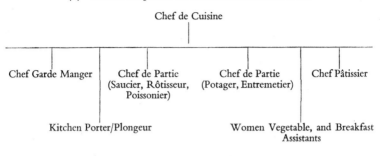

Chef de Cuisine

Chef Garde Manger | Chef de Partie (Saucier, Rôtisseur, Poissonier) | Chef de Partie (Potager, Entremetier) | Chef Pâtissier

Kitchen Porter/Plongeur

Women Vegetable, and Breakfast Assistants

KITCHEN BRIGADE

(III)   Possible Adaptation for Smaller Establishment

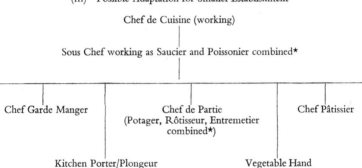

Chef de Cuisine (working)

Sous Chef working as Saucier and Poissonier combined★

Chef Garde Manger | Chef de Partie (Potager, Rôtisseur, Entremetier combined★) | Chef Pâtissier

Kitchen Porter/Plongeur

Vegetable Hand

that little remains but a broad division into larder work, pastry work and the main kitchen work and where there is frequent intermingling of these branches of work under an assistant.

Adaptations due to modern trends

Apart, however, from the reduction of the number of sub-divisions and the simplification of the partie system to meet the requirements of establishments of smaller size and more modest menus, there are other factors which increasingly affect the staffing and the organisation of the kitchen.

There is, for example, a noticeable trend towards the purchasing of perishable commodities in a prepared form ready for cooking. In the case of the poultry cleaned, dressed and trussed and where meat ready butchered into, for example, equally portioned cutlets is concerned

★ Obviously other combinations of duties are possible and linking all these sections, i.e., sauce, fish, soup, roast and vegetables under one cook with an assistant is common.

there is a tendency for the work of the hotel butcher and poultry man to dwindle and disappear and for the work of the garde manger to be greatly streamlined. As is mentioned in Chapter 5 when dealing with the duties of the chef entremetier, the pre-cleaning and pre-preparation of vegetables (including also the development of deep freezing, canning and dehydration techniques) has so far affected mainly the unskilled vegetable-room helpers but its effects on cookery techniques and the arrangement and equipping of the kitchens and stores is by no means over. Progressive managements and chefs de cuisine are increasingly interested in methods which will both improve cooking and simplify staffing, storage and catering equipment (Chapter 10 deals more fully with such trends).

The development of kitchen equipment has made excellent progress in this country though this is perhaps largely due to the development of expensively equipped kitchens in spheres of catering other than hotels and restaurants; for example, in industrial catering where much money has been spent on kitchen plant. New and better types of apparatus are causing changes in the way in which kitchens are operated. The result of all the advances in these fields of pre-prepared food processing and the development of modern cookery and storage equipment has not yet been fully felt. It is likely, however, that the best developments and adaptations in kitchen organisation will be brought about by those who not only make a careful study of the work involved in the light of new facilities, products and techniques, but also have a full appreciation of the evolution of professional cookery on the large scale through the perfection of the partie system.

Because of the varied conditions of scope of work, equipment, reliance or otherwise on convenience foods it is difficult to lay down hard and fast rules regarding the size of brigades and the number of cooks required. One London hotel of 100 rooms doing a good restaurant trade augmented with businessmen's lunches may employ a chef de cuisine with eight cuisiniers (cooks, chef de partie) with three commis/apprentices whilst some of the giant hotels may have as many as 100 in each hotel divided amongst several kitchens.

The kitchen staff of the smaller non-partie system establishment

In England, America and even France and other Continental countries, the smaller establishment employing a working staff with one or two assistant cooks, cannot be regarded as operating even as an adaptation of the partie system.

The organisation of kitchens in, for example, country inns, small sea-side hotels and private hotels can seldom conform to the same sort of pattern as that determined in the case of big hotels and restaurants who adhere to traditional French style cookery and menus for a large number of guests.

In the small licensed country hotel, satisfactory catering of a national character is perfectly capable of achievement with a man or woman cook in charge; providing such staff have sound training and experience in their more restricted field. Where good English fare is appropriate a high-grade working woman cook may be a much more satisfactory proposition than a male 'chef'. In such cases a kitchen staff might consist of a sound working head cook with a reliable 'second' and possibly a third to deal with pastry and desserts together with assistance from unskilled or 'on the job' trained semi-skilled kitchen hands. This will be a better arrangement than some bogus, pretentious emulation of a 'partie system'.

4   The chef de cuisine and his staff in the partie system

The Chef de Cuisine is often described in the most luxurious establishments as the maître chef des cuisines or maître des cuisines and, commonly, in English establishments as the head chef. Purists object to the designation 'head chef' because its literal translation of 'head chief' involves a redundancy of expression. The term head cook or master cook has not, in the past, always carried the same kind of dignity as the French expression but with the growing reputation of British cookery and catering a wider use of the English term for this top post and suitable English terms for his subordinates could become more widespread and there is no reason other than custom why it should not.

Chef de cuisine (head chef)

The chef de cuisine in the large establishment is much more a departmental manager than a working craftsman. He will be selected for his position and will retain it more for his organising and executive abilities than for his culinary skill though it is obvious that he should have such skill and a large appreciation of fine cookery as part of his background. Nevertheless, his principal function is to plan, organise and superintend the work of the kitchens.

His 'blue-print' for the major part of his activities is the menu which he will prepare for the management in accordance with the costing and catering policies laid down. He will either have full responsibility for staffing within a general kitchen labour cost policy or will have major responsibility for staff selection and dismissal in conjunction with the Personnel Department. Whilst in large hotels and restaurants, food buying may be dealt with by specialist buyers, sometimes stationed at the principal markets, the chef de cuisine often has heavy responsibility for ordering food stocks if not actually himself effecting the purchase. He will also be concerned with the plant and equipment of his kitchens at least in an advisory capacity.

Thus the executive responsibilities of the chef de cuisine can be considered under the principal headings of:

(*a*) Food and food costs (through menu planning and ordering).
(*b*) Kitchen staff.
(*c*) Kitchen plant and equipment.

Under his control all three must be co-ordinated to produce good food efficiently and economically.

Within his organisation, moreover, high craft skills and artistry of cookery must be developed. Because of the complexity of the operation he organises and the skills and art he must foster, the chef de cuisine enjoys a unique standing. His status is normally second only to that of the manager and he will expect, and is normally accorded, complete control of his domain. Within the establishment's general policy, particularly in regard to cost, he will be given considerable freedom to operate and control in his own way. Hotel and restaurant etiquette, for example, might prohibit the entry of staff up to the manager into the kitchens without the consent of the chef de cuisine and except in the matter of overall policy direction would preclude managerial interference with the chef's executive control.

It is clear, therefore, that in addition to the craft skills and technical knowledge acquired as a result of apprenticeship, technical training and experience, the chef de cuisine must additionally acquire managerial qualities and administrative knowledge, particularly in regard to the organisation of work, control of staff, the efficient use of machinery, costing and food control. At the same time, his craft skills in regard to food should desirably have been expanded into a full understanding of gastronomy so that his menus and dishes may be planned by him and executed by his staff in accordance with aesthetic considerations as well as commercial ones. He must be aware of (and, perhaps, prompt and stimulate) modern developments in manufacturing and processing foods for his use and perfecting equipment for his kitchens. Present trends indicate that the chef must increasingly concern himself not only with cookery but with the techniques of meal presentation in the widest sense. This calls for a degree of merchandising skill and, on occasion, showmanship.

The duties and responsibilities of the chef de cuisine are so wide that it may be said that they may best be appreciated through noting the contents of the other chapters of this book.

Sous chef

The sous chef, or under chef, is the principal assistant of the chef de cuisine. In the large establishments, sous chefs will have no sectional or partie responsibility but will aid the chef in his general administration and in particular in supervising the work of preparing food and in overlooking its service at the hot-plate servery. Where a considerable kitchen operation is involved, there may be more than one sous chef. The position of sous chef is, of course, regarded as an intermediate step between control of a partie and the ultimate control of a kitchen. In smaller organisations one of the principal chefs de partie such as the chef saucier (sauce cook) or chef garde manger (larder cook) (p. 40) may act as sous chef.

Where there is only one sous chef he will, of course, stand in for the chef de cuisine when the latter is off duty but more importantly he will tend to act as the direct supervisor of practical kitchen activities when the chef is engaged at work within his office, that is to say, when the chef is occupied by menu planning, checking records and figures or is engaged in similar administrative routines. The sous chef is able to supervise at the servery during meal service times and can make ad hoc staff changes during the working day to relieve pressure. He is desirably something of a disciplinarian, particularly during the arduous work conducted at the fast tempo of the kitchen, so needs firmness as well as an understanding of people and the tasks they must perform.

Additional sous chefs will be borne upon the chef de cuisine's staff when the brigade is sufficiently large to warrant it and particularly when there are separate service points for different restaurants within an hotel or when an establishment has frequent and sizeable banquet services.

In the largest establishments it is possible for there to be as many as four to six sous chefs, particularly is this so when separate kitchens are set up for, say, grill room, restaurant, banquet service and buttery.

Chef de partie

The chef de partie is a working cook in charge of a clearly defined section of activities within the kitchen. As mentioned above, a chef de partie of the more important sections, particularly the sauce and larder, may have the status and duties of a sous chef in addition to sectional responsibilities; in any case these two chefs are usually regarded as among the leaders of the 'brigade' as the kitchen staff is generally known.

All the chefs de partie may be regarded as supervisors or foremen of their sections as well as skilled craftsmen. They must, for example, plan and organise their work and staff and normally they will prepare daily indents for commodities (usually signed by the chef de cuisine). The chef pâtissier, the chief pastry cook, also normally has special status because of the importance and difficulty of his duties.

The importance of parties and the work of chefs de partie and their assistants is recognised by variations in rates of pay according to the complexity and amount of work involved.

Commis

Dependent on the partie concerned, the sectional chef will be assisted by one or more trained cooks who have not yet reached full chef status. These assistants or commis should have completed their apprenticeship or training, but will still be gaining experience before taking full partie responsibilities. Nevertheless, the first commis, as the senior of the assistants is called, should be capable of taking charge when his chef de partie is off, and as second in command should take considerable responsibilities under his chef.

Apprentices

On each partie there will also be found apprentices or trainees who will, whilst learning, also be helping in the practical day-to-day work of food preparation and cookery.

In French brigades learners and apprentices were styled aides de cuisines.

Other assistants

The chefs de parties, their commis and their apprentices are concerned with craft work only. As will be seen later, unskilled operations are largely undertaken by porters, kitchen hands, vegetable preparers and the like.

The craft status of the skilled men and of those apprenticed to him are maintained as carefully in the kitchen as they are in other industries and trades where craft skills are valued as being of high importance.

Non-cooking kitchen staff

In addition to the various chefs de parties, cooks, commis and apprentices carried on the staff of a chef de cuisine there are other functionaries who are regarded as an integral part of the kitchen brigade and the partie system. Some staff of this kind work in the main kitchen itself and others in departments ancillary to it.

Le secretaire de cuisine (kitchen clerk)

The number of clerks employed in an hotel or restaurant kitchen will depend on its size and volume of trade. Apart from supervision of the checking system at the servery and after service terminates, clerical work in the kitchen is mainly a matter of recording the receipt and issue of goods so that there may be, in the largest establishments, for example, a clerk attached to the garde manger concerned with the receipt of perishable foods, principally meat, fish, poultry,

game and with recording the subsequent issue of food portions prepared from these items. The work of such a functionary may extend
into the control of cold stores and to the control and registering of
items for the pastry department.

A kitchen clerk is also likely to be attached to the chef de cuisine as
a personal assistant in the office duties falling to the chef. This clerk
often carries out also the duties of aboyeur (*see below*). As in the case
of sporting terms (such as 'le football') of Britain being used in France,
it may be noted that at least one French hotel manual refers to 'Le
Keetching Clerk'.

Aboyeur (order announcer—literally 'barker')

The aboyeur ('barker') is stationed at the servery during the time of
service of meals and on receipt of the written order chits from the
waiting staff calls out the orders to the different parties, possibly using
in the case of those in the pastry and larder detached from the main
section a loud-speaker system.

The language of the hotel kitchen is French and the loud calling of
the aboyeur and the equally loud responses of the parties makes its
distinctive contribution to the hubbub and clatter of the busy service
period which strangely gives to the uninitiated visitor an impression of
confusion and turmoil. The aboyeur must, of course, be a person of
some culinary knowledge, if not experience, for he must have a command of the cookery repertoire and be able to recognise the appropriate
garnish for all dishes. In some establishments a sous chef may undertake
the duties of aboyeur. The duties of the aboyeur are further elaborated
in Chapter 18, *Kitchen Records and Control* (p. 278).

L'econome (storekeeper)

The storekeeper or l'econome as he is known in the French brigade
has not only an important responsibility in the receiving, recording
and issuing of stores but must also have a good knowledge of grocery
to deal adequately with the wide range of commodities under his
control. In addition to the normal range of grocery items he will need
to be familiar with foods from all parts of the world including many
which are not in ordinary demand in the average retail grocery store.
Additionally, he will need experience in the arrangement and storage
of grocery items from the point of view of avoiding spoilage and
deterioration. It hardly needs emphasis that personal integrity is a
vital factor in the character of a storekeeper and in those of the porters
and assistants, which, in the case of the biggest establishments, may be
allocated to him.

Cold and perishable stores attendant

In establishments of importance doing considerable trade, the storage of meat, poultry, etc., in refrigerated storage and of fruits and bulk butter in cool store is likely to be separated from the grocery store and under the control of a separate functionary. This type of stores attendant may well be a kitchen porter who has received 'house' or 'on the job' training in the care and issue of foods of a perishable kind needing cold storage.

Kitchen porters

The unskilled work of a large kitchen is considerable and involves the employment and organisation of a staff often larger in numbers than the chefs de partie and their commis. Responsible for the bulk of unskilled work in the kitchen are kitchen porters under a head porter who acts as foreman responsible to the head chef. He overlooks the work of the kitchen porters generally, though any allocated to parties will come under the instructions of the appropriate chef de partie.

Apart from obvious duties such as the carrying of kitchen loads and cleaning, porters will assist in vegetable preparation and in unskilled kitchen work generally.

Some staff graded as kitchen porters have specialised functions. Of these the two most prominent traditionally were the plongeur (less commonly known as the casserolier) who is responsible for the scouring of the cooking vessels of tinned copper and other metal and the charbonnier. This latter worker is, however, fast disappearing as solid fuel stoves are replaced by gas and electric for his principal duty was to keep each partie supplied with coal.

It was the charbonnier who often coupled with this main duty that of taking round the traditional drink of beer to the chefs twice a day at lunch and dinner service.

Plongeur or sculleryman

The wash-up for metal kitchen vessels and implements is, of course, separate from the washing-up arrangements for plates and table silver. The latter are dealt with by the silverman (argentier) who usually comes under the control of the maître d'hôtel.

The kitchen scullery is known as the plonge and the sculleryman as the plongeur or casserolier in a kitchen with a French-style brigade and culinary programme. In such kitchens most of the cooking vessels are made of copper lined with tin and keeping them scoured in a busy establishment is both a full-time job and a heavy one (see Chapter 11).

Terms for the pot washer such as le vaisselier and le passe-plats are not nowadays in common use in kitchens in this country.

Kitchen hands

In addition to kitchen porters, large kitchens employ as kitchen hands unskilled or semi-skilled women workers attached to parties or in the stores and vegetable rooms for tasks ranging from making butter pats, replenishing hors d'œuvres raviers, vegetable peeling, fruit salad preparation and in assisting at the servery, particularly at breakfast.

Cafetier (still-room man)

The still-room, though it is often under the supervision of the maître d'hôtel, may be regarded as an ancillary department of the kitchen for in it are prepared non-alcoholic beverages, in particular tea, coffee and other warm drinks but not soda fountain items which have separate service arrangements. Toast is also prepared in the still-room.

The range of work of the still-room will also include the portioning of butter (though this may also, when convenient, be done by a member of the store-keeping staff or even the garde manger). Traditionally, dirty glasses were washed in some still-rooms but there is a trend in more modern establishment to rationalise work so that the washing of utensils is separated from the service of any items of food.

Still-room staff are unskilled in the sense that they need to be trained only in a limited number of fairly simple processes and in the operation of simple machinery.

5 The chefs de partie and their work

The essence of the partie system and a feature immediately notice-able to most newcomers is the degree of specialisation which exists among cooks. In purely British establishments such as the English inn, specialisation has never enjoyed the same development. This is prob-ably because English restaurants have been run largely on the plan of a daily set menu (the old 'ordinary' or English inn version in former times of the table d'hôte). Indeed a simpler kitchen organisation will suffice to provide good simple fare.

On the other hand, kitchens in large modern hotels and restaurants require of their cooks a high degree of specialisation. French restaurants in every part of the world are organised for à la carte service from a menu which may include a hundred items or more and some of these items may change almost daily according to season. It was both to make this type of meal service possible within a reasonable time be-tween ordering and placing courses before the customer and to attain and uphold the high standards which custom and competition demand that the partie system was developed.

The tendency to eliminate a substantial amount of unskilled and semi-skilled food preparation by having a good deal of preliminary work done by the supplier will, undoubtedly, continue. Receiving into kitchens pre-prepared vegetables, butchered short cuts and also using foodstuffs processed in various ways is likely to cause adaptations of the functions of individual parties, a new blending of their functions collectively and, in some cases, radical re-organisation. Such trends have not, however, yet caused the disappearance of the partie system.

Arranging the work of the partie

It will be seen that the work of the various parties differs in type and magnitude but there are certain features common to each. In the case of each chef de partie the menu or menus (for often there will be commitments for table d'hôte restaurant, à la carte restaurant, grill room or buttery and for banquets) will be his blue-print. The French of the menu, discussed in more detail (p. 197), is, from the point of view of the chef de partie, technical jargon which he must understand because from it he learns the precise nature of his work for the day. Studied in advance, the menu linked with an estimate of the number of customers and a further estimate based on experience of the likely demand for the various items, enables the chef de partie to compose his indents for the stores for commodities for his partie.

Chefs de partie seldom receive written instructions for their work other than the menu. For a soup cook, the presence of consommé Celestine, for example, on the menu is sufficient intimation that he must order flour, eggs and the other ingredients needed to prepare the pancake garnish for this particular form of clear soup in addition to the soup's basic constituents (or, alternatively, to receive pancakes from the entremetier). Despite the fact that the chef de cuisine may already have made overall estimates of food required it is still commonly a partie responsibility to ensure that accurate sub-orders are placed on the stores and these are normally submitted through the chef de cuisine or a responsible sous chef for approval.

Supervising his staff

The chef de partie having his terms of reference from the menu and having made his order for food will then allocate work amongst himself, his commis and his apprentices. Though much of this work may fall into a pattern or regular routine it still remains necessary for a chef de partie to cultivate some qualities of foremanship in order to plan and organise successfully the practical work of his team. This responsibility and task varies in difficulty, of course, according to the size of the particular partie.

Again, as a full craftsman of standing, the chef de partie will invariably have an apprentice, improver or trainee of some kind attached to him and his ability to hand on his craft skills is not only a factor of importance to his own establishment but to the industry in general and is a regular feature of his normal day-to-day work with which he must learn to cope sympathetically.

The principal chefs de parties are as follows:

Chef saucier (sauce cook)

If he does not enjoy the title and status of sous chef the chef saucier is undoubtedly regarded as following next below. His standing in the kitchen is rivalled only by that of the chef garde manger (larder cook) (and, also, of course, by the chef pâtissier (pastry cook), who, however, is a specialist regarded as distinct from the other sectional chefs).

The reason for the importance accorded to the duties of the chef saucier is directly related to their complexity and the vital role they play in executing the requirements of the menu. It has been suggested that the word saucier is derived from the Italian salsa, salt, the fundamental seasoning in savoury foods.

The work of this chef de partie involves, of course, much more than the preparation of sauces, important though the actual sauces may be, and, indeed, the chef saucier is not ordinarily responsible for all sauces prepared in the kitchen because, for example, the chef poissonier (fish cook) undertakes this branch of cookery in regard to the accompaniments and garnishes of fish.

The saucier's work may, perhaps, best be summarised as comprising the cooking, garnishing and dishing of all meat, poultry and game dishes with the exception of those that are plainly grilled and roasted (which are cooked by the rôtisseur). This means that he is responsible for braises, bouillis, entrées, poêlés, which are included on the table d'hôte, à la carte and banqueting menus throughout the establishment.

In some hotels one of the chef saucier's assistants who was primarily responsible for dishes en cocotte was designated Cocottier, but today this separate functionary is seldom encountered.

The sauce partie will normally be responsible for at least one of the plats du jour or specialities of the day.

Link with other parties

In producing his dishes, assisted by one or more commis and apprentices, the chef saucier will not only have to prepare his own mis en place but for many items will receive prepared commodities from other sections. He will, for example, receive his tournedos ready cut and dressed from the boucherie, and escalopes for, say, escalopes de veau Holstein will be sent as required to his corner ready flattened and breadcrumbed from the garde manger (larder). When entreés require Italian pastes, nouilles or vegetables as garnishes on the same dish, their accompaniments will be sent to the saucier by the chef entremetier.

Thus the chef saucier is not only the preparer of his own foods but the assembler of the food prepared and sometimes cooked by others. This is true to some extent of all the parties in the kitchen, because their efforts under the chef de cuisine are all interlinked and interrelated.

It is, however, the chef saucier who has the greater proportion of such assembly work and in the sections of the menu which have a great impact on the customers.

Scope of work

When one considers the enormous range of entreés, relevées and garnitures included in standard professional cookery books and culinary repertoires, it is apparent that the work of the saucier covers a wide

and varied field. Though he and the chef de cuisine can, and do, refresh
their memory as to the appropriate garnishes for classical dishes by
turning to standard books of reference there must be, additionally, a
fund of training, experience, skill and artistry to draw on from himself
so that the formulae may be properly interpreted. Most working chefs
quickly abandon the recipe book but will keep by them a repertory of
dishes which they will use to the end of their working days.

In order to illustrate the work of this department and how it is linked
with the other sections of the kitchen, I give below two dishes which
amongst many others will be prepared and assembled by the chef
saucier indicating in each case the components of the dish that will be
contributed by other sections.

Côtelette de mouton reforme. A panéed lamb cutlet, i.e., one that has been
flattened, trimmed, egg and breadcrumbed but with, in this case, a
little chopped ham added to the breadcrumbs. These cutlets are sautéed
in butter and accompanied by a Reforme sauce which is made by
blending a demi-glace with a little red-currant jelly and, traditionally,
Poivrade sauce, and with a garnish of the following cut in short
Julienne size: cooked salted tongue, egg white, mushroom, truffles and
gherkins. To dish the above, the saucier receives the prepared crumbed
cutlets from the larder together with the ready-cut dry garnish. He,
himself, prepares the basic sauce, cooks the cutlet and assembles and
dresses the dish.

Tournedos ninon. This rather rarely encountered version of Tournedos
involves sautéing the little round steak from the tail-end of the beef
fillet in clarified butter, setting it on a bed of pommes Anna and topping
it with a small puff pastry bouchée which is filled with pointes d'asperges
and Julienne truffles cohered with butter. It is accompanied by Madeira-
flavoured demi-glace or sauce Madère. Here the saucier will cook and
assemble the dish but will receive the raw tournedos already dressed
from the larder or boucherie, the pommes Anna and other vegetable
garnish prepared and cooked by the chef entremetier and the bouchées
from the pastry.

Chef garde manger (larder cook)

The chef garde manger is in charge of the larder. The word larder
has in professional kitchens a much wider significance than in domestic
cookery. The larder is not simply a place where food is stored but a
place where the raw materials of cookery are prepared and dished.

In the very largest establishments the larder work may be further
broken into sections, and in one or two instances it is possible that the

sub-sections may even enjoy a degree of independence of the chef garde manger, i.e., in some organisations the boucherie might be directly controlled by the chef and the sous chefs. This is certainly rarely true in the smaller houses, and to note the sub-sections within the garde manger will both indicate the wide range of this chef de partie's duties and explain why he enjoys a status in the kitchen brigade comparable with that of the chef saucier.

The garde manger is normally accommodated adjoining, but not separated from, the main part of the kitchen. It will have its own cooking facilities which may, in some circumstances, be within the main kitchen itself. According to the size of the establishment its sub-sections too will be separate to a greater or smaller extent. The principal heads of the sub-sections are as follows:

Bouchier (butcher)

Boucherie in hotel work differs in many important regards from that commonly encountered in the retail meat trade. In the professional kitchen the boucherie, which is in the hands of full-time butchers if the volume of trade and the size of establishment warrant it, or in the hands of the chef garde manger or one of his assistants, may include the dissecting of quarters of beef and carcasses of lamb and sides of pork, but it will certainly involve the dressing of meat either for joints such as contrefilet or petits détails (small cuts) like noisette, côtelettes or tournedos.

Charcutier (pork butcher and sausage maker)

Charcuterie involves speciality pork butchery and the preparation of pork products and sausages and kindred made-up items. The charcutier is also usually responsible for the rendering and clarifying of dripping. Again the extent to which the charcuterie work is separated from that of the butcher and is assigned to another member of the staff of the garde manger depends on volume of work.

Volailleur (poulterer)

Here again where there is an extremely large commitment, the poulterer who is responsible for the plucking, cleaning and dressing not only of the poultry but game birds, hares and rabbits may be separated from the fishmonger and the larder proper.

Poissonier (fishmonger)

The hotel fishmonger prepares fish not in the style of the tradesman in retail trade for he must have the raw materials ready for the immediate attention of the appropriate chef; either the chef poissonier or in some instances, where cold dishes are included, for the chef garde manger himself.

A wide range of products of sea, river and lake will normally come to him for treatment which includes skinning, filleting and portioning. Fish such as eels, oysters, lobsters and crabs will demand his attention as well as the ordinary range of river, sea and shellfish.

Hors d'œuvrier (hors d'œuvres cook)

Where the work justifies it the preparation of hors d'œuvres of all kinds is organised separately. The range of dishes for this section can be great and can involve the regular preparation of commodities such as Bismarck and rollmop herrings from the raw state, the various varieties of vegetable salads (potato, Russian, etc.) found on the hors d'œuvres voiture (trolley) and the innumerable varieties of meat and fish raviers (side dishes). The dressing and re-dressing of raviers for hors d'œuvres is often entrusted not only to a chef hors d'œuvrier and assistants of the chef garde manger but to semi-skilled hands, often women workers trained only in assembling prepared material and in decorating raviers.

General larder work

The general work of the garde manger can be divided into two parts:

1. The items for which the garde manger is solely responsible.
2. The items which he produces to be cooked and worked on by other parties.

The garde manger's own dishes include all those commonly found on a cold table and comprise not only the cold joints but also galantines, ballotines and cold fish dishes and salads. Sandwiches, too, are the responsibility of the garde manger with the exception of some of the speciality hot or toasted sandwiches such as club sandwiches (ordinarily dealt with by the chef rôtisseur).

Mayonnaise sauce and its derivatives, vinaigrette sauce and other dressings and sauces for cold foods are also undertaken by the chef garde manger.

Saladier (salad maker)

The person responsible for the preparatory work and assembling of salads usually works in the garde manger.

An example of the work done by the garde manger for other parties has been indicated in outlining the work given to the chef saucier. The garde manger similarly provides the fish cook with many fish items ready for cookery and items for garniture for other corners of the kitchen as they are required.

Chef potager (soup cook)

If one considers the remaining parties in sequence roughly corresponding to the manner in which the courses of a meal appear on a menu, one would begin with the chef potager. This chef de partie, again assisted by commis and apprentices according to the size of the establishment, is responsible for the preparation and making of all the soups for the establishment and for the garnishes accompanying the soups. Because he prepares for the early course of lunch and dinner, the chef potager and his assistants sometimes begin duty (and finish it) a little earlier than the other cooks.

The work of the potager is, of course, important for the obvious reason that the soup will usually be the overture, as it were, for the meal and will create the first gastronomic impressions. This partie's importance within the kitchen brigade is also supported by the fact that the repertory of soups including consommés (clear soups), crêmes and veloutés (cream soups), purées, broths, bisques (shellfish soups), and many speciality and national soups is extensive. Consommés alone can be composed with differing flavouring essences and garnished in hundreds of ways.

The chef potager can, of course, be supplied by other parties with some of the garnishes required. He may, for example, receive material not only from the garde manger but may, for consommé Celestine, for example, receive pancake from the chef entremetier (via, perhaps, the chef pâtissier who prepared the appareil (mixture) or be supplied by the chef rôtisseur with the appareil for making diablotins which, like tiny Welsh rarebits, garnish the consommé of that name, and stock (or material for stock) from the chef poissonier for fish soups.

There still remains, however, for the soup corner itself, a substantial amount of garnish preparation involving skilful use of the knife and other culinary tools. Particularly prominent is the need for producing vegetable adornments of a wide variety of shapes and sizes.

Like all cooks, a cultivated palate is an important requirement because the adjustment of seasoning and the finishing of a potage, requires personal judgment as well as technical skill. This chef de partie, like the saucier, works normally in a section of the main kitchen.

Chef poissonier (fish cook)

The chef poissonier is responsible for the cooking, garnishing and sauce-making for the fish courses of a menu with the exception that deep fried fish is normally dealt with separately. (This frying may, indeed, be undertaken by a semi-skilled assistant cook who has been trained simply in that relatively narrow field.) The grilling of fish also may possibly be undertaken either by the grill cook or one of the grill cook's subordinates.

It has already been noted that the basic preparation of fish is undertaken either by the hotel and restaurant's fishmonger or by the chef garde manger or one of his assistants. This means that cleaning, including scaling and gutting and also when necessary, skinning, filleting, portioning and breadcrumbing are carried out not by the chef poissonier himself but by a fishmonger or chef garde manger on his behalf. It sometimes is arranged, however, that a commis poissonier be detached for part of the time to assist in these preparatory functions. The subordinate engaged in egg and crumbing is called, in a French brigade, the panadier.

The chef poissonier and his commis and apprentice helpers work, as in the case of the sauce partie, on a stove section in the main part of the kitchen. This chef de partie is responsible for the cooking, garnishing, saucing and dishing of fish dishes featuring fresh-water fish and sea-water fish, which in turn embrace shellfish such as crab, crayfish, shrimps, scollops, lobsters and mussels. Oysters are ordinarily served either direct from the fishmonger or the garde manger or a convenient cool place, and only if oysters have been cooked, are they dished direct from the chef poissonier's corner.

Methods of cooking fish are varied including as they do poaching, à la meunière (shallow frying in butter), en poêle (see p. 319) and, of course, in elaborate dressings. The repertoire of fish dishes and their accompanying sauces is, again, enormously wide so that considerable experience, training and palate judgment are required from this important chef de partie.

Chef rôtisseur (roast cook)

English cooks have long enjoyed a high reputation for the interest they have taken in roasting and the consequent skills they have acquired in this method of cooking. Even when continental kitchen brigades were the rule, it was quite usual to find in many top establishments, that roasting was under the supervision of a British roast cook or chef rôtisseur.

The work of the roast cook has, in the last half-century, changed outwardly more, perhaps, than any other section. The type of spit roasting which Arnold Bennett described so vividly and accurately in his novel *Imperial Palace*, which was first published in 1930, is seldom found even in high-class establishments today, for roasting by the open fire has been largely replaced by oven roasting which many consider to be virtually baking. Spit roasting has in the present era been revived but this has been due to the exploitation of electrical apparatus which tends to be featured more 'in the room' as a speciality feature for chicken rather than to be behind the scenes for roasting other birds and joints on the rôtisseur's corner. That the spit was linked with the chef's work is emphasised by the fact that his name is supposedly derived from the Italian 'rota', something turned.

Whilst the methods and equipment for roasting may have changed, the scope of duties of the chef rôtisseur have remained similar and include several processes quite distinct from roasting. This partie is, for example, commonly responsible for deep frying of foods of all kinds, including fried potatoes and the rôtisseur may have an assistant, le friturier (frying cook), for the task.

The chef rôtisseur is normally also responsible for savouries such as Welsh rarebit and for hot sandwiches of the club sandwich type. For tasks of this kind he may well have assistants, including in the case of deep frying, semi-skilled assistants, concerned with this narrow range of duties alone. The roast corner is also occupied with the preparation of stock, for the gravies which accompany the roasts and other dishes supplied from that corner.

Foods to be roasted cover a wide range of poultry, game and meat but exclude the baking of pies. The joints, the poultry and the game to be cooked by the rôtisseur are given the basic preparatory treatment in readiness for the oven in the larder or the appropriate 'shop', i.e., by the butcher or poulterer. It can, however, happen that here again a commis from the roast corner may be seconded to the larder for some part of the day to assist in the cleaning and trussing of poultry or the dissection, trimming and tying of joints of butcher's meat.

It is generally recognised that the dishes prepared by the roast cook are not as complex as many of those completed by the saucier or poissonier. Nevertheless, considerably more than simple roasting is involved. Game is varied and its garnishes vary too. In addition to experience in roasting, skill and familiarity with the culinary repertory is required to cope with the range of savouries and the production of good gravies. Knowledge and judgment is of over-riding importance in gauging the correct cooking of roasted items of varying sizes and kinds. These factors, alone, call for a man of parts for a roast cook's duties. Additionally it has to be borne in mind that this section of the kitchen tends to be most exacting physically. In big hotels the roasting trays heavily loaded with birds or joints need strength and knack to handle comfortably and skilfully.

The roast 'corner' is another of those parties which is sited in the main stove section and of necessity the cooking apparatus for roasting, for deep frying and for the finishing of savouries under a salamander (top heated griller) are grouped together and can make this section one of the hottest.

Trancheur (carver)

In many establishments the carver or chef trancheur may be under the control of the rôtisseur. The trancheur normally is skilled only in carving not in cooking. He may operate only behind the scenes at the hot service counter or may alternatively be stationed 'in the room' and patrol the restaurant with a heated voiture.

Chef grillardin (grill cook) and Chef savourier (savoury cook)

In some establishments the work of the grill cook is simply undertaken by a subordinate of the chef rôtisseur. Where a separate grillardin is established he might be expected to deal with the savouries and combine the functions of grillardin with that of savourier (savoury cook). Again it is a matter for a particular brigade organisation whether or not a grillardin will deal with the grilling of fish and the trend for some years now has been for fish to be grilled by the poissonier using a completely separate salamander for this purpose.

The grillardin today, therefore, is tending to be a semi-skilled, speciality cook or a commis rather than a full chef de partie of experience. His duties relative to those of other chefs are narrow but dealing with grilling whether using traditional media like charcoal or more modern grills using electricity or gas call for care, experience and judgment.

Chef entremetier (vegetable, egg and noodle cook)

The entremet course is, on the modern menu, the sweet which is the responsibility of the chef pâtissier and not the chef entremetier. Traditionally an important entremet course on traditional menus in France was, however, the entremet de Legumes when skilfully prepared and cooked vegetables were presented on a dish apart. An entremet was originally something sent to the table between courses and this practice still survives in France as far as vegetables are concerned.

The entremetier in the kitchen brigade today is, therefore, concerned mainly with vegetables with additional responsibilities for the cooking of eggs, pâtes, rice and farinaceous dishes such as gnocchi. When these are served as a course they are cooked and assembled on the chef entremetier's own corner but he may be responsible for passing vegetable garnish to another partie for the completion of a dish destined to be sent to the room by, say, the chef saucier; for example, the vegetable accompaniments, including tomato and French beans, of a Tournedos Nicoise.

The cooking of eggs forms an important part of the work of this corner. Particularly prominent are omelets of all kinds which are so frequently ordered by customers not only on their own merits on the menu but, sometimes, as a substitute for a table d'hôte item which is not favoured.

The pâtes (usually Italian pastes but also nouilles (noodles), not to be confused with the pastes of meat, poultry, fish and game, prepared by the garde manger) are also cooked by the chef entremetier. Items such as cooked spaghetti and rice may be sent to another chef to garnish other dishes as, for example, nouilles which customarily accompany Hungarian goulash. But rice, Italian pâtes and the like are also in the same way as eggs, featured as a preliminary course of a luncheon menu.

The cooking of pancakes either for service from the kitchen or to be sent in for speciality cooking from the guéridon (service side table) for serving by the maître d'hôtel or his staff is also undertaken by the chef entremetier or his commis and apprentices. Pancakes are commonly made from a batter supplied to the entremetier by the chef pâtissier.

Important though these items are they are not more so than the vegetables prepared and cooked as accompaniments to the main meat, poultry and game dishes. Unfortunately in Britain where meat, poultry and game have been regarded as the main bricks in the menu structure, vegetable cookery was in the past honoured relatively less. To some extent this was reflected in an attitude towards the chef entremetier which appeared to rank him at somewhat lower level than other chefs de partie.

This attitude should no longer exist, for it is certain that the cooking and service of vegetables is of the greatest importance to the culinary reputation of an establishment. What is more, the proper cooking and dressing of vegetables demands not only great experience and skill but also a similar familiarity with a wide repertoire of methods as is the case in other parties.

Because of the nature of the commodities to be cooked by the entremetier, the amount of food (particularly when required for table d'hôte purposes) to be handled by him usually in volume is greater than with other parties. This may create the impression that the operation of cooking masses of vegetables in bulk may be crude and less skilled than other smaller processes. Nothing could be more erroneous; for, on the contrary, the management of cooking vegetables well for large numbers calls for particular knowledge, skill and judgment and should never be entrusted to an unskilled and disinterested cook.

To facilitate vegetable cookery, that part of the work which is required for the set table d'hôte or function meals is often organised separately from the à la carte vegetable service.

It goes without saying that the peeling and cleaning, trimming and other basic treatments of vegetables which are, at best, semi-skilled operations only can be, and are, undertaken by unskilled kitchen hands of either sex (p. 38).

Modern processing methods such as deep freezing, dehydrating and canning are tending to remove such basic preparations from the kitchen but the skills of assembling, cooking, garnishing and flavouring remain. One has only to note the numbers of vegetables commonly featured on menus and the numbers of ways of dressing them as listed in the standard culinary repertoires to appreciate that vegetable cookery is work demanding the highest skill.

Chef pâtissier (pastry cook)

The chef pâtissier in a large and important establishment has a status different from, but certainly not less than, the chef saucier and the chef garde manger. Like the chef garde manger, however, the work of his department is normally separated from the main body of the kitchen and is not only self-contained in the matter of cold storage and specialist machinery and equipment for making ices and the like but is also equipped with its own baking and cooking facilities.

The chef pâtissier is responsible for all hot and cold sweets for lunches, dinners and functions and for pastries served at tea-time (or other occasions). He is also responsible for the making of pastes like short and puff pastry, fritter batters and also noodles and Italian pastes for supply to other corners of the kitchen.

The number of hotels and restaurants which nowadays operate their own bakery plant is dwindling though formerly this work might be organised by a boulanger (baker) under the chef pâtissier or separately and directly under the control of the chef de cuisine. In modern establishments where baking is normally restricted to a limited quantity of bread, rolls, batons, croissants and brioches, the work is likely to be in the hands of one of the chef pâtissier's subordinates.

However regrettable it may seem to gourmets, the art of making

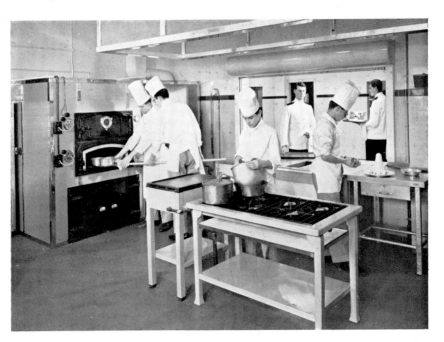

A corner of a well-appointed pâtisserie or pastry kitchen at the Scottish Hotel School

The service area of the Scottish Hotel School kitchens designed along hotel lines but with additional space which enables training to be effectively performed

A corner of a garde manger partie at a hotel and catering training centre

The smaller gas kitchen at the Scottish Hotel School

various kinds of ices such as bombes, biscuits glacées and the many varieties of ice cream is also tending to disappear from all but the most exclusive hotels and restaurants and the practice of obtaining these items from the factory is now common. Such work formerly was in the hands of a chef glacier who was one of the assistant chefs to the pâtisserie. Though Sorbets and water ices are not, perhaps, as extensively featured as they were in the days of longer and heavier menus, these items are the ones nowadays most likely to be made in the pastry section itself. The service of ices and those sweets which are based upon ices has, of course, developed strongly and these, from whatever source the ice cream is obtained, are prepared and assembled in the pâtisserie. They include the sweet omelet en surprise and the soufflée surprise (ice cream with the hot meringue exterior) and speciality dishes like Pêche Melba, Poire Helene and Puits d'Amour. Spun sugar, dipped fruits and petits fours of all kinds to accompany this type of sweet course are all prepared within the pâtisserie.

Arts of the pastry which were formerly developed extensively to satisfy a wealthy and leisured clientele included work with pulled and coloured sugars to make flower baskets and similar decorative centre pieces, work with pastillage (fondants and icing sugars reinforced with gum), the fashioning of nougat and praliné into boxes and decorative objects containing chocolates or friandises and the carving of blocks of ice into sculptured pieces using heated irons.

High kitchen labour costs and the changing public in the restaurants are among the factors which have caused some of these arts to wane.

There is still an élite corps of men skilled in sugar work but many pâtissiers keep it alive more as a personal craft and hobby than as a creative feature of commercial realism. Though the sugar basket, which if properly stored has a reasonably durable life, can still be an aid to business in high class and function catering, an art such as ice carving seems almost to be a forgotten skill.

The work of the pâtissier has always been high-lighted by the beauty of the cold sweets, ices and their accompaniments, but the work of the department is made up of a considerable volume of substantial activity which, though less spectacular, still requires great skill and experience. In big houses one or more cuisinier will do no more than prepare pastry itself like short and puff pastry for the making of pies, flans, etc. Semi-skilled assistants will prepare fresh fruit for fruit salads for service not only at lunch and dinner but at breakfast. The chef pâtissier is, therefore, like the garde manger something like a chef de cuisine of a speciality kitchen and in addition to his own skills must co-ordinate and organise the work of a number of subordinates.

RELIEF, DUTY AND OTHER CHEFS

Chef tournant (relief cook)

The chef tournant is simply the relief chef de partie. His duty is to take over from any chef de partie as demanded by the normal incidence of holidays and days off. Attitudes to the chef tournant vary amongst chefs de cuisine. It is quite common for it to be regarded as an opportunity for an experienced commis to gain his first experience as a chef de partie because it is thought he will have fresh memories of all the parties round which he has circulated as an apprentice or commis. Usually, therefore, le chef tournant is a young and 'up and coming' cuisinier. Occasionally, however, the appointment may go to an older man of long experience as a prelude to appointment as sous chef. This post can be useful for older men because there is a definite tendency for chef de parties, after their all-round training, to specialise in one partie either from choice or accident.

Chef de garde (duty cook)

The term chef de garde means, simply, the chef 'on guard' or the duty cook and the task may be undertaken by any chef de partie (or even experienced commis) in the kitchen. The working hours of the ordinary chefs de partie and their assistants were at one time invariably 'split' and, indeed, in many establishments there continues to be a break in duty following the service of lunch and up to 5.30 p.m. or 6.30 p.m. when the immediate preparations for the service of dinner begin. During this period (and in late evening periods) when the bulk of kitchen staff are off duty, there remain behind one or more chefs de garde (duty cooks) with appropriate commis and apprentices de garde to continue the work which cannot be delayed until the remainder of the brigade return to duty.

In large establishments, separate chefs or commis de garde will remain in the pâtisserie, the garde manger and at least one in the main section of the kitchen and who may see to the affairs of more than one of the kitchen parties.

Chef de nuit (night duty cook)

The chef de nuit is similarly a chef whose main duties are to take over when the main kitchen staff leave. A separate chef de nuit may be retained in the garde manger but normally one person suffices if given a roving commission.

The chef de nuit does not necessarily remain on duty throughout the night but only until such time as the possible need for late meals has ceased.

Chef de banquets (banquet chef)

In the largest establishments completely separate arrangements may be provided if not for the complete cooking of banquet and function meals at least for their assembly and service. The chef given responsibility for special service of banquets may be known as the chef de banquets.

Breakfast cook

The 'traditional' chefs de partie normally appear with their commis in time to prepare the service of lunch. The cooking and service of breakfast in hotels is commonly entrusted to a speciality cook whose range is limited to the needs of breakfast. He (or sometimes she) does not rank as a full chef de partie, but nevertheless needs to be of good skill within the limited field.

It will be apparent that the breakfast cook as an appendage to the normal kitchen brigade is normally dependent upon British custom (spread wider, too, by American habit) for on the Continent, except as required originally by British visitors, provision for cooked breakfast was unnecessary. Café complet (coffee with rolls, croissants, butter and jam) was served mainly in the guest's own room from small floor kitchens. The way in which the work of the breakfast cook and his semi-skilled assistants is organised must be considered a distinctly British addition to a traditional brigade.

The mis-en-place (preparation) for breakfast including the boning, rinding and slicing of bacon and the preparation of the various types of fish normally eaten at breakfast time is, of course, ordinarily carried out in advance by a subordinate of the garde manger and semi-skilled assistants may be carried on his staff for this purpose. Similarly, the preparation of fruit compôtes and fruit salads is a matter for assistants in the pâtisserie. The breakfast cooks and helpers are left with the relatively simple task of assembling and cooking breakfast dishes. In these dishes the cooking of eggs in their various forms and the grilling and frying of fish and bacon are amongst the principal functions. Toasts and beverages are the responsibilities of the still-room which is mentioned in a separate section (p. 38).

In high-class hotels, of course, a substantial amount of breakfast cookery may be de-centralised on to the various floor kitchens.

Chef communar (staff cook)

In many small establishments, food for the hotel and restaurant staff may be prepared according to its nature by the different chefs de partie.

In larger houses a separate section of the kitchen or a completely separate kitchen may be allocated to the production of staff meals.

Staff meals ordinarily imply meals provided for the 'rank and file' wage-earning staff such as uniformed staff, chambermaids, waiters, lower grade clerical staff, etc. The chef communar and his staff will prepare and cook meals principally for this type of employee.

Catering of this nature should be influenced by nutritional factors as well as those designed to give pleasure and will be the concern not only of the chef de cuisine under whom the chef communar operates, but also the management of the hotel who must regard it as an important personnel management feature contributing to staff well-being, welfare and efficiency.

In addition to supplying wage-earning employees with meals, the chef de cuisine in bigger establishments is also responsible for catering for the couriers' room. The name of the couriers' room is derived from the days when travellers were accompanied by couriers and attendants and such rooms in hotels still afford facilities for personal servants, such as chauffeurs and ladies' maids accompanying guests.

It is, however, today common for the couriers' room to be combined with the function of catering for 'superior staff' or, put another way, the servants of guests are often afforded dining facilities in the 'superior staff' dining room. Whether the couriers' room or superior staff dining room becomes the responsibility of the chef communar wholly or partly and whether the different chefs de partie contribute to the dishes provided for this grade of staff is, of course, a matter for management policy to decide.

It is common for supervisory and executive staff of departmental managers' grade and above to be given dining facilities in the restaurant or in their own quarters from the ordinary en pension or table d'hôte menus. In the case of more junior executives some restrictions may be imposed as to selection of the higher cost items on the menus.

6   Management and foremanship in the kitchen

In recent years management has been taken much more seriously and formal studies have been incorporated into many courses of hotel and catering training. In America, and some other parts of the world, chefs who reach the most senior posts are called 'executive chefs', and this term gives emphasis to the type of managerial work that is involved in being the head of a large and complex department. Apart, however, from executive duties which clearly devolve upon the head chef, there are other supervisory responsibilities for senior subordinates in the kitchen, who must acquire qualities and skills to exercise effective foremanship. The chef de cuisine, in short, is and must undoubtedly act as a departmental manager; while sous chefs and chefs de partie must, to varying degrees, act as foremen.

Chefs' fundamental management functions

The fundamental functions of management which have to be undertaken by the chef de cuisine as a departmental manager may be summarised as follows:

(a) *Planning.* He must determine his course of action in a given set of circumstances.

(b) *Organising and co-ordinating.* The chef de cuisine must allocate work amongst the various parties and sections. At the same time he must establish and foster sound working relationships in the midst of satisfactory working conditions.

(c) *Motivating* or actuating the working groups to achieve the objectives required by his plan is also a function of the chef de cusine. He must give leadership, inspiration, direction and example to the chefs de partie and their teams.

(d) *Controlling.* What is achieved or produced must be evaluated against the requirements of the plan. In controlling, the chef de cuisine will be taking such corrective steps as are necessary to ensure that the results will be as planned.

Planning

The chef de cuisine, for example, must plan the activities of his kitchens for the day, week or month in accordance with the requirements of the restaurant or other type of service and in such a way as to dovetail them into the activities of others such as the maître d'hôtel. His plans must, therefore, be flexible owing to the uncertainties, inevitable in many cases in hotel, restaurant and catering operations, of the requirements. (Unexpected arrival of a large party or a change in the weather bringing (or preventing) business are amongst examples of catering uncertainties.)

In the light of these requirements, however, work has to be allocated to the parties and sections of the kitchen and co-ordinated with stores and restaurant. Such allocation will ensure that there are sufficient cooks and other workers to deal with the work on each partie, that there are materials to hand in correct quantities, and that table d'hôte or à la carte production is available as required by the restaurant.

Thus the chef de cuisine through his key staff such as sous chefs, chefs de partie and kitchen clerks must be in a position to control production, assess progress, alter plans as required (often on the spot) or to re-allocate staff if necessary.

Organising and Co-ordinating

It cannot be too strongly stressed that co-ordination of activities in the kitchen must ensure effective fusion with other departments of the hotel or catering establishment but, in particular, a harmonious relationship must be established with the maître d'hôtel and with his staff. Achievement of efficient service (the plan) is difficult without close co-operation between the two department heads, the chef de cuisine and the maître d'hôtel. Experience shows that all too often friction between these two heads of departments result in bad restaurant service. Deterioration in relationship between the two departmental managers concerned is unfortunately seldom confined to the two main personalities but can, and is indeed likely to extend to their respective staffs. This exacerbates, even when it does not cause, 'up the wall' relationships.

Motivating

Motivating includes creating and maintaining in each member of the kitchen (and restaurant) staff the desire to achieve the objective set out in the plans. Mention has been made of the supervisory function of the important chefs de partie, particularly men like the chef garde manger or chef pâtissier. In motivating it is, thus, vitally important to start by making each chef de partie realise that he is an integral and important part of the management team. It is equally important that each chef de partie is made aware that he has the active support of those above him in the chain of responsibility. Those higher in the chain must indeed appreciate that he is a vital link in it as the individual closest to the operatives—the working cuisiniers, commis and aides. In consequence, chefs de partie must be relied on for support in a supervisory or foreman capacity and in turn must be given the help, encouragement and confidence to enable them to function properly at such supervisory or foremanship level.

Controlling

Clearly it is not really enough that the chef de partie is technically well endowed as a craftsman, important though this is. He should also have the capacity to lead his section; particularly where the section is a substantial one, such as the pastry or larder as has been mentioned. That qualities of leadership are required is a fact too often forgotten or ignored when such staff appointments are made.

The main chefs de partie must be able to handle staff, delegate and place responsibilities. They must cope with complaints and grievances within their sections, co-operate with superiors and opposite numbers in charge of other sections and other departments, maintain morale and enforce discipline. A chef de partie has great responsibility for training new staff, or 'old staff' in new jobs or new techniques. He must, moreover, seek to develop potential chefs de partie or future chefs de cuisine who are members of his section. He must plan his part of the kitchen operation and control production through his section. At the same time, he must maintain quality in production, eliminate waste and be generally cost conscious.

Awareness of responsibilities

The first step towards improved management in the kitchen is for the chef de cuisine and his supervisory staff to be fully aware of the managerial responsibilities of their respective positions and to implement their managerial or supervisory functions as outlined in this chapter.

Progress in this regard may be slow and there will be many pitfalls, but these are to be expected. After all, management concerns human beings and one must deal with individuals with different personalities, different qualifications, different abilities, different personal problems as well as different work problems. It is the function of management to weld these diverse personalities into a soundly motivated and efficiently working group; to deal with problems as they arise and to ensure that the results desired and, indeed, planned are in fact achieved.

Some aspects of management

In the present era the study of management in industrial, commercial and vocational fields of activity has, as emphasised in this chapter's opening paragraph, come to be regarded much more seriously. The development of facilities for study of management both 'on the job' and in courses of study (from short, week-end study groups to longer periods of training) has been accompanied by a somewhat alarming and forbidding mass of descriptive jargon.

Aspects of management such as work study, communications, industrial psychology, as well as the more familiar features, have tended to create the impression, as far as the ordinary man in the street or chef in the kitchen is concerned, that there are a welter of new problems, new studies and new difficulties to overcome. Most people concerned with management training would, it is certain, wish to stress that all that is new in the modern approach to management is the way in which age-long problems are investigated and described.

An old kitchen dictum like 'a place for everything and everything in its place' is an older-fashioned and simpler way of expressing a precept which is today emphasised as a result of, for example, work study. No chef worthy of his salt has ever neglected to study the tasks which confront him and his staff. He has sought to simplify the component parts of each job, to reduce unnecessary movement of personnel and material and, in doing such things over the ages, he has basically differed not a whit from his modern counterpart, who will describe his activities in terms of work study, work simplification and so on. What is, of course, true is that today there are more specialists and consultants and advisers who, after detachedly observing or studying kitchen processes like other industrial activities, can often make substantial contributions to revising and rationalising work in the kitchen.

Chefs and caterers would be most unwise to reject the aid which the development of such specialist services has made possible or will make possible. There is a strong inclination on the part of many in old occupations and traditional crafts to stress that their work is unique rather than to appreciate the many similarities between what may superficially appear different activities.

Lessons learned in a bakehouse, in a retail store, in a factory, or even in an office, often surprisingly have a common application one to the other and often have an application within an hotel, a restaurant and other type of catering establishment. This is especially true of specific human activity for, despite many characteristics, there is a basic consistency about human behaviour, motives and reactions, and the chef and cook is not as different from other craftsmen as he so often thinks.

Value of experience
   It must be apparent that the art of management can hardly be acquired

from reading books alone. Much less will it be mastered through the medium of one chapter in a Manual of the Kitchen such as this. Management may be studied, but the practice and perfecting of techniques of management undoubtedly involves experience. The progressive chef will be gaining by experience of human beings and of technical problems involving human beings from the early days of his apprenticeship to the end of his career, but he will undoubtedly gain maximum value from such experience if he augments it with thought, reading, study and discussion.

Whilst an enormous field of management and foremanship must remain untouched in a work of this nature, there are two facets which should be stressed:

Personnel management

Inanimate objects, plant and equipment constitute problems for management, and particularly so in their relationship with people who will use them. Inanimate objects, however, like stoves and tables may be fixed in position without any regard to the vagaries of personality. How different are the problems of dealing with the human element in the kitchen or anywhere else for that matter. Thus to some the very term staff management or personnel management seems almost an unnecessary qualification of the word management for they see managerial problems as basically human problems and as invariably involving the staff as the human element in the operation being managed. Clearly, however, personnel management is recognisably today a specialist activity, largely concerned with the recruitment, allocation and well-being of staff. In larger establishments these functions will be handled by a specialist and this is, of course, the case in many units within the hotel and catering industry. Yet the chef or caterer must on no account regard the presence of a staff manager or personnel manager as a reason for himself not being concerned with the human beings on his staff. Whether his own task of staff management is supported by a personnel officer or not, the chef must be closely concerned with his staff as individual personalities and certainly not as mere 'units of labour'.

Recruitment

Having the right man in the right job is to be half-way towards securing a contented craftsman or other worker. Attracting the right man and satisfying oneself that he is the right man are problems by no means as simple as they appear. Other sections of this Manual have indicated the importance of giving status to the different tasks of the kitchen, and it cannot be too strongly stressed that the standing of the job performed will be, to many people, as important as, or more important than, the pay attached to it.

The development of the partie system has in itself made a substantial contribution to what is today known as 'job evaluation'. Where the traditional partie system is operated, the staff engager, who will normally be the chef himself, will know:

(a) The type of man required.
(b) From where he may be obtained (whether by promotion or from outside recruitment).
(c) The experience and qualifications he should have.
(d) The tasks he will have to perform.

There are undoubted advantages, however, in recording this sort of information or job evaluation on job analysis sheets or cards for filing in the staff office or in the chef's office, both as an aide-memoire to the chef, and certainly as a guide to a staff engager. Such aids are particularly necessary if, for any reason, staff is being recruited from a detached head office and the chef is not available for on-the-spot advice.

The technical requirements for the job do not, of course, exhaust the features of staff selection, and it will be apparent that the chef, like any other executive, must study methods and techniques of interviewing and must be concerned with character (involving the taking up of references) as well as with technical aptitudes.

Staff efficiency

A logical extension of evaluating the job, in order properly to fill it, is the preparation of brief notes either in the form of a sheet of instructions, or even a leaflet or small manual which outlines the nature, times and details of the duties to be performed. Even in the case of chefs' or cuisiniers' tasks where the broad duties are traditionally clear, such as in the case of a chef saucier or other chef de partie, there is likely to be value in handing the newly engaged man a résumé of his duties as specially conditioned by the custom of the hotel or catering establishment in which he is engaged. In the case of workers at lower levels in ancillary departments like stores, fishmonger's shop, wash-up and the like, there is very great value in having an employee leaflet indicating the work of the section as a whole and preferably including details of the component jobs.

Welfare and leisure

The chef de cusine must be concerned, therefore, with ensuring that his department is conducted so as to give appropriate human dignity to all members of his staff, however humble the tasks they perform. Whilst he, in company with the management of his establishment, must be concerned with the pay for the job being competitive with that in other industries and appropriate within the industry itself, he must, if the right staff are to be attracted and retained, also have regard to other factors, particularly:

(*a*) Changing facilities.
(*b*) Dining facilities.
(*c*) Rest room and recreational facilities.
(*d*) Clear duty, day off and holiday rotas.

Such are amongst the special factors which, unfortunately, are too often unsatisfactory as far as kitchen staff are concerned.

The provision of a suitable place for cooks and other kitchen workers to change and to have a shower is clearly most desirable, and it is equally most important that a suitable, quiet dining area is available for kitchen staff just as it might be for other types of workers.

Special problems exist in the catering industry in regard to time off and the provision of facilities for leisure time. The catering industry is today nearer other industries in the total number of hours worked by its staff, but there remain many problems connected with the distribution and 'spread' of hours. Week-end and evening working and, particularly, pressure during holiday periods impose special difficulties. Many of these problems are reduced to insignificance when kitchens are fully recruited and when clear-cut arrangements are made and announced in advance for working hours and days off. The executive chef who takes pains to compile a realistic duty, days off and holiday rota will be amply repaid for his trouble in the satisfaction of his staff and the reputation of his kitchen. Similarly, where staff spend an hour or so of rest on the premises, as is so often the case in the hotel and catering industry, it is of the greatest possible value to provide a bright and attractive staff rest-room, with due regard to the value of such recreational amenities as games, radio and books.

The foregoing by no means constitute the sole staff and welfare factors with which the chef, in conjunction with the manager and the personnel manager, need be concerned, but they are certainly features of special significance in hotels and catering establishments.

Training staff

The preparation of job evaluation sheets and employee guide sheets are important basic steps in 'on the job' training, which is referred to in Chapter 19, p. 288. Training must closely concern the departmental manager and the foreman. It will have amongst its prominent aims:

(*a*) Making the most effective use of men and materials.
(*b*) Ensuring efficient use of plant and equipment.
(*c*) Preventing accidents and loss of time through accidents.
(*d*) Encouraging high morale through job satisfaction.

Status and designation

The hotel and catering industry is one with an extremely high rate of labour turn-over, and there is little doubt that within the kitchen there are humdrum tasks like peeling and washing up which can easily appear meaningless, trivial and even degrading. Much can be done to improve the morale of people engaged on unskilled and semi-skilled tasks by giving thought to an appropriate designation for the task (terms like 'veg man' are certainly not happy choices), and the efficiency and effective performance of simple tasks can be improved by proper training, so that unnecessary dirt and drudgery may be eliminated. Terms like 'kitchen hygiene assistants', 'kitchen assistants' and so on, given to those who clean pans and equipment or undertake basic food preparations like vegetable peeling may help to improve morale and to attract and keep staff. This is particularly likely if an appropriate designation is supported by provision of trim, clean working uniform and decent working conditions.

The chef as executive must compete for staff who may be attracted by other occupations in, for example, department stores, factories and offices, and where welfare measures and job status have been thoughtfully fostered. One of the greatest mistakes that the chef can make is to look back into the past when kitchen staffing was made easier through unemployment and through men's fear of losing a job.

Ultimately the health and well-being of the kitchens, and the hotel and catering industry as a whole, must hinge upon the ability to recruit staff on equal terms with other and similar industries. It is, thus, necessary to interest staff, pay them and look after them in such a way as to retain them in face of outside competition. The chef as a departmental manager and the chef de partie as foreman must, therefore, keep abreast of managerial techniques, not only to ensure proper staffing, contentment and efficiency in his own department or section, but also to help build a flourishing and efficient business.

Banquet service kitchen, Grosvenor House, London, W.1, is an up-to-date installation enabling numbers to be served swiftly and efficiently

The service area of the kitchens of D. H. Evans' Restaurant, Oxford Street, London, also planned by kitchen equipment layout specialists to cater speedily for large numbers

Young people entering kitchen work today can augment their daily practical activity with part-time study at technical college. Girls, though not yet fully accepted as apprentices in many of the largest hotels, play an important part in other fields of professional cookery

7   The cookery craftsman's tools

The chef and his kitchen have both shared in the technological progress of the second half of the twentieth century. Today they use equipment that former masters like Soyer and Escoffier had barely begun to envisage. Yet the fact remains that the immediate tools which the chef uses personally and which he owns and carries with him wherever he may work have changed little over the last hundred years.

The chef's personal tools

As in the case of many traditional crafts in which the implement held in the hands must do the work, the craftsman by process of acceptance and rejection, early established his ideal requirements in the kitchen. The chef's personal tools are relatively small in number and of them his knives are by far the most important. Whatever his partie the chef will require knives of various sizes with which to trim and to cut vegetables for garnish, to bone meat, to fillet fish, to slice and to carve. For these and other tasks, the chef has learned by experience what type of knife is best suited for the purpose. Yet it must be stressed that craftsmen remain individualists and many a fine workman will reject a perfectly adapted couteau d'office in favour of a worn-down table knife to which he has become accustomed.

All good professionals, however, have one thing in common; dexterity with the knife. They have been taught from the earliest days of apprenticeship to realise the value of using simple tools, particularly knives, effectively. The professional chef knows that careful selection of his personal knives is important in helping him achieve dexterity in, for example, the cutting of garnishes. This not only conserves his time and energy (and thus, of course, affects his employer's labour costs) but aids artistry because it ensures neatness of décor and also because speed in the basic operation allows more time for finishing touches.

Deciding what tools to own is a matter of personal choice (though some are obviously necessities). Just as some good golfers are strong advocates of a modest range of clubs whilst equally good players rely more heavily on a multitude of irons, drivers and other 'special purpose' aids, so chefs differ in choosing their range of tools.

In making their selection, however, most chefs choose carefully. An overwhelming number prefer the best French knives for cutting garnishes, trimming and paring and mincing. British knives of best Sheffield steel have, however, a strong following for uses linked with larder work particularly, for carving and boning. It is not mere traditionalism which caused chefs generally to reject the fancy shapes of hollow-ground stainless steel with pretty handles for they have found many of the fanciful shapes ill adapted to their special needs and unable to stand up to the work of the kitchen.

The craftsman in the kitchen, as in other spheres, is well advised to adopt early the strict rule of neither borrowing nor lending his implements.

Here are the more important knives and tools from which the chef is likely to make his own personal selection:

Couteau d'office. The couteau d'office is a small knife normally of the traditional French shape, i.e., a broad heel tapering to a point. It is used for trimming and turning vegetables. The blade is seldom longer than 4 in. and the size usually preferred is 3 or 3½ in. (It must be stressed, however, that personal idiosyncrasies are strong as far as this tool is concerned, even ground-down table knives, as has been observed, being used.) The couteau d'office must, however, have a pointed end for it is used for tasks such as removing the hard pith where the stalk joins the tomato and in removing blemishes in root vegetables or in removing carrot tops.

Apart from cleaning and peeling, the couteau d'office is used for the skilled task of 'turning' vegetables. Having peeled and cut the vegetables to rectangular segments, the couteau d'office is used to trim off the square edges giving an olive shape to enhance the appearance of vegetable garnishes such as bouquetière and jardinière.

The use of the knife for this purpose is not learned from books but is passed on by the chef craftsman to his apprentices.

It is, however, worth recording that the point only of the knife is used in 'turning' and the axis of movement should be from the wrist down so that the hand and tool move as one when making the round downward cuts towards the thumb of the other hand which is holding the piece to be 'turned'.

Filleting knife. In size this knife usually comes between the couteau d'office and the small cook's knives. The length of the blade most favoured is 6 or 7 in. The filleting knife is of the traditional broad-heeled, pointed-end French shape, but is more slender than the larger cook's knives and resembles more an elongated couteau d'office. The filleting knife as its name implies, is chiefly used for removing fish from the bone or in trimming meat. It is also suitable for tasks such as removing membrane from the fillet of beef, where a thin, pointed knife is required.

Cook's knives (1).

In addition to the couteau d'office and the filleting knife, the chef normally has at least two more knives of French style:

Slicing knife. The size of cook's knives range from small ones with 5 in. blades up by 1 in. lengths to blades 12 in. long but most favoured for slicing purposes are those with a 9 in. or 10 in. blade. It is here that the real value of the traditional French shape—broad heel tapering to a point—is shown. With only a little practice, the apprentice can soon be taught to slice neatly large masses of segments, slices or dice using the gliding toe and heel movement of the knife and controlling the garnish to be cut with the left hand. The fingers of the left hand holding the foodstuff are slightly tucked under enabling the left hand safely to guide the knife's action.

Here again the use of the knife is imparted by one craftsman to another and is not a subject for 'book learning' but one or two points are worth recording. (*a*) The beginner must learn to hold a knife correctly by grasping it lightly but firmly with the fingers around and under one side and with the thumb along the other. It must be stressed that the knife is designed for the *handle* to be used and the forefinger should not press along the top of the blade. (*b*) With the cook's knife in particular, the blade will necessarily be cutting against a resistant surface and this should always be a wooden chopping board. The knife should not be used against metal and other hard surfaces. Today, when kitchens, to comply with hygiene regulations, have work tables with impervious surfaces, the use of proper wooden chopping boards is extremely important. (*c*) Have a clean, unlittered board on which to work. (*d*) Stack what is to be sliced on the left and stand squarely in front of the board. Have no vegetables or other materials to be cut between you and what you are cutting. (*e*) As the garnish is made, stack it on the right-hand side out of your way. (*f*) Be comfortable. Height of working bench is important here. The good kitchen will have work tables of different sizes to meet the needs of different sized craftsmen.

When cutting garnishes it will help if it is remembered that it is the heel of the knife which is used more than the point, which is rather a pivotal part. The cutting in the heel and toe action is actually made with the forward movement.

When slicing with a small knife (or even a large knife for small articles) a somewhat different action is used. The small knife is moved quickly up and down whilst the guiding hand holding the vegetables to be cut ensures that the required thickness is achieved. This up and down technique needs considerable practice and depends on a good knife and a good surface of chopping board.

Chopping knives. Chopping knives are of exactly the same appearance as French cooks' knives but range in size from 11 in. to 14 in. and are extra heavy. Again, the choice of chopping knife for size and weight is a matter for individual preference. The technique of using the chopping knife for preparing a fine mince is to hold the knife parallel with the body and with the fingers of the left hand steadying the top of the point end. The knife is then rocked from one hand to the other with the knife moving across the board away from and then towards the body.

A less common mode of mincing is to use two equally weighted knives held at right angles to the body with tip pointing away and chopping alternatively up and down.

In addition to chopping fine garnishes this heavy type of knife is, however, widely used for severing through bone joints of poultry, or the removal of bony parts of fish. For such purposes, of course, the knife is brought down sharply in one stroke.

Palette knife (2). The palette knife derives its name from its similarity to the knife used to clean the artist's palette. It ranges in size in 1 in. stages from about 5 in. to 12 in. blade lengths. A popular size for general use in the chef's own personal kit is a 9 or 10 in. blade. The blade of this knife is rounded at the end and has no sharp cutting edge. Its use in the kitchen is, like the artist's, for the scraping of bowls, slabs and trays but additionally, it has wide use for turning and removing articles during cooking and for smoothing and finishing surfaces such as in the dishing of purées or in icing cakes.

Boning knife. The usual blade size for a boning knife is 6 in. and this blade differs from the French cook's shape, having no depth of heel and with the blade curving backwards at the tip giving a rounded point, as it were, at the top. The knife is grasped like a dagger for this point is the part of the knife which does the work of searching out the bone and cutting away close to it. In boning, unless great care is taken, accidents can happen because cuts frequently must be made towards the body and it is important that these cuts should only be obliquely towards the body, thus if there is a slip the knife will pass harmlessly by. Boning knives, like others used by butchers, are usually selected from the Sheffield range.

Carving knives. The most common carving knives are the long, flexible knives (3a) which are quite straight and have a rounded point. These sometimes have light hollow grounding and range in size from 10 to 14 in.

There is a type of French larding knife (3b) resembling an elongated filleting knife called the *Tranchelard* which is also used for carving and which has its adherents though normally the Sheffield models are preferred in this country.

Knife steels (4). It is, of course, extremely important to keep knives sharp so that they may do their job effectively and safely. It is fre-

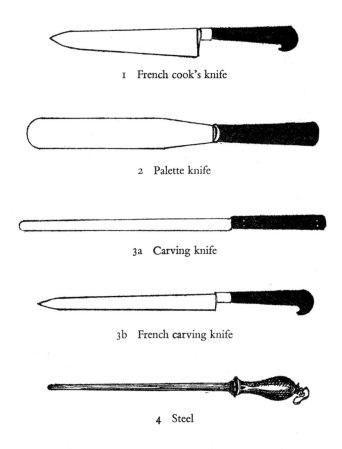

1   French cook's knife

2   Palette knife

3a   Carving knife

3b   French carving knife

4   Steel

quently the blunt knife which causes accidents because bluntness encourages unusually hard pressure. Knives should be sent to an expert as necessary (often not more than once or twice a year) for re-setting or re-grinding but it is important that they are not allowed to be ground away prematurely. The chef should, however, have his own steel, normally 10 to 12 in. in length with which he may keep a keen edge on his knife blades.

When using the steel it should be held with the thumb on top of the handle on the same side as the fingers which firmly but lightly grasp the blade. The reason for this is that the steel need only be held steady and there is more possibility of the thumb being nicked if it is projecting on the under side of the steel in the event of the knife slipping during the sharpening process. The use of the steel is not learned from books, however, but by observing and imitating a good butcher or larder chef.

Some chefs carry a carborundum to give a new edge to their knives but this is not recommended as it results in excessive wear of the knife and soon produces an uneven edge.

Couteau canneler. This little knife of similar length to the couteau d'office has a serrated edge which enables a grooving cut to be made and facilitates the preparation of fancy garnishes with these grooved edges. There are also small knives which give a single grooving cut and which are particularly well adapted for decorating lemons. Another small knife also exists which enables the zest of the lemon to be peeled off without taking the pith of the lemon away with it.

5   Cook's fork

Peeler

Despite the fact that bulk vegetable peeling of, for example, potatoes, is usually done by unskilled kitchen hands, a peeler remains a necessary part of the chef's kit and though quite satisfactory results may be achieved with the English, North-Country style implement, there is no doubt that the French peeler is better adapted for quick, easy and good results. The English type is single-edged and consequently has right- and left-hand models whereas the French has a short edge with a double-edged blade where the peel strip passes through. At first the user may find the French model somewhat less handy but when the correct angle at which it is used has been mastered it is usually infinitely preferred. It is particularly suited for use on long vegetables such as asparagus, cucumbers and the like.

Cook's fork (5)

The cook should use a fork with great caution. Normally a palette knife is a safer tool for manipulating items during the cooking process for there is then less danger of meat tissues being penetrated with consequent loss of juices. But the fork when it is employed in, for example, carving should pierce the fat or wind through the string or, in the case of a bird, be inserted between a bone joint rather than piercing the flesh. It should not, under any circumstances, be used to test whether the meat is done. Cook's forks are normally two-pronged (the French style having rather longer prongs). They should have straight, thin tines and the handle should be complete with guard.

Other small tools

Few chefs attempt to carry personally all the small tools used, even though they may be required quite frequently. Those which are selected as personal belongings must remain a matter of individual choice. Other small equipment includes (*a*) Apple corers. (*b*) Can openers of various styles (though in the busy kitchen the larger models for fixing to wall or bench are preferred). (*c*) *Poultry Secateurs*. These, shaped like garden secateurs, are designed to clip through bone joints but are much less favoured amongst chefs than chopping knives referred to above. (*d*) *Kitchen Scissors*. These include scissors used for trimming fish. (*e*) *Parisienne Spoon or Vegetable Scoops*. The round vegetable scoops designed to produce various sizes of roundels also include a range which produces an oval- or olive-shaped garnish. (*f*) *Trussing Needle*. These range in size from 6 to 12 in. and are employed according to the size of the piece to be trussed. When using the trussing needle, it should be threaded as in an ordinary needle with free running string and a knot, knotted at the eye. The string should remain attached to the ball and severed when the trussing is completed. This helps to avoid yards of loose string which tends to cause tangling.

It is from the foregoing that the chef normally selects the tools which will belong to him personally and which he will carry with him as a permanent part of his kit. The leather sheath formerly worn on a belt over white working dress is seldom found today but chefs would do well to have a protective wrapping of, say, baize with pockets sewn in to accommodate various implements. Bunching them into a kitchen rubber, though common, indicates a lack of concern with tools reflecting only too often a slipshod approach to craft. Pride and care of personal equipment is an integral part of pride of craftsmanship.

There are individualists who increase their range of personally owned equipment to include some of the larger and more unusual items but they are rare characters. Following the small knives and tools which form the chef's own kit is a range of items which are used in the hand and in most cases require some degree of skill, however slight, in their manipulation. These further tools and items of equipment are seldom, however, carried by the chef but are rather part of the kitchen's furniture—constituting indeed a section of the batterie de cuisine.

Non-personal kitchen tools

Parsley choppers (quatre lames) (6)

Consists of four curved blades topped by a wooden handle equipped with two handle knobs which permit a rotary action for rapid chop-

ping. Though there are single-blade models, the commonest is the four-blade type, hence the French description, *quatre lames*. The tempered steel blades are about 12 in. long and when in use should be scraped from time to time to keep them clear of clinging material being chopped. Blades require grinding at regular intervals.

6   Four-bladed parsley chopper

Choppers and cleavers

There is very little difference between the chopper (7) and the cleaver. The latter being slightly longer but much deeper than the chopper. Both implements are used in butchery and are consequently

to be found in the garde manger or the butcher's shop of an hotel or catering establishment.

The chopper is used where the bone is relatively soft as in lamb or for penetrating hard or

7   Chopper

gristly parts of meats. The back of the chopper is also used to crack bones. In size it is about 10 to 15 in. in length.

Meat saw (8)

The meat saw is simply an ordinary bow-type with usually a 14 in. blade; though sometimes the saw is adjustable to different sizes. The saw is used for severing through bone only and should not be used to cut through meat itself. In careful butchery work, it is preferred to the chopper because it avoids bone splintering.

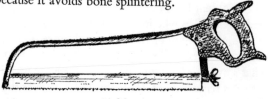

8   Meat saw

Cutlet bat (9)

This is a frequently used tool in the garde manger where it is employed not only for flattening raw meat cuts such as cutlets, escalopes and entrecôte minutes, but also for flattening fish. The bat should be kept moist during use. When flattening the food it is tapped smartly at the same time as the bat is allowed to slide sideways off the food. This is repeated with the bat sliding, after tap-

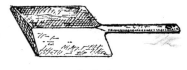

9   Cutlet bat

ping, in all directions so that the piece is flattened by a few actions of this kind and not broken down by continual blows.

Whisks (*Fouets*)

(*a*) *balloon type* (10). The balloon type of whisk is made of strong, flexible, tinned wires, curving out from a handle (normally wood) where they are bound together with thin copper wire. The balloon

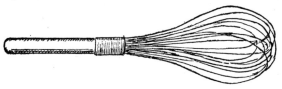

10   Balloon whisk

whisk is a large one about 16 to 18 in. in length and is used almost entirely for the whipping of whites of egg and cream. It should not, indeed, be used for sauces or mixes of a con-

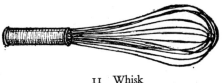

11   Whisk

sistency thicker than cream. Its design makes it an ideal tool for incorporating air, especially when whisking by hand.

(*b*) *General-purpose whisk* (11) is of similar style to the balloon type. It consists of the same kind of strong, flexible tinned wires, bound to a handle and is used widely (in sizes from 6 to 18 in.) for all kinds of preparations requiring beating to ensure smoothness or whipping for lightness. Such whisks are not used for mashing or the breaking down of solid foods into purées.

Professional chefs have not found other styles of whisks such as the flat, flipper type or small rotary beaters suitable for their manual whisking though all good kitchens now use, of course, power-driven mixers which have whisk attachments of the balloon type.

Wooden spoon (12)

Wooden spoons ranging in size from 8 to 18 in. are usually made from hard beech wood. The bowl is only slightly concave and tapers to an extremely thin outer edge. Unlike the wooden spatula they are not made for strength and consequently the wooden spoon is not the appropriate instrument for use in sauce making where the *roux*-thickened liquid tends to clog in the spoon bowl thus losing part of the thickening agent. Additionally, when this clogged matter is scraped off it does not mix smoothly.

12   Wooden spoon

In the professional kitchen, therefore, the use of the wooden spoon is limited. It tends to be confined to use in thickened liquids or syrups where an ingredient like meat or fruit may have to be lifted out and where an iron spoon might discolour or give a metallic taste.

Spatulas (spatules)

Wooden spatule (13). The spatula is a flat piece of wood (usually hard beech wood) made in many sizes from 8 in. to 4 ft in length. Its shape can, perhaps, be most simply described as that of a flattened spoon or spoon shaped without a bowl.

13   Spatula

It is used like a whisk or as a preliminary to the whisk for all kinds of mixing for smoothness and in breaking down mixes where consistency is too thick for the whisk to operate properly. A typical use is for the making of a sauce from a *roux* base. In this case, all the stirring is done by the spatula and the whisk need only come into play at the last moment for final stirring.

Iron spatule (14). This implement is made from tinned steel or iron and consists of a flat rectangular piece of metal with a long shaft bent back at the extremity for hanging. The tool roughly resembles in shape a child's sea-side spade though there is sometimes a hole in the centre to

help movement and flow of liquid in which it is used.
The iron spatule is a stirring implement. It clears the
bottom of vessels lifting the sunken ingredients in, for
example, a soup or sauce when used with a 'figure of
eight' movement. Because of its scraping action it is
important that both spatula and pan are properly tinned
to avoid discoloration. Sizes vary from approximately
1 to 3 ft in length.

Skimmer (ecumoire) (15)

This metal instrument is traditionally made from
tinned steel and consists of a round, slightly concaved
perforated disc set on a long handle at only a slight
angle. The almost horizontal plane enables the tool easily
to take off scum from the surface of stocks. The skim-

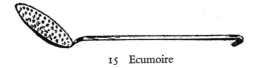

15 Ecumoire

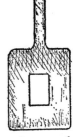

14 Iron spatula

mer is also the proper instrument to turn over vegetables which have been pushed to the side of a cooking
vessel by boiling water. It is also useful for removal of
pieces for testing. This tool should be used for vegetable testing and removal in preference to a wire
skimmer because the wire tends to cut and penetrate delicate foods.

Ladle (louche) (16)

This metal instrument traditionally made from tinned steel is now
frequently found to be made of aluminium and stainless steel. It consists of a hemispherical bowl riveted at right angles to its handle which
is turned at the end for hanging. Though the bowl is attached at right
angles the handle slopes away to a slightly wider angle though remaining almost vertical to the bowl.

The ladle has several im-
portant uses including the
skimming and serving of
sauces, soups and gravies and
including napping or coating

16 Ladle

with sauce. It is the ladle (not the spoon) used at the appropriate angle which enables a quicker and more even spread of sauce to be achieved in 'napping'. It is one of the most useful implements; for though one can make sauces without its use, it is difficult without it to test consistency or to serve and certainly no other tool is properly adapted for skimming them.

The ladle should not, however, be used for serving stews or liquids containing pieces of food which may be broken with a ladle and where a serving spoon would be more appropriate.

Ladles range in several sizes with bowls from 2 to 8 in. The most useful are (*a*) 2½ in. diameter bowl holding approximately 3 oz of liquid when two-thirds full. This size, therefore, can be reckoned as sufficient for one portion of sauce or gravy or to coat one portion of fish, etc., (*b*) 6 in. diameter bowl holding about 7 oz is sufficient for one portion of soup.

Serving spoon (cuillère à service) (17)

This is another metal implement traditionally made from tinned steel but now often made of aluminium and stainless steel. It is simply

17   Serving spoon

a very large spoon of anything from 12 to 18 in. long but is used solely for serving and never for stirring. Its rather shallow bowl is adapted to the serving of stews and vegetables, etc., without the danger of ingredients being broken.

Steak tongs (18)

A metal tool, usually steel, the tongs are normally about 18 in. long. These simple, springy tongs held together by a cross piece which pushes through a side bar when pinched together are used for placing and removing, turning and testing meat in grilling. A fork or implement which could pierce the flesh must never be used as it causes juices to exude through the incision

18   Steak tongs   made.

Ice pick (19)

The ice pick is used more frequently by kitchen porters or apprentices rather than chefs. This wooden handled metal implement bears a superficial resemblance to a steel but its sole purpose is to pierce blocks

19   Ice pick

of ice in order to break them into pieces of required size. It is important that the ice pick is kept exclusively for this purpose and not abused by being misemployed to prise open boxes, etc.

Wire skimmer (spider-araignée) (20)

The araignée is similar in shape to the perforated skimmer but the slightly concave disk is in this case formed by heavy tinned wire. The discs range in diameter from 7 to 9 in. with handles ranging also from 12 to $13\frac{1}{2}$ in. As mentioned in the paragraph on perforated skimmers,

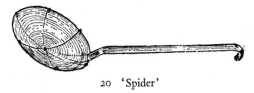

20   'Spider'

the spider should not be used in conjunction with boiling water for it is intended for use entirely with deep frying. In frying, it is used for the turning and removal of food from the *friture* though it is not used to fry soft articles of food which are laid on the wire drainer.

Mushroom (champignon purée presser) (21)

The mushroom is so named because of its shape which is almost exactly like that of the typical fungus. Made from hard wood it consists of a slightly domed, circular piece of wood with a handle attached to the flat underside. Normally it is about 5 in. in diameter and is simply used to press or rub food through a sieve.

This tool should not be confused with the flat-bottomed vegetable presser which would not be encountered in a first-class kitchen but is

21   'Mushroom'

used by incorrectly trained cooks in place of a mushroom. The rounded shape of the mushroom is properly adapted to give the correct leverage to the hand when the tool is used in vertical but rounded movements. This enables the food to be pushed through the wire spaces without clogging and 'building up' between the sieve and mushroom. This spoiling and solidifying of the food tends to occur when a flat-bottomed vegetable press is used.

Hatelet skewers

These skewers are hardly kitchen utensils, yet they are used by the chef garde manger. They are silver or plated skewers of a decorative kind used to decorate cold pieces montées for the buffet table. They are employed to finish decorated hams and to help in the assembly of cold fish dishes, etc.

Other kitchen appliances
Mandolin (22)

The mandolin consists of a rectangular wooden frame fitted with a handle. Within the frame are bolted two steel plates. The top plate is fixed and the lower, which has a knife edge, is adjustable to form a wide

and thin aperture against the fixed plate by tightening or otherwise a side wing nut. The blade may be horizontal or set at an angle to facilitate cutting. This implement enables vegetables, mainly root vegetables, like potatoes and carrots to be sliced. The article to be cut is held in the hollow of the hand and pushed downwards against the knife blade which has been adjusted to give the required thickness. The action of sliding up and down against this blade with the one hand whilst holding the handle of the instrument in the other, has prompted the name of Mandolin for this kitchen aid.

Those unused to the Mandolin can easily cut themselves if they fail to employ the correct technique. The push should be made with the ball or cushion of the thumb on the palm of the hand itself with the fingertips kept high and out of reach of the knife. The hand should give the vegetable a slightly circular movement so that it

22   Mandolin

cuts evenly and not at an angle. Mandolins are obtainable in different sizes and styles but a common size is approximately 12 in. long by 4 to 5 in. wide.

Mar-For slicer (23)

The Mar-For slicer is close kin to the Mandolin but instead of a handle, is supported by a metal stand which keeps it steady at an angle convenient for use. Instead of two pieces of metal as in the Mandolin, the Mar-For consists of three flat pieces and a fourth cross piece. The centre plate is the fixed one holding the frame together and the two end plates are adjustable in a similar way to the adjustable blade on the Mandolin.

The cross piece consists of a bar running through the side frame, adjustable to be flush on one side with the centre plate, but on the other having a row of small, wheel-shaped knives about $\frac{1}{8}$ in. apart and set vertically. This device enables straws or Julienne style garnish to be cut when the vegetable is pushed with straight downward strokes against the outward pointing wheel blade. The other adjustable plate has a corrugated edge so that when the slicer is reversed and the stand clamped to the other end, vegetables cut on it will similarly have a corrugated surface. If the hand is turned at right angles alternately during slicing, *gaufrette* or lace style slices can be achieved.

23   Mar-For slicer

All the foregoing items have one common factor. They are designed to be handled or manipulated by the chef or kitchen craftsman.

Whatever secondary uses they may have, the appliances remain primarily *tools*, albeit non-personal ones. Care in their use and maintenance will enable maximum benefit to be gained from them. The acquisition of the correct manipulative skills in employing even these larger implements of the kitchen is an essential for the properly trained chef.

8

Batterie de cuisine

The term batterie de cuisine has been translated as kitchen furniture. Some British chefs have suggested that the description batterie de cuisine refers specifically to articles made of copper, usually tin-lined, and which comprise an important section of the craftsman's apparatus. Today, however, the designation batterie de cuisine certainly is used to describe all the cooking utensils in the kitchen.

Metals in the kitchen

It is naturally no accident that kitchen craftsmen have shown preference for certain metals for various uses over the years. Their preferences have been determined naturally by the performance of the metal. In cooking, efficient conduction of heat is of supreme importance. Silver is the best conductor of heat amongst those metals which have been reasonably commonly used for cooking and if silver is given a figure of 100%, copper is not far behind with 73%. Aluminium is 31%, tin rates 15% and iron or steel 11%. Apart from limited use in chafing dishes, silver is today too costly to be employed in cooking.

Metals used in the batterie

Copper. This has a high melting point, 1,985°F as against the 449°F melting point of tin. Its weight is almost exactly that of wrought iron but three times that of aluminium.

It is not surprising, therefore, that many pans were and are made of copper. Unfortunately it has some drawbacks. For example, copper exposed to air which contains carbon dioxide forms a thin, bluey-green skin of verdigris which is poisonous. Hence the inside of copper cooking vessels are lined with tin, a metal which resists corrosion well by air and water and does not harm food which comes in contact with it.

If a little bottled sauce or similar acid or vinegary material is on the outside of a copper pan for a while and then removed, the copper underneath will be brilliant. If it is left there for some considerable time the edges will begin to show faintly with verdigris. For this reason, some pans like bains-maries (double saucepan) are tinned on the outside as well, and others like trout pans which usually contain vinegary liquor (court-bouillon) and are also sent to table are tinned inside and out.

The technique of cleaning copper and tin-lined copper is considered in Chapter 11, *Maintenance in the Kitchen*, p. 148.

The great French chef Urbain Dubois contended that 'the chief luxury of a kitchen consists in possessing plenty of stewpans' and from the context it is clear he meant copper ones, 'well tinned inside and bright as sunshine outside'. Certainly, the batterie of copper vessels should be one of the kitchen's great assets and thus should be accorded constant care by the chef and his staff.

Stainless steel

So far the cost of stainless steel has discouraged its use in the manufacture of moveable cooking vessels for professional kitchens though it has been extensively adopted for table surfaces and sinks and it is widely used in fixed boiling pans such as steam-jacketed, tilting vessels. Because of its relatively poor conductivity, stainless-steel pans used in domestic kitchens have been given an external layer of copper at the bottom and this aids in spreading the heat. Few professional chefs are, however, prepared to yield the traditional tin-lined copper in favour of stainless steel at this stage of its development.

Aluminium

Aluminium was first put to kitchen use in 1883 when Charles Martin Hall, who invented the modern process of extracting aluminium from its ore, produced cast aluminium kettles and found that kitchen utensils were to be his first successful line commercially. Aluminium is a relatively soft metal but is light, low priced and rust-free. Compared with cast-iron and steel, aluminium has high conductivity and the metal has been used with considerable success in vessels used for boiling, frying and baking.

Some prejudices existed at one time owing to a belief that aluminium was harmful and that small quantities could find their way into prepared food and injure health. Research and investigation over the years appears not to support this prejudice and as long ago as 1955 Dr G. W. Monier-Williams, who was then in charge of the chemical laboratories of the Ministry of Health, collected and examined for the Minister all the information available on the subject of the use of aluminium cooking vessels and came to the conclusion that 'while aluminium salts are undesirable as ingredients of baking powders there is no convincing evidence that aluminium cooking vessels are harmful'. Perhaps the discoloration, indeed blackening, after a period of use tends to evoke questions about its being harmful. Such discoloration is, in fact, without effect on the food but undoubtedly appears unpleasant. Fortunately the discoloration which is really a film of microscopic thickness can readily be removed by boiling in the vessel concerned an acid product such as apple parings.

Any fat which settles into this soft metal often takes days to come out (if ever it does) and this together with the discolorations mentioned make it unsuitable for white sauce making and other processes where the retention of pure white colour is important.

Cleaning of aluminium is discussed in Chapter 11, *Maintenance in the Kitchen*, p. 148.

Iron

Iron and steel because of their tendency to rust and become corroded and because of relatively low conductivity have a restricted use in the professional kitchen. Iron is still widely favoured where frying or 'griddle' frying with fat is concerned for in such forms of cookery the vessels are not cleaned with wet techniques and rusting is not a problem.

Design

There are, in fact, 'vessels of all shapes and sizes'; tall and narrow, short and shallow, long and thin, different kinds of handles and all sorts of covers. These differences have developed because the various pots have definite uses and functions. If liquor is to be reduced rapidly a large but shallow pan will get rid of it much more quickly than a long and narrow one. The tall, narrow pot will, on the contrary, keep things hot longer because the smaller surface area does not allow for much evaporation. A salmon fits a *saumonière* but this vessel would not be chosen for a stew. A pan with a long handle will not go into an oven as easily as one with two side loop handles (called lateral handles). Some covers fit inside, some outside and some not at all. There is a reason for every shape and every shape should be chosen with a reason. Spatulas are made of wood because metal scraping against metal will cause discoloration. Covers are tinned because they come into contact with the food. The angle of the ladle to its handle is of paramount importance for its effective use. The shape of the mushroom, the mesh of the sieve, the shape of knives, everything and everywhere there is reason derived from long experience of our craft of cookery.

The text and illustrations in this section of the Manual are intended to indicate the reasons behind the design and also the reasons prompting choice of material as well as to aid the professional cook in becoming familiar with a wide range of tools and utensils.

It has already been observed that the angle at which handles should come away from the main structure is important. It may also be noted that pans made of copper by a reputable firm will nearly always be correct in detail, but imitations in other metals which sometimes have to be used in schools and kitchens for reasons of economy, are often wrongly shaped and angled. It is necessary to insist on correctly shaped pots, pans and utensils and not to be tolerant of less efficient substitutes.

To give a fuller picture, mention is made of sizes but these sizes have not been laid down by any one firm nor by the industry. They are simply approximations of sizes which are most usual to give a comparative height and breadth.

Iron and steel items of kitchen furniture

Friture (frying kettle) (24)

Fritures which are constructed from heavy, black, wrought-iron, untinned steel are oval bottomed, vertically sided vessels, fitted with handles at the narrow top ends. These handles project well and allow plenty of space so that they remain cool and may be grasped when the vessel has been used and contains hot fat. They are made in many sizes, the smallest being 12 in. × 8½ in. × 5 in. and the largest 28 in. × 17 in. × 8 in.

Fritures are supplied completed with a drainer made of wire, which just fits the kettle. Drainer handles are, of course, made high to project well out of the fat. There are sometimes two hooks on these handles which fit over the rim of the vessel to allow the fat to drain away. This wire grill is for use with soft articles of cooked food like

24   Friture

croquettes to help in immersion and removal from the hot fat. The drainer is never used for the frying of other articles (filleted fish, potatoes, etc.) and particularly not for batters.

Iron frying pan (poêle à frire) (25)

The heavy wrought-iron frying pan is a familiar enough object in the kitchen. It ranges in size from diameter 7 in. to as large as 16 in.

Important features of the pan area are: (*a*) that the bottom should be perfectly flat to ensure even cooking, and (*b*) that the slightly sloping sides should not meet at the base at a sharp angle but should be coved or rounded for ease of cleaning.

25   Frying pan

Iron frying pans should never be washed and, indeed, no liquid whatsoever should ever be put into them. The cleaning technique consists of regular and thorough wiping immediately after use with a dry cloth or clean absorbent paper.

Thorough cleaning can be effected by spreading coarse salt over the bottom and heating. This absorbs dirty fat. After the soiled salt is tipped out the pan should again be wiped and three parts filled with clean fat which should be heated to smoking point. This gives the pan a 'skin' which stops food from sticking during subsequent frying.

The pan is, of course, used for shallow frying such as sautéing of potatoes or onions and the tossing in butter of certain vegetables. The pan is also used for shallow frying of fish, for meunière (though the oval-shaped meunière pan is often chosen) and in the making of brown and black butters. The iron frying pan should not be used in place of the sauteuse or plât sauté for the more prolonged forms of shallow frying or for sautéing small cuts of meat such as tournedos and noisettes.

Omelette pan (poêle à omelette) (26)

The omelette pan closely resembles an ordinary frying pan and, indeed, an ordinary frying pan is sometimes reserved for omelette making when the sides are sufficiently rounded. For the distinguishing feature of the true omelette pan is the curved side which helps to give an appropriate shape when the pan is tapped at the time the omelette is being finished and rolled. Pans vary in size from 8 in. at the base (one-portion size) to 10 in. (two- to three-portion size), 12 in. (four- to five-portion size) and even larger.

26   Omelette pan

In the authentic omelette pan, after the first distinguishing feature of the rounded side, the handle is important. This is usually attached with three rivets. It rises in a curve slightly from the side and then straightens almost to the horizontal so that it is practically parallel with the base. This angle facilitates folding and turning out the omelette.

The rules for cleaning iron frying pans apply here and where it is important to preserve the 'skin' on any iron frying pan it is especially vital in the case of an omelette pan. For that reason an omelette pan should be used for no other purpose whatsoever and in the professional kitchen the chef entremetier makes sure that his apprentices and aides learn this lesson and strictly comply with it.

Pancake pan (poêle à crêpe) (27)

Pancake pans which are again similar to the ordinary frying pan are distinguished by having sides that are not so deep and which slope outwards at a wider angle. Because of the tra-
ditional size of pancakes, the base diameter of the pan remains constant at about 7 in. Their purpose is normally confined to the cooking of pancakes and all the rules regarding cleaning the iron frying pan and the omelette pan apply here. It is, however, true that sometimes the

27   Pancake pan

pan is used to fry a double portion of eggs though strictly speaking a smaller pan with a larger handle is normally employed for frying single or double egg portions.

Meunière pan (poêle à meunière)

This pan of heavy wrought iron is virtually an oval frying pan with grip handles at each narrow end and its shape is designed to accommodate fish such as trout, sole, plaice fillets, which can thus lie side by side across the width of the pan. The size ranges from 16 in. × 8 in. to as large as 32 in. × 12 in.

Baking sheet (28)

The flat baking sheet is usually of black wrought steel and as it is made to fit the oven, is sometimes supplied with it. The flat sheet is given a right-angle edge on three sides simply by the sides being turned up to form a 1 in. rim. This leaves the fourth side open so that baked goods can be easily slid from the

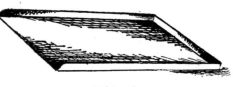

28   Baking sheet

sheet. Though varying sizes may be found to fit various ovens, the standard is normally called the '28' because it is 28 in. in width.

Tinned steel

Colander (29)

Colanders have been developed for domestic kitchens in a variety of materials including plastic. For professional use in catering establishments, however, tinned steel has retained its popularity though aluminium and stainless steel have been found suitable by many chefs. The colander is simply a hemisphere shell with a three- or four-ridged

29   Colander

bottom. The bowl is pierced with holes something less than $\frac{1}{4}$ in. diameter and ranges in size from 9 in. to 18 in. in diameter and in depth from 6 in. to 12 in. The colander is especially adapted for straining liquor from vegetables, farinaceous items and the like and with holes perforating the sides it is better suited for this purpose than a sieve or other form of strainer.

Vegetable drainer (passoir) (30)

This item of equipment is also normally made of tinned steel. It somewhat resembles a conical strainer though it has a more rounded

30   Passoir

bottom. In addition to a long handle on one side it has a lateral handle on the other which enables the strainer to rest within a saucepan. Its bowl is pierced with holes about $\frac{1}{4}$ in. in diameter. The passoir is exclusively for rechauffer (reheating) work, particularly of vegetables. The technique is to place the food in the passoir and then stand it in boiling salted water. This technique has long been a feature particularly of busy à la carte services but is perhaps being given fresh significance in the present-day treatment of frozen foods. In size it is normally $9\frac{1}{2}$ in. in diameter and 4 in. deep.

Conical strainer (chinois)

There are two types of conically shaped strainers—the chinois fin (31) and the chinois gros (32). It is generally understood that the name chinois is derived simply from the fact that the conical shape is similar to a Chinese coolie hat. *Chinois fin.* The chinois fin is made from tinned metal and wire gauze and is normally in three sizes of diameter, 5 in., 7 in. and 9 in. The fine

31   Conical strainer (fine) chinois of wire gauze and tinned metal is

sufficiently rounded at the point of the cone to accommodate the bowl of a small ladle or the tip of a small whisk.

Chinois gros. The chinois gros is also in three sizes, 7 in., 8 in. and 9 in. The features of the strainer are the long, almost straight handle, but sloping very slightly upwards from the horizontal and the rimmed or ringed top which enables the strainer to fit into the neck of a bain-marie (double saucepan) or into a wooden triangle placed on top of a wider vessel.

The coarse strainer is made from tinned, perforated metal and is of much stronger construction. Both the strainers are used for 'passing'
thickened sauces, gravies, etc. (The

32 Conical strainer
     (coarse)

term 'passing' is used more commonly than straining in the kitchen.) In the case of the fine chinois the technique is to pour the thickened liquor to be passed into the strainer and then facilitate its flow through by tapping the top lightly with a ladle. Only occasionally and as necessary, light pressure may be given to push solid matter through the mesh with the ladle or whisk. The technique in using the coarse chinois is similar, though more frequent rubbing with the small ladle is allowed in the stronger construction. Because the coarse chinois is designed more for the passing out of small particles than of pushing them through, gentle tapping should, however, suffice.

It is important to remember that the fine chinois is relatively fragile and easily becomes mis-shapen and broken. It should, therefore, be washed immediately after use and put away. It should never be flung to await attention in the sink or plonge tank where the risk of damage is great.

Soup machine

This is a large contrivance of several parts, each of which can be replaced independently. Its structure does not lend itself to easy description but it is simply a device for assisting the passage of a large quantity of purée-type soup through a curved and perforated based container by manipulating wooden rollers on a long shaft. Different gauges are normally supplied.

The only points which need to be made regarding this apparatus are:
(*i*) the machine should only be used for soup for it is not a satisfactory

way of passing thicker purées, (*ii*) like all 'passing' implements, its perforations need thorough cleaning and the whole machine, being large and relatively complicated, should be washed immediately after use.

Frying basket (panier à friture) (33)

Made of heavy-gauge tinned ware, this is a round basket with straight vertical sides having a handle also of wire. It is made in various sizes usually ranging in diameter from 8 in. to 12 in. and in depth from 3 in. to 6 in. It is a convenient receptacle for frying for it is easily removed if the fat surges too vigorously upwards. Its wire open construction makes it ideal for draining whilst the handle allows for the free tossing and salting of crispened articles. Most raw foods are first placed in the basket for frying and removed from the fat when the temperature has lessened. They are then drained and re-dipped in hot fat later.

33   Frying basket

There are available, of course, various sizes and varieties of frying baskets, chip shovels, etc.

Nest frying basket (34)

This metal implement consists of two ladle-shaped parts made from tinned wire. The fitting of one into another allowing only about ½ to ⅓ in. space between the basket-type bowls permits potato nests to be made and fried.

34   Nest frying basket

The outer basket is first heated in the fat and lined with straw, lace or similar cut potatoes which have not been washed. The smaller basket is then also heated in the fat, pressed in, and the side spaces filled with more potato. As the handles fit tightly together the bowls may be kept tightly pressed whilst the potato nests are then fried in deep fat and which after draining can be removed intact.

Double wire grill or fish grill (grille à poisson) (35)

This is another wire implement consisting simply of two grids hinged together and capable of being clipped together at the handle. For grilling fish on an open grill, the wires, which are set about ⅔ in. apart, are first wiped (the grill should never be washed) and the oiled fish placed on to one grill and held immovably in position by folding over the other side and clipping the handles together with a wire ring. It is placed on the open griller and when the fish is cooked on one

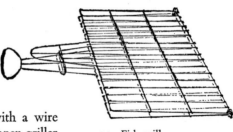

35   Fish grill

side the whole grill is turned to cook the other. When opened the fish is easily removed by a palette knife. The size of the grids are usually about 12 in. square.

Saladier (salad basket) (36)

This is another article of tinned wire construction and the traditional model is rounded urn-shaped with a narrow neck quite open at the top to which is attached a hinged handle. This handle enables thoroughly washed lettuce to be shaken free of moisture and to hang for draining. Its usual size is a top diameter of about 8 in. and depth of about 13 in.

There are today variants of this traditional size including double hinged baskets and those made of collapsible mesh but as the lettuce can be held quite satisfactorily in position in an open basket through centrifugal force when swung, the traditional shape is perfectly satisfactory.

36   Salad basket

Wire rack (pastry rack) (37)

These wire stands consisting of a simple rectangle on short feet vary

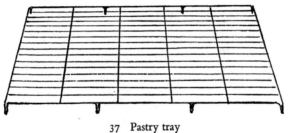

37   Pastry tray

in size from 12 in. × 9 in. to 24 in. × 18 in. They are used particularly in
the pastry both for cooling goods removed from the oven and also
in fondant work and sugar dipping. They are also used in the garde
manger for chaud-froid and aspic work and, indeed, for any operation
where a coating is required to drain away from the article being
coated.

Copper utensils

Despite its relatively high cost, tin-lined copper remains widely used
throughout professional kitchens and is still favoured by chefs above
all other types of vessels for work on the stoves. The reasons for the
efficiency of copper were mentioned earlier in this section but its great
advantage may be re-emphasised. It is a good conductor of heat and
thus evenly and efficaciously permits the transfer of heat from the stove
to the food cooked.

It will have been noted that copper affects food cooked in it and the
copper salts formed can be highly dangerous and hence the tin lining
of copper cooking vessels. Lining requires renewal from time to time
because of the wear and tear caused by stirring and cleaning and it is
most necessary to review the copper ware regularly to ensure that
copper is not becoming exposed beneath the tin lining. Another disadvantage is that copper tends to discolour easily and to keep it a
bright, burnished appearance requires attention.

The dominance of copper ware in the professional kitchen is still
such that to many chefs the term batterie de cuisine implies the range
of copper vessels. They are kept in the kitchen or in the 'plonge' on
open shelves (étagerès) which were formerly of cast iron but now are
found in other metals including stainless steel.

Stockpot (Marmite) (38)

Copper stockpots vary in size from those of 5 gal. capacity and in
a further half dozen sizes up to 38 gal. They are as broad as they are
high and depth and diameter range from those of 12 in. up to 24 in.
The vessels are easily recognisable being of cylindrical shape with two
side handgrips and fitted with a tap on the lower part. It is the tap
fitting which usually requires attention for it is fitted on the inside
with a perforated piece of metal which acts as a grid to prevent the
tap pipe itself becoming blocked but which in turn requires checking
during cleaning processes. Even more importantly, care has to be taken
to ensure the safety of the key in the tap which is only too often a
separate and detachable fitment. The stockpot is, of course, used almost
exclusively for the making of clear meat, bone or poultry stock. The

stockpot is often cover-
ed by a tin-lined circu-
lar lid also fitted with
two lateral handles.

In the French kitchen
it has already been
noted that the plongeur
(scullery man) has
sometimes been called
the casserolier and this
is because cooking ves-
sels generally are in
France referred to as
casseroles. This term
may quite properly be
given to a large variety
of pots and pans which
are certainly not cas-

38   Stockpot

seroles in the narrow, oven cooking sense used in the domestic kitchen
or even in the professional kitchen for methods en casserole.

Large pots (casseroles) (39)

This type of large pot ranges in size from 12 in. diameter by 8½ in.
depth and of 3 gal. capacity up to those of 16 in. diameter by 10½ in.
depth and of 8 gal. capacity and has three intermediate sizes. It will be
seen from these dimensions that this
vessel is wider than it is high. This
makes it especially suitable for use
in clarifying consommé. The wide
pan affords easy access and space to
remove grease and scum and the
relatively large area exposed to the
atmosphere has the effect of reducing the heat of the contents so that
gentle simmering can be achieved
easily by applying the requisite
amount of heat. This vessel also has

39   Casserole—large pot

a flat, round cover with lateral handles. The narrow rim of the cover
is usually 1 in. high and enables it to fit over the outside of the pan. A
cover of this kind can additionally be used when turned upside down
as a large sauté pan.

Large stew pan (40)

This differs from the large pot or consommé pan being cylindrical

and taller in relation to its diameter than the former type of vessel. It has two side grips but its cover is of sunk pattern type fitting on the inside and with a central loop handle. Made in six sizes ranging from diameter 12 in. by depth 9 in. to diameter 22 in. by depth 14 in., this stew pan has many uses for work on top of the stove including sauce making, boiling and the like.

40   Casserole—large stew pan

Poêler pan (braising pan)

The poêler pan is made in four sizes from diameter 9 in. by depth 5 in. to diameter 14 in. by depth 7½ in. and is fitted with a long handle almost horizontally. Its cover fits tightly over the outside with a handle set in a sunk depression in the middle of the cover. It will be noted from the dimensions that this type of pan is much shallower than the other casseroles described. In fact, the casserole description is really apt in this instance because the pan is used for poêléing meat and poultry, a process which involves surrounding the vessel with heat. The depression in the fitted cover was traditionally used in hot ember cooking to hold the hot fuel or alternatively it can be used to hold water to cool the contents.

Stew pans (russes)

1. *Deep* (41). These are cylindrical, deep pots, fitted with long almost

horizontal handles on the one side with a lateral grip on the opposite one and also accompanied if required with a deep, sunk pattern cover. It is normally made in at least six sizes ranging in diameter from 6 in. to 14 in. and in depth from 4½ in. to 9 in. With all sorts of uses from boiling to stewing, the

41   Russe stew pan (deep)

deep russes can be described as the all-purpose kitchen pans which 'do all the donkey work'.

2. *Shallow* (42). This type is precisely the same except that it is shallower and has no lateral grip opposite the long handle. Made in half a dozen

sizes ranging from 6 in. to 14 in. in
diameter and in depth from 3½ in. to
8 in. its uses are similar to the deep
type.

3. *Tall russes pans.* This variety made
in about four sizes of diameter 6 in.
up to 12 in. is deeper than it is wide

42   Russe stew pan (shallow)

—and it is sometimes fitted with a flat, sheet lid. It is especially adapted
for despumating (the boiling out) of sauces. Its tall shape means that
there is the minimum of evaporation and the relatively small surface
area facilitates the removal of scum.

Braising pan (brasière) (43)

This is a rectangular-shaped, straight-sided vessel fitted with two side
handles and a deep sunk, tight cover which fits on the outside and has
one central looped handle. It is
made in at least six sizes ranging
from the smallest of about 12 in.
long by 9 in. deep. In the braising of meats, a steady heat is
needed for cooking and the
close-fitting lid helps retain all
the juices with minimum evaporation. Apart from normal
braising purposes, however, this
shape of vessel is also useful for
boiling salt meats such as ham

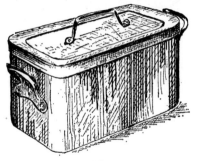

43   Braising pan

and tongues. It is also the type of pan to be used when roasting large
birds such as turkeys, geese or capons where deep sides afford protection during the lengthy cooking.

Roasting tray (plaque à rôtir) (44)

This is simply a tin-lined tray of rectangular shape with short,
straight, vertical sides. Strong steel handles are fitted on each short side
and these lateral grips project upwards and outwards. They are made
in at least six sizes from a
small one of 14 in. × 9½ in.
× 2½ in. to a large one of
24 in. × 18 in. × 4 in. This
type of tray is used for
roasting small joints or
birds and where the

44   Plaque à rôtir

protection given by the short sides suffice. It is important that the right size of tray be selected so that it can be adequately filled; for in roasting the intense heat quickly causes the fat to burn if there is an area of the copper vessel left unfilled. This in turn will cause the joint to be scorched and spoil the sediment to be used for the gravy.

Owing to the high cost of copper, increasing use is being made of thick-gauged wrought steel for roasting trays. This cheaper type gives reasonable results.

Oval roasting tray (45)

This is of similar construction except that the shape is oval and the low rim comes up at somewhat of an angle. On the smaller sizes

the side handles, which are situated at the narrow ends, drop downwards. Ranging in size from about 8 in. × 5½ in. up to 18 in. × 10¾ in. with rims ranging in proportion from 1⅜ in. to 2½ in., the trays are used for single birds or small à la carte joints. The

45   Oval roasting dish

fish cook also uses them for poaching in the oven the larger cuts of fish. The entremetier (vegetable cook) employs them, too, for the roasting or baking of potatoes.

Grilling trays (46)

These heavy, copper trays lined with tin, range in various sizes from 12 in. × 10 in. to 32 in. × 20 in. and are simply rectangular sheets whose four sides are turned up at a slight angle to give rims of approximate

½ in. depth. The corners are slightly rounded and are, of course, leak-proof. The trays are obviously not used for true grilling but for cooking small articles under the salamander or for holding other articles which

46   Grilling tray

are to be given an au gratin finish. Those with sufficient depth may be used by the chef poissonier for poaching fillets or thinner cuts of fish au four (in the oven).

Sauteuse (sometimes called a vegetable stew pan) (47)

This type of relatively shallow pan is of tin-lined, heavy-gauge copper and resembles a shallow saucepan with rather sloping sides. Its use is by no means confined to vegetables for it is employed on many

occasions, as for tossing foods in butter
or in sauce, for the reduction of liquids
by rapid evaporation or for the poaching
and cooking of delicate or soft foods,
which might be crushed or broken in a
taller vessel. It does not really resemble
a frying pan (its sides are much deeper
and it is, of course, copper) and it must

47 Sauteuse

be stressed that it certainly should never be used as a frying pan. Customary sizes range from diameter 6 in. to 18 in. and in depth from $1\frac{5}{8}$ in. to 5 in.

Sauté pan (plat à sauter, sautoir) (48)

This is a shallow, flat, round tin-lined copper vessel with straight vertical sides. These sides are shallower than the sloping sides of a sauteuse. The sauté pan is provided with a long handle and with a flat sheet type cover.

The pan is designed especially for
the sautéing of meats particularly in
those cases where an accompanying
sauce has to be made by deglacéing
or rinsing the sediment within the
saucepan. Beginners in professional
cookery are sometimes confused because some sautéing processes result

48 Plat à sauter

in a dry, shallow-fried dish such as sauté potatoes. In other instances 'sautés' are of stew-type appearance such as filet de bœuf sauté Strogonoff. The explanation is, of course, that the sautéing of meat, kidneys, etc., is frequently accompanied by the preparation of a co-hering sauce in the sauté pan.

The flat cover is used in two ways which are both characteristic techniques employed by the chef saucier. The first way is the expected one of use as a lid when the pieces are large and need long cooking or when they have to be cooked 'à blanc'. The second use is where several pieces are to be cooked at once as, for example, in party catering or banqueting. In such cases the underpart of the cover which is tinned is oiled and the seasoned small cuts (noisettes and tournedos, perhaps) are arranged round. This enables the whole number to be slid off the cover into the hot fat of the sauté pan simultaneously. This is not done merely to save time but to ensure that all the pieces are cooked at the same moment. Importantly also, this ensures that each article is sealed in the same degree of really, hot smoking fat. An experienced chef can cook as many as thirty noisettes at a time using this technique. If thirty were to be placed in one at a time this would either mean that the last would enter the pan at a temperature so lowered by the preceding twenty-nine as barely to simmer and in consequence the pieces would stew instead of being sautéd or that pieces would become cooked at different times.

Bain-marie

49   Bain-marie

50   Bain-marie

The term bain-marie in British kitchens is now used in reference to the large bath of heated water in which pots are kept hot and also to the specially adapted pots themselves. Bain-marie pans made of tin-lined, heavy-gauged copper are like extremely narrow, deep saucepans. The larger size (49) has two side handles and smaller ones (50) have long, high handles which facilitate storage close together in the water tank. Both have a deep, sunk pattern lid fitting in the inside and equipped with a knob on top for easy removal. These pans are *never* used for cooking but solely for hot storage of sauces and gravies, etc., in a well of boiling water. Sizes vary considerably ranging from ¾ pt capacity to 8 pt capacity in the long-handled style and with a similar wide range of the large two-handled type. There are also even larger two-handled bain-marie soup pots of several sizes up to about 24 pt capacity and which are used, as the name implies, for the hot storage of soups.

Turbot kettle (turbotière) (51)

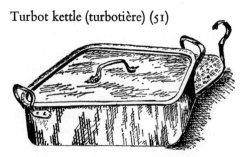

51   Turbot kettle

This tin-lined, heavy-gauged copper vessel is diamond-shaped with shallow vertical sides. This shape is especially adapted to accommodate whole turbot and is constructed customarily in lengths 24 in. to

26 in. The pan is equipped with side handles at each end of the longer width with a sunken type cover fitting on the inside and with a central looped handle. It is also accompanied by a drainer of perforated tinned steel also fitted with two handles in which the turbot can be gently lowered into and removed from the court bouillon (stock).

Salmon kettle (saumonière) (52)

This tin-lined copper vessel is long and narrow with rounded ends adapted for poaching whole fish of salmon shape or large cuts of round fish. It is fitted with handles, drainer and cover in the same way as the turbotière and it is used in the same manner as that vessel. The smaller

52   Salmon kettle

type of fish kettle used for truite au bleu and which ultimately themselves enter the restaurant for service from the guéridon (service side table) have a hinged type drainer and a half loop which clips over the side of the kettle so that the fish may lie out of the liquid for easy service. Sizes range from 10 in. to 30 in. in length, from 3 in. to 9½ in. in width, from 3 in. to 7 in. in depth.

Copper vegetable boiler (53)

Though this pan may be obtained tinned inside (in which case it may be used for other purposes) it is not normally tinned either inside or out when it is designed for its customary use which means that it is confined solely to blanching and cooking green vegetables (peas and French beans particularly). It is a round vessel and its flat, round base curves to meet the vertical sides. Broader than it is tall, it has a heavy rim at the top and two side, grip-type handles. The broad base is designed to give plenty of rapidly

53   Copper vegetable boiler

conducted bottom heat to boil the water fast. Sizes range from 12 in. diameter × 7½ in. depth to 20 in. diameter × 11 in. depth.

Sugar boiler (poêlons à sucre) (54)

Another untinned boiler, this too must be confined to its proper purpose of sugar boiling and must on no account be used for the

preparation of sauces, meats and milk. Sugar boilers are made in about three sizes and are round, saucepan type vessels with long handles and a rim lip for pouring. Diameters are usually 6 in., 7 in. or 8 in. and depths 4½ in., 5 in. or 5½ in. The pots are not tinned mainly because the high temperature needed for sugar boiling would cause the tin plate to melt.

54   Sugar boiler

Copper mixing bowl (bassine chaudron) (55)

The copper mixing bowl with one ring handle is normally untinned. It is used by the pâtissier particularly for beating egg whites. There

is sometimes a tendency for the egg white to take on a faint tinge of green colour because of direct contact with the copper hence some chefs today prefer to use stainless-steel bowls or to have the copper ones tinned—though whipping is not quite so successful in a tinned bowl as the egg tends to become 'grainy'.

55   Copper mixing bowl

Moulds

Dariole moulds (moulle à dariole) (56). The best type of dariole moulds are made from thick-gauged copper, tinned inside and are intended for a single portion of either savoury moulds in aspic or for charlottes, bavarois, créme caramel, etc. They do not vary greatly in size, being usually from 2 in. to 2½ in. in diameter and from 2½ in. to 3 in. deep. These round, flat-based moulds have straight sides, sloping slightly outwards to an open end to facilitate turning out.

Charlotte moulds (moulle à charlotte) (57). These moulds are also best made from tin-lined copper for they are used for both hot and cold charlottes where the centre filling is surrounded by biscuit, bread or a jelly lining either aspic or sweet. These are also plain, flat-bottomed, straight-sided moulds sloping to give slightly greater width at the open end for ease of turning out. The 4 in. diameter size (depth 2¾ in.) is regarded as a four-portioned mould, the 5½ in. diameter mould (depth 3¾ in.) usually yields six portions and 8 in. diameter (depth 3¾ in.) is an eight-portion mould.

Savarin mould (moulle à savarin) (58). These tin-lined copper moulds are virtually flat, round rings though they are sometimes made hexagonal or with flat or concave tops but always form a ring shape with a hole in the centre. They are used for proving and baking the savarin yeast mixture and also for aspics, turbans and mousses and for the moulding of rice. They are normally employed when, after turning out, some

56   Dariole mould

57   Charlotte mould

58   Savarin mould

59   Timbale

60   Jelly mould

61   Dome top bomb mould

other preparation is to be placed in the centre such as fruit for the savarin.

Timbale mould (moulle à timballe) (59). This is a tinned copper mould similar to, but very much deeper than, the savarin and sloping to open slightly to permit easy turning out. It is rounded at the top and is particularly used in cold larder work for mousses and aspic and, unlike the savarin, the hollow centre is seldom filled when served. There are several sizes each as wide as it is deep, ranging from 3 in. to 5 in.

Jelly moulds (*moulle à gelé*) (60). Customary sizes of tin-lined, copper jelly moulds are 4 oz, $\frac{1}{2}$ pt, with some larger models. They are fabricated for various fancy shapes, oval and round, but it is customary for the decorative work to be in tiers to facilitate the moulding in layers of different colours or varieties of fruit.

Ice pudding mould (*moulle à bombe*) (61). Bombe moulds are somewhat inaccurately named for they are much the shape of an artillery shell. Made from tinned copper, the round sides slope gradually and then turn to form a dome. The bombe mould is equipped with a lid having a collapsible handle which fits closely on to the outside. It stands on a small, round foot which may be unscrewed. It is used to mould ice-cream bombes and the technique is to line the inside of the mould with

ice-cream (chemiser), and then fill the centre with fruit or another variety of ice-cream or other preparation. There are a variety of sizes but the most usual are a 4 in. to $4\frac{1}{2}$ in. diameter and 3 in. to $3\frac{1}{2}$ in. depth.

Tall ice pudding moulds (*moulle à bombe haut*) (62). These are tinned moulds much taller than the other moulds and tapering to a dome shape and with an extra side added to the mould to enable it to stand upright in the freezing cave. This mould is not 'chemised' but is used principally for ice-cream pudding mixtures of two to three colours. It is normally made in 1 pt size but there are also $1\frac{1}{2}$, 2 and $2\frac{1}{2}$ pt sizes.

62   Bomb
      mould

Tin-plated steel or iron

Biscuit mould (*moulle à bisquit glacée*) (63). This tin, rectangular mould consists of three sections, a deeper centre piece with two lids fitting

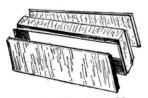

over a lip so that both inside and outside is flush with the centre piece. The technique is to line the bottom lid with paper, overlapping the edges and made fast to the centre piece and then place the ice-cream mix inside (this may be in coloured layers of Neapolitan or of plain variety). The top is fitted with grease-proof paper

63   Biscuit mould

and shut tight on to the centre piece prior to the whole mould being set to freeze.

Pastry and pie moulds

Raised pie moulds (64). These tin moulds vary in shape and fancy design but normally consist of two oval or oblong sides which fit together

with two pins securing each end.
Their use is the making of cold pies
with hot-water paste. The technique is
to put the mould together, stand it on
a baking sheet and work the paste in
from the bottom around the sides.
When filled and topped with further
decorative trimmings on the surface,
it is baked. When cold the pins are
removed and the sides are then easily
pulled away. Sizes are usually 14 in.

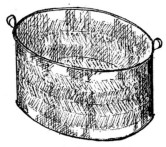

64   Raised pie mould

or 16 in. in length if oblong and 9 in. or 10 in. in length if oval. The
depth is from $3\frac{1}{4}$ in. to 4 in.

Tartlet moulds (65). The French-type tartlet moulds are of simple, round
pattern ($2\frac{3}{4}$ in. to $3\frac{1}{4}$ in. in diameter), without lip and with straight sides
coming up to an angle of 45° and are used where the pastry is baked
with the filling. The proper technique is to assemble several tins
together, place over them one layer of pastry and press with a piece
of floured dough (or a smaller floured patty tin). If a rolling pin is then
run over the tops, the pastry can be cut off against the sharp edge of
the tins.

65   French tartlet mould   66   Patty tin   67   Barquette

Patty tin (66). These tins of 2 in. to 4 in. diameter have their straight
sides at an angle of 35° and rounded over at the end to form an outside
rim. This enables them to be used where the pastry is first cut with a
crimped cutter and 'thumbed up' or machine blocked to give a fancy
edge.

Boat-shaped patty tins (*moulle à barquette*) (67). These are similar to patty
tins but are sharp-pointed, oval shapes 4 in. to $4\frac{1}{2}$ in. in length. They
are cooked empty for later filling with savoury mixtures.

Flan ring (68). Flan rings are made from tin
and consist of a simple round hoop with each
rim turned over for strength. The ring should
be quite plain and never fluted. It should be
1 in. only in depth. The technique is to place
the ring on a baking sheet, line with plain
paste, roll off the edges with a rolling pin and

68   Flan ring

'crimp up'. Just before the flan is baked the ring is removed to colour the paste (some cooks at that stage like to gild the outside with egg wash).

Cake hoops. Cake hoops are similar but deeper and are always lined with several thicknesses of paper. Sponge tins for making Genoise have bottoms and are not to be confused with flan rings. So-called flan rings that are fluted, have push-out bases and so on, are never found in good-class kitchens.

Wooden implements

Rolling pin

Most experienced pâtissiers advise against the loose-handled variety of rolling pin because one does not so readily sense the pressure on the paste being rolled. Thus, loose-handled pins are not so effective for gauging evenness and thickness. A good straight pin with or without handles is to be preferred.

Chopping blocks and boards

One or two points should be made about chopping blocks and boards. Under present statutory hygiene regulations preparation tables and work benches should be topped with impervious material such as stainless steel or laminated plastic. Chopping and cutting boards are, therefore, particularly necessary for the protection of knives as well as for effective working.

It must be remembered that the chopping board is designed only to take the force of the chopping knife or parsley mincer and that where a cleaver or chopper is to be used a heavier block is necessary.

Chopping blocks or boards (particularly the former) should not be washed with water for this causes softening of the wood and subsequent tendency to splinter and warp. The butcher's block (and similar surfaces) should be dry scraped with the specially provided scraper and/or should be cleaned with a wire brush. The technique is to sprinkle the surface with clean sawdust and remove by vigorous scrubbing with the wire brush in the direction of the grain.

69   Sieve

Sieve (tammis) (69)

The sieve should not be confused with the strainer nor, because its French designation is the *tammis*, should it be confused with the tammis cloth which is known as the *étamine* in France. Sieves are made of circular, wooden frames and the round gauze strainer is fitted in with a ring of wood pressing in to form a taut, straining surface.

The gauze may be wire or of hair or nylon. The lighter hair and nylon sieves are used principally for 'sieving out', i.e., processes such as passing flour where it is intended that foreign material should be left behind. In that case passing is assisted simply by tapping or agitating the sieve. When sieving for 'breaking up' such as in sieving potatoes and other vegetables, the material to be passed is pushed through with the champignon (q.v.).

Tammy cloth (étamine). The tammy cloth is so useful and so frequently used that, despite the fact that it is not a utensil, it should not be omitted from present consideration. A tammy cloth is made from calico by cutting lengths of approximately 1 yd from 27 in. wide rolls. The technique of using is to place the cloth over the receptacle, push it in to fit loosely inside and then pour in the sauce to be passed carefully so as not to dislodge the cloth. The chef now needs help from another, for two persons are required to lift the cloth at each end and to hold it fairly taut. The ends of the cloth are then gathered together. Each person with the left hand over the right to hold his own end of the gathered cloth, then pulls and turns (never relaxing the tautness of the cloth) in the opposite direction to the other. This twisting continues until all the sauce has been forced through the cloth.

Another way of using a tammy cloth is where passing through a fine chinois has not sufficed to make a sauce or purée fine enough. Then the cloth is stretched out, the thick sauce placed in and the cloth gathered up. With two wooden spatulas held against each other, the ingredient is forced through. Each in turn pushes his spatula forward and allows the other person to push it back again. The underside of the cloth is frequently scraped with a pallet knife.

Muslin (mouseline). Pieces of muslin, one, two or three thick, are used in the passing of clear gravies and consommés. They should never be used with pressure as with a tammis cloth.

Jelly bag and stand. The stand is made of wood and is four sided, wider at the bottom than at the top. It is fitted with a door and shelf inside on which is placed the receptacle to receive the jelly. It is enclosed so that air will not cool the thin trickle of jelly and to exclude all dust. The jelly bag is made of thick flannel material, shaped like a cone. This is placed in the open top of the stand and secured with four tapes to each outstanding corner. The hot jelly is poured in and left to drain through. It is *never* disturbed, or it may become cloudy.

Nylon jelly bags are now also obtainable.

The foregoing has covered the main items of the type of batterie de cuisine that would be found in an adequately furnished professional kitchen. The way in which these utensils are recognised, used and maintained by chefs and their staffs can make or mar their effectiveness. These utensils, perfected and adapted for their purposes over the years complement the skills and knowledge of the craftsman. In turn, the craftsman should know and respect these inanimate *aides.*

9   Kitchen and food service planning

The plan or layout of a kitchen should be determined by a clear catering policy; even though the plan is often limited by space available. In turn the policy adopted and space and layout required for the kitchen to carry forward that policy is affected by many things. Determining factors include: the type of business done, whether a hotel is primarily for residents or does a busy chance trade, the type of district it is in and consequently its type of customer, seasonal pressure of trade and the possibility of expansion. These points (and there are others) must be considered when a catering establishment as a whole, including the kitchen, is in the project stage for chefs often complain, perhaps not without justification, that kitchens too often seem to be added to hotels or hospitals, for example, as an afterthought and tend to be passed over during early planning.

In determining kitchen layout, as well as organising the subsequent work within that layout, certain fundamental intentions remain constant whatever the type of catering operation. Traditional kitchen organisation along partie lines is compatible with the effective achievement of these fundamental aims. On the other hand basic intentions behind planning kitchens and food service must not be obscured by 'traditional' thinking.

Basic intentions might be summarised as:

1. Reception by the catering unit or kitchen of commodities in various forms and either by partial or complete preparation followed by cooking, reheating, portioning and other dispensing methods, conversion of this food supply into meals.

2. Regulating the supply of food in meal form because of limitations such as economy, time, locality and quantity but in such a way that the quality of the food and service is acceptable and, indeed, attractive.

All other aspects of food service planning hinge on these two considerations but unfortunately subsidiary or intermediate factors of detail and design may be introduced in such profusion and at such an early time that basic issues tend, too often, to be fogged and obscured. Too early a pre-occupation with detail can result in poor designing, subsequent operating confusion and even failure.

Efficient and intelligent interpretation and fulfilment of the main considerations must depend not only on floor areas, bricks and mortar, but also on study of present-day trends and anticipation of future developments in catering techniques.

The traditional partie system of kitchen operation and well-tried methods of food preparation and cooking will certainly not be immune from technological and economic influences of the day. Escoffier himself observed in the preface to *A Guide to Modern Cookery* that 'social customs and methods of life alter so rapidly, that a few years now suffice to change completely the face of usages which at their inception bade fair to outlive the age'.

Amongst significant current trends in cooking, kitchen organisation and food service the following are readily recognisable:

1. Improved pay for catering staff especially those employed in the kitchen and shortage of skilled operators and unskilled assistants alike have tended towards the development of higher pay. Probable consequences of this are:

(*a*) Greater mechanisation.
(*b*) Simpler operations.
(*c*) Increased use of 'convenience' foods.

2. Greater emphasis on marketing and merchandising reflected in:

(*a*) Selling prices based less on meal production costs and more upon the value to the customer of the total food service being offered.
(*b*) Increasing development of specialities either of foods, dishes or forms of service capable of giving individuality and character to an establishment.

The outward forms of luxury hotels and restaurants may remain least affected by these considerations but even at this top level there are clear signs of adaptation in approach to kitchen plans and planning designed to deal with higher paid and scarcer staff and in the increased exploitation of pre-prepared commodities. At other levels of hotel keeping and catering generally, the trends mentioned are already noticeable.

In terms of kitchen layout and equipment such trends seem destined to lead to closer relationship or contact between the actual point of food service and the customer. This should further stimulate the demand for faster cooking applicances and conversely render unnecessary much of the hot-food holding equipment or hot-cupboard storage. The holding of cooked food in hot cupboards only too often does, in fact, contribute substantially to poor food and the more frequent preparation of food in smaller quantities for immediate service is already finding favour with customers.

The chapter on menu planning indicates that the menu is the blue-print of the catering operation and similarly may be accepted as the starting point when planning. The points of importance in determining menu policy hinge on decisions made on the type of the establishment and the scope and style of catering to be provided. There must be complete clarity regarding:

(a) Those for whom it is intended to cater.
(b) The reason for their patronage.
(c) Any service demands which the foregoing points, (a) and (b), will impose (examples might be late-night service, gourmet standards, etc.).

At one time, once the menu's form had been decided, equipment requirements were estimated largely on its scope and style. Already, at the present time, much deeper consideration has to be given additionally to the role which the kitchen itself has to perform in executing the menu plan. Food supplies may be received in many different forms and in varying degrees of preparedness and as more and more of the chef's or caterer's supplies become 'convenienced' for him the role of the kitchen in relation to the menu will require even greater consideration.

'Convenienced' foods are already a reality to a wide number of progressive hoteliers, caterers and chefs. Meat, fish, poultry, vegetables and fruits are obtainable quick-frozen and in prepared and/or portioned forms. Dehydrated products, bakery pre-mixes, prepared soups and sauces are now available to caterers in addition to canned goods which have long been used by them. The packaging of cordials in pliable plastics and experiments constantly being made on new methods of preservation suggest that changes in traditional forms of supply are by no means over. Increasing use of 'convenience' foods displacing or supplementing unprocessed commodities must have a profound effect upon planning and equipment (see also p. 109). Certain types of equipment such as those concerned with vegetable preparation may be reduced or eliminated. Storage facilities may require adjustment. De-hydration and other forms of processing will enable storage areas to be reduced and the use of quick-frozen products will require appropriate provision of refrigeration.

Modern food service and kitchen operation must be planned not only in accordance with the concepts of work flow and culinary principles, but also to take these changes into account.

Information required. As will be seen from the above, before beginning kitchen planning answers to various questions are needed in the light of modern trends. Typical queries will also include:

1. What type of meal will be offered?
2. How many persons will be served?
3. When will these meals be required? Will the main meal be a.m. or p.m., i.e., will it be a lunch or dinner service?
4. How many sittings are there to be for each meal?
5. What will be the extent of still-room service requirement, i.e., what quantity of tea and coffee for lounge as well as restaurant will be required?
6. Is allowance to be made for special functions?
7. Will 'convenience' foods be used?
8. What area of floor space is available?
9. What is the position of windows, ventilation, drainage, water supply, etc.?
10. What type of service is proposed—cafeteria, waiter or waitress service?

Area required. It is possible that kitchens have sometimes been reduced in size in order to provide more space and increased seating in the restaurant. The pity is that this measure does not necessarily increase trading capacity of restaurants, for it is the kitchen as much as the dining room which determines the number of customers to be dealt with during a service period.

Cramped inadequate kitchens must inevitably lead to delays and faults in service. These flaws may ultimately deter customers. Quite apart from an unfortunate influence upon volume of trade and repeat business; inadequate kitchen facilities must adversely affect staff. It will already be apparent that there are many elements which tend to make the calculation of kitchen areas a controversial matter, about which experts themselves differ.

Briefly stated, kitchen areas desirably vary according to the type and number of meals provided. As the number of patrons increase, so the area of the kitchen relative to the seating capacity may tend to be reduced. Accordingly, information about numbers alone is not sufficient to plan a kitchen nor to calculate its area. Knowledge of peak load is essential and this must either be a result of experience or, in the case of new establishments, intelligent forecasting.

In dealing with hotel and restaurant kitchens, these premises generally require kitchens out of all proportion in size to the actual seating capacity of the restaurant. This is mainly due to the length of time during which meals are available. Under certain circumstances, the size of hotel and restaurant kitchens may be as much as 40% of the restaurant area although one American authority (J. O. Dahl, in his pre-war work on *Kitchen Management*) suggested that they 'usually occupy about 25% as much space as that allotted to the dining room'.

It has been suggested that between 10 to 12 sq. ft should be allowed for each customer per meal in calculating restaurant space but clearly rate of meal service or 'customer turnover time' will condition such calculations. Kitchen space estimates have been as low as $2\frac{1}{2}$ to 4 sq. ft per catering unit for a kitchen catering for 1,000 (*Architects' Journal*, Gas Supplement, 14th January, 1960) to as much as 9 or 10 sq. ft per head per meal served in the case of small establishments such as, for example, fifteen- to twenty-bedroom guest houses; though some would consider a figure of this kind appropriate even in the case of more substantial hotels. G. C. Tanner, writing in the *Architectural Review* (October, 1960) on the hotel kitchen, also stresses that there are no hard and fast rules for calculating kitchen areas but suggests as a useful 'rule of thumb' at sketch plan stage '6 sq. ft of floor area per person accommodated in the dining room'.* Because of such variable factors it is not really possible to deal with the kitchens of hotels and restaurants as constituting a group. Small à la carte restaurants may have relatively tiny kitchens, whilst some hotels may have large ones compared with the dining area.

Perhaps all that can be said with certainty is that a lower area per head suffices for 'straightforward' kitchens such as those planned primarily for one purpose such as banqueting or a relatively simple operation such as industrial staff catering and that a higher rate for calculating kitchen floor space must be used when preparation and stove work becomes more ambitious and complex as in high-class à la carte work. Possibly also in hospital kitchens where provision for several types of diet may be required.

No firm rules as to area can thus be given but the following may be used as a rough indication of kitchen space possibly required for hotels and restaurants offering waiter or waitress serviced meals.

In attempting to estimate kitchen areas on the basis of total daily catering capacity, it is similarly difficult to lay down a hard and fast scale. The following tables are thus intended for broad guidance only:

* Tanner states that this figure is arrived at by assuming 50% of the area allowed in assessing the size of the dining room (i.e., 12 sq. ft per person, which includes tables, passageways, etc.). Dining area, however, varies from as low as 10 sq. ft to 18 sq. ft for a luxury hotel.

APPROXIMATE INDICATION OF KITCHEN REQUIREMENTS

Numbers eating in busiest period	Kitchen area desirable per customer, sq. ft
100	5 to 9
100 to 250	4 to 6
250 to 500	4 to 5
500 to 1,000	3 to 4
Over 1,000	2½ to 3

Note: Area reductions may be made when, for example, convenience foods (frozen, etc.) are fully exploited. The lower figures relate to such simpler operations and the higher for more complete catering.

TABLE 1 (a)

POSSIBLE AREAS ON A DAILY BASIS OF CATERING CAPACITY

Total meals per day	Restaurant area, sq. ft	Kitchen area, sq. ft	Total catering floor space, sq. ft
100	375	150	525
250	560	215	775
500	950	300	1,250
1,000	1,500	500	2,000

(b)

Seating capacity	Restaurant area, sq. ft	Kitchen area, sq. ft	Estimated possible number of meals per hour
50	700	300	75
75	1,000	400	115
100	1,250	500	150
125	1,750	750	190
200	2,750	1,200	300

Out of the total kitchen area, up to approximately one-quarter may be required for storage; with the remaining three-quarters of the space devoted to food preparation, cooking and serving.

For school meals—service kitchens, the Ministry of Education (*Building Bulletin* 11) makes suggestions concerning kitchen areas which may be found helpful also to those concerned with catering for industry and other forms of staff and welfare catering. For example, in the case of secondary schools, catering for 150, an area of 550 sq. ft is suggested for the kitchen. 1,730 sq. ft is proposed for a kitchen catering for 600 similar pupils.

Other suggestions include:

For 250 secondary school pupils a kitchen area of   800 sq. ft.
„ 450   „   „   „ „   „   „ „ 1,350 „

These areas are much more generous than those which have been commonly used in commercial ventures for it must be remembered that the possibility of 'staggering' meals in school catering is very much less. Even so there are many chefs, caterers and kitchen planners who would feel that figures quoted for hotel and restaurant kitchen areas in the foregoing tables are less than sufficient. It would certainly be dangerous to use any figures merely on 'rule of thumb' lines and it should be stressed that they have been used to illustrate and attempt to illuminate the subject rather than to indicate precise rules for calculating.

Because of the factors involved and the variations that exist even between similar establishments, it will be appreciated that it is thus difficult to reduce to an exact science the calculation of area requirements. Architects and kitchen engineers tend to have their own formulae for calculating kitchen space requirements and some may have 'rule of thumb' adjustments to allow for the difference in scope.

It is also important to remember that in the matter of area as in other details, initial planning is not a matter for any one man. Often it can involve the user (hotelier or restaurateur) and his chef and maître d'hôtel. Their terms of reference have to be reconciled with site limitations and the views and advice of consultant, kitchen engineers and the like, whose activities are co-ordinated by the architect.

(IV) CONVENIENCE FOODS AND METHODS DIAGRAMMATICALLY EXPRESSED

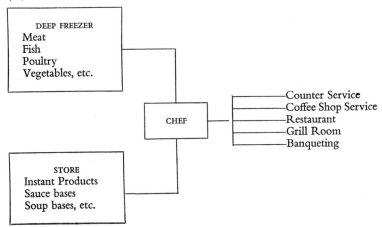

DEEP FREEZER
Meat
Fish
Poultry
Vegetables, etc.

CHEF

Counter Service
Coffee Shop Service
Restaurant
Grill Room
Banqueting

STORE
Instant Products
Sauce bases
Soup bases, etc.

The chef's role in kitchen planning

A chef may, however, never have a decisive voice in determining the space to be allotted to his activities and it is, indeed, surprising how often planners neglect to consult him in regard to this and other aspects of kitchen design.

Despite these circumstances there can be no doubt that the chef and his senior staff should have an interest in the whole concept of the kitchen. They should be prepared to play their part in providing terms of reference and appropriate briefing on culinary and catering aspects in planning, constructing and equipping their work-place. Though architects, engineers and hotel directors are often strongly criticised by chefs and other catering executives for faults in designing and planning it is probably true that some part, at least, of the blame could be ascribed to insufficiently informed and insufficiently articulate chefs. Wisdom after the event is no substitute for the intelligent anticipation of the trained and experienced man.

Passages and ancillary offices

Before considering in greater detail factors within the kitchen itself, it should be remembered that passages to and from the kitchen must be kept clear and unobstructed, both for the entry of goods, exit of containers and movement of staff. Other matters also not to be overlooked are that an office should be provided for the chef, and a dining room and cloakroom for kitchen employees.

The flow of work

Disposal of equipment in the space to be provided and even some detailed arrangement within the kitchen is best considered before deciding the area of the room. Only too often kitchen planners. engineers and caterers find the area allocation is done first and their detail work must follow.

The basic fundamentals of kitchen design may be illustrated by the diagrammatic progress chart (v) p. 111. This indicates that efficient operation of an hotel kitchen depends on smooth work flow based on work study.

To obtain a continuous flow of goods from section to section as illustrated (v), the design of each section must be considered carefully to ensure that paths within its bounds do not cross more than is necessary.

(v) Goods and Work Flow

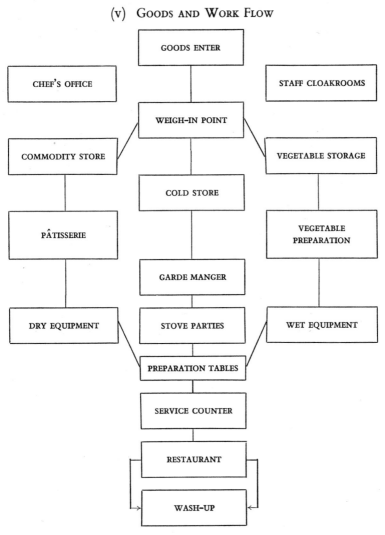

A well-planned layout largely depends on the following require-ments which, if properly provided for, establish good basic kitchen conditions:

1. Incoming supplies and raw materials (checking and weighing).
2. Food storage.
3. Food preparation.
4. Cooking.
5. Servery arrangements.
6. Pan-wash (plonge) arrangements.
7. Crockery and cutlery wash-up.

Intelligent disposition of preparation machinery, sinks and work benches may make a great difference to the total daily 'kitchen mileage' covered by the food, and also, more important, to unnecessary 'travelling' by the kitchen staff. Thus, the perfect kitchen from this point of view is one in which raw, and cooked material needs the minimum of movement and requires once only to cover the same route. Once each section is satisfactory, therefore, they must be arranged to comply as nearly as possible to the flow illustrated.

This, at first, may seem reasonably simple but in many cases the task involves modernising an existing old kitchen or laying out a kitchen within the confines of existing premises. This can present difficulties in arriving at any kind of work-flow system and often the best has to be made of limited opportunities. Layout becomes even more of a problem, when the siting of new plant has to be governed by, for example, existing drainage.

Further early factors in kitchen planning

A decision must be made as to the type of fuel to be used. It is not always advisable to install a complete gas, electric or solid fuel installation. In some instances a combination heated by different fuels may be an advantage. The next chapter deals more fully with fuels and cooking apparatus.

When planning a kitchen, careful attention must be given to lighting, wiring, ventilation, plumbing and hot and cold water services and appropriate specialists should be consulted at an early stage.

Storage

Coupled with the basic aim of achieving smooth flow from stores to preparation, preparation to cooking, cooking to servery and from the servery to the restaurant and then back to the wash-up is the need to provide storage space appropriate to the size of the kitchen. Various types of stores are necessary and these include dry goods, meat and cold storage of fish and dairy produce.

Dry commodity storage, vegetable stores and the cold store should desirably be in close proximity to the receiving point where food is brought into the building.

It is difficult to give precise guidance on the amount of storage space required as much depends on the type of food purchasing policy followed. Modern trends are to smaller stores for vegetables because of using processed items whilst for dry goods, space required is affected by marketing policy, proximity to suppliers and similar factors. Total storage for food and equipment should not generally exceed one-quarter of the kitchen area and the commodity or dry goods store is seldom more than a room representing 8% to 10% of the total kitchen area. Another guide (Tanner, writing in *Architectural Review*, October, 1960) is 0·2 sq. ft of vegetable storage per person accommodated in the dining room and 0·4 sq. ft of commodity (dry goods) storage on a similar basis.

Food containers and storage

In many kinds of catering it is desirable that wherever possible the same container should be capable of use for both cooking and dispensing. Moreover, there are obvious advantages in having containers standardised to allow for interchange between various uses.

Among the possibilities in regard to storage must be reckoned:

1. Increased storage provision at 0°F for quick-frozen foods both to accommodate:
   (a) Uncooked foods such as fish, meat, poultry, vegetables and fruit, frozen desserts.
   (b) Prepared or cooked foods such as confectionery and baked goods, ready-cooked individual items and completely cooked meals.
2. Increased storage provision for dehydrated, dried, canned, plastic wrapped and ready-mixed products such as:
   (a) Soups and sauces.
   (b) Vegetables, fruits, potatoes, confectionery and pie fillings.
3. Reduction in provision for storage of vegetables, fruit, meat, poultry and fish at chill temperatures, i.e., 20°F to 35°F.

Preparation and cooking

The different types of food (fish, meat, vegetables and pastry) should have their appropriate preparation space. The equipment necessary for cooking the food should be sited close to the appropriate preparation point, e.g., boiling pans, close to vegetable preparation; pastry ovens, close to pastry preparation and so on. Preparation areas of the future will be profoundly affected by 'convenience' and pre-processing techniques.

Vegetable preparation

If quick-frozen and/or dehydrated vegetables are fully exploited, the vegetable washing and cleaning area can be drastically reduced to cope with salad preparation only. Peelers and sinks for potatoes will continue to be required in some operations but the availability of 'instant' dried potatoes and quick-frozen potatoes may satisfy the demands of some establishments.

Preparation of fish, meat and poultry

It is possible for all types of fish to be obtained in ready-to-use form enabling preparation areas to be restricted to simple washing facilities and a work bench. Breaded, ready-to-fry portions can further reduce preparation time.

Most types of poultry are already available in oven-ready form. Portioned joints may be obtained ready for cooking. Poultry cleaning and dressing areas are, under such circumstances, unnecessary.

Meats, similarly, can be obtained in jointed form and many butchers to the catering trade are ready to supply meat portioned for cooking. Certainly a significant trend is in the availability of an increasing range of quick-frozen portions. Prepared offal, sausage meats, canned products (especially pie fillings) are amongst those items available which can reduce preparation areas.

Type of cookery

Haute cuisine will remain in evidence in establishments where the guest is prepared to pay appropriately for it; and the stockpot and fonds de cuisine are not destined to be eliminated from good cookery. There seems little doubt, however, that the improved products, dried, canned and frozen (which have already met with a good response in the domestic market) cannot be ignored by chefs and caterers.

Whatever raw materials are used, however, consideration must be given to the different cookery processes summarised as follows:

1. Roasting and baking.
2. Boiling.
3. Grilling and toasting.
4. Steaming (vegetables, fish, puddings, etc.).
5. Deep frying (fish, chips, etc.).
6. Shallow and griddle frying.
7. Making of soups, stews, stocks, etc.
8. Plate and food holding in hot cupboards.
9. Beverage making (tea, coffee, milk and other hot drinks).
10. Heating water for culinary purposes.

Apparatus requirements

Having considered the proposed kitchen and its task in these general terms, cooking apparatus can be selected and sited.

Cooking and serving high-quality food in large quantities, and to a strict time schedule, is an exacting task, even under the most favourable conditions. By the correct choice, disposition and use of cooking equipment, purely physical strain can be greatly eased. Moreover, the favourable environment of an adequately equipped kitchen leaves greater scope for exercising skill, maintaining quality and controlling costs.

Economical cooking often depends on using apparatus specially designed for its purpose, and suitably deployed to meet average conditions. In a new kitchen it is especially important to guard against putting in too much equipment. The ideal is to prepare, cook and serve food with the minimum of appliances in active use. The effect of this policy is to keep down capital outlay as well as running costs.

In improving an old kitchen it is, of course, important to note the capacities of existing appliances and particularly the uses to which they are put. Modern fuels, such as electricity and gas can deal more efficiently with most cooking processes, and therefore, in many cases smaller equipment will suffice.

Categories of apparatus

In selecting equipment it is obviously necessary to know the cooking capacity of the various items. Amongst the most important pieces of equipment likely to be required are:

1. Ranges or cookers.
2. Roasting and general-purpose ovens.
3. Boiling tables.
4. Bains-marie and hot cupboards.
5. Steaming ovens.
6. Boiling pans and vegetable boiling pans.
7. Pastry ovens.
8. Water-boiling apparatus.
9. Deep fryers.
10. Grills/toasters/salamanders.
11. Stockpot stands.

Catalogues of kitchen manufacturers and engineers may be consulted for details and, of course, advice and information may be obtained from area Electricity and Gas Boards.

Efficient and robust apparatus should be installed and before selecting equipment it is advisable to try to visit other hotels and catering establishments where cooking equipment has recently been installed so that first-hand and up-to-date knowledge can be obtained.

When deciding on the type and size of the apparatus required, in a good class restaurant or hotel kitchen, provision will have to be made for à la carte menus in addition to table d'hôte service. Additional equipment may also be necessary to deal with special dishes. Furthermore, in restaurants and hotel kitchens where parties and banquets are catered for, allowance may have to be made for equipment to deal with abnormal requirements.

Present equipment trends

Chefs and caterers are becoming aware of the advantages of wheel-mounted kitchen equipment, manufactured wherever possible in unit form, to provide flexibility.

Cantilevered equipment is increasingly recognised as having many advantages in accessibility, convenience, hygiene and strength and offers scope for considerably more exploitation.

The reduction in preparation work as a result of using pre-prepared or processed foods cuts the time between the initial handling of food and its final presentation to the customer. (Quick-frozen vegetables for instance require less cooking time than the market-bought variety.) The need for equipment for quantity preparation tends, therefore, to give way to the provision of equipment for faster cooking of smaller quantities.

Amongst items of catering equipment being increasingly used the following may be mentioned:

(a) The trunnion kettle or tilting steam-jacketed boiler is tending to displace the traditional stew pan.

(b) The self-generating steam oven is increasingly favoured where frequent batch cooking of food is required.

(c) New developments in ovens give improved temperature control and forced convection ovens are now designed to give greater speed and more even temperature.

(d) Micro-wave cookery working on electronic principles now brings the possibilities of high-speed cooking and reheating techniques to the service of the caterer.

Siting the equipment

The positioning of ranges or cookers is vitally important. It is nearly always advisable to install stove equipment on an island site with a ventilation canopy above. Bains-marie and stockpot stands should be close to the ranges. Boiling tables, steaming ovens and vegetable boiling pans should also be near the centre of the kitchen and within

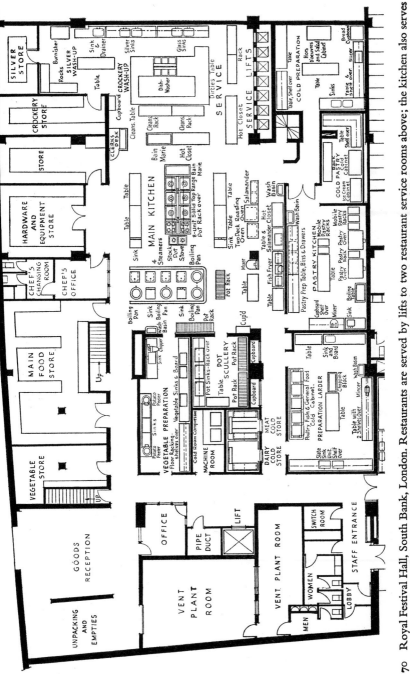

70 Royal Festival Hall, South Bank, London. Restaurants are served by lifts to two restaurant service rooms above; the kitchen also serves the staff dining room at same level. *Architects:* Robert H. Matthew, A.R.I.B.A., and J. L. Martin, F.R.I.B.A.

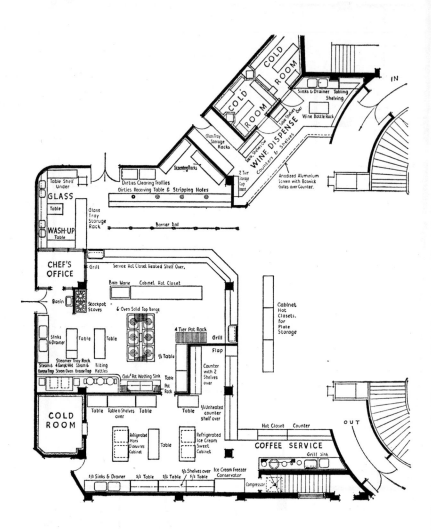

71 Grosvenor House Great Room, Park Lane, W. One of two services connected with the Great Room. For full banquets both services are used. Washing-
up is done in the second service. Of interest is the considerable number of appliances
and the central cabinet hot closets which are removed during exhibitions. When
in use service area is entirely enclosed by large semi-circular removable shutters.

easy access of vegetable preparation tables. Here again it is advisable to provide a canopy over the equipment. The deep fryer should be conveniently sited near the main ranges and service point, but it is desirably provided with a separate extract canopy.

Quick-service cooking equipment such as a contact grill, toasters, griddle plate, etc., may be desirable in the still-room or at a service point near the restaurant or where late or 'out of hours' meals may be served. Additional hot cupboards in or near the main restaurant may also be required for hot storage of plates, coffee cups, etc. The still-room should have a café or quick boiler and suitable equipment for providing hot and cold drinks.

Easy-to-clean preparation tables constructed of stainless steel topped with laminated plastic or some other impervious material should be positioned near the apparatus. Chefs should make themselves familiar with statutory requirements regarding hygiene. It is, for example, now imperative for preparation tables to have impervious surfaces. See also Chapter 13.

Table and work surfaces must be sufficiently high. It is better to err on the side of their being too high rather than too low, because shorter employees can increase their level by using such stands as slatted boards or even a box but one can do little about a surface that is too low. Unfortunately, opinions differ about the ideal work bench height (possibly because personal size varies) and something between 3 ft and 3 ft 3 in. is usual.

Sinks

Sinks and draining boards should be fitted wherever possible along external walls to facilitate drainage. This has the added advantage that any windows will then provide as much natural light as possible for kitchen staff.

Similar considerations regarding height apply. Sinks might even be slightly higher for certainly they should be provided with duckboards or slats for dry standing. Detachable tops for sinks may be found useful (especially in vegetable rooms) for giving extra preparation space.

Different types of sinks should be provided according to their particular function:

Stainless steel for glassware, crockery and cutlery. (*Note.* Dishwashing machines are usually fitted for dealing with the bulk of crockery and cutlery.)
Stainless-steel sinks for vegetable preparation. (Porcelain may be used for this purpose but does not always stand up to heavy work.)
Galvanised sinks for pot washing.

Slate-lined sinks for fish preparation.

Wash-hand basins must be provided in compliance with statutory requirements.

In approaching the general plan for the kitchen and ancillary offices, other matters in which, the chef will be interested are as follows:

Flooring

Many developments have taken place in floor surfaces and the mind should not be closed to the possibility of making use of new materials. Most chefs, however, tend to agree that standard, kiln-fired quarry tiling provides an extremely satisfactory kitchen floor surface. Terrazzo and granolithic chips, bedded in concrete are also good hard-wearing floors. Important requirements for the floor area are:

(*a*) Ease of cleaning.
(*b*) Good appearance and the facility of not readily showing dirt.
(*c*) Coolness and non-slip surfaces for foot comfort and safety of the kitchen worker.

Skirtings and corner should, of course, be coved to facilitate cleaning.

As all kitchens must be equipped with drains it is important to ensure that floors are properly sloped to drainage outlets to ensure speedy and efficient flow-away.

Walls

Kitchen walls should meet the following needs:

(*a*) Be clean and easy to clean.
(*b*) Be of attractive and hygienic appearance.
(*c*) Reflect light.

There are many wall surfaces including plastics and washable paints which give good results in kitchens. Nevertheless, wall tiling (whatever the glazing finish, i.e., matt or high gloss) deservedly retains high popularity, and to tile walls at least up to 5 ft or 6 ft is desirable. Above the tiling, sound absorbent and anti-condensation treatment is advisable. Where cost is a factor, such special protection may have to be limited to sink and stove areas.

Lighting

Many existing kitchens are in basements or semi-basements and in any case are seldom sited to obtain the best natural light. Artificial lighting is almost invariably required. This is clearly a matter in which expert advice should be sought. Particular attention needs to be paid to the lighting under canopies and for sinks and work tables. There is not only the question of the intensity and type of lighting required for comfortable and efficient working but the problem of colour distortion must be considered; vitally important when food is to be effectively dished.

Colour

Colour generally is now recognised to be important: (*a*) as an aid to efficiency in matters such as light reflection and the promotion of cleanliness and also (*b*) in regard to promoting staff efficiency through helping to provide an encouraging and pleasant place to work in. Advice should be sought (from the architect or, where no architect is employed, from the British Colour Council, 13 Portman Square, London, W.1, regarding the reflective value of colours and their most effective use.

British Standards exist for paint colours, and it is possible to achieve precision in colour selection by using British Standard references. It is, in fact, difficult if not impossible to give a Table showing the reflective value of different paint colours without quoting the code numbers, and it must be emphasised that the British Standard number is a reliable guide irrespective of paint manufacturer. The following list consists of an extremely limited range from a vast number of available colours and shades and has been selected by the author merely to give a general indication of colour values. There are, of course, inevitably apparent alterations in appearance according to the 'finish' of surfaces whether 'matt' or 'gloss'. The list itself shows how descriptions vary and the colour designations used in 1960 of two manufacturers have been used to illustrate this. These makers are indicated by the initials I.C.I. for Imperial Chemical Industries Ltd, and I.P. for International Paints Ltd. It is interesting to note that these two manufacturers name a different British Standard colour 'Wedgwood Blue' which illustrates the difficulties in comparing colour by name alone.

With regard to selecting colours, it is suggested that those in the list with a reflective factor of less than 56% are not suitable for extensive wall areas in kitchens but only for emphasis in outlining architraves, skirtings, etc. Indeed, for major wall areas in kitchens it is thought that colours only above 72% should be contemplated if light, airy work-places are required.

Colour can play a most important part in creating effects of spaciousness or otherwise. Henry Hillier, senior lecturer in Interior Design and Decoration at the Glasgow School of Art, and who teaches this subject also at the Scottish Hotel School has stressed that 'the cool colours of the spectrum seem to recede progressively as their tones become lighter—range after range of mountains fading into the distance until finally the tone of the furthermost range is indistinguishable from the sky. The "hot" colours of the spectrum, on the other hand, reds, orange, yellow, seem to advance and appear nearer at their highest intensity'. Hillier points out that these observations applied architecturally give the decorator an opportunity to modify 'faults' where structural alterations are impossible. The same expert has also stressed how moods can 'be induced or initiated by the appropriate use of colour'. This is of great significance in creating an effective or efficient place of work. For such reasons the architect with training and sympathy for colour or the design consultant who specialises in this field can be of real practical service in helping to create a functional kitchen.

TABLE 2

REFLECTIVE VALUES OF A LIMITED RANGE OF COLOURS

British Standard colour No.	Example of maker's description	Reflective factor, %	Author's notes
B.S.4 – 046	Off White (I.C.I.) Bone White (I.P.)	84 do	
B.S.4 – 052	Ivory (I.P.) Buttermilk (I.C.I.)	84 do	
B.S.4 – 055	Acid Yellow (I.P.) Jasmine Yellow (I.C.I.)	72 do	Pale Yellow
B.S.3 – 040	Straw (I.C.I.) (Yellow/ Red Group)	72	
B.S.1 – 015	Zephyr (I.C.I.) (Red Group)	72	Pink Shade
B.S.6 – 070	Almond Green (I.P.) Goblin Green (I.C.I.)	72 do	Pale Green
B.S.7 – 081	Glacier Blue (I.P.) Narvik Blue (I.C.I.)	72 do	Pale Blue
B.S.7 – 075	Horizon Blue (I.C.I.) (Blue/Green Group)	72	Pale Bluish Green
B.S.2 – 026	Mellow Buff (I.C.I.) (Yellow/Red Group)	64	Pale Pinkish Yellow
B.S.5 – 058	Quaker Grey (I.P.) Gossamer (I.C.I.) (Green/ Yellow Group)	56 do	Pale Grey or Greenish Yellow hue

British Standard colour No.	Example of maker's description	Reflective factor, %	Author's notes
B.S.4 – 047	Stone Grey (I.P.)	56	Pale Stone (Greyish Yellow)
	Silver Gleam (I.C.I.)	do	
B.S.9 – 094	Flake Grey (I.C.I.)	56	Pale Grey
	London Grey (I.P.)	do	
B.S.0 – 088	Lime (I.C.I.) (Strong Colours Group)	56	Greenish Yellow
B.S.2 – 027	Mushroom (I.P.)	42	Light Pinkish Brown
B.S.1 – 016	Pink Haze (I.C.I.) (Red Group)	42	Pink
B.S.0 – 009	Citron (I.C.I.) (Strong Colours Group)	42	Light or Greenish Yellow
B.S.5 – 059	Greenstone (I.C.I.) (Green/ Yellow Group)	42	Light Yellowish Green
B.S.6 – 072	Apple Green (I.C.I.)	30	
B.S.0 – 006	Poppy (I.C.I.) (Strong Colours Group)	20	Light Red
B.S.0 – 012	Pacific Blue (I.C.I.) (Strong Colours Group)	12	
B.S.3 – 044	Golden Brown (I.C.I.)	12	
B.S.0 – 006	Post Office Red (I.C.I.)	9	
B.S.3 – 038	Congo Brown (I.C.I.)	7	
B.S.0 – 013	Anchusa (I.C.I.)	5	Strong Blue
B.S.3 – 039	Chocolate (I.C.I.)	2	Chocolate Brown

Ceilings

The treatment of kitchen ceilings in order to obviate moisture condensation is somewhat easier with the paints available today. Ceiling heights need no longer be excessive, for air change by artificial ventilation is a common means for promoting light and airy work-places. Nevertheless, the nature of a kitchen is such that loftiness can be a help psychologically as well as practically in aiding better lighting and ventilation for a hemmed-in, oppressive room is to be avoided at all costs. On the other hand higher kitchens are noisier kitchens unless sound deadening materials are used. Thus a floor to ceiling height of not less than 10 ft may be considered reasonable.

Having given general consideration to floor, walls, light, colour and ceiling, the shell of the kitchen, including its departments, has been given form and some final points which might be made regarding this shell are:

(a) It should be able to withstand fire hazards.
(b) It, and its departments, should be on the same level and they all in turn should preferably be on the same level as the restaurant.
(c) It should, where possible, have outside exposure.

Vegetable preparation

Separate provision away from the kitchen should be made for vegetable storage and vegetable preparation so that there is no question of bringing vegetable or garden soil into contact with other foods. A danger in vegetable storage is deterioration through close packing in warm, unventilated corners. Vegetable bins or racks of open construction are usually found to be best for storing vegetables so that they are kept as cool and as exposed to circulating air as possible. Galvanised tubing is suitable for vegetable racking and is to be preferred to wooden, slatted shelves. (Moveable shelving mentioned below in the paragraph on *Kitchen stores* in this chapter may also be considered for use here.)

As in the case of the commodity store and larder a north or east aspect is to be preferred for vegetable storage. This latter seldom occupied more than 5% of total kitchen area even in old-style kitchens and using modern techniques the space allocated may be even less.

In the adjacent preparation section an electrically operated potato peeling machine is usually justified together with adequate tank, sink and preparation tables.

Larder storage

Larder storage together with refrigerated storage is usually linked with the garde manger. Natural (as distinct from refrigerated) storage for foods should, for preference, be sited facing north and such storage should have natural window or outside ventilation. Windows should be fly-proofed with wire gauze. Slate, tile or marble shelving to give a cold and easily cleaned surface is desirable for larder storage. Left-over perishable foods should, of course, be kept in the refrigerator or artificial cold store for maximum safety.

Bread storage

A bread store should be well ventilated and provided with shelves of open construction to permit maximum exposure of the goods to air circulation. (See below and also vegetable storage above.) Shelves should be arranged for all bread to be stacked methodically with new deliveries going to the rear so that older loaves are used first. An adequate amount of shelving is important; for bread should not be stacked too high or too close.

Plonge

Chapter 11, (*Maintenance in the kitchen*) dealing with the work of the plonge indicates its requirements. Wherever possible at least one copper-lined tank should be provided for the washing of copper vessels. There should be adequate racking for clean pots and space for those awaiting treatment.

Kitchen stores

The dry stores should be proof against vermin of all kinds. Materials proofed against gnawing of rodents should be selected where possible. The storeroom should be lockable, well ventilated and long and narrow rather than square in order to economise in floor space. Obviously a primary consideration is the provision of adequate and conveniently arranged adjustable shelving for tinned and packaged items. Adjustable shelves allow the maximum utilisation of space.

Shelving equipped with wire trays and capable of being mounted on wheels is obtainable. This racking is completely aerated, allows food to be wheeled into the kitchen itself when required and, most importantly, allows the whole shelf to be pulled out for cleaning.

For items stored in bulk, bins with close-fitting lids are provided and these also should be mounted on wheels so that they can be moved for easy cleaning. Careful thought should be given to the layout of the storeroom beginning with the convenient positioning of scales at the entrance to check goods received and issued. The basis of stores layout is to ensure that those goods most frequently handled are most conveniently to hand.

Equipment, cleaning and other stores

In addition to commodity storage (l'économe) and vegetable store, it is also important to make adequate provision for the storage of spare utensils and equipment, cleaning material, empty returnable containers and the like.

Conclusion

The problems of catering and kitchen management are many, and only experience can teach the chef and caterer how to avoid the pitfalls in kitchen planning. It will be appreciated that this chapter has merely outlined the subject from the chef's or caterer's point of view and that it is a subject in which architecture, engineering and business economics play at least as great a part as the knowledge of cooking and kitchen management.

I O Equipment and fuel
in the kitchen plan

The consideration of appropriate cookery equipment for the modern professional kitchen will inevitably lead to a consideration also of the type of fuel to be used. Though solid fuel and oil both have their place under certain circumstances, there is little doubt that in most instances the choice of fuel for professional cookery lies between electricity and gas. Many chefs and caterers would, however, contend that the choice is not *between* appliances using one fuel or the other but of building up the most effective blend of equipment irrespective of fuel. There are, for example, keen advocates of 'combination' equipment such as electric ovens in a gas-topped range. It is true, however, that certain benefits may be derived from the exclusive use of one fuel in that a favourable tariff or special prices may be arranged. Each individual project, therefore, must be considered on its merits and the 'all in' scheme weighed against the 'combination plan'.

Electricity

When considering equipment for hotel and other professional kitchens, chefs and caterers cannot ignore the reasons which support the choice of electricity. Before turning to actual items of equipment, the following may be noted as among advantages claimed for an electric kitchen:

1. Cleanliness and better atmosphere in the kitchen.
2. Easy control of apparatus.
3. Improved working conditions for kitchen staff.
4. Greater flexibility in planning.
5. Saving in labour (no handling of fuel, stoking or ash removal).
6. Saving in space, in equipment and storage of fuel.
7. Long life of pots and pans.

Odours or fumes sometimes associated with some other fuels are not present for there are no products of combustion at all. Food is cooked under hygienic conditions and natural flavours are retained. Ease of operation is a feature of electric cooking. Further, the air in the kitchen is less likely to become vitiated for electric heating elements do not require oxygen. This is important, for it reduces the need for costly ventilation schemes, and savings can be effected in labour, cleaning and re-decorating.

Response to demand for heat

With regard for the 'responsiveness' of boiling plates, many chefs are convinced that gas is more suited to a sudden demand for 'special dishes' and find some inconvenience in the time lag of an electrical boiling plate. But a boiling plate seldom has to start from cold other than early in the morning, and during the principal working hours can economically be kept ready for instant use by running continually at low heat. Under such conditions, and using suitable utensils with ground flat bases, the electric boiling plate can give satisfaction. Some economy in operation may be achieved by using up the residual heat remaining after the plate has been switched off, though this is not a factor of great importance in commercial catering.

As to the actual electrical installations, it may simply be mentioned that supply leads should preferably be brought up from the floor in screwed conduit, this being finished off about 9 in. from floor level. Between the solid conduit and the terminal boxes of the apparatus the leads should be carried in flexible galvanised conduit tubing. It is the modern practice for every item of equipment to embody its own fuses, switches and pilot lamps. This is a great advantage when planning island units, and leads the chef and his assistants to practise economy while giving flexibility of control with switchgear immediately to hand. Adequate provisions must clearly be made for a main distribution board from which the various kitchen circuits are branched off, and including a main circuit breaker.

Gas

There is similarly available from the gas industry a wide range of reliable, efficient and economical equipment. Gas itself is a convenient fuel, labour-saving, flexible and free from smoke, and like electricity, it is brought right to the point of use, thus eliminating the need of storage for fuel, fuel handling or ash clearing.

Solid fuel

Twenty-five years ago many chefs regarded gas and electric cooking apparatus as 'new fangled' and were distrustful of "it". Solid fuel equipment particularly in the form of traditional coal ranges fired by the 'charbonnier' was not only widely used but was generally regarded by the traditional chef as ideal and irreplaceable.

In the past quarter of a century, however, kitchen craftsmen have been completely won over to modernisation and their suspicions tend now to be reserved for solid fuel installations. Yet it would be quite wrong to believe that coal, coke and similar fuels no longer have any use in the professional kitchen. It would be equally wrong to suppose that no advance has been made in the design and construction of stoves and ranges to burn such fuel. Efficient solid fuel cooking apparatus is today being made which still fulfils a useful function in modern kitchens and which is, in fact, particularly appropriate and useful in certain areas and types of establishments, such as country hotels.

What is over is the day of the old-fashioned black-lead open fire range. In recent years it is the stove with a low rate of fuel consumption and with heat retention features that is considered when solid fuel is to be employed.

Oil

Unlike solid fuel, oil is generally accepted by chefs and caterers as a 'modern' fuel though its application in water heating, steam raising or for central heating is more readily appreciated by chefs and caterers. Yet cookers adapted to or designed for oil burning can be considered under certain circumstances such as, for example, when oil is being purchased and stored for heating and water heating purposes, where solid fuel is not desired and when electricity or gas is not available.

Steam

Steaming ovens, boiling pans and other apparatus needing a supply of steam may be served by the installation of a boiler to generate steam for these and other purposes, such as heating wash-up water. In addition to solid fuel and oil-fired boilers there are types designed for gas firing, while it is also possible to adapt solid fuel boilers for gas heating. Gas-fired boilers are, of course, automatically controlled and their efficiencies are high. They have the additional advantage, owing to cleanliness in operation and the fact that fuel is piped directly to the point of use, of being suitable for positions which might be impracticable for some other fuels.

Cost considerations

As a general rule the capital cost of electric cooking equipment is greater than that of other solid fuel or gas appliances. When all the advantages and attendant savings are taken into consideration, however, it is usually found that any extra capital outlay is quickly recovered.

In addition there is another factor to be considered when comparing schemes using different fuels; that is the overall cost of food preparation. This includes the total overhead charges (rent, rates and taxes, interest charges, maintenance, depreciation and wages) plus the cost of raw materials, i.e., food and, finally, the cost of fuel. The latter is generally such a comparatively small item that its importance is overshadowed by the other charges; for example, the cost of electricity (in an all-electric kitchen) being something between 3% and 5% of the cost of the complete meal.

Oil

The cost involved when oil is used for large-scale cooking is indicated by the following examples:

1. Cooker in small hotel for 50 people with table d'hôte menu, choice of two main courses, cost of oil   4s. 7d. per 24 hr.
2. Hotel catering for 100 persons with à la carte menu, cost of oil   5s. 8d. per 24 hr.

When taken in quantity, oil is available at a cheaper rate and the above figures are based on oil at 1s. 4d. per gallon (1961).

Solid fuel

For the operating cost of a modern, solid fuel, heat storage cooking range an example is provided by a cooker designed to cook for 80 to 100 people (the Esse Major) having a hotplate area of $5\frac{1}{2}$ sq. ft approximately and two ovens, one of 20 in. × $23\frac{3}{4}$ in. × 21 in. and another 20 in. × $23\frac{3}{4}$ in. × 22 in.

For this cooker the fuel consumption over twenty-four hours is 45 lb.

Siting freedom

An obvious point in kitchen design which has been stressed in the preceding chapter is that equipment must be sited to obtain a proper flow in the kitchen: from 'goods in' to the stores and then the sequence to preparation sections, to cooking apparatus and to servery.

As electrical equipment does not need special ventilation to dissipate other than the odours of cooking and as the equipment is portable, it is easily assembled in the right place and correctly related to other items. Equipment run on other fuels often necessitates more ventilation and may have to stand in a fixed position.

Cleanliness

Even electric and gas appliances will in time be dirtied by the ordinary grease of cooking if they are not properly maintained. Cleaning is, however, easily carried out. It is only necessary to wipe down the cooking surfaces whilst the equipment is still warm, with an occasional use of a mild abrasive.

Food can only be burnt on to an electric stove where it comes into direct contact with the element guards, or the enclosed element surfaces such as boiling plates. Modern gas equipment is also 'streamlined' and functional so that keeping it clean is easy.

Design and scope of equipment

In table d'hôte cooking much of the boiling and stewing is of large quantities. These are conveniently done in separate appliances such as steaming ovens and boiling pans leaving only a small number of utensils of various sizes for placing on the boiling top. In à la carte cooking, on the other hand, smaller scale boiling and stewing operations seldom necessitate separate appliances, other than a stockpot.

With regard to the design of cooking apparatus, many points are common to all, irrespective of the type of fuel they burn. Main considerations may be summarised as follows:

Ranges. As utensils in hotel and catering establishments are usually comparatively large, the hob height on which they stand should be kept to a minimum and the most useful working height is now generally agreed to be 34 in. The chef or his aides should be able to see into the utensils without having to stand on a platform and the chef's arm when stirring utensils should not be at a higher angle than 45°.

In any kitchen the key appliance is the cooking range which is, in effect, a combination of boiling table and oven and more often incorporates other features including grill, bain-marie, etc.

Features of gas ranges

There are two main types of gas range, the open-top range (similar to the domestic cooker in design, but larger) and the solid type 'heavy duty' range. The ovens of either type can be internally heated or partly or wholly externally heated. Either type can be built on the unit principle, the units being put together to form as large a range as is needed.

The open-top gas range is suitable for the smaller restaurant kitchen where cooking is lighter. In this type, boiling burners are arranged under an open hotplate grid and it is possible to have some burners for fast cooking and others smaller for sauce making and simmering. There is, however, a marked trend towards the single-size burner with good control characteristics.

Ovens, which are thermostatically controlled to give automatic regulation of heat, can be of various widths 18 in. and upwards to 30 in. They are normally internally heated and fitted with swing doors. Experienced chefs generally prefer to have the grill separate, but it can be part of the range, in which case space must be left over the oven to accommodate it.

The solid-top gas range is specially designed for the heavy continuous work of professional kitchens. The boiling top is solid, thus giving a stable surface for utensils, and has removable rings like those of the traditional coal range. Burners have been constructed to give an intense core of heat obtainable up to 1,000°F at a central spot or 'bull's eye' with a gradual reduction of heat as the edge of the hotplate is neared. Fast cooking can, therefore, be carried out at the centre and gentle simmering at the edge, while the right heat for the job in hand can be obtained simply by shifting the position of the cooking utensil.

The hotplate of the solid-top gas range is generally lower than that of the open-top type (about 34 in. from the floor) as utensils used on the solid tops are heavier and taller. Ovens are similar in both types of range. Solid-top ranges normally incorporate semi-externally or externally heated ovens and are generally fitted with drop-down doors. External heating gives the chef a little more control of the oven atmosphere and is useful in some kinds of cooking.

Direct or internally heated ovens are those which have a visible flame. In the indirect, externally or sole-plate heated ovens the burners are usually placed beneath a sole-plate and the heat enters the oven through vents or enters round the edges of the sole-plate. Direct heat ovens give various temperatures from top to bottom thus enabling different foods to be cooked at the same time. The constant heat of the indirect oven makes it suitable for large kitchens where the oven is used for one kind of food at a time.

The solid-top cooker is constructed on the unit principle for grouping into ranges for wall or island siting. Most manufacturers also supply open burners to units of the solid-type construction and an open burner section is usually considered advisable on groupings of four units or more.

Where space allows it can be advantageous to have both open and solid types of range in the kitchen for different types of work.

Special roasting ovens are often needed in large kitchens in addition to 'general purpose' ovens. Larger gas-heated ovens are manufactured to meet this requirement which have double doors and are fitted with a number of shelves and drip pans to catch fat.

There are two types of roasting oven; one designed with à la carte service in mind and one considered suitable for table d'hôte operation. Many chefs advocate that table d'hôte ovens should have side swing doors as each of the shelves in use will tend to be occupied by large dishes. Table d'hôte often involves serving sequences of small numbers of portions from large dishes, i.e., big roast joints, large baking trays of roast potatoes, or Yorkshire puddings, etc., for which general-purpose roasting ovens are suitable.

On the other hand, many chefs consider that à la carte ovens should have a drop door of small projection. A la carte cooking involves large numbers of small dishes and general practice is for each oven to contain one type of plat whether it be a roast, braised or baked item, spaces above being retained for finishing off dishes being cooked on the hob. The actual dimension of a chef's à la carte oven is usually 24 in. × 24 in. × 15 in. internal height. If the internal height is any greater than this, it: (1) wastes space, and (2) the drop door will project too far and it will be impractical for operators to place into and remove dishes from the oven. Electric ovens are made to meet these two needs.

Combination units

It is worth stressing that the two kinds of boiling table (the solid top and the open top) and the two kinds of oven can be combined to give a choice of four different kinds of range units. One of these combinations, that which incorporates a solid-top boiling table and a direct-fired oven, has not always occurred to the minds of cooks but it is a development they have greatly welcomed.

It is useful, too, to have ovens and boiling plates separately mounted on stands or legs. This allows the height of boiling tables to be adjusted and allows cooks to work separately. It tends to be more expensive to arrange appliances separately, however, besides occupying more space.

Electric multiple boiling tops and solid tops

The height of hob should obviously be the same as other parts of the cooking range. Hobs used in connection with general-purpose roasting ovens should, when electrically heated, invariably be of the multiple plate type.

Electric solid boiling tops consist (as do gas ones) of a centre hot spot with heat graduating to the outside so that chefs who work rapidly during the preparation of sauces, soups and small boiling processes do not have to operate any heat control switches. As with other solid tops, they merely bring the items to the boil on the centre hot spot and move the cooking vessel to the correct hob temperature to maintain boiling or simmering point. Thus for table d'hôte cooking multiple boiling tops may well suffice whereas the demands of à la carte service are best met by solid tops.

Solid fuel range

Modern solid fuel ranges are now completely closed, finished in vitreous enamel and are controlled by a thermostat or a precise manual control to give the chef the cooking conditions which he chooses. They burn smokeless fuels such as coke, anthracite or Phurnacite and have a closed firebox. The fuel is poured in through a feeding hole in the top from a hod.

The old disadvantage of dirt is eliminated or greatly reduced because the occasional shaking of the fire can be carried out without a cloud of dust. Ash is collected in an ashpan in which it is removed for disposal in the outside bin.

Where a thermostat is provided this is set at the beginning of the day. Apart from occasional shaking of the bottom grate and occasional re-fuelling, no further attention is required as oven and hotplate temperatures are then maintained at the desired value.

On a typical model, the solid-machined hotplate gives a graduation of heat from fast boiling at the rate of about 1 pt per minute at the hottest spot. The hotplate and simmering panels provide a full range of temperature conditions. As the hotplate is of massive construction it can take a heavy load without much loss of heat. In using this type of hotplate, it is, of course, essential that cooking utensils have heavy machined bases. Hinged heat-retaining bolsters are provided to cover hotplates and retain the heat when the hotplate is not in use.

On this type of solid fuel range the ovens are of cast-iron construction and heated externally. They are vented to the flue to take away steam and cooking smells.

They are clean in operation because as the oven walls are hotter than the atmosphere of the oven, grease and dirt tend not to be deposited on them.

Heavy construction ensures that there is the minimum drop of temperature when a heavy cold load of cooking is introduced into the oven. Moreover, the entire oven space is available for cooking as there are no hot spots in the neighbourhood of the heating elements or burners.

The fire burns at a slow steady rate and in this way abstracts the maximum of heat from the fuel. Cookers are heavily insulated to conserve heat and to ensure that the heat is used for the required purpose and not wasted.

When siting a solid fuel, heat storage cooker in relation to other equipment, similar principles apply as for cookers using other fuels.

For small kitchens, single units consisting of a firebox and oven can be used but for larger kitchens multiple units can be built up with cookers either in alignment side by side or arranged back to back to form an island group.

One or two special requirements must be borne in mind when installing solid fuel cookers:

(a) *Provision of flue.* A suitable chimney must be provided and the cooker must be located so that it can be connected to a fairly short length of flue pipe. The flue pipe should slope upwards towards the chimney avoiding sharp bends. As smokeless fuels are used, chimney cleaning is minimal and is a simple operation as the flue does not go round the oven. It runs, in fact, from the firebox over the oven to the chimney and all that is needed is for flue dust in this short length of cooker flue to be swept into the fire about once a week.

(b) *Ventilation.* The cooker has to draw in air from the kitchen so any ventilating arrangement must not cause suction in the kitchen as this will interfere with the free burning of the fire. If an exhaust fan only is provided for ventilating the kitchen an opening must be provided for free entry of air to the kitchen to replace that which has been extracted. It should not be possible for kitchen staff to close this opening.

(c) *Fuel storage.* Provision must, of course, be made for fuel storage which will be convenient both for delivery and in use.

Oil-burning ranges

Oil-burning cookers are generally designed on the lines of modern solid fuel cookers and provide a similar service.

Oil, however, is a fuel which can be piped to the cooker so that bringing in solid fuel and carrying out ash are completely eliminated.

The cooking performance is similar to the solid fuel models from which they are adapted and, for example, the solid machined hotplate gives a graduation of heating from fast boiling at the rate of about 1 pt per minute at the hottest spot and provides a full range of temperature conditions from fast boiling to simmering. Because of similar cooking conditions, cooking utensils must have heavy machined bases.

A thermostat is provided to control oven temperature as required by the chef. In addition, a time clock can be supplied which turns up the thermostat in the morning so that the cooker is at its full operating temperature when the kitchen staff arrive. It is automatically turned down at night when the day's work is done. In establishments where no cooking is required on certain days as, for example, in factory canteens, the automatic time clock can turn the cooker down to idling conditions for these selected days.

To ensure efficient burning of oil, the burner is provided with a fractional horse-power motor and fan to assist the draught. Oil is supplied to the burner through a safety valve which is controlled by the thermostat.

Installing an oil cooker

Similar general principles apply when installing an oil cooker (or a range of oil cookers) as are applicable to cookers burning other fuels but there are one or two special requirements.

(*a*) *Chimney*. As for solid fuel a suitable chimney must be provided and the cooker must be located so that it can be conveniently connected to a chimney with a short length of flue pipe sloping upwards towards the chimney and avoiding acute bends.

(*b*) *Ventilation*. The same requirements must be met as apply in the case of solid fuel cookers.

(*c*) *Fuel storage*. An oil storage tank must be provided outside the kitchen with a supply pipe connecting it to the cooker. The tank itself should be located so that it can be readily filled by road tanker. Advice should always be sought from the oil supply company before the position of the tank is finally fixed. Only clean oil must be fed to the cooker and a filter must be included in the supply line from the tank to the burner. It should be so located that it is easily accessible and it should be of such a type that it can be easily cleaned.

Oil is available at a cheaper rate when taken in quantity and the size of the tank should be chosen in consultation with the suppliers of the oil so as to take advantage of the cheap bulk rates. Arrangements can be made with the oil suppliers for the tank to be kept regularly topped-up so that the management does not have to worry about checking on fuel level and ordering.

Deep fat fryers and frying ranges

Though many chefs still follow methods involving 'blanching' or par-frying, there are manufacturers of electric equipment who consider that the practice is out-moded and that modern fryers should be of sufficient capacity and of a design to fry each setting of, say, fish from start to finish in four to five minutes.

It is claimed that fast frying by electricity means crisper and better chipped potatoes, saves kitchen time and thus cuts down current consumption. Fryers should have automatic temperature control, pan covers and fume extraction. Ventilation of fryers possibly requires more thought than that of other appliances. All surfaces touched by the fumes from frying become fouled with grease and require frequent cleaning. An electric fryer lends itself well to heating and ventilation and substantial claims are made for its cleanliness and efficiency. Correct frying temperature can be maintained, for electric heating can be applied evenly over the whole base of the pan with automatic temperature control to ensure that the fat does not rise appreciably above it. Whilst 410°F is often used for browning chips, the closer the oil temperature is kept to 375°F for steady frying the less frequently have the frying fats to be changed.

Heating by enclosed elements also reduces the risk of fire but one important point often forgotten should be mentioned here. A fusible link damper should be provided in the ducting to operate in the event of fire. This fire precaution is not included by the manufacturers, but it should be installed by the installing contractors.

Satisfactory gas-heated deep fat fryers are also available and can be constructed on the unit principle so that ranges of any size can be built up. They are usually thermostatically controlled to save fuel and prevent overheating of the fat, and, indeed, if the fryer is not under constant supervision it should always have a thermostat fitted to control temperature.

In a comparatively new design—the 'cold-zone' fryer—the side walls are heated, but the lower part is kept at a reduced temperature. Particles of food, therefore, falling into the bottom of the pan do not become charred, nor do they get deposited as black spots on the food. This form of heating also saves fat.

Boiling pans

Boiling pans for soup, vegetables or puddings can be independently heated by gas or electricity if they are not steam-heated. Some of the latest types are of stainless steel or are die-cast in a special aluminium alloy (though other cheaper materials can also be employed). Water-jacketed pans of tinned copper are designed for custards, milk puddings, etc. Boiling pans are of varying capacity from 10 gal. upwards; a large number of smaller pans are usually found more convenient in use than a smaller number of large pans.

A boiling pan is designed to permit all forms of bulk boiling and stewing to be done without fear of burning. A steam jacket operated with pressure is obviously the most suitable form of heat application, but next to that electricity scores in that the heat can be dissipated evenly round the pan to provide the heat jacket. Indeed, electricity has one advantage over steam in that no pressure is involved and maintenance cost should be low.

Grillers and toasters

Intense radiant heat is required from a griller. This can easily be obtained with electricity without being accompanied by any smells. Thus, food which is placed in close proximity to the source of heat, does not acquire a distinctive flavour from the fuel.

Grills may be required to *grill* meat, fish, tomatoes, etc., to *toast* tea-cakes and bread or to 'salamander' (or glaze) cooked dishes. Gas-heated grills can be obtained which, by adjustment, will perform any of these operations. The heat-resisting grill frets used in their design are extremely speedy; one small type, for example, can deal with 360 slices of bread, each 4 in. square, per hour. Bottom cooking plates or branders are now incorporated into grilling appliances and enable food to be cooked on them by heat transfer from the plate itself as well as from heat sources above. Thus, food may be completely cooked without turning.

Some gas grills have vertical radiants in pairs facing each other, so that the food is cooked or toasted on both sides at once. Continuous rotary toasters have been devised to meet a demand for toasted dishes. In one type of gas toaster the bread is fed on to an endless power-driven chain and passes between vertical radiant surfaces.

The 'silver' grill on which chops and steaks are cooked on bars over a glowing heat are nowadays commonly heated by gas. Coke is little used for this purpose and the author has not heard of a new coke grill having been installed in recent years. Charcoal enjoyed a considerable vogue for a year or so but its popularity is now waning.

More manufacturers are producing the under-fired gas grill and still more widely used is the grill with grilling hearth used in all classes of restaurant for speedy grilling.

Pastry ovens

Special ovens for pastry baking are generally used in large kitchens. Some types of baking require a moist or steamy heat, others a drier baking atmosphere. Thus, control of ventilation is required. Similarly, separately heated and ventilated 'decks' allowing for different kinds of baking to be carried on simultaneously are also desirable in large establishments. Thus, gas-heated pastry ovens are of two main types— one in which a number of tiers are heated by one system of burners so that the same temperature is obtained throughout; and one in which each tier is independently controlled. This latter type is more flexible and running costs should be lower as sometimes only one tier need be used.

Pastry ovens vary from inexpensive makes finished in galvanised iron and black paint to the standard vitreous enamel-finished appliance of better appearance and longer life. Thermostatic control is an integral part of these ovens and one manufacturer controls the top and bottom heat of the compartments by separate thermostats.

Steamers

The first essential in a steamer or steaming oven is that the operating temperature should be kept up to boiling point and that heat control should be automatic. The cook too often imagines that the more steam comes from the vent, the faster the steaming process is taking place. This, of course, is not correct. As long as the oven is full of steam and up to 212°F that is all that is necessary. Automatic temperature control, practicable with gas and electric models, ensure both these requirements with a minimum of fuel consumption. Manual control, on the other hand, usually means the total load being on the whole time. For example, the electric running load to steam a cubic foot oven of potatoes is approximately 4·5 units per hr and that for pudding 3 units per hr, whereas if reliance is placed on manual control 9 units per hr in both cases is usual.

To enable oven temperature to be maintained at 212°F, the oven must operate at a slight pressure so that the temperature control can be set just above boiling point. Furthermore, operation at slight pressure does speed up steaming time by a good 20 per cent.

The oven should be fitted with valves to ensure that all cold air is evacuated and, of course, the oven should have its own ball valve control water feed. The water feed should be broken down from mains pressure by means of a header tank.

Electricity lends itself to the heating of steaming ovens as the water can be heated by immersion heaters and direct heating by gas is also efficient.

When raising steam by gas, burners heat a water pan with an automatic cold water feed tank which maintains a constant level of water in the interior pan. But, of course, steamers can usually be heated most economically and effectively from a steam supply. Steam is used at atmospheric pressure or at $\frac{1}{2}$ lb per sq. in. Temperature is controlled by thermostat or pressure stat. The steaming ovens are fitted with removable perforated trays or wire baskets to choice.

Hot cupboards and bains-marie

Doors of hot cupboards should be easy-sliding for it is an advantage if they can be operated by the knee when the operator's hands are full. Construction of the hot cupboard should be rigid so that unevenness in the floor does not make the doors bind. Adjustable feet should be supplied for hot cupboards and doors must be removable for easy cleaning of the slide channels.

Heating should be even throughout the whole cupboard area and as electricity does not need an excess of oxygen, elements can be placed where required. An even temperature is thus obtained without any hot spots for these tend to cause cracking of the glazing.

However, hot cupboards and serving counters can be steam-heated, or internally or externally heated directly by gas. Indirectly heated hot closets are usually selected for use where food may have to be kept uncovered. Where direct heating is used, gas also is suitable.

Hot cupboards are obtainable with solid tops or with surfaces containing carving wells and bains-marie. Where space is restricted a taller hot cupboard fitment can be used such as two separate hot cupboards of normal height one above the other. Like the long lower types this can have doors opening on both sides. Hot cupboards can be combined with boiling tops if desired. If it is considered suited to the layout of the equipment, the bain-marie can be a separate piece of equipment, mounted on legs and fitted with a draw-off tap. Thermostatic control can be added. Gas 'mobile' bains-marie fitted with a 'plug in' safety type of gas connection are also available. For cafeteria service, bains-marie with fitted containers are particularly useful.

Some chefs and caterers seem to be prejudiced against the 'dry' bain-marie and research is now in progress to attempt to determine whether there are any apparent disadvantages in its use. When fitted with its own burner and thermostat, it would appear to give service comparable with the water-filled type.

Stockpot stands

Of strong construction, electric and gas-heated stockpot stands are designed to withstand heavy usage. Gas stockpot stands are available with open-top burner or solid-top burner and also in multiples of the single unit. The height of the stand is normally 24 in. but some are available at 18 in.

Water boilers for tea and coffee making

There are three main types of gas heater water boiler on the market: bulk, expansion and pressure. The nature of the demand will determine the type of boiler selected. Prolonged continuous service throughout the day and evening calls for boiling water at short notice at any time; this can be provided by a 'continuous flow' heater, either expansion or pressure. For a service limited to a specific period, e.g., when teas are served, a bulk boiler of adequate capacity will be found efficient. Counter sets, or café sets as they are often called, consisting of a water boiler complete with milk and coffee urns, the latter being fitted with gas-heated water jackets, are popular in all classes of establishment. Gas-heated coffee percolators are also available and glass vacuum coffee makers are used extensively. Similar still-room apparatus with electric heaters is also available.

Hot water washing up

Either storage or instantaneous gas or electric water heaters may meet the hot water requirements of some kitchens. Storage heaters, as their name implies, have a storage cylinder or tank as an integral part of the appliance; thermostatic control keeps the stored water at a pre-selected temperature. The storage heater is normally selected for washing up in the plonge or plate wash. Instantaneous heaters heat the water as it runs through the appliance; there are types to serve one point or larger (multipoint) heaters to serve several points. A small instantaneous gas heater, for example, will supply about $\frac{1}{2}$ gal. per min. raised to 100°F; a large multipoint about $1\frac{1}{2}$ gal.

Small instantaneous water heaters are chosen for use at isolated hand basins rather than for washing-up and, indeed, they are not suitable for that purpose. The large multipoint is often selected because when wall-mounted it takes up no floor space and because of the fact that for its output it is relatively inexpensive. These factors often outweigh its somewhat short life; though machines similar in appearance but of slightly greater output and more robust construction are nowadays available.

Also in the field of instantaneous heaters are gas models made by the manufacturers of café boilers. These have thermostatic control and are quite suitable for connection to dishwashers.

Gas is also being used to heat the water in dish-washing machines and sanatising tanks. For the purpose of rinsing crockery and utensils in water hot enough to kill any germs there can be installed a sink which incorporates a gas burner beneath it; the water can thus be raised or kept at a sanatising temperature of 170°F.

Refrigerators

For substantial cold storage and large refrigerators, electricity is usually demanded but in small establishments the capacity of the large-size gas refrigerator may suffice. The largest type of gas refrigerator has a 10 cu. ft capacity.

Other kitchen tools and aids

In addition to cooking and refrigeration, other essential kitchen services are needed. Those powered by electricity include:

Lighting, telephones, lifts, ventilation, food trolleys, coffee mills, bread and butter machines, ice-making plant, slicing machines for meat and vegetables, potato peelers, knife cleaners and polishers, silver burnishers, dish-washing machinery.

It is, in fact, taken for granted that all auxiliary equipment such as potato-peeling machines, dough mixers, meat and bread slicing machines and dish-washing machines, etc., will be electrically operated.

Sample installations

In quoting suggestions for equipping kitchens with both gas and electric equipment, it must be stressed that such schedules are guides only. Equipment requirements vary widely according to the particular wants and nature of the business. Obviously much depends on the number of chefs, the type of menu, the charge for food and so on. Only in a few cases are requirements likely to be similar or capable of standardisation and these instances tend to occur when all the relevant facts are known beforehand as in the new unit in a chain of restaurants of standard policy, or in units of standardised catering services such as in, for example, hostels, hospitals or in school meals service. Generally, it is impossible to stipulate hard-and-fast schedules of equipment and the guides which follow, while giving some lead, must clearly be treated with considerable reserve.

As an example of equipping a modern kitchen in the light of the general planning factors already considered, here are suggestions for an electric kitchen for an hotel catering for 200 to 250 guests. Suitable items to be installed with their respective loading are as follows:

TABLE 3

REQUIREMENTS OF ELECTRICALLY OPERATED EQUIPMENT FOR A
MEDIUM-SIZED HOTEL CATERING FOR 200 TO 250 GUESTS

Quantity	Equipment	Electrical loading, kW
	Dry Equipment	
2	Double oven ranges (unit type)	68·8
1	Double pan fish fryer	18·0
1	Open bath bain-marie	6·0
	Wet Equipment	
2	6 cu. ft steaming ovens	18·0
2	20 gal. boiling pans	18·0
1	16 gal. stockpot	3·7
	Auxiliary Equipment	
2	22 in. × 20 in. grillers	16·0
	Pastry Room	
1	Double deck pastry oven	14·0
	Servery Equipment	
1	7 ft 6 in. hot cupboard with à la carte top	9·0
1	6 ft hot cupboard with plain top	6·0
1	120 pt café set with 2 gal. side urn	8·8
	Wash-up Room	
1	Dishwasher, 1,500 pieces per hour	13·8
	Total Loading	200·0

Naturally the foregoing selection might well be amended in the light of policy as evidenced by, for example, the style and price of the menu, but the items listed should permit a satisfactory table d'hôte service to be operated.

In such an installation it would be appropriate to arrange the 'wet' and 'dry' sections in island form, leaving the outer walls available for 'stores', and the various preparation and ancillary sections. Indeed, a 4-unit control range rather than the pair of double oven ranges would be preferred by many caterers.

The uses of the above equipment need not be detailed, for cookery apparatus has already been considered and there is nothing mysterious or highly technical about operating such apparatus when fuelled by electricity.

In addition to the example of equipping the 200- to 250-guest hotel, the following two tables of the British Electrical Development Association give further guidance in estimating requirements.

TABLE 4

REQUIREMENTS OF ELECTRICALLY OPERATED EQUIPMENT FOR A HIGH-CLASS HOTEL KITCHEN CATERING FOR 150 PERSONS PER MEAL

1 3-oven chef range with ovens of 5 cu. ft capacity each and a total of about 1,100 sq. in. of boiling plates
1 Open-type bain-marie
1 Stockpot of 16 gal. capacity with stand
1 Griller with 400 sq. in. grilling area
1 6 ft hot cupboard with heated top and bain-marie
1 Automatic water boiler of 90 pt capacity
1 Refrigerator, 100 cu. ft capacity
1 Water heater of 100 gal. capacity
1 Mixing machine, 10 qt capacity, with attachments
1 Potato peeler of 14 lb capacity
2 Six-slice automatic toasters
1 Coffee brewer, 20 pt capacity.

TABLE 5

REQUIREMENTS OF ELECTRICALLY OPERATED EQUIPMENT FOR A POPULAR RESTAURANT KITCHEN CATERING FOR 100 PERSONS PER MEAL

1 4-oven general-purpose range with ovens of 7 cu. ft capacity and a total of about 1,600 sq. in. of boiling plates
1 Open-type bain-marie
2 Griller-toasters with a total area of 800 sq. in.
2 Steaming ovens each of 6 cu. ft capacity
2 20 gal. vegetable boilers with steaming attachments
1 Stockpot of 16 gal. capacity with stand
1 2-deck pastry oven with an area of 1,300 sq. in. per deck
2 8 ft hot cupboards with heated tops, one being fitted with bain-marie

2 Café sets of 160 pt capacity with 2 gal. milk and coffee urns
1 Coolroom, 250 cu. ft capacity
1 Water heater of 200 gal. capacity with attachments
1 Mixing machine, 30 qt capacity with attachments
1 Potato peeler of 28 lb capacity
1 Slicing machine
1 Dish-washing machine, capacity 1,000 to 1,500 pieces per hour.

The following are tentatively suggested as outline requirements for similar establishments where gas has been selected as the main fuel:

TABLE 6

POSSIBLE REQUIREMENTS OF GAS EQUIPMENT FOR A MEDIUM-SIZED HOTEL KITCHEN CATERING FOR 200 TO 250 GUESTS

Quantity	Equipment
1	4-oven solid-top range
1	Steaming oven
1	Salamander
1	Stockpot stove
1	8 ft hot closet with doors both sides
1	Café boiler with coffee and mild service urns
	Possible auxiliary equipment
1	Single pan deep fat frying unit

Note.—Gas-heated bain-marie, boiling pans and pastry oven may also be required.

TABLE 7

POSSIBLE REQUIREMENTS OF GAS EQUIPMENT FOR A HIGH-CLASS HOTEL KITCHEN CATERING FOR 150 PERSONS PER MEAL

Quantity	Equipment
1	Oven range (3 or 4 ovens)
1	Open bain-marie
1	Salamander
1	Single unit deep fat fryer
	For Service
1	6 ft hot cupboard
1	Café set with coffee and milk urns

Note.—Gas-heated water heater, water boiler, stockpot stove may also be required.

TABLE 8

POSSIBLE REQUIREMENTS OF GAS EQUIPMENT FOR A
POPULAR RESTAURANT KITCHEN CATERING FOR 100
PERSONS PER MEAL

Quantity	Equipment
1	Oven range (2 ovens)
1	Medium-size steaming oven
1	Salamander
	Service
1	6 ft hot cupboard
1	Café set with coffee and milk service urns

Note.—Bain-marie vegetable boilers, stockpot stove, pastry oven, are also likely to be required amongst gas-heated equipment.

Advice and aid

The gas industry takes a great deal of trouble over the problems of chefs, hoteliers and caterers and through the Gas Council and the various boards (as well as through individual manufacturers, engineers and suppliers) is able to provide much advice as well as service. The special pride taken by the gas industry in their kitchen service is un- doubtedly influenced by the fact that chefs themselves are generally well disposed to gas cooking equipment. Chefs usually praise the ease of control of heat and find gas 'responsive'. Equipment can give heat quickly as required, be adjusted speedily to lower heat or, when not needed, is soon cold (and, consequently, does not unnecessarily over- heat the kitchen). In short, since the day in 1841 that Alexis Soyer had gas equipment installed in the Reform Club kitchens most chefs have come to regard gas cooking appliances as affording efficient modernisa- tion of traditional plant and, being used to it, normally work well with it.

As for electricity, chefs today are certainly becoming more adven- turous in their approach to electric cooking equipment. They are more ready than formerly to give a fair trial to, for example, heavy duty ranges using this fuel. The Electricity Boards and the British Electrical Development Association take pains to aid chefs and caterers and to disseminate useful information about electricity and electrical appli- ances. Many chefs, however, remain critical of some electrical equip- ment because of the problems of residual heat (for which cooks require to learn appropriate techniques). Nevertheless, much electrical equip- ment, particularly the oven, is invariably well received and, of course, modern kitchens rely heavily, as has been observed, on electric power for mixing machines, peeling, chopping and the like. The new forms of training (including that of hotel schools and of apprenticeship involving Technical College attendance) are helping to ensure a more balanced and open-minded approach which should lead eventually to the maximum exploitation of electricity as well as gas in modern kitchens.

I I   Maintenance in the kitchen

One of the problems which arise when considering the matter of kitchen maintenance in its widest sense is that of deciding where the responsibilities of the chef de cuisine and his principal lieutenants begin and end; for it is of importance to determine the responsibilities of the chef and his staff towards kitchen maintenance as against the duties of the hotel engineer and other maintenance personnel.

Maintaining and keeping the kitchen in a clean condition is primarily the chef's responsibility whatever the manner in which he may delegate parts of it. It assumes today greater significance than ever because:

(*a*) Kitchen cleanliness is governed by statutory requirements more stringent than ever before.

(*b*) It has, perhaps, never been so difficult in certain areas to recruit the staff needed to keep the kitchens clean in the traditional manner.

Mechanical equipment

In the larger establishments the upkeep of kitchen installations and mechanical equipment will seldom present major difficulties to the chef because his department can receive a substantial amount of the service and aid needed from the engineer.

As far as maintenance of mechanical equipment is concerned all that is really required is an efficient system of regular checking:

(*a*) By the chef or his nominee so that faults and repairs needed may be promptly reported.

(*b*) Less frequent, but nevertheless regular, inspection from the engineering and maintenance section.

In this second category is placed, of course, those inspections by manufacturers under maintenance contracts, or as part of the sale guarantee or renting agreement.

In the medium- or smaller-sized establishment, engineering services may be on a small and even negligible scale and, further, there may be in the more modest establishments a reluctance to have maintenance agreements made under contract with manufacturers. Under these circumstances even greater vigilance is necessary by the kitchen staff under the direction of the chef to ensure that all working equipment is kept in proper repair and, of extreme importance, that safety devices where applicable are complete, are in working order and are in use.

There are in many kitchens members of the brigade de cuisine who often have considerable 'flair' for effecting 'on the spot' repairs and adjustments to kitchen machinery but in general it cannot be too strongly emphasised that there are great dangers in 'self-help' of this kind. A prudent rule is that chefs, kitchen clerks and kitchen porters should confine themselves to noting, checking and reporting faults where they occur rather than attempting repairs which they have not been properly trained to do.

Policy decisions as to whether kitchen plant and machinery shall be maintained under contract by manufacturers is not a customary one for the chef except in a few cases when the maître chef in a top establishment may have been given wide executive powers within a budget. Even where the chef will have no responsibility for deciding such matters his advice seen in the light of his experience and knowledge as a user will hardly be ignored and it is for him, therefore, to take a lively and intelligent interest in this sphere.

Maintenance log books

A good means of ensuring that electrical, manually operated and other equipment is kept continually under check and review by responsible staff is for a maintenance log book to be kept under the general direction of the chef de cuisine. (In small establishments it would be appropriate for the chef himself to be responsible for it.)

The form in which the log book is drawn up is of secondary importance but should make provision for the following:

1. A complete list of all equipment having moving parts either electrically or hand driven and also cooking or other equipment in which deterioration and wear through use is possible.

2. The items listed should be grouped according to the frequency with which routine and major inspections are either: (*a*) recommended by the manufacturer, or (*b*) considered advisable by the management (or as possibly advised by the hotel engineer).

3. An indication of the person or persons responsible for carrying out: (*a*) routine inspections; (*b*) major inspections; (*c*) reminders of dates when major overhauls, etc., are due.

4. The log should accordingly be ruled out against the list of equipment in columns with date headings. This will provide for brief comment and initialing under each date-headed column indicating that inspection has been carried out and what action, if any, is necessary.

Provision should also be made of space in an adjoining column to indicate when action has in fact been taken and the job completed.

5. A column or columns should also indicate any special point to be particularly noted, e.g., that safety devices and safety notices are properly affixed and functioning.

A sous chef, head kitchen clerk or even head kitchen porter when sufficiently responsible and intelligent may be given responsibility for carrying out the more frequent, regular routine checks though it should desirably be a senior member of the kitchen staff or the chef himself who completes the log as a result of personal inspection at least once or twice during the year.

General repairs book

Apart from mechanical equipment, the kitchen department contains much that requires supervision and attention. Floors, wall tiles, paintwork, plumbing, cupboards and fixtures, locks and keys, are amongst the items which can aid or impede efficiency and improve or mar working conditions.

POSSIBLE LAYOUT OF A MAINTENANCE LOG BOOK

Equipment	Make and ref. no.	Where sited	Sous chef's quarterly check. Date. . . .	Initial of sous chef checking	Chef de cuisine's initial

Here again in the largest establishments building and decorative maintenance will present little or no problem to the chef who will have the backing of the organisation possibly represented by a resident clerk of works. But even in these circumstances, and certainly in the case of smaller hotels without so many sources of support, it is important that the need for repair and maintenance is noted immediately and recorded.

POSSIBLE ARRANGEMENT OF A GENERAL REPAIRS BOOK

Item requiring repair	Where sited	Type of repair required and urgency	Reported by	Date	Chef de cuisine's initial	Date

A simple system of recording (it need not be more elaborate than a simple exercise book) is a convenient and effective means of ensuring that necessary action is taken. Such a book kept by the chef or his representative can be divided quite simply into two columns; one for items requiring urgent or immediate attention and another which provides for the noting of matters which can be accumulated for attention during the off-season or quiet period. A simple record of this kind not only ensures that minor items are not overlooked and develop into major ones but is also useful as an historical record, proof against changes of staff and indicating recurring sources of trouble where they exist.

There may be those who consider that the introduction of paper records for matters of this kind increase labour and are merely manifestations of 'red tape'. Certainly nothing elaborate involving massive clerical chores is recommended, but it cannot be too strongly emphasised that in these, as in other matters, it is unwise to rely on memory alone.

From the foregoing it should be apparent that the chef and his staff should be vigilant and interested in the maintenance and efficiency of the kitchen and its ancillary departments; but their rôle is rather that of watchdogs than of executants.

Usage control

On the principle that prevention is better than cure it is, perhaps, appropriate and it is certainly convenient to mention in this section the importance of controlling the use (and often the abuse) of kitchen plant, fabric, services and fuel. Control of this type may not strictly speaking constitute maintenance but it is certainly a strong contributory factor in reducing the demands of maintenance services.

Control of light and fuel

It is, for example, of the greatest importance that the chef de cuisine and his leading assistants should be able to read meters for gas, electricity and (where applicable) water consumption. It is, in fact, surprising how many men and women in charge of sections where there is considerable consumption of one or all of these elements:

(*a*) Do not know where the consumption meters are sited.
(*b*) Would not be able to interpret them if they did know.

The type of tariff under which electricity or gas is consumed will most generally be a top management decision but it is a matter in which the chef may take an interest and may proffer advice based on personal experience.

His most important function, however, is to keep an eye on consumption and to control it through:

(*a*) Regular meter checks.
(*b*) Personal and diligent supervision in the use of appliances.

There is usually scope for minor economy in the use of, for example, electricity by training and instructing kitchen staff in the way to use residual heat remaining when the electricity supply is turned off or turned down in ovens and ranges.

Today, where gas, oil and electricity are increasingly supplanting solid fuel, saving can be effected by ensuring that heat is not turned on before it is required (incidentally this often measurably improves working conditions for staff who enjoy a cooler work-place during the earlier hours of morning preparation).

To enforce regulations regarding the turning off of lights and machinery after use is a positive contribution not only towards fuel economy but also in preventing overwork and overheating of appliances.

Using machinery

In using mechanical appliances there is often a surprising tendency for older members of the kitchen brigade to over-estimate the knowledge and aptitude of more recent recruits. There is strong evidence to support the belief that not only accidents to operatives but damage to machinery is caused through insufficient preliminary instruction of new staff in the use of quite simple apparatus.

Instruction charts

Some of the most successful and progressive companies in other fields have demonstrated the value of 'on-the-job training' and the provision of simple visual aids or instruction charts for tasks apparently simple but often baffling to new employees.

The chef de cuisine must not forget that he exercises managerial and executive responsibilities which should cover such points. He should ensure that he satisfactorily delegates to competent staff the duty of ensuring that apprentices, kitchen hands and all who have to use machinery even as simple as potato-paring machines are given proper preliminary instructions. He will be wise, too, if he takes steps to see that clear, succinct working instructions together with safety notices are prominently displayed by mixers, slicers and all other mechanical devices.

Routine points for checking in smaller establishments

In large hotels the chef himself will not as a rule be closely concerned with minor routines (though he should ensure that they are covered). In smaller establishments he may well find it necessary to check the following:

1. Knives and tools are ground and reset.
2. Water softening installations are recharged.
3. Grease traps are cleared and gulleys cleaned and disinfected.
4. Chimneys and flues are swept.
5. Refrigerators are defrosted.

Cleanliness

The chef's main responsibilities, however, probably lie in ensuring that the kitchens and ancillary sections are properly maintained so far as cleanliness and working order are concerned. The chapter on hygiene indicates the importance of scrupulous cleanliness in the kitchen and its ancillary departments. It indicates some of the main dangers and similarly indicates the remedial action needed. Obviously, the prevention of food poisoning is an important reason for maintaining a perfectly clean kitchen. Additionally, other factors should be borne in mind as supporting the need for well maintained and clean premises. These are particularly:

1. *Aesthetic reasons.* Food, particularly in hotels and restaurants, is a source of pleasure as much as a biological necessity. It is, therefore, of great importance that it is produced in surroundings that cannot

possibly spoil appearance and flavour. Dirt, decay and bad smells are, apart from any hygienic factors, aesthetically taboo in a kitchen because they are both directly capable of impairing taste and appearance.

2. *Craftsmanship*. Indirectly, but equally importantly, such dirtiness encourages a slip-shod and uncraftsmanlike approach to the task of food preparation. Obviously, a kitchen and its sub-sections cannot function at the peak of their efficiency in a dirty and untidy condition.

3. *Staff working conditions*. Thirdly, but by no means least, is the need for kitchens to be kept thoroughly clean in order that they shall be pleasant places in which to work. Some of the old, dismal hotels of the past, ill-lit and ill-ventilated, were not only dangerous and distasteful from the customers' point of view, but were drab and dispiriting places to work in. Much is said about the chef being an artist and there may, therefore, be some who were tolerant of 'artistic' disorder but no chef today worthy of his name would permit himself or his staff to work in dirty and poor conditions if he could avoid it.

There are many who suggest that the atmosphere of the place of work is a factor equal in importance to salary and prestige in recruiting suitable craftsmen. Cooking and the place in which it is done can easily become dirty, that is why from the standpoint of staff welfare and contentment as well as from the standpoint of hygiene and aesthetics, it is vital for the kitchen to be clean.

Cleaning routines

Much is heard today of work study. Certainly good management at all levels must involve careful assessment of the tasks to be done, close watch of the way in which they are being carried out and constant vigilance to ensure that all necessary steps are taken to eliminate unnecessary time, movement and effort. In simple terms, the object of work study is to ensure that necessary jobs are accomplished as quickly, as efficiently, as cheaply and as happily as possible.

Good chefs have applied such thinking to kitchen work from time immemorial though they have not, perhaps, used the jargon of management currently in vogue.

It is, however, true that tasks more directly concerned with cooking may tend to dominate the interest of those in charge of kitchens and that the devising of cleaning routines, porters' duty rotas and the chores of unskilled and semi-skilled kitchen hands may be delegated to a head kitchen porter, a kitchen clerk or a junior sous chef and not reviewed with the desired frequency by the chef.

General principles affecting cleaning

As kitchens, though often conforming to a general pattern, differ widely in plant, equipment, area and pressure of work, it is impossible to give standard routines for maintaining them in a clean condition. It is equally difficult to make 'rule of thumb' rules to cope with this problem.

There are, however, one or two general principles which should be borne in mind when considering cleaning routines. They are as follows:

1. The tasks should be devised and ordered to meet real requirements of hygiene and efficiency. It is just as important to cut out unnecessary 'spit and polish' as it is to ensure that needed work is covered.

2. The work routine is a vital one and it is important to ensure that a rhythmic pattern of cleaning from hour to hour, day to day, week to week and from section to section is clearly established.

Having made sure that cleaning tasks are not mechanically repeated at intervals because 'they have always been done', in other words, having analysed the needs and retained only essential work it becomes important that tasks are carried out in a regular order and at regular times. This helps:

(a) To obviate lapses of memory on the part of the cleaner.
(b) Aids the chef or the supervisor delegated by him readily to recognise what should or should not be going on at a given time.

3. Unnecessary cleaning may be caused by out-moded equipment, unsatisfactory techniques of cooks and others, and poor design or layout of plant including work benches. Thus, before completing plans for cleaning routines every effort should be made to correct the faults of plant layout and work techniques which can create unnecessary dirt and disorder.

4. Cleaning routines should be divided amongst specific individuals and for specific times. As it is not desirable for washing down and cleaning to be mingled with active cooking or food preparation or during service time when disruption and disturbance might ensue, routines should budget for alternating unskilled tasks such as vegetable preparation with cleaning.

5. It is obvious that staff normally concerned with cleaning such as kitchen porters and female kitchen hands will, from time to time, require to be diverted from regular routines to cope with special tasks caused through mishap or to undertake unusual work created by special or additional demands in the kitchen. But the fact remains

that a clear framework of activity for each member of the staff is needed.

Recording routines

It is important that routines for unskilled and semi-skilled staff are outlined on paper and not merely communicated by word of mouth. Even where work routines are not displayed on kitchen notices it is still desirable for them to have been noted or kept for reference in the chef's office. The value of written records of work routines can be gauged from two main factors:

(*a*) Continuity and the ease of handing over duties both at operative and supervisor level.

(*b*) The discipline of noting down the cleaning requirements is a positive help in analysing, assessing and reviewing what needs to be done and the best time to do it.

Reliance on word of mouth, day-to-day orders, alone tends to lead to muddle and uneven results and even when at its most effective makes great demands on the supervisor who has to be more than ordinarily zealous to ensure that the work is done.

6. Cleaning routines should be devised for work which occurs frequently (operations like washing work-surfaces are often necessary several times a day), and for work of a less frequent kind such as the special cleaning of ovens and plant, involving partial dismantling.

Routines, therefore, should provide for the cleaning of floors, wall surfaces, lights, rafters, ceiling fitments, fixed kitchen and cooking plant, cooking and preparation equipment including manual and power driven machinery, work benches, tiling and the interior shelves of cupboards and bench fitments.

Techniques and appliances

In preparing routines to cover these needs it is desirable at the same time to review the techniques, the appliances and the materials used in cleaning. Many acres of kitchen flooring are hand scrubbed annually and it is always worth calculating whether labour (usually the most expensive commodity in the kitchen) can be saved by the introduction of a scrubbing machine.

In the same way, the selection of soaps and detergents for floors, tiles, work benches, etc., should not be left to chance. When a decision has been made as to the product to be used then clear instructions should be given and recorded as to strength and quantity necessary for the various chores. Pre-dilution, in the stores, of some detergents is often advisable not only on grounds of economy but also to ensure maximum effectiveness. The mode of collecting and using materials should be covered under the general term of cleaning routines.

It may seem a minor matter to refer to tools as simple as scrubbing brushes, cloths, squeegees, mops, swabs and buckets but it is obvious that if the appropriate tool is not selected and if it is not subsequently kept clean and properly and conveniently stored that much of the effectiveness of the cleaning operation will be vitiated. Thought given by the top man in the kitchen to these matters will prove to be rewarding. It is a melancholy fact that the cleaner tends usually to be of extremely conservative habit and the manager or supervisor will undoubtedly need to exercise pressure and persuasion in many instances in the matter of using the most appropriate type of tool in the most effective way.

Specialised cleaning

The plonge

The function of the plongeur is outlined in Chapter 4. It should be faced squarely that the work in the plonge consisting of scouring and cleaning of the metal cooking vessels can hardly be regarded as an attractive task. It is not surprising, therefore, that labour for this work is not always easy to obtain and that there is usually a substantial 'turnover' of operatives working in the plonge.

The 'plongeur' (literally one who plunges) is the kitchen porter who has the important task of cleaning the pots and pans. For copper pots traditional procedure was to have two deep sinks, one at least fitted with a steam jet so that the water could be heated to boiling point. Pans were placed in this water to which soda was added before heating with the steam jet. The plongeur had a long hook with which he could fish out the pans from the hot water. He then cleaned them with a pickle made of one-third salt, one-third silver sand and one-third flour mixed with vinegar to a paste. Traditionally, he did this either with the bare hands or with the skins of used lemons, rubbing all over the pan inside and out to bring up a shine and effectively removing all particles of food. This pan was then dipped into the sink again and straightaway rinsed and sterilised in the second sink of hot, clear water. Finally, it was wiped dry and placed on the *étagères* which are open shelved iron or steel racks. Pans should be placed in order of size, each group together and the handles pointing all one way. This operation is still carried out in many plonges today.

Increasing use is now made of wire wool or steel wool in conjunction with ordinary washing soap or a detergent. This newer mode of cleaning is even more effective if the plonge is equipped with a copper-lined rinsing tank. If the rinsing water in this type of tank is acidulated by the addition of vinegar, this helps to keep the copper vessels free from discoloration. Scouring powders (with or without added detergents) are also favoured in some kitchens. Whether traditional techniques, wire wool or scouring powders are used, preliminary soaking and detachment of debris is needed.

As it may be difficult to avoid fairly frequent labour turnover in this department the simple technique chosen to deal with metal pans should be clearly outlined and it may be helpful to have them displayed within the section.

Although pot washing can hardly be glamorised, it should not be accepted that the plonge must inevitably be a steamy and unpleasant place to work in. If properly ventilated, with adequate floor drainage, suitable duckboards and conveniently positioned racks for clean and dirty pans, much can be done to improve working conditions. It is imperative to provide the plongeur with suitable working dress, with facilities for frequent change of overall and with suitable waterproof apron for added protection. A good type of working dress does much to improve the self-respect of the operator and it is worth the little extra laundry expense.

Treatment of pots and pans

Large size, deep 'plunges' are essential to deal with tin-lined, copper vessels, iron, aluminium and other metal, heavy-duty kitchen vessels. Similarly, adequate facilities for really hot water are imperative, and steam injection into the washing-up water is often a most effective way of ensuring adequate heat.

Efficient pan cleaning can probably best be achieved by a three-tank technique. In the first, pans cleaned of food debris by preliminary scraping with a rubber, plastic or wood spatula are placed to soak. Remaining debris, when softened by soaking can then be further cleaned by spatula or scraper and given a major clean in tank number two containing hot water and soda. The cleaning agents used in this tank will depend on the type of pan under treatment and a note regarding cleaning agents is appended below.

In the third tank the clean vessel can be given its final rinse before being placed on the rack to drain and dry.

Cleaning agents for pots and pans

Methods and materials for cleaning pots and pans vary according to the metal. It is desirable, therefore, to avoid 'mixing' equipment and to rely on one main type, i.e., copper, but if copper and aluminium vessels are both held then separate washing arrangements (at least washing in separate batches) will have to be made. The batterie de cuisine consists of a mixture of metals:

1. *Copper.* Copper cooking vessels are, of course, lined with tin. The whole pot should be immersed in very hot water with a little soda (as mentioned, preliminary soaking and scraping is often desirable) and then, as necessary, scoured with a little powdered bath-brick or similar abrasive. Green discoloration of the copper can be removed with vinegar and salt.

It is, of course, important that the pots be re-tinned when the lining begins to wear through.

Metal polish may also be used to give brightness to the *exterior*.

2. *Aluminium.* The danger of using washing soda in cleaning aluminium vessels has, possibly, been overstressed. If the contact with the metal is brief as in ordinary washing up and the water is moderately hot, there is little danger of the metal being attacked. It is, however, important that aluminium pots should not be left to soak in a water to which soda has been added nor should they be allowed to come into contact with boiling soda water. It is, perhaps, advisable not to allow soda in the plonge where aluminium vessels are in the majority.

Modern detergents and plain soap and water are perfectly suitable and steel wool and mild abrasive powders are also useful for thorough cleaning.

Care must be taken not to pit or score the metal (which is relatively soft and therefore metal scrapers should not be used).

Ordinary metal polish may be used if a brighter finish is required for an external surface.

Aluminium should not be cleaned with a zinc plate and soda solution in the way that silver plate and cutlery is sometimes cleaned because it does not in any case work well on aluminium; but more importantly because it will probably lead to attack on the metal surface.

3. *Cast-iron.* Some iron cooking vessels such as omelette pans should not be wet washed but simply wiped clean with clean paper or clean cloth (salt may be used in bad cases).

Otherwise iron vessels do not require special treatment and can be satisfactorily washed with hot water with the aid of a little soda and other soaps and detergents as may be required. Abrasive powders and metal scourers may also be used.

It is important to dry iron and steel pans thoroughly after cleaning.

4. *Stainless steel.* Stainless steel is still not widely used for cooking

purposes in professional kitchens. Though increasingly used for food service purposes these service dishes are usually returned to the plate and silver wash rather than to the plonge. Should stainless steel require washing in the plonge and kitchen sections it can be effectively cleaned with hot water and soap and any of the modern detergents.

Plate and silver wash

These sections, though adjacent to the kitchen, normally come under the jurisdiction of the restaurant, though the maître d'hôtel usually appreciates that the chef de cuisine requires access to those sections in order to obtain silver for dishing.

Items requiring special cleaning techniques

All kitchen equipment and utensils need regular cleaning and care. The following are examples of the type of items that need other special checking.

1. *Butcher's block.* Apart from the normal methods of scrubbing and scouring, the larder and/or butcher's shop is likely to have chopping block and butchery block which, to remain effective, should not be softened by using wet techniques. Meat blocks of this kind should be treated after use with a metal scraper, preferably by a wire brush which tends to produce a roughened surface.

2. *Stoves, stove tops, etc.* Heavy-duty solid tops should be kept wiped clean during the day and an effective way of ensuring good appearance is, when still hot, quick rubbing with a coarse material in a heavy wad. Sacking is effective for this purpose. Obviously, damp or wet cloths will be ineffective and because of the rapid generation of steam will be dangerous if used for this purpose.

When cold, the range of stoves and ovens can be more thoroughly cleaned. Oil and grease may be removed. Bath-brick or similar mild abrasive powder remains a useful medium for cleaning stove exteriors but more modern detergent/abrasive mixtures are increasingly used.

The interior of ovens should receive regular attention. Shelves should be removed and the oven thoroughly cleaned with soda and hot water, or other grease solvent.

3. *Dry wiping of pans.* Iron omelette pans and stove tops or griddles used for griddle or hotplate cookery should not be washed but should be kept clean by wiping. Should a pancake or omelette pan become crusted, salt in conjunction with paper or dry cloth may be used to remove any incrustation. Once a pan has been properly maintained it usually acquires a patina which will permit ready cleansing by wiping with a clean cloth.

4. *Graters, whisks, mincer plates and sieves.* Graters, whisks, perforated mincer plates and sieves need special checking and attention for obvious reasons. Metal graters and wire sieves should be thoroughly washed in hot water immediately after use. Hair sieves should be carefully washed and allowed to dry thoroughly in a warm corner.

5. *Pastry brushes.* Pastry brushes must be thoroughly washed and allowed to dry after use. Stand them in hot water to which soda or detergent has been added and then clean thoroughly using a clean swab so as to clear to the roots. After thorough rinsing, shake well.

Inspections

The chef will, of course, delegate routine inspection for cleanliness to his responsible aids including sous chef, chef de partie and head porter. If he wishes cleanliness to be a feature of his establishment he will, however, show personal interest by himself inspecting for cleanliness from time to time. It is particularly important that attention be directed by these means to danger spots, particularly those where food débris and dirt might conceivably contact food which will not subsequently be sterilised by heat in cooking. Such danger spots, as has been indicated, include the attachments to mincers, such as the perforated plates, the perforations to sieves and strainers and the rough surfaces of graters.

Cleaning routines as kitchen maintenance

There are aspects of cleanliness which have not been dealt with in this section though of vital importance. Cooks', kitchen hands' and porters' clothing, for example, towels and other hand-wiping appliances all have the greatest significance but are considered in the Manual under the heading of personal and kitchen hygiene. Obviously, cleanliness as part of kitchen maintenance is dominated by the hygienic aspect (the note above regarding sieve and mincer danger spots are indicative of that aspect) but it is linked with efficient and agreeable working conditions and efficiency and effectiveness of the kitchen and its plant.

Planning to avoid excessive maintenance and cleaning

The chef if he is wise will not hesitate to adopt a questioning approach to cleanliness. He will not see it as something detached from the work of his culinary craftsmen but as something directly resulting from their work or necessary to it.

Because he will find it hard to get a reliable and constant flow of labour to deal with, for example, the dirt caused by certain types of solid fuel, the chef of the twentieth century has turned more and more to switch or tap controlled fuels which are not only more convenient in use but eliminate much cleaning. The chef is similarly more and more examining the use of commodities that have been pre-prepared in the factory so that there is less garden soil, for example, to cope with in the vegetable preparation room and in the ancillary departments of the kitchen.

That prevention is better than cure is, in short, the present positive approach of the modern chef and caterer to the cleaning problem. Better not to create mess rather than to have effective means of clearing it up. Planning cleaning routines, therefore, can never be divorced from the planning of schemes, processes and layouts to eliminate it.

12   Kitchen accidents and their prevention

It is a fact not perhaps as well known as it might be that more accidents (many of them fatal) occur in the home than on the roads of this country. Such domestic accidents often concern the very old and infirm or the very young; but many have simply to do with negligence or carelessness linked with the ordinary hazards of cooking, heating and the use of electric power, gas and other fuels. It is apparent that accidents of the kind that may occur during food preparation and cookery in the home may also occur in professional kitchens. Indeed, risks in hoteliers' or caterers' kitchens are likely to be increased by the heightened tempo and volume of work and by the abundance of equipment and machinery of greater size and greater complication than is encountered in smaller-scale cookery.

General causes of accidents

Before dealing with specific dangers in kitchens or food-preparation rooms it is as well to note three general factors which encourage the incidence of accidents in the professional kitchen. These may be summarised as:

1. Excessive haste.
2. Use of heat and hot equipment.
3. Use of machinery.

The state of intensive activity which occurs at service time in the busy hotel kitchen, for example, has been described as the coup de feu. Whilst activity reaches its height at these service times, kitchens even during other hours tend to be busy places in which speed is counted a virtue. Many of the measures to increase the speed and the expeditious accomplishment of tasks are, however, likely to reduce rather than increase accidents. For example, the correct handling and use of the French cook's knife will both increase efficiency and speed and reduce the possibility of mishap. The dangers generally lie not in the development of swift techniques but in rushing about the kitchens or attempting to perform a task with undue haste. The temptation to quote the tag 'more haste less speed' is irresistible for it permits one to add a rider 'more haste more accidents'.

It is thus imperative that, whilst kitchen staff are trained to execute their duties efficiently and expeditiously, the atmosphere in the kitchen should be ordered and calm. Even during the busiest periods it is vital that increased pressure and tempo of work should not be linked with dashing about or the glorifying of what many chefs describe as being 'up the wall'.

As far as heat, heated equipment, power and power-driven equipment is concerned, there are two general points that should be made at the outset, for they indicate that accidents can happen for two diametrically different reasons. The first point concerns lack of familiarity with the equipment and absence of skill in using it which can result in fat fires at the stove, cut fingers at the working bench and disastrous results from using machines without guards. On the other hand, and as regards the second point, there are undoubted dangers in the case of those operators who are skilful but have become over-familiar with their tools, equipment and working processes and whose consequent over-confidence may result in negligence and subsequently accidents of the kind that can befall the tyro. One knows only too well of cases like the still-room maid who after using a bread-slicing machine for years, yet sustained an accident and lost the tip of a finger in using it.

It is not, perhaps, appropriate here to delve too deeply into Freudian aspects of injuries sustained nor to seek to discuss at length 'accident proneness'. Suffice it to say that there seems to be an unmistakable link between on the one hand, minor accidents (even major ones, too) breakages and machine damage and, on the other hand, staff morale and contentment. This may be made manifest through individual staff mishaps at times of personal difficulty or with staff accidents and breakages as a whole when morale is generally low. Conditions of stress, anxiety or conditions of poor staff/employer relationship are almost bound to have a distracting effect which, in turn, can be a considerable factor in causing accidents. Calmness, in other words, is not merely the elimination of undue haste but demands the active promotion of a happy working atmosphere.

Cause of accidents

Having noted the general tendencies and conditions which may lead to accidents, the following may be listed as being particular points to be noted:

Structural and building faults

Accidents due to faults in the fabric and structure of kitchens, adjacent corridors and ancillary departments are common. They are so common, in fact, as to make it well-nigh impossible to deal exhaustively with every conceivable situation; but the following indicates some of them.

Floors

Particular attention should, for example, be directed to faultiness of flooring such as:

(a) Broken or missing tiles.
(b) Displaced or broken gutter coverings.

Accidents from tripping, particularly when carrying vessels containing foods and liquid can be serious and a frequent cause is deteriorated floor covering, such as a displaced tile. Additionally, however, floor hazards which must be checked by the chef and his staff include grease or wetness on the floor or unfamiliar projecting objects—even a broom or a saucepan left in an unfamiliar place. The area around greasetraps and gutters should be particularly checked for the presence of grease due, for example, to exudations from uncleared greasetraps.

Walls, ceilings and windows

Structural defects of walls and ceilings are less common in causing kitchen accidents but faulty doors, unfamiliar projections from walls or damage to windows affecting lighting are amongst items which should be checked and guarded against.

Fire

Fire risks within a kitchen must be regarded as special ones because the very nature of the cooking operation involves the use of intensive heat. There is, moreover, often an abundance of electrical machinery for food preparation and faults in wiring must be regarded as a possible cause of fire. In addition to constant vigilance to guard against outbreak of fire it is vitally important that the kitchen is properly equipped with emergency fire-fighting equipment and that staff are rehearsed or drilled in action to be taken in the event of fire. In accordance with the responsibility as allocated by management the chef or caterer will undoubtedly be carrying out procedures which have the approval of the fire-fighting organisation within the area of his Local Authority.

A common cause of outbreaks of fire in the kitchen is from igniting frying fats. Another is from cloths or clothing catching fire when using open-fire cookers such as salamanders and grills. Oven fires from foods catching during baking are also by no means infrequent. Whether such outbreaks spread and cause major damage and injury may largely depend on action taken before and during the accident by the chef and his staff. Hence, everyone in the kitchen must be properly instructed in the use of the chosen fire-fighting equipment such as fire blankets, sand, chemical and foam extinguishers.

Machinery and equipment

In some ways machinery causes the most dramatic kind of accident because of its suddenness and often swiftly mutilating effect. The amputation of fingers by mechanically propelled knives or choppers and the crushing or mangling of hands are still unfortunately likely to occur in many kitchens. It is not practicable here to detail each and every possible cause of mishap through using kitchen machinery but the following general points may be made:

(*a*) Manufacturers' instructions should be clearly displayed together with safety warnings. These should be kept in an obvious position adjoining the machine, preferably under glass or sufficiently protected to prevent fading and damage to the instructions.

Accidents from improper use of slicing, mincing, whisking, beating and bread-cutting machines are almost invariably due to the operator failing to observe the makers' instructions and/or to carry out the customary safety precautions as required by the chef or kitchen manager.

(*b*) *Safety guards*. It is astonishingly often that despite all instructions to the contrary, machines are operated without safety guards being in position.

(*c*) *Failure to use feed stick or pusher*. Feeding in meat or other material to be minced involving the use of a wooden plunger or feed stick is all too often aided by some other instrument such as an ice pick, steel or knife which can cause great damage to the machine. Alternatively, the hands or fingers are used with consequent personal injury.

(*d*) '*Saving time*'. Accidents on mixing machines are caused through trying to dislodge material adhering to the side of the bowl with hands or instruments whilst the machine is in motion or even attempting to change the beaters without waiting to switch off.

(*e*) *Loose stockpot taps, etc.* Loose taps or cocks to stockpots, urns, or boiling pans which can inadvertently be turned on by someone brushing against them are by no means unknown as causes of scalded feet. Valves and steam joints in steam-heated equipment may become defective and faults may also occur through the blockage of condenser pipes in steamers or wet steam ovens. Cereal grains swelling in condenser pipes causes excess water to accumulate and in steam ovens of older design may result in an abrupt escape of steam into the face when the steamer door is open.

General accidents

Apart from specific kitchen hazards there are many perils linked with the usual human element. Climbing on to an unsteady structure of boxes to reach an otherwise inaccessible object such as an item of stores stock or a piece of equipment or attempting to lift too heavy a load, are amongst the kind of accidents caused through human folly, error or even misplaced zeal. Running in the corridors and elsewhere and cannonading into others who may be carrying loads are linked with the factor of excessive haste already mentioned. Leaving saucepan handles projecting from the stove which are consequently brushed against and knocked over by passers-by remains a common cause of mishaps. Leaving saucepan handles to become hot over fire or burners resulting in burnt fingers and dropped pots is also still prevalent.

Using hand tools

The section of this Manual dealing with the use of hand tools and knives gives positive instructions in their proper use which should help minimise mishaps. There are some particular errors which may, however, be mentioned here. These include:

(a) *Misuse of tools.* An extremely common example of such misuse is attempting to open tins with a knife or tool other than a tin-opener and severing box wire with knives or tools other than a wire cutter. This type of accident can equally well be placed under the heading of 'saving time' by which is meant ill-judged attempts at haste.

(b) *Attempting to dissect frozen meat.* In larder work, accidents with knives can be caused by attempting to cut food, particularly frozen meat which is frozen hard and from which the knife so easily may slip.

(c) *Clothing.* Cooks' dress is specifically dealt with in this Manual under the appropriate heading. It is well adapted for kitchen use and generally jackets, aprons and caps, etc., protect the body rather than cause damage. Footwear is, however, a common cause of accidents and gum boots and other rubber-soled shoes have a marked tendency to slip on tiled floors which may have become wet or greasy.

Lighting

Reference has already been made to possible obscuring of natural light but it must be remembered that kitchens are often entirely lit by artificial means. It is essential that the lighting requirements should be measured by lighting experts and appropriately met for it should need no emphasis that it is essential at all times to see what one is doing. It is thus even more imperative that lighting conditions should be good when fire, knives and power-driven machinery are commonplace.

Electrical and gas equipment

Taps and leads on gas equipment must be particularly checked. It is most important also that gas burners should be kept clean so that no obstructions may be caused by dirt. Most accidents with gas are caused through carelessness in leaving burners on or in failing to report defects in the taps or leads or burners.

Cleanliness and general maintenance is equally important with electrical machinery but here it is also wise to be aware of the location of safety switches and of instructions for their use. Wiring, too, and the dangers of exposed live equipment must be borne in mind.

Both gas and electrical equipment is perfectly safe when properly used and maintained. The approach to these and other types of equipment is not so much a matter of guarding against accidents arising from possible faults as the positive approach of keeping the equipment in first-class working order so that no question of faults arises.

Reporting accidents

It will, of course, be obvious that accidents involving staff and equipment may well become the subject of insurance claims, compensation demands and of litigation in the courts. It is thus vital that an immediate and accurate record is made on an accident report form which should be signed personally by the chef or caterer and passed to the management of the establishment. Amongst other items, the form should provide for information regarding:

1. The person involved and/or machine damaged.
2. Where the accident occurred.
3. What supervision was in force.
4. Names of any persons witnessing the accident.

It may also be desirable for the chef or departmental manager to attach a confidential note or memo giving any supplementary information about the accident and why it occurred.

Accident book

Whether or not the establishment's own accident report forms, book or other records are maintained, it may be necessary that an Accident

Book (Forms B.1.510) under the National Insurance (Industrial Injuries) Act, 1946, should be kept. This is a statutory requirement for business premises employing ten or more insured persons to which any of the provisions of the Factories Act, 1937, apply. This Accident Book (obtainable from H.M.S.O., price 9d., excluding purchase tax) is drawn up in the form approved by the Ministry of Pensions and National Insurance and must be kept in a place readily accessible at all reasonable times to any injured employee and any bona fide person acting on his behalf.

The purpose of the Accident Book is to assist an injured person in giving notice of accident to his employer as required by the regulations made under the Industrial Injuries Act, 1946 (Sec. 25 (1)), and an entry in this book, if made as soon as practicable after the accident happens, will be sufficient notice of the accident for the purpose of the Act. Particulars of an accident may be entered in the book either by the injured person himself or by someone on his behalf (if the latter, the address and occupation of such a person must also be given). The book provides for the following information to be given:

1. Full name, address and occupation of the injured person.
2. Signature of the injured person or other person making the entry.
3. Date when entry was made.
4. Date and time of accident.
5. Room or place in which accident occurred.
6. Cause and nature of injury (with clear information about the work or process being performed at the time of the accident).

In addition to giving notice of the accident to his employer (the entry in the Accident Book is enough for the purpose) an injured person wishing to obtain National Insurance Benefit must ensure that a claim is lodged within twenty-one days at a local office of the Ministry of Pensions and National Insurance. If the accident prevents the injured person from working, he must, when seeing the doctor, obtain a certificate and this certificate may be used by him for making the claim.

Employers are required to take reasonable steps to investigate the circumstances of every accident recorded in the official Accident Book and if there appears to be any discrepancy between the circumstances found by them and the entry made by the injured or person acting on behalf of the injured, the employers are required to record the circumstances so found.

First aid

The foregoing give some indication of typical causes of accidents to people and to machinery in the kitchen. Despite all precautions, fires do break out and thus it is vital to have fire-fighting equipment and a drill or fire-fighting procedure drawn up beforehand to meet any circumstances which may arise. In the same way cuts, burns, fainting and other personal mishaps will occur even in the best-ordered kitchen. It is thus important that similar steps are taken to provide first-aid.

A first-aid box or boxes must be conveniently sited. It is also desirable to have nominated one or two suitable staff members at least who may be given some basic instruction in rendering first-aid. Such instruction can be provided through an organisation such as the St John Ambulance Association (in Scotland the St Andrew Ambulance Association) and/or the British Red Cross.

It is not considered appropriate within the scope of this Manual to detail steps to be taken in the case of each and every type of accident or mishap but it is stressed that it is particularly vital that provision should be made for treating cuts, scalds and burns, shock (including electrical shock) and that all who work in the kitchen are aware of the siting of the first-aid boxes, the names and section of those with first-aid skills and the quickest and best means of summoning further medical attention. It is strongly recommended that in addition to the provision of such items as bandages and medicine, a concise first-aid manual should be included in the first-aid kit. *First Aid*, the authorised manual of the three organisations mentioned above, is recommended as ideal for this purpose.

In concluding this section dealing with accidents and taking measures to prevent them, it cannot be too strongly stressed how closely accident prevention is linked with general staff relationships and staff management. The well-ordered and contented kitchen, free from undue haste, anxieties and free from physical neglect and dirt, will not only be a pleasant place in which to work but generally a much safer place in which to work. Again, just as welfare in other directions is compatible with, indeed necessary for, good business so are measures for the protection of people, plant and equipment against damage and mishap equally important for efficiency. Such measures constitute good business practice, for time lost through illness from any cause, or work impeded by the breakdown of machinery or equipment, results not only in impaired operating efficiency but in actual commercial losses. Measures to ensure welfare in this as in other directions is certainly to the advantage of the employer as it is necessary to the health and contentment of his staff.

A dictionary definition of hygiene is: 'principles of health, sanitary science' and the word hygiene is, in turn, derived from Hygea, the Goddess of Health or health personified. It is thus obvious that the observance of the principles of health must be part and parcel of every-day living. Attention to hygiene in the broadest sense should begin from the earliest days of a child's upbringing so that clean and healthy living is made a matter of instinctive action.

There are, however, certain industries, professions and vocations and consequently certain places of work where hygiene, particularly in its more commonly understood sense of clean practice, is of much more than ordinary importance.

The kitchen is one of those places where hygiene requires particularly close attention. Chefs, cooks, other food handlers, kitchen assistants and kitchen porters are engaged in a vocation where it is their duty and craft need to understand the importance of hygienic practices and the appalling dangers which lurk behind neglect and misunderstanding of the rules of clean working.

To illustrate the need for especial care in hygiene matters in the kitchen it is only necessary to mention the alarming growth in the number of notified outbreaks of food poisoning which rose steeply in the ten years from 1940 to 1950 from comfortably below 100 to little short of 4,000. It was in this decade that the practice of eating away from the home rose correspondingly sharply. Although no proof exists of a link, many consider it significant that the growth at that time in the reported cases of food poisoning (which in some instances resulted in death) was at least not unconnected with the increased amount of catering done from professional kitchens as distinct from cooking in the home.

Certainly the potential dangers revealed during this period did not pass unmarked by hoteliers and caterers themselves. Thus they, together with medical officers of health and representatives of kitchen workers, began to study the promotion of health through hygiene.

Legislation

In fact, a working party of the catering trade with this kind of representative membership and which first met in November, 1948, issued a report in 1951 which pin-pointed many of the dangers, suggested measures to improve conditions and put forward a standard code of practice. From this beginning similar work has been carried on in more recent years by the Food Hygiene Advisory Council set up by the Ministers of Health and of Food, Agriculture and Fisheries, and more detailed legislation to promote hygiene in the catering and food trades has been passed.

Today the statutory requirements, that is to say, those things which must be done because they are the law of the land, are outlined in Food Hygiene (General) Regulations, 1960, which came into effect on 1st October, 1960. These amend and consolidate those regulations which were introduced on 1st January, 1956, as a result of the Food and Drugs Act, 1955. It is encumbent upon those with senior responsibility in catering such as hotel managers, catering managers and executive chefs to be aware of the provisions of the regulations and also the various requirements of the Local Authorities, and it is their moral responsibility as well as their professional duty to see that they are carried out in the spirit as well as to the letter.

Many progressive people both inside and outside the hotel and catering industry believe, however, that the statutory requirements are minimal and that a code of practice actually followed should be stricter than the basic legal requirements.

Ordinary cooks and kitchen workers usually find difficulty in interpreting the formal language of Acts of Parliament and statutory regulations. For those actually on the job, it is desirable therefore to lay down simple, concise and practical rules of conduct and especially to explain them.

Help in hygiene instruction

It is in matters like hygiene that the work of technical colleges makes so vital a contribution. There is hardly a better way of demonstrating the importance of clean food than by clear explanation of the principles and facts in the college classroom supported by a follow-up in proper procedure on the job itself. This is achieved in, for example, National Apprenticeship schemes where the young apprentice cook is released weekly to attend technical classes or where the recruit to cookery has had initially a full-time basic training in the hotel and catering department of a technical institution.

Even where this ideal has not been achieved or for some reason is not capable of achievement some basic instruction in hygiene is desirable. This instruction can often be obtained through the co-operation of the Local Authority's officers, such as the Medical Officer of Health or the Health Inspector and also through other bodies. The Royal

Society for the Promotion of Health, St John Ambulance Brigade (or, in Scotland, St Andrew Ambulance Brigade) are amongst those organisations who can advise or provide lectures or short courses for all grades of staff.

Large organisations such as B.O.A.C. and British Transport have issued, in the past, concise working instructions for catering staff and this is obviously a most effective way of reaching each member of the organisation particularly when supported by displayed instructions in the ancillary departments of kitchens including washrooms and toilets. The Ministry of Health have issued posters promoting hygiene and advantage can also be taken of the excellent publicity material supplied at modest cost by the Central Council for Health Education.

Causes of food poisoning

Food poisoning is usually caused by the negligence or ignorance of the person preparing food. Certainly it never happens without a reason. Whilst, therefore, it may not be necessary for the craftsman cook even up to and including the chef de cuisine to have anything remotely resembling a detailed knowledge, for example, of bacteria, it is most important for such kitchen staff to be aware of the causes, dangers and results of food poisoning. Textbooks on this subject exist but many of these are, because of unfamiliar terms, forbidding reading to those engaged in hotel and catering cookery.

This section of the Manual is not intended to provide exhaustive and authoritative detail on the specialised subject of food poisoning but to provide a summary of information. This may serve to bring home to kitchen staff the realities of food poisoning and to alert them to factors causing outbreaks.

Despite the unfamiliar and forbidding terms encountered in even a slight approach to the study of bacteria (almost as alarming to practical craftsmen as the troubles they cause), some reference to those bacteria which may cause food poisoning must be made.

Bacteria

Bacteria are micro-organisms so small that they can only be seen with the aid of powerful magnification. They occur everywhere in our surroundings and in living creatures and whilst some are harmful to man others are harmless and even helpful. Of the harmful kind some gain direct entrance to the human body through, for example, being inhaled, others invade food and live in it.

Food poisoning or infection is caused by two groups of bacteria. The first group comprises those bacteria transmitted by the food and which directly cause the illness. The second group consists of bacteria which have formed poisons within the food and this may be described as the toxin type.

BACTERIAL FOOD POISONING—GROUP I

The commonest symptoms of food poisoning caused by this first group are of diarrhoea and vomiting. The infections caused are as follows:

Dysentery. The dysentery organisms (there are several of them belonging to what is called the *Shigella* group) produce classic symptoms of diarrhoea and vomiting sometimes with mucus or even blood in the faeces and, possibly, with some fever. Dysentery bacteria take some eighteen hours to incubate.

Salmonellae. Salmonellae bacteria owe their name to an investigator named Salmon and not to the fish. The symptoms are similar to those of dysentery, varying in severity, sometimes being most severe and with accompanying septicaemia.

Source of bacteria are the bowels and the symptoms are headache, fever, aching all over, diarrhoea and vomiting. The incubation period is from twelve to twenty-four hours and the duration of illness from one to eight days. Foods usually implicated are sliced cooked meats, meat and poultry, salads, 'warmed-up' foods, synthetic cream, ice-cream, improperly processed canned foods and duck eggs.

Typhoid and paratyphoid. The source of bacteria, which is of the Salmonella type, is the bowels. The symptoms of diarrhoea, vomiting, fever, etc., are characteristic of typhoid. The incubation period is from seven to twenty-one days and the duration of illness is four to six weeks. Foods usually implicated are water, raw milk and other diary products, salads, 'warmed-up' foods, synthetic cream, ice-cream and shellfish.

Enteric fever. Normally enteric fever is caused by a *Salmonella* bacterium (in this country, the typhoid or paratyphoid); it is also occasionally caused by other varieties which on rare occasions may cause symptoms of acute gastro-enteritis. The symptoms are fever, fluctuating temperature, headache and, initially, there is frequently constipation, although later probably turning to diarrhoea and other complications.

Infantile enteritis. Because formerly this tended to break out in the warmer weather it was called 'summer diarrhoea' but it may occur at any time of the year. Occurring amongst children it may be caused by the bacteria Salmonellae or *Shigella* already mentioned, or in babies by certain types of *bacterium coli*. When infants are brought together as in hospitals and clinics an outbreak can be most serious and may be accompanied by fatalities.

Virus diarrhoea and vomiting. The symptoms closely resemble dysentery or *Salmonella* infections and the disease has been called 'winter vomiting' and 'infectious diarrhoea and vomiting'. Though no virus has actually been isolated, the disease has been traced to faeces.

THE TOXIN TYPE—GROUP 2

In this group, poisoning is caused due to bacteria producing toxins in food which is then consumed.

Botulism. This is caused by Clostridium botulism toxins. The source of infection is soil and intestines and the incubation period is from twenty-four to seventy-two hours. The duration of illness is either death in twenty-four hours to eight days or slow convalescence over six to eight months. The poison attacks the nervous system and the symptoms are dizziness, double vision and paralysis.

Fortunately, this is a disease of extreme rarity in this country. It is fortunate because it is highly dangerous with a high rate of mortality. It is caused by contamination of food by soil bacteria and is thus associated with foods that have contact with the soil such as root vegetables.

The foods which are usually implicated include improperly processed, canned and bottled vegetables, fruits, meat pastes, etc. It is thus important that foods of this type which may have to be stored are properly sterilised under steam pressure.

Clostridium welchii. The bowels are the usual source of infection and the symptoms are severe abdominal pain, cramp, collapse, diarrhoea and vomiting.

The incubation period is from eight to twenty-two hours and the illness usually lasts from twelve to twenty-four hours. The foods usually implicated are made-up dishes (especially those 'warmed-up', gravy, stews, etc.).

Found in the faeces of animals, a common place of contamination is the slaughter house. In the case of meat thus affected, subsequent boiling or stewing will kill the bacteria but not the spores which will germinate, multiply and produce their poison if the meat is kept in a warm place overnight, and this is particularly possible when pastry or fat on the top has helped to produce ideal conditions. Alternatively, bacteria in affected meat may be kept alive because the meat has not been cooked through. This is possible, for example, in the case of under-done roast beef. Where the joint is kept warm for a period, as when it is allowed to cool slowly or if it is kept overnight without refrigeration, the toxin will be produced by the bacteria developing from the germinating spores. In restaurants or other catering establishments where meat is carved from a joint which has been roasted on a previous day and the slices reheated in stock or gravy such slices are capable of containing the toxin.

It is thus particularly important in the case of meat cookery to ensure that food is consumed immediately it is cooked or, if it has to be kept, that it is cooled rapidly and then kept properly refrigerated. It will, of course, be apparent that some of the techniques developed to cope with large-scale catering like pre-cooking, and subsequent re-heating are not only to be deplored for taste and quality reasons but also because they are accompanied by special dangers.

The symptoms occur from ten to twelve hours after contaminated food has been eaten and they consist of severe stomach pain with accompanying diarrhoea which occurs until there is (virtually) nothing left to pass. Because of the time taken for the symptoms to develop, their onslaught is usually in the early hours of the morning.

Staphylococcal. The Staphylococcal bacteria are found in the nose, throat and on the skin. If food becomes contaminated and is left to stand overnight in a warm kitchen a poison is produced by the growing Staphylococci. It is thus apparent that dangers can be reduced by: (*a*) reducing the amount of handling, by (*b*) making full use of refrigeration to keep cooked food or (*c*) ensuring that food is consumed immediately after preparation. It is obvious also that there are special dangers in foods which have to be handled after preparation or after cooking such as in the case of dishes which are decorated or left to set.

Foods which are frequently involved include custard, pastries, pies, cooked ham and other cooked meats, gravies and dressings, synthetic cream, ice-cream, improperly processed canned foods.

The incubation period is from two to six hours and the symptoms of severe abdominal pain and vomiting usually occur about four hours after the eating of contaminated food. The illness lasts from six to twenty-four days.

Mixed infections

Apart from food poisoning traced to specific toxin-type contamination, there are infections where because of inadequate storage conditions large numbers of bacteria have multiplied and produced their toxins. Where there are no specific organisms present the symptoms are usually more vague. Diarrhoea and vomiting may occur any time after eight hours and up to twenty-four hours from the time the contaminated food was eaten. Here again, proper storage and refrigeration of food will reduce the danger of toxin development.

Sources and spread of infection

From the foregoing it will be apparent that though it is possible for some of the dangerous organisms to be transmitted from, say, the soil it is more usual for infection to be spread by human or animal carriers. Staphylococci, for example, are found in the nose of most human beings and are also commonly on the skin and clothes. Similarly, *Clostridium welchii* are found in the excreta of all animals. The extent to which *Shigella* and *Salmonella* are carried in humans and animals is more variable but can grow rapidly as cases occur.

Even when infection has an animal source other than human, its spread is nearly always accomplished by human agency. It is spread by bacteria in the faeces or urine of carriers whether permanent or temporary and from those suffering or convalescing from a case of food poisoning. From the faeces and urine, transmission is by fingers, flies and food. The author was once associated with the making of a film which was able, graphically, to demonstrate how easily, for example, bacteria pass through toilet paper on to the finger-tips. *Shigella* and *Salmonella* live on the skin, particularly under finger-nails for a long time. It is thus obvious how necessary it is both to have provision for handwashing (especially after toilet use) and how important it is to ensure that the facilities are used.

Statutory requirements

Because of the grave dangers attendant on negligent handling, preparation, cooking and service of food, legislation exists to reduce and control risks. It is difficult for practical craftsmen always to extract essential information from Acts of Parliament and statutory publications. The full regulations contain a great deal of reading which makes difficult going for the average cook. Moreover, they are concerned with aspects of clean and safe food in markets, dairies, slaughter houses, vehicles and so on, with which the ordinary chef or caterer would not directly be concerned. On the other hand, it has to be borne in mind by those in responsible positions in the industry that ignorance of the law cannot constitute a defence in the event of prosecution.

Registration of premises and compliance with bye-laws

There are two general points which may be made regarding the Food Regulations. These are that premises used in connection with the sale, preparation or manufacture of food for sale must be registered with the local authority and secondly, that subject to the provisions of the Act a local authority may make bye-laws to ensure clean food or clean methods of food preparation. It must be stressed, therefore, that caterers require not only to learn of the main provisions under the Act of Parliament but also the local requirements of their own authority.

Special provisions

Among the matters which chefs and caterers should particularly note are special provisions that apply to the preparation and sale of ice-cream and also the possible provision that may be made by a county council or local authority for cleaning shellfish, i.e., subjecting the shellfish to appropriate germicidal treatment for which a charge may be made.

Notification of outbreaks

The caterer should also note that medical practitioners are required to notify the Local Authority should he become aware of or suspect a case of food poisoning and must provide the Authority with full details.

Officers of the local authorities

The Authority is usually represented in all matters relating to clean food by the medical officer of health and his staff, including health inspectors and food inspectors. The medical officer of health of a district has powers to take samples of food, to stop the sale of food until tests have been made and to condemn food. The Authority's authorised officers have a right to enter premises at any reasonable hour to carry out their duty. It is, thus, clearly important for hoteliers, caterers and their senior staff to seek help and advice from the officers of the Authority and to co-operate with them in every way possible to promote public health.

Designation of food

In addition to the provision concerning clean and safe food, there are also obligations regarding the designation of food offered for sale and chefs should particularly note, for example, the restrictions that apply to the use of the word cream. This word must not be used either alone or in a description which includes the word cream to describe anything which resembles cream but is not cream or any article of food (for example, cream bun) containing such a substitute substance.

Food hygiene regulations

However, within the provisions of the Act those which most immediately concern the chef and catering staff are those regulations governing food hygiene and they should also be aware of the fact that the Food Hygiene Advisory Council set up by the Ministry under the Act may produce further a Code of Practice for the guidance of those concerned with food preparation, cooking and food purveying generally. Under the Act the Minister may also make further regulations to ensure clean food conditions and practice.

As a result of this legislation, the Food Hygiene Regulations, 1955, came into operation on 1st January, 1956. These regulations were amended and consolidated by new ones which came into effect on 1st October, 1960. These Food Hygiene (General) Regulations, 1960, should be in the hands of all chefs and caterers (they are obtainable from Her Majesty's Stationery Office) who would also be well advised to obtain the H.M.S.O. Handbook, *Clean Catering*, which gives further detailed guidance about appropriate measures for the promotion of clean and safe food.

Points summarised

The basic regulations provide for a number of essentials which may be summarised as follows:

1. No food business must take place in unsanitary premises or any place which would expose food to the risk of contamination.

2. Articles or equipment used in connection with a food business must be clean. They must be made of such materials and in such a way as to:

   (*a*) Enable them to be thoroughly cleaned.
   (*b*) Prevent, in so far as is reasonably practicable, matter being absorbed by them.
   (*c*) Prevent, so far as is reasonably practicable, any risk of contamination of the food.

3. Anyone engaged in the handling of food must:
   (*a*) Keep clean all parts of his person liable to come into contact with food.
   (*b*) Similarly keep clothing and overalls clean.
   (*c*) Cover any open cut or abrasion or any exposed part with a suitable waterproof dressing.
   (*d*) Refrain from spitting.

    (e) Refrain from smoking and snuff-taking not only whilst handling food but whilst in any food room in which there is open food.

4. The regulations lay down the mode of transporting food and the wrapping of food and in this connection prohibit the use of certain materials including printed materials (other than special wrapping paper) to contact food other than uncooked vegetables.

5. Cooks or any other food handlers must inform employers if aware that they are suffering from or are carriers of any infections likely to cause food poisoning. In turn the employer must notify the medical officer of health. Infections specifically mentioned in the regulations are: Typhoid fever, paratyphoid fever or any other *Salmonella* infection or dysentery or any Staphylococcal infection.

Chef proprietors or any other 'one-man business' naturally report direct to the medical officer of health.

In addition to the foregoing, there are a number of further specific regulations concerning food premises, equipment, first-aid materials, accommodation, facilities, repair, etc.

The more important provisions of this kind may be summarised as follows:

6. *Sanitary conveniences*
    (a) Toilets in food premises must be clean and sufficient and so sited that no offensive odours can reach food rooms.
    (b) Toilets (and this term implies a place which contains a sanitary convenience) must be well lit and ventilated.
    (c) No room containing a toilet shall be used for food purposes and no room directly communicating with a room containing a sanitary convenience may be used either for the handling of open food or even for the cleaning of equipment used in connection with the handling of open food.
    (d) Near every sanitary convenience and toilet in food premises there must be displayed a clear notice reminding users to wash their hands after using the convenience.

7. The drainage system connected with sanitary conveniences must be similarly isolated from food rooms and:

    (a) No fresh-air intake from the soil drainage ventilation pipe must be sited in a food room.
    (b) Any inlet into such a system situated in a food room must be trapped.

(c) No water supply cistern to a food room must supply a toilet other than through an efficient flushing cistern or similar equally efficient flushing device suitable for preventing water supply contamination.

(d) Water supply itself must be sufficient to cope with the Food Hygiene Regulations generally and be clean and wholesome.

8. Wash-hand basins must be provided for food handlers on food premises in places convenient and accessible for them. The basins must be properly maintained and provided with an adequate supply of hot and cold water (or of hot water at a suitably controlled temperature).

Wash-hand basins so provided for use by food handlers must be furnished with soap or other suitable detergent, nail brushes and clean towels or other proper hand drying facilities. These must be used only in connection with personal washing.

9. Suitable and sufficient first-aid materials must be provided in an accessible position for food handlers and must include bandages, dressings and antiseptics.

10. Accommodation for clothing must be provided for food handlers and lockers or similar suitable facilities are to be included.

11. Facilities must be provided other than the wash-hand basins for washing food and equipment and utensils. Sinks for washing equipment must receive an adequate supply of either hot or cold water. Sinks that are designed only for the rinsing of vegetables (and also the washing of fish, tripe, animal casings and fruit) may be provided with cold water alone. Similar conditions in regard to the provision of detergents and drying facilities apply to sinks for washing equipment and utensils.

12. Food rooms must be properly lit and ventilated and they must not be used for sleeping purposes nor communicate with a sleeping place.

13. Food premises including walls, floors, doors, windows, ceilings, woodwork and other parts of the structure must be kept in sufficiently good repair and condition as to enable them to be effectively cleaned and so as to prevent infestation by rodents, insects and to prevent the entry of birds.

14. Proper provision must be made for the removal of refuse and neither solid nor liquid refuse nor filth must be allowed to accumulate in food rooms.

15. *Storage of cooked or partly cooked food.* Certain food must be kept at a temperature of not less than 145°F when it is served for immediate consumption or if the temperature is allowed to fall to less than this

145°F it must be cooled to one below 50° as quickly as possible and under hygienic conditions. It must then be kept below this temperature until served or re-heated for service. (The list of foods excluded from this provision was increased by the Regulations of 1960.)

Penalties for offences

Penalties are imposed for those guilty of offences against the Food Hygiene Regulations and penalties mentioned include both fines and imprisonment or both.

It should be noted that the foregoing summarises some of the more important features under statutory regulations and should serve as a guide for employees and for minimum standards of clean practice. Employers and executive staff such as the chef or catering manager must, however, ensure that they become acquainted with the full regulations themselves in order that they may study the precise legal requirements.

It is also desirable to carry out the terms of any Codes of Practice published by the Food Hygiene Advisory Council. Pending such publication, Codes of Practice recommended by the Royal Society for the Promotion of Health may be used as forming an appropriate guide to ethical conduct in clean catering.

Chefs and caterers may obtain much help and guidance from reputable manufacturers of sanitary products and, even more important, would find that the Royal Society of Health and the Royal Institute of Public Health and Hygiene are also active in ways which are helpful to those in the catering profession. The latter body, for example, conducts short courses in food hygiene and the handling of food and also offers an examination for a certificate in this subject.

Complying with the regulations and promoting hygiene

If the causes of food poisoning as outlined earlier are thoroughly understood by executive chefs and catering managers they will be, in turn, better equipped to bring home to all grades of kitchen staff the perils which are very real. All concerned should then be ready to take the necessary precautions to prevent food contamination and food poisoning and to comply with the law of the land as enacted by Parliament and as further provided for under the various bye-laws of Local Authorities.

Positive measures that are required to promote hygiene in the kitchen can be best considered under the three following headings:

1. The proper handling and storage of food before, during and after cooking.
2. The proper maintenance of premises, tools and equipment used for or in connection with the preparation, cooking and storage of food both before, during and after meal service.
3. Personal cleanliness from every aspect on the part of the food handler and the kitchen worker including the provision of proper clothing and adequate hand washing and similar facilities.

Checking the food itself

It cannot be emphasised too frequently that once the dangers of food poisoning are recognised, one is measurably nearer taking adequate precautions. The recognition of defects in certain types of food is, as might be anticipated, a specialist task involving training and experience over some years. This is particularly true, for example, of the detection of disease in meat. Fortunately, so far as the chef and caterer are concerned, meat comes under inspection arrangements of health inspectors employed by Local Authorities and there is consequently, nowadays, no need for cooks themselves to have detailed knowledge of inspection points in meat of the kind that some years ago was taught to military cooks on the assumption, presumably, that they might have to slaughter their own livestock and carry out their own checks.

In regard to processed food including meat, fish, vegetables, fruit, etc., which are packaged in cans, it is not vital that every cook should be any more knowledgeable than that he should be able to isolate suspected consignments. In such instances the assistance of the appropriately trained officer of the Local Authority should be sought in case of the need to make condemnation of suspected food. Indeed, most suppliers would require evidence of condemnation by such an Authority if there was to be any question of replacement or refund.

In the author's opinion, therefore, it is hardly necessary for the chef or caterer to be expert in judging the nature and causes of, for example, 'the blown can'. It would seem to be a far safer principle to seek expert assistance when confronted with this phenomenon.

The following simple rules should be observed on the part of the chef (and his appropriate subordinates) in regard to foods entering kitchen and kitchen stores.

1. Food in its natural, i.e., unprocessed state, should be clean, look clean and have a sweet smell. The natural foods which perhaps need special care in checking are:

(a) *Meat.* Meat is, of course, subjected to inspection at points of slaughter and at meat markets, cold stores, etc., but it is still important to ensure that it is in sound condition when coming into the kitchen or kitchen meat store. Expert inspection should be sought if there is any discoloration and bad smell (bone taint, for example, is sometimes not betrayed until meat is dissected). A special watch should be made, both at the time of delivery and also during the time that the meat is stored prior to cooking, against fly blow and deterioration through decomposition. Some of the positive points by which to recognise sound meat are dealt with in the section on buying.

(b) *Fish.* Similar vigilance is necessary in the case of fish where deterioration is rapid if packing or cold storage is not adequate.

(c) *Vegetables and fruit.* It is most important that vegetables to which will inevitably be adhering garden soil should not be allowed to come into contact with other foods until they have been washed and prepared in the vegetable store and preparation room. It will already have been noted that there is danger of bacterial contamination from soil. For hygiene reasons as well as culinary and aesthetic ones, bruised, damaged or rotting vegetables or fruit should be rejected.

(d) *Dry goods.* It is true that certain items such as bread are, on the whole, more resistant to the multiplication of bacteria than other foods such as cooked meat or cream in cream cakes, but the relative safety of drier foods should not engender complacency. Indeed, some dried foods become potentially highly dangerous once their preparation into dishes begins and one needs only to think of dried egg which when reconstituted, is particularly susceptible to contamination under certain conditions.

Dirty and damaged bread should be rejected as should musty smelling or weevily flour and particularly any foods such as cereals or sugars which bear the slightest trace of attack by rodents. Wrappings and packings should be intact and tins should be unrusted, uncorroded and any sign of 'blow' regarded as unsafe until the contrary has been proved.

To summarise, it may be said that the evidence of the chef's own senses of smell and sight which (together with taste, men of food will particularly cultivate) will lead to automatic rejection or setting aside for expert investigation of any suspect commodity.

Food in preparation, cooking, service and storage

Foods of all kinds, it is clear, can become dirtied or contaminated at any stage up to actual consumption by the guest. Hygiene precautions in regard to food should, therefore, be maintained rigorously throughout its period in the kitchen or kitchen store. Points particularly to be borne in mind are: (1) the need to avoid contamination of food in the first instance, and (2) the need to kill or prevent the growth of any bacteria already present.

The prevention of contamination is, of course, a prime purpose of all hygiene and those measures concerned with the cleanliness of the person and of the premises and equipment have already been made clear. Here let it be sufficient to re-emphasise that food should be protected from dirt by being kept in clean vessels or containers, in clean premises and properly protected against dust, insects, rodents, etc.

Storage temperatures

In keeping food both before and after it has been cooked it will now be appreciated how valuable it is that the cook can understand that bacterial growth is linked closely with temperature. At very low temperatures such growth either stops or is considerably slowed and at very high temperatures such as at boiling point and above bacteria are either destroyed or their further development is prevented. Thus the advantages of storing food in refrigerators or cold-store room is apparent and the safety of thorough cooking at high temperatures is underlined. By the same token it is now apparent that keeping food in the moderate warmth of the kitchen and even on the hotplate is potentially dangerous. In the case of re-heated meat and fish dishes, for example, there can be an enormous and dangerous rate of multiplication of bacteria when such a dish has become contaminated from any cause whatsoever and the dish has been left in the warm kitchen or non-cold storage overnight.

In looking after food, therefore, vigilance to protect it against contamination in the first instance must be supported by: (1) full use of adequate cold store, and (2) great care in ensuring thorough cooking. Particularly is such vigilance needed in the case of made-up dishes, warmed-up and re-heated foods and when food has been handled and not eaten immediately after heating. Moreover, after cooking, if food is not to be eaten straight away then it should be cooled rapidly to below 50°F.

A special word might be said in regard to gelatine; for aspic jelly and similar gelatinous material is a particular feature of buffet food and cold pies. Gelatinous material of this kind is such a favourable medium for cultivating bacteria that it is used in the laboratory for this purpose. Special precautions need to be taken, therefore, in regard to this type of dish. Any food which has been exposed on buffet tables where it so easily can be contaminated by dust, air, breath, sneezes and coughs should most certainly be used on the day prepared for use.

Premises, tools and equipment

It is obvious from other sections of this Manual that the design and equipment of the kitchen and the ancillary departments will have been strongly influenced by the need for clinical cleanliness in regard to food storage, preparation and cooking. Surfaces of walls and floors should be washable and kept clean and scrupulous cleanliness should be observed in the case of food shelves and preparation tables. Surfaces on which food is prepared should be of impervious material such as stainless steel, laminated plastic or marble. Sinks and tanks in which food is rinsed, soaked and stored should similarly be of non-corroding metal or of porcelain in an undamaged state.

Disposal of waste

A most important feature of the kitchen premises are the facilities for the disposal of waste food which in itself is a possible means of contaminating other foods and also attracts flies and vermin. It is important to have clean food-waste bins (with tightly fitting lids) standing on a hard surface outside the kitchen so that both bins and the area on which they stand can be kept clean, disinfected and deodorised. Food refuse bins should be washed internally as well as externally at regular intervals and scalded out.

Wash-up

The provision of proper facilities for washing-up is vital. The cleaning of cooking vessels has been dealt with in the section on the plonge. The plate wash and cutlery wash is not normally under the control of the chef de cuisine but it may be noted that washing-up techniques should include sanitising procedure. There is more than one way of rendering plates and cutlery sterile but immersion in rinsing water of 180°F or over is generally considered to be the most effective and the most practicable.

Use of disinfectants

Chemical methods of sterilising by the addition of agents to the water is somewhat more subject to human error. Sterilising agents such as, for example, the quarternary ammonium compounds can, however, be extremely effective for dealing with swabs, wiping knives, benches, etc., and also for keeping ice-cream scoops safe.

Chefs should not accept unquestioningly the merits of all the branded products sold for cleaning and sterilising purposes and in particular they should learn to distinguish between detergents which are simply for cleaning purposes and sterilising agents which are intended to render cleaned surfaces or articles safe from infection. Where preparations of either type or both types are used it is important to check that the proper concentration of solution is employed.

Hand washing

Food premises must comply with statutory requirements in regard to hand washing facilities. It will, of course, be apparent apart from legal requirements, that a wash basin with adequate hot water, soap and nail brush should be provided for use adjacent to the toilet. Hand-drying arrangements can often undo the good here and ordinary roller towels allowed to become wet and soiled are particularly unsuitable and dangerous. The patented type of rollers which give access to clean portions by pulling down, electric warm air driers, individual towels or disposable paper towels are all types of hand drying which can be considered to give satisfactory results.

Precautions against contamination by insects and vermin

A deal of good-natured jesting is sometimes directed against the title of 'Rodent Officer' by those who think that the designation should be simply 'Rat Catcher', yet the fact remains that controlling infestation by rats and mice in agriculture, in food stores and in kitchens as well, even, as in ordinary domestic surroundings requires skilled attention. The same is true of attacks of insect pests who often find in kitchens ideal conditions for breeding and feeding.

It is not considered within the scope of this Manual to do more than indicate the normal precautions that the chef and the caterer should take in the kitchen to combat the possibility of infestation by rodents and insects and it is stressed that detailed advice and, indeed, action where necessary, *can* be sought and *should* be sought from the appropriate officers of the Local Authority. The question of the best means of destroying rats and mice when detected is best left to the expert. It is, however, important that the chef or caterer and his staff should be able readily to detect the presence of pests.

Rodents

Invasion by rats and mice may usually be detected as follows:

1. *Holes and scrapes.* The beginning of holes can often be detected by

little piles of earth or debris made by the rat. These are known as scrapes.

2. *Smears*. This is the term used to denote marks made by fur touching a wall, a projection or a surface when rats or mice pass along a frequently used run. The passage of rodents is seldom made without trace because the fur is greasy and sometimes dusty; moreover, smears may also be left by the tracks of their feet.

3. *Runways*. These are simply the tracks beaten down by rodents frequently using the same route.

4. *Gnawing marks*. Apart from eating food, rodents gnaw anything else that is not too hard. This activity prevents the front teeth, which continue to grow throughout life, from becoming excessively long. It is well to look for gnawing marks, therefore, not only in foods such as cheese, butter or chocolate, but on wood, soap and even lead piping.

5. *Marks of feet and tail*. These tell-tale signs may be encouraged by laying whitening matter such as flour. Such marks can also be seen in dust or mud or spilt cereals.

6. *Droppings*. Droppings not only indicate where the animals run but where the infestation is active. Ships' rats and house-mouse droppings dry quickly and consequently their freshness may be difficult to detect. Common rat droppings when fresh are moist and can give a guide to the magnitude of the infestation. Unfortunately, the common rat tends to leave its droppings away from the runway in definite places.

7. *Disappearance of bait*. Rats and mice need food and if this is unobtainable, there will be no infestation. In the well-run kitchen, therefore, food should be stored in containers proof against rodents and waste should be placed in covered bins until collection. Daily removal of waste should be arranged wherever possible.

In order to test whether rodents are in fact present, baits (which should *not* be poisoned) may be put down and inspected. Bread mash, sausage rusk, flours and sugar are materials which can be used for this purpose.

8. *Damage*. Despite being listed as the eighth point, this may be the first sign of rodent infestation. Damage may be caused not only by the gnawing for food into, say, cereal or sugar sacks but also as a result of the quest for nesting material.

Preventing rodent infestation

A secondary factor encouraging rodent invasion is suitable shelter and entry facility. In addition to securing food in proper containers, the following precautions should be taken:

1. Anything such as rubbish or cartons or other objects leaning against a wall and which might provide cover should be removed promptly.
2. Similarly, holes made through walls for cables, gas pipes, drains, etc., should be filled. The filling must be rat-proof, and concrete to which glass has been added is appropriate.
3. Airbricks, gulleys and manhole covers should be inspected regularly and broken fittings renewed.
4. Accessible windows to larders, for example, that may be left open at night should be covered with wire netting.
5. Wooden doors and frames to kitchen areas should be protected against gnawing by metal kicking plates and any gaps caused by worn steps should be attended to.
6. Finally, drains and sewer connections should be checked for these are frequent entry passages for rats.

All these measures should be properly carried out by a reliable builder or similarly skilled labour carried on the hotel's (or catering establishment's) staff as distinct from self-help efforts by kitchen staff. Inspections should be made by the chef or caterer at regular intervals.

Combating insect pests

Cockroaches. Cockroaches belong to a group of insects which include crickets, grasshoppers and locusts. They are of a class of pest which has been described as 'visitors' because they live in crevices in the structure of buildings or other harbourages even in the ground outside and make journeys within to gain their food.

Three kinds of domestic cockroaches are found in Britain:

1. *The German cockroach (Blattella germanica L.)* which is also called the steamfly or 'Croton bug'. This is a yellowish-brown insect, growing to about half an inch long with large wings. It commonly infests large buildings especially those warmed by central heating.

2. *The Oriental cockroach (Blattella orientalis L.)* or 'Black Beetle', grows to 1 in. and is shiny, dark brown in colour. The male has wings covering two-thirds of its abdomen but the female has much fore-shortened ones. Though once very common, this type is now less frequently found than the German cockroach in modern buildings but is often enough encountered in kitchen and bakeries of older construction.

3. *The American cockroach (Periplaneta americana L.)* or 'Bombay canary' is reddish brown in colour with a margin of yellow on the

thoracic shield. The insect grows to $1\frac{1}{2}$ in. in length and both sexes have large wings.

Because of their size and their activity at night, cockroaches are generally easy to detect. Moreover, an unpleasant 'roachy', foetid smell is associated with them.

Their flat bodies enable them to lie concealed in cracks and crevices during the day, but they emerge at night to feed. They will eat almost anything (wool, leather, book covers as well as food) and leave their smell wherever they have been.

Whilst it is possible for cockroaches to act as carriers and transmitters of disease germs through having fed on contaminated material, they are not suspected of carrying infection as commonly, for example, as the house fly. It is, however, obviously important to eradicate them because of the smell, the soiling by excrement, the destruction of food by nibbling and the general revulsion they cause.

As in the case of rodents, it is best to entrust their control and destruction to experts for complete eradication is difficult to achieve. Treatment over a period is necessary because insects and eggs are usually well protected in their remote harbourages. Fumigation is the one method that can be relied upon to eradicate in a single day but because of its drastic nature this measure must be handled by experts.

Flies. There are several types of house fly and of blow fly. However, both house flies and blow flies are readily recognisable and their ability readily to spread disease is nowadays generally appreciated. Their methods of feeding have been shown visually through enlarged motion pictures and these are an excellent way of emphasising to kitchen staff the dangerous as well as the repulsive aspects of the fly's habits. The regurgitation and defaecation which accompanies feeding is seldom forgotten by those who have viewed magnified moving pictures, and vigilance against flies can be effectively improved by constant propaganda of this kind.

Local spraying to kill, including the use of residual insecticides (i.e., those which remain effective on windows and walls over a period) obviously have their value. Useful also is protection of food by flyproofing larders and the use of muslin and plastic covers to protect food. It is even more important, however, to attempt to control breeding and this is more difficult.

Scrupulous cleanliness not only in the kitchen and its departments but in the area outside is necessary to restrict breeding. Particularly is this cleanliness important near swill-bins and dust-bins. These should stand on washable hard standing, for earth and soft ground generally contaminated by rubbish and food waste provides an ideal opportunity for fly breeding.

It is, however, more than likely that flies will penetrate kitchens from breeding grounds away from and out of the control of the establishment and that insecticides and mechanical methods of killing will often, in any case, have to be used to combat such invasions. Persistent entry of flies (both blow fly and house fly) should receive expert attention over and above the routine anti-fly measures of kitchen staff.

Ants. Ants which are normally encountered out of doors do, on occasion, invade food stores and are particularly attracted by sugar products. Some types have a large range and it is most unpleasant to see these little insects swarming over and near food. It is even possible that disease germs might be carried by them after their visits to sources of water such as drains, moist excreta and so on.

To repel ants complete cleanliness and effective storage under cover is vital and the use of barrier insecticides of the powder type, coupled with cleanliness can be effective. Unfortunately, with serious interior infestations the destruction of nests is the only certain method of complete eradication and this may be difficult to achieve since nests are often inaccessible.

Other insect pests. There is, of course, a vast range of insect pests which can invade foodstuffs in store but happily these are not so commonly encountered in kitchen stores because of measures already taken at docks, warehouses and by packers before commodities are distributed to shops and caterers. Weevils in flour, cheese mites and so on soon betray their presence and appropriate clearing out and preventive measures may then be taken.

Wasps and bees. Where serious invasions of wasps or bees take place it will be advisable to obtain assistance in the destruction of the nest or colony. Generally, however, the intrusion of wasps is an occasional kitchen nuisance which can best be met by the same 'proofing' (particularly in the pastry departments, etc.) as is used against flies.

Disinfectants in kitchen hygiene

In pursuing the goal of clean food, clean kitchen and clean equipment, the chef and the caterer and their staff will rely a good deal on new and traditional cleaning aids and methods. Hot soap and water and the scrubbing brush (together with elbow grease) will go far in ensuring cleanliness of utensils and apparatus but it is often necessary to consider the use of chemical disinfectants.

The chef or caterer today unless he has had the advantage of some instruction in the laboratories or classrooms of an hotel school or technical college may have some difficulty in assessing the functions and claims of the various types of disinfectant now advertised. He would certainly be wise to seek expert advice when in doubt. The following points should be regarded as giving broad guidance only.

Desirably, chemical disinfectants should have the following properties, they should:

(*a*) Act rapidly on as many types of organisms as possible.
(*b*) Have an effective degree of penetration (this will vary according to surface tension).
(*c*) Be active and efficient in low concentration because of the cost factor.
(*d*) Be active in the presence of organic matter.
(*e*) Be stable for storage purposes.
(*f*) Be of a price permitting reasonable use.

Types of disinfectant

Types of chemical disinfectant commonly encountered in catering establishments are as follows:

1. *Oxidising agents.* Some disinfectants destroy bacteria by oxidising them and are also able to combat spores. This type is effective but they are unstable and hence storage problems arise. Their effectiveness is inhibited also by the presence of organic matter as is found in the solid debris left in washing-up soil. Disinfectants of this type include sodium hypochlorite, potassium permanganate, hydrogen peroxide and halogens (for example, chlorine in drinking water).

2. *Chemical agents—hydrolysis.* Such chemical disinfectants are not today considered very practical because they are either strong acids or alkalis, highly corrosive and generally difficult and unpleasant to use.

3. *Derivatives of coal tar.* These are effective disinfectants which are reasonably pleasant to use. They include carbolic acid, lysol and some alcohols.

4. *The quarternary ammonium compounds.* There has been a considerable development in the marketing of this type of disinfectant which is used in modern detergents which also emulsify grease.

5. *Other types.* In addition to the foregoing some of the traditional methods of preserving foods may also be regarded as disinfectants. Essential oils, for example, such as clove oil which with others were used to mask the flavour of decomposition as well as to arrest its progress are active when pure but slow down bacterial growth rather than destroy it. The salts of heavy metals also act as disinfectants but

their effectiveness is due, in part, to the toxic effect of the metal such as the mercury in mercuric chloride. Formalin is well known over a long period as a preservative and disinfectant. Strong brines and syrups also have a preservative value and slow up or arrest the process of decomposition due to bacterial activity. Finally, there are many modern drugs and antibiotics.

Effectiveness of disinfectant

The effectiveness of disinfectant varies and may be improved by:

1. Heat. For example, hot lysol is much more effective than cold.
2. By lowering the surface tension of whatever is to be disinfected and this can be achieved by using detergent either beforehand or mixed with the disinfectant. By emulsifying the grease it affords the disinfectant an opportunity to reach its objective and to work.

Similarly, the efficiency of disinfectants is impaired by:

1. The presence of organic matter such as is found in washing-up water and which can include food soil, fragments of cloth such as wool, cotton or silk, mucus, pus, flesh fragments, blood or wood. These act as barriers making it difficult for the chemical to reach and destroy the bacteria.
2. The presence of grease giving the bacteria a protective barrier.

Finally, it may be observed that a disadvantage of chemical disinfectants is that if they are over-concentrated they may affect tissues and heavy concentration may have to be avoided on account of those with sensitive skins.

Personal hygiene

The foregoing factors which have been concerned with the food itself, its protection against dirt, insects, vermin and the importance of having clean premises, equipment and the like, are clearly of great importance. Equally clearly they depend to a large extent on the constant interest and vigilance of the human being working in the kitchen. The chef, the caterer and their staff of cooks and kitchen hands must be concerned to see that all the measures to promote hygiene are observed effectively.

Yet perhaps the most important form of precaution is that in which the operative himself renders himself safe by personal measures of cleanliness. Contamination is so often, indeed almost invariably, caused by human agency that it would not be exaggerating to say that the human being is the greatest potential danger in the kitchen.

There is, however, another aspect of personal hygiene which is of importance. This aspect is the comfort and well-being of the individual at work. It is always an added point to stress that many of the measures of hygiene and cleanliness which protect the customer and others, also promote health and a sense of well-being in the person practising them.

The type of dress to be worn and the measures to be taken in keeping it clean and in good order have already been dealt with in this book. It need not be further stressed that work in many sections of the kitchen induces perspiration, the gathering of cooking odours (fat frying for example) on the person and that the daily bath or shower is doubly necessary in the case of a kitchen worker as is the daily change of underclothes.

Care of the feet can make a vast difference to the efficiency and contentment of the kitchen worker. Apart from wearing properly fitting shoes maintained in decent repair, socks should be given equal attention. Over-tight socks can cause foot discomfort and damage just as ill-fitting shoes. They should be changed at least once a day and whilst regular bathing and showering is essential, many hotel and restaurant employees have found it advisable not to soften the feet by prolonged soaking in water but to keep them as dry as possible even using surgical spirit and talcum powder for hygiene purposes. Cooks and other members of the kitchen staff should not hesitate to seek proper advice about foot care from qualified chiropodists and foot clinics.

Although the cook wears a white cap, the hair preferably should be kept short and regularly washed.

Care of the mouth and teeth are also vital to the health and well-being of the cook. Some mouth infections (one thinks of Vincent's disease) are highly contagious and expert advice should be sought if there is any puffiness or soreness of the gums or a tendency for the gums to bleed. Whilst it may not be necessary to remind adult staff of ordinary mouth hygiene rules, young workers and apprentices should certainly be made aware of the importance of regularly cleaning the teeth after meals and on retiring at night.

In regard to the maintenance of health generally, it is certainly worth stressing again that whilst the cook must taste frequently for seasoning that he must guard strictly against picking at food and eating except at proper meal times. A great deal of indigestion and more serious stomach troubles have undoubtedly been caused by failure to take proper time for meals and through eating on duty in a hurried way. Whilst the cook must be temperate in eating he must also be temperate in drinking. Over-indulgence in both food and drink is usually accompanied by a reduced vigilance in other directions including the proper maintenance of good standards of hygiene.

Staff should constantly be reminded about the importance of clean personal habits. These include, particularly, washing the hands after visiting the toilet. Such reminders should not be merely verbal but supported by notices (in or near appropriate places) and, even better, by bold slogans or posters.

Final thoughts on the subject of hygiene in the kitchen, in the hotel and catering industry generally and of the personal hygiene of staff within the industry should certainly not be one of mere concern with meeting statutory requirements alone. It is of great social importance that all employees in the industry, particularly employees like chefs, caterers and others in executive positions, should develop a professional conscience and a professional code in ensuring clean food and clean practices. This should go further than the meeting of minimum legal requirements.

In professions concerned with health like medicine, nursing, branches of science, dentistry and so on, the wearing of white is first of all a matter of functional necessity but it has also become symbolic to the general public of a concept of clinical cleanliness. White dress in such professions is a badge which conveys confidence to the public and pride to the wearer. Such an approach involving this pride and conveying this feeling of confidence must be actively pursued by those who wear the white dress of the professional kitchen.

The approach to hygiene by the chef and his staff must be interested and positive. The chef must try to convey both to his apprentices and older workers that hygiene in the kitchen is not a matter of observing dreary regulations but a vital part of culinary aesthetics, health and happiness. The chef of tomorrow, if not of today, must certainly regard hygiene as one of his major professional responsibilities and one which he is glad to accept.

14 The menu and menu making

It is said that the written bill of fare originated in Britain when it was realised that dining could be made more enjoyable by anticipating the dishes to come and by tuning appetite according to the various courses. Whether, in fact, the British bill of fare came before the continental menu or whether it occurred first in Chinese, Egyptian or other early cultures need not worry today's chefs. For the professional man of the kitchen as for his customer, the menu is as permanent a feature of dining as the heat with which the food is cooked.

Yet the menu to the chef has a significance differing from that which it has for his customers.

To the customer the purpose of the menu is virtually unchanged from that which it had for the mediaeval diner who may first have consulted one in England. It tells the customer the scope and order of the meal. To a gourmet it may have a significance approaching that of poetry; to a more matter-of-fact eater its importance may be even as mundane as indicating merely the price that will ultimately be paid for the food served. But for both these extremes and for those customers of the hotel or restaurant who fall between the extremes, the menu must fulfil its function of informing the eater accurately about the food to be offered him. The chef, hotelier and restaurateur must not lose sight of this central fact. Whatever the language in which the menu is composed, whether it be in traditional and classic French or in the language of the country, its terms should be precise and accurate and intended to illuminate rather than to obscure.

Kitchen blue-print

For the man of the kitchen, however, the menu is the summary or digest of all his activities. The maître chef in composing a menu is therefore not only producing information about a meal for the benefit of his clientele but is evolving a blue-print or basic plan on which the kitchen operation will develop. Thus, clarity and accuracy are as important to chefs as to the customers. The various parties receiving advance copies of the menus will plan their work according to its requirements. From their point of view as much as from the customers' it would be disastrous if the language was ambiguous or lacking in meaning.

Menu jargon

The making of dishes and the language of menus are, if not the same thing, inextricably linked together. Professional hotel and restaurant cookery of Western civilisation has been developed largely under French influence yet deriving the items for its repertoire from a variety of sources. Terms which are now firmly within the tradition of hotel kitchens may be derived from French domestic, bourgeois and regional cookery or have been borrowed from alien areas, such as peasant soups from Italy, peppery stews from Hungary, plainly cooked dishes from England, cold items and hors d'œuvres from Russia and Scandinavia or sweetmeats from Turkey and the Middle East. By whatever way, items like minestrone, borstch, goulash and Baklava have found their way into the international hotel menu, they have all in the process been refined and adapted in the hands of skilled chefs of the French tradition.

In creating dishes to a high and uniform standard it became obvious to the serious craftsmen of the kitchen and to discriminating diners who travelled not only from hotel to hotel but from country to country that it was of the greatest importance that dishes should be recognisable by name, by content and by appearance wherever they were served. Hence, the evolution of menu language which, though apparently French is both more than and less than French in that it is virtually a technical and artistic jargon. The names of the dishes do not merely describe the central item but indicate to the knowledgeable the method of cooking and accompanying sauces and garnishes.

Comparison with other crafts, trades and sports has been made before but it is, perhaps, worth recalling that, albeit in a simpler way, Italian has been used as a universal musical code, that English has international usage for many sports and that a dead language has been retained for its use in pharmaceutical descriptions.

French, in short, has not been imposed on the menu for showy or pretentious reasons but has naturally been used to codify dishes because of the vital part that French practitioners have played in developing professional cookery.

At this stage let us examine the way in which menu language has grown and how it may be used and interpreted.

Basic food vocabulary

It goes without saying that the central factor of menu writing or menu understanding is a good vocabulary of French words for food and cookery processes. For example, words like bœuf for beef and braisé for braised, appear regularly and frequently in menus both simple and complex. Without learning a comprehensive range of French words for fish, various cuts of meat, poultry, game, vegetables, fruits, cereals and other commodities the menu is bound to remain something of a mystery. But that is only a beginning. It must be remembered that in one of the cookery repertoires (Saulnier's *Repertoire de la Cuisine*) most used by working chefs, more than 350 methods of serving sole are listed and that other sections are equally formidable. Thus to learn, for example, that the French word for sole is the same as the English one is but a first step amongst many that must be taken if some of the more important of these 350 sole dishes are to be understood.

Of course, no one—not even the most eminent of chefs—is expected to memorise the meaning of all the thousands of 'classic' French dishes. What a competent chef will aim to do is to recognise the more commonly met items, be completely familiar with the French for principal commodities and be able to interpret and use the reference works and repertoires at his hand.

Describing cookery processes

The importance of knowing the French words for basic cookery processes for menu compilation and interpretation purposes has been stressed already. In addition to straightforward descriptive terms, such as rôti, sauté, poêlé and the like, there must be included in this category phrases which indicate not an elaborate garnish and sauce but a simple mode of dressing or serving. In pommes sautées the sautéing of the potatoes describes the cooking process of 'jumping' or tossing in shallow fat, in rognons sautés (kidneys sauté) or bœuf sauté, the word takes on an added significance because when meat is sautéed it is invariably 'finished' by cohering with sauce, cream, butter, wines or a combination of these items so that the final dish is not at all of the character of the dry, shallow-fried sauté potatoes. Differences of this kind where the same word appears to describe a somewhat different end product can cause scepticism in the uninitiated but really serves to emphasise that some understanding of cookery processes is needed for proper menu interpretation.

Besides the example of sauté potatoes, however, could be placed many others much more straightforward and where straight translation will immediately yield the meaning. Étuvée used in conjunction with, say, peas or the innumerable cases where vegetables are au beurre are of this kind. In this group, therefore, it would be true to say that menu understanding requires little more than knowledge of French food terms and some acquaintance with cookery.

National descriptions

Not only, however, are cooking processes described straight-forwardly but are sometimes linked with the country in which that style of cooking has predominated. À l'anglaise inevitably means extremely simple cooking but according to context might apply to plain boiling or the traditional English way of dressing roast meat. In other cases, too, the style of cooking or dressing will vary according to the food with which the designation is linked. Thus, à la française with peas, i.e., petits pois à la française denotes peas stewed with lettuce and onion, though one will obviously not expect to find these vegetable ingredients in a rice pudding à la française in which the French touch is achieved with beaten eggs. Hongroise will indicate the use of paprika and Hungarian methods. Italienne suggests pasta accompaniments and Italian-style cooking and so on.

Association words

A second category of dishes are somewhat less simple unless one has the key to the convention. These are the kind which though not simply a descriptive French version of a cooking process still yield clues to those with a knowledge of French and have a knowledge of commodities and their places of origin. Such dishes might be categorised as those using 'association' words. One of the simplest examples is in those dishes where 'association' words indicate a mixture of vegetables as an ingredient to or accompaniment of a dish. Thus, potage cultivateur or potage santé amongst soups readily disclose their meaning. In entrées of, say, lamb cutlets or other small cuts the words aux primeurs or printanière indicate the presence of first spring vegetables and bouquetière, jardinière and similar words show where an assortment of trimmed vegetables, irrespective of season, will provide the garnish.

Indicating shape and cut of garnish

Less easy unless initiated are ways of describing vegetable garnishes by virtue of their cut. Paysanne, indicating a 'rough' slicing of vegetables which has now lost its original peasant 'roughness' and has become as neat as any other, may be fairly easy as will be macedoine. It may nowadays be forgotten that these little cubes, whether of fruit or vegetables, were named after the cluster of small islands comprising Macedonia, but macedoine has been used for so long that it is generally readily recognised. So, too, julienne where the fine strips are known by this name to many, even outside the kitchen. Less so, however, are the tiny cubes of brunoise (diced vegetable). Monte Carlo garnish where the cut is intended to simulate coins is also an 'association' description easily memorised once known.

Geographical clues

Some 'association' words seem less straightforward because they require some geographical or horticultural knowledge. Of this sort potage Argenteuil is a good example. This soup and other dishes with the Argenteuil designation involve asparagus—strictly with the especially luscious asparagus originally developed in the Argenteuil area. Similarly Périgord indicates the presence of truffle, Florentine an accompaniment of spinach, and Chantilly the addition of whipped cream, all because of the association of a commodity with a town or geographical area.

The chef and menu names

It is, of course, obvious that whatever the origin of the dish and however it came to be named, that the chef has a great deal to do with the dish and its place on the menu. Even dishes derived from provincial and bourgeois cookery, as has been remarked, undergo some tidying up or refinement both from the point of view of the cook and the menu composer. Some dishes, however, owe a great deal more to the chef than this. There are two categories of dish in the naming of which the chef is directly involved. First, there is the dish which he himself invents or perfects and which is named after him and secondly there is the dish which because it has been derived and perfected by a chef is given its name by the chef. This second category is, of course, capable of further sub-division because the great chefs of the past were inventive men and the multitude of their creations were given names usually according to some general idea or concept. It may, therefore, be more convenient to consider the approach to dish-naming by chefs by their sections.

Dishes named after chefs, however, form a small division of their own and it is, perhaps, an indication of a surprising modesty and lack of flamboyance that has made this a relatively small group. Typical of this kind of dish is filet de sole Dugléré in which the name of the master chef is permanently associated with the dish of his creation. Examples of other dishes named after chefs either because they invented it or to honour them are, Faisan Carême, Tournedos Vatel and cold Paupiettes de Sole Escoffier.

Historic occasions

Poulet sauté Marengo is often cited as typical of a dish both honouring and arising from an historic occasion. Shortage of ingredients on the eve of battle prompted inspired improvisation and earned the dish a lasting place in classic cookery. Another battle, Creçy, is linked with carrots which apparently abounded near the scene of the fighting.

Naming dishes after patrons

Having created or distinctly adapted a dish sufficiently to give it a new individuality, the chef and restaurateur may have given it a name which he hoped would not only distinguish it on the menus of his own establishment but ultimately earn a lasting place in the culinary repertoire. Chefs of the past as of the present were, of course, stimulated in their inventiveness by either the special occasion or by the special customer or by a combination of both. Thus it is that menu names have been inspired by such considerations.

Honouring gourmets

In the Middle Ages persisting until late into the nineteenth century it was, perhaps, the male gourmet who inspired the creativeness of chefs and consequently prompted the naming of dishes. As evidence of the way in which the more things change the more they remain the same thing, one may note the association between the rich and prosperous men of affairs and richness and prosperity at the table. Many dishes 'à la financière' cloak with anonymity the financier whose gastronomic interest had influenced the chef. In other cases the financier emerges by name immortalised in dishes such as Sole Colbert. Here the dish derives its name from Jean Baptiste Colbert, the 'father' of France's financial system, yet whose fame as a minister in the seventeenth century holds its own with difficulty against his reputation as a patron of science, literature and art—including gastronomy. Kettner, in his *Book of the Table*, avers that 'the Sole of Colbert is now of a surety more to mankind than all his statesmanship'.

Sole Colbert was amongst the recipes listed in the works of Antonin Carême, chef to the Prince Regent, and the recipe is annotated 'Sole, from the inventor'. This clearly indicates that Carême himself does not claim the credit for this dish but whether one may further assume that Colbert himself had done more than inspire it is less certain.

Talleyrand and Richlieu are prominent amongst other famous statesmen-gastronomes to give their names to a number of dishes.

Though not a statesman, Brillat Savarin was of some prominence in the legal profession but in his case his fame rests indubitably on his gastronomical masterpiece *Physiologie du Gout* and though this is a philosophical rather than a practical work, he describes at least one method of cooking and certainly provides evidence of a more detailed occupation about matters than mere inspiration. The Savarin sponge mix clearly owes its name to this man of food. He, perhaps, more than Colbert, typifies the 'man of the world' figure who, though not with certainty a practical culinary creator, may well have had an influence more than inspirational.

Artists, men of letters and composers

Because of the affinity between the arts one not infrequently finds painters who have written well, writers who have painted well and this mélange of talent not infrequently embraces cookery and dining also.

It was not merely to honour his musical compositions that dishes such as Tournedos Rossini were named after the great Italian man of music. He was active in table matters. We have besides Tournedos Rossini, Omelette Arnold Bennett and Œufs sur la Plat Meyerbeer. Victor Hugo, Verdi and Rabelais are amongst many from letters and music to give their names to food. Alexandre Dumas, Père, even essayed to enter the ranks of professional cookery writers with the *Dictionnaire de la Cuisine*, but like the English journalist, Sala, whose book the *Thorough Good Cook* has more literary than practical merit, would have been better advised to have remained the influence behind the scene rather than a would-be chef.

Whilst gourmets and rich bon-vivants and financier food fanciers may have provided active menu inspiration in the sense that they were informed and intellectual consumers there is, of course, a wider category of those who have given their names to dishes on the menu. Royalty, statesmen and politicians, generals and those who gained the kind of fame which has evoked the admiration of their fellow-men including chefs. In some cases the naming of a dish after a famous personage may have an association additional to or distinct from an act of dedication or homage. It is, of course, to be expected that Henry IV of France's famous remark about a chicken in the pot should have caused the linking of his name with dishes mirroring this concept.

Not only are individuals linked with dishes but categories of individuals (sometimes where one particular person had been originally in mind) also provided and still provide dish designation inspiration for chefs. Hence the many dishes à la Royale, à la Princesse, Maréchal, Cardinal, most of which were brought into being on occasions or functions when an eminent royalty, soldier or churchman were to be present or were to be honoured.

À la maison. Chefs and the general public alike no longer favour menu designations which refer vaguely to the 'style of the house' and 'in the fashion of the chef' as being altogether too vague. Furthermore, there is a lingering suspicion that such designations permit an elasticity of execution that may mislead. This suspicion may or may not be justified but certainly the 'fashion of the house' has caused the permanent inclusion of several famous dishes in the culinary register.

Even before the days of hotels, Soyer devised in London's Reform Club, a mode of cooking and garnishing breadcrumbed, lamb cutlets which have now enduring fame as Côtelettes d'Agneau à la Reforme. Where the à la maison has become a specific maison and method, all valid objections can be over-ruled. Pommes Delmonico, Salad Waldorf Astoria, Pommes Voisin, all such dishes named after famous establishments in which they reached perfection comprise a respectable and distinctive section in our catalogue of dishes.

Feminine menu influence

One of the significant parts played by the great chef, Escoffier, and the great hotelier, Ritz, was their contribution in persuading respectable women as distinct from demi-mondaines into dining in the restaurants of hotels. Ritz created the settings in which this social change could take place and Escoffier led the spearhead movement which acknowledged women as having taste, discernment and a right to be catered for at intimate dinners and on more formal public occasions. During those early days of the twentieth century and even after the death of King Edward VII, women became steadily more articulate in menu matters and exerted ever-increasing influence. This influence was typified by women of the theatre, opera house and concert platform who became personal friends of Escoffier and his more eminent colleagues in the kitchen. Sarah Bernhardt and Nelly Melba not only gave their names to dishes which have been created as testimony to their artistry but also actively concerned themselves with food. Many of the leading feminine personalities of the Escoffier era may be credited with some gastronomic knowledge over and above their simple power as artists to inspire the chef. The names of Rachel, la Belle Otero, Mary Garden, Duse, Bernhardt and Melba reveal on the feminine side what names such as Hugo, Bennett, Dumas, Rossini do on the masculine— creative artists who have inspired good food and interested themselves in it.

It would, of course, be wrong to think that the feminine influence prevailed only towards the end of the Victorian era for though there was a distinctive and almost spectacular emergence of women into gastronomy at the turn of the century and after, there were other periods when women, or at least one or two of them, had managed to make their mark. It is true that they were not perhaps quite so 'respectable' for it was a mistress of a French monarch, the Dubarry, who not only gave her name to food but who also is credited with promoting the standing of women cooks through the creation of that 'invisible' culinary order, the Cordon Bleu. It is, perhaps, ironic that the dish with which her name is chiefly associated, i.e., Crème Dubarry, is believed to have been associated with the whimsical concept of cauliflower sprigs being comparable with the powdered, white wigs of the Dubarry epoch.

The foregoing indicates but does not exhaust the influences which have been brought to bear on the naming of dishes. They will serve to show, perhaps, that though sometimes fanciful, they have seldom been completely without reason or without logic.

Menus in French

Whether, in fact, more modest establishments should base their cooking on the French tradition and whether their menus should continue to be composed in French has been hotly debated within the hotel and catering industry for many years. Few would dispute, however, that cuisine at international, tourist level is unlikely to relinquish its tradition of menu composing in French because this tradition is rooted, not in mere convention, but in the whole art of professional cookery. This language though puzzling to the customer is meaningful to the trained chef and of the greatest value and convenience to him.

Menu planning considerations

Whatever the language in which the menu is written, however, the chef de cuisine or caterer will have to take into consideration a number of vital factors. These may be summarised as follows:

(1) Cost and price policy.
(2) Season and availability of supplies.
(3) Type of customer.
(4) Menu balance.
(5) Skills and capacity of kitchen staff and the size of the brigade.
(6) Plant and equipment available for cooking.
(7) Publicity and business promotion aspect of the menu.

There are two types of menu: à la carte and table d'hôte. The à la carte is a larger selection of dishes each independently priced from which a customer can compose his own meal by choosing 'from the card'. Naturally, à la carte selection by the customer may involve waiting some minutes for dishes like grills and sautés unless choice has been made in advance. The table d'hôte literally the host's (or hotelier's) table, is the set menu at fixed price with much less choice or even no choice at all.

The points listed above which are not necessarily in order of importance, must be given careful thought by the menu planner but these points themselves will have varied application according to whether the menu is for breakfast, lunch or dinner and according to whether the meal is one for a function or for routine table d'hôte and à la carte service.

As the art of composing a menu might be considered as an outward manifestation of the whole art of cookery and catering it is obvious that a whole volume might be devoted to menu planning. Certainly, many sections of this Manual deal with topics which have relevance to the bill of fare. Whilst this chapter cannot deal exhaustively with the menu maker's art which should be founded on a comprehensive knowledge of cookery and the kitchen it may, perhaps, usefully pinpoint some of the more important factors. As a convenient way of examining menu-making, further consideration might be given to the seven points already listed.

Cost and price policy

It was sometimes thought that the food cost was almost the sole price factor in the meal and certainly the most important one but most caterers today are agreed that the cost of food is strongly linked with the cost of labour. Costing and pricing policies may, therefore, be increasingly determined by the management who, because of their concern with labour, may make decisions relating to the use of processed and pre-portioned foods.

When labour was less scarce and less well paid its significance was less marked and many chefs were left free to base their menu on a food cost basis only. It seems unlikely that this simple, single consideration can ever determine the menu plan as it formerly did; but at this point it need only be stressed that the modern menu-maker will be primarily concerned with devising a menu to produce the desired profit. Whilst his management may have taken the labour and overhead factors into prior consideration (thus leaving the chef or caterer with only the food prices to take into consideration from day to day) it would be a naive caterer indeed who did not recognise that food alone was only part of the menu cost.

Portion control

It is, however, the part with which many chefs and caterers may continue primarily to concern themselves. In creating a bill of fare the chef will consider food in relation to the size portions which are to be served and the weight of the cuts of meat, fish and poultry must be clearly established (even if subject to regular review) and the portion size of even the less costly elements must not only be pre-determined but carefully controlled.

Price stability

One of the cost aspects in à la carte menu composing may well be the maintenance of price stability over a period and chefs and caterers have to give consideration to fixing prices for relatively cheaper items such as potatoes which give sufficient margin not only to cushion against fluctuations in the cost of that vegetable itself but also in variations of price which the chef may have to pay for other items like meat, fish and poultry which will accompany it. Price or cost balance has also to be achieved in table d'hôte menus or in the menus when they are part of an all-in en pension tariff so that awareness of prevailing prices, market gluts and shortages and seasonability from the price standpoint are matters of prime importance to the chef.

The accounting system of the hotel, restaurant or catering establishment will be designed to reveal ultimate profitability or otherwise of the food service but it cannot be stressed too emphatically that records and accounting systems can do little more than measure performance and reveal where action is needed. Measures to put right loss of profitability may be many and varied but correcting common faults such as uneconomic or erratic menu planning must be the kitchen's responsibility. Supervision by the chef and the harnessing of his staff's culinary skills constitute the practical action which follows accounting revelations of lack of profitability.

In addition to warning tocsins sounded by the records there are also warning signals of a practical kind even closer to him that the chef or caterer must heed when dealing with his menu. Such signs are to be found in larder left-overs, accumulation of stocks in the dry goods stores, plate waste and dishes which do not 'go'. The study of these points must support a profitable kitchen operation in addition to a positive policy of featuring dishes or creating dishes that can attract custom and promote business.

Season and availability

Seasonal gluts particularly of vegetables are probably less important to the chef catering from a cost aspect than in former times because of the developments that have taken place in marketing and distributing processed goods.

Nevertheless, in countless operations maximum advantage of what is abundant and fresh will continue to be taken to gain a cost advantage.

Over and above this consideration, however, is the important one of gastronomic appeal. Those who live in the temperate north are aware of the interest of changing weather which accompanies the passing of each season of the year. The rhythm of spring, summer, autumn and winter becomes bound up with the pattern of living. It is not far-fetched to suggest that nature's arrangement of the foods that come to perfection at various times of the year has significance in terms of both health and enjoyment. The strawberries of early summer, chestnuts of winter, the tender vegetables of spring are anticipated early by diners of discrimination irrespective of price. Even though new and more perfect means of capturing freshness in processed or preserved products are achieved so that what once could only be savoured during a few weeks of the year in its natural form may be held virtually in that state for a twelvemonth it is unlikely that seasonability or seasonal variations in menu can be abandoned. Light, cool, fruit desserts will be demanded in hot weather and substantial stews will have their major appeal when winds are bleak. The wise chef must continue to recognise seasonal change in menu making for gastronomic and nutritional reasons even when factors of cost and availability no longer arise so acutely.

Consideration of season in menu making is not, therefore, simply a matter of exploiting foods that are in season and are available and cheap but of weaving into the fabric of the year's bill of fare a rhythm and variety of foods that have appeal because they suit the conditions of the time and the human instinct for variety. The kitchen staff must continue to know much about the foods that are at their best in their own locality and in their own country but also must be aware of the seasons in other lands. The modern chef must pay heed to the fruit crops of South Africa and California as well as to the yields of the orchards of Kent. There is nothing complex about designing a menu in sympathy with season but simple though it is it demands a knowledge of food and an instinct for balance.

Processed food

In terms of kitchen organisation for which the menu is the blue-print, it has been noted that the principal effects of using processed

foods is in the allocation of labour, space, storage facilities and equipment for less space is needed for handling vegetables and fruit, fish,
meat and poultry. This can lead to the concentration of certain kitchen
activities, particularly in the larder. When vegetables, fish, meat and
poultry are supplied in processed form, the chef's need to allocate this
work to different sections diminishes. Thus the work of the kitchen
staff can become increasingly concerned with final cooking and presentation. Many chefs who at first deplored certain products because
they believed them 'artificial' or that they reduced the chef's role now
have a different view because they recognise that usually only the basic
chores have been eliminated and that the top skills of cooking,
'finishing' and garnishing still remain in the hands of the chef. Indeed,
they permit even greater care and concentration on the finer points and
can help widen the scope of menus. But if 'ready-to-use' foods are to
form an increasingly dominant section of restaurant food supplies, the
problem of individuality in their presentation will be of major concern
to many caterers and chefs, particularly where 'popular' priced menus
are concerned. The need to maintain a menu's individuality can be met
by the development of recipes and dishes based either on the suggestions
and pointers provided by the food manufacturers or on the ingenuity
and skill of the chef himself or on a combination of both. Chefs and
their customers recognise that the avoidance of sterile standardisation is
essential though it is recognised that the essence of culinary traditions
has been to devise certain methods of food preparation and cookery in
order to ensure that a similarity of presentation was achieved.

Type of customer

In many establishments menus both à la carte and table d'hôte require
to be of wide enough appeal to meet the demands of a clientele ranging
from babies to octogenarians and designed to satisfy the finicky
appetite of the semi-invalid or the robust hunger of the sportsman on
holiday. The chef in the de luxe hotel has traditionally designed menus
of such great scope that they have embraced all possible kinds of
customer with a wide margin as far as nutritional needs and the satisfaction of hunger is concerned. In other kitchens, whether in restaurants, hotels or in catering in schools, canteens or hospitals, knowledge
of the type of customer to be catered for or the type of customer it is
desired to attract are of paramount importance. The immature palates
and larger appetites of schoolboys and schoolgirls impose menu-
making conditions quite different from those which confront the
caterer responsible for the meals of a large office dining room in which
women secretarial staff might predominate.

Considering the customer involves thought being given to a number of points which include:

1. Nutritional considerations (with which the appropriate chapters in this Manual deal).
2. Meeting local tastes.
3. Attracting custom and promoting business.

Such points require no great elaboration here, but it is as well to remember constantly that the menu makers' own tastes and culinary scope may sometimes have to be restricted rather than expanded in deference to determined customer conservatism. One chef caterer of great experience, resourcefulness and attack sorrowfully abandoned an attempt to introduce interesting plats du jour and early suppers of modest price but classical characteristics in a restaurant in which the 'plaice and chips high-tea' had been a money-spinner for years. In this north-west of England town one or two new establishments with an adventurous approach might have succeeded in attracting a new following and a new clientele but business could as easily be lost in launching too abruptly new-style menus in an established business involving too violent a departure from customers' known demands.

There are times when the chef caterer may deplore his customers' tastes and he should never cease to seek to educate them unobtrusively and progressively. There is little doubt, however, that in many instances this can best be achieved by: (*a*) Preparing, cooking and serving as superbly as possible, that which is known and which the customer likes. (*b*) Gradually introducing minor variants on an optional basis. (*c*) Occasionally introducing new items only as an alternative to proven favourites.

Violent assaults on customers' dining habits are seldom successful in either commercial or welfare catering.

Menu balance

Much is heard about balancing a menu but unhappily this may mean different things to different people. For the dietician it involves nutritional balance, for the hotel accountant cost balance may be all important and to the chef gastronomic balance involving colour, texture and flavour will be implied.

Nutrition is separately dealt with in Chapter 15 and the need to achieve satisfactory balance in this respect is acknowledged to be of over-riding importance at whatever level of catering. Achieving economic balance is also vital even when in some forms of welfare catering a subsidy may be used to achieve it. But as André Simon once observed, 'man is not a test-tube' and in this he echoed something similar to Ude, the great chef of Victorian times, who averred that cookery could not be done like pharmacy. It might equally well be said that man is not merely a unit in an accounting system. Thus the chef's approach is mindful of cost and nutrition but it is gastronomic balance and appeal to taste which predominate in his case. Such balance and appeal are not only important factors in themselves but are necessary also to the achievement of success in nutritional and economic balance.

Gastronomic balance in menu making demands from the chef a wide knowledge of foods in their raw state and a wide repertoire of dishes in their prepared and cooked form. It also calls for the development of an 'instinct' for putting food components together which can only be compared with an instinct for other forms of creation. Composing an essay, a song, a picture, a letter depends on craft skills but also on a vital interest in and sympathy with, the subject. So it is with menu composition. Nevertheless, a number of tangible factors are involved. These include: (*a*) *Colour.* An experienced menu composer can spoil his bill of fare by colour monotony. The appearance in sequence of dishes, for example, in which brown is predominant can induce boredom in the diner even though the dishes, individually, are good. In the same way, a cream soup should not be followed by a blanquette or fricassée and even when it comes to the dessert course involving sweet rather than savoury flavours, a colour change is desirable. Agreeable colour contrast is not, however, solely a question of having one course varying from another but of achieving appropriate colour composition in the principal courses of the meal and where more than one item is featured. It is relatively easy to introduce the green of leaf vegetables and the tints of root vegetables from white, yellow to the ruddier tints of carrot and beetroot but sometimes the colour effect of potatoes and these second vegetables are strongly conditioned by cooking and the menu writer must be mindful of the colour values of plainly boiled potatoes as against those en robe, deep fried or rissolé. Many classic garnishes automatically take care of such problems yet at the same time it is surprising how often there is a failure to exploit to the full the visual virtues of food in appetite creation.

Texture and flavour

It could reasonably be advanced that considerations of texture and flavour might be dealt with separately because each factor has its own value. Most practical men of food, however, regard the two as inextricably bound together. Just as the gelatinous body of good soup stock is a necessary vehicle for the effective carrying of flavour so generally is the texture and consistency of food linked with its taste and seasoning. In writing a menu it is, therefore, vital to provide not only changes of colour and taste within each course and from course to course but also to provide variations of consistency and texture in the various preparations. At its most extreme the faults in providing a broth followed by a stew accompanied by mashed potatoes and macedoine of vegetables to be completed by a rice pudding is obvious. The general effect of 'sloppy' consistency is exaggerated in such an example though unfortunately such menus are by no means unknown. However good each individual item might be, to assemble components of similar consistency and texture can only tend to create boredom for the palate.

The question of flavour contrasts may again be regarded as too obvious to dwell on yet there are many pitfalls awaiting even flavour-conscious chefs. Whilst few would deny mulligatawny soup a place on luncheon menus, its strong flavours make the choice of what is to follow one to which thought must be given and there is little doubt that delicately poached fish, for example, could hardly hope to make much impact following the curry-stuff of such a preliminary.

Within the courses traditional accompaniments and classic compositions whether they are as simple as apple sauce and roast pork or as refined as lamb cutlets Reform often solve, or partially solve, the flavour contrast problem. Emollient sauces with fatless, white fish, sharp sauces with fatty meats, poultry and game are elementary flavour designs but the exercise becomes more complex when several courses need to be woven together. Generally, the menu creator will seek to awaken appetite in the opening courses and, if the menu is to be long, progress gradually from the milder flavours of the pasta, egg, fish items to the more robust impact of meat entrées and roasts. Often, too, the partnership between the food and accompanying wine will be a problem which will require nice judgment from the chef as much as from the maître d'hotel and flavour and texture will have much to do with the way in which the food and drink can be happily married.

Capacity of the brigade

It is one thing to compose a menu which reads well and as a fragment of literature, satisfactorily evokes a flow of gastric juices. It is quite another thing to translate the menu into reality with the aid of staff and kitchen. The greatest establishments operating a full partie system will seldom be limited by considerations of craft skills and even of cooking plant and equipment. In such cases it will rather be a matter of the maître chef exploiting to the full the talents of the 'stars' of his team and high-lighting specialities perfected by them.

There seems little doubt, however, that chefs de cuisine and caterers must become increasingly accustomed to planning menus requiring smaller but more efficient kitchen brigades. They must be prepared to give thought to the demands of the actual meal service even more than to the preparation of the food in the kitchen for there can be no ignoring the trends implicit in the development and use of processed and 'convenience' foods towards speciality restaurants and the greater emphasis on cooking food in the general restaurant area itself. 'Seen' service, as the latter is usually termed, is linked with the availability of foods in a ready-to-use presentable form and involving new deployment and usage of staff. In more modest operations and especially in catering establishments other than hotels and restaurants the menu which is to be the blue-print for the kitchen must, in any case, be one completely adapted to the available skills. One has seen only too often the utter folly of introducing on to a canteen menu hotel-type dishes which have quite defeated the resources of the good, plain cook. Better by far to settle for a decently made shortcrust than to demand puff pastry from staff lacking confidence and experience in the latter's preparation. Simple dishes well finished and attractively served that are well within the competence of the cooks must always be chosen in preference to pretentious items which have not been part of the team's experience.

Equipment

As in the case of staff, the large and elaborate establishment, whether it be an hotel or a well-equipped industrial canteen, may be immune from real strains on the resources of its equipment. The problem may simply be making the maximum use of an abundant provision. In many operations, however, kitchen area and equipment limitations will become major factors when planning a menu. Thought will have to be given to avoiding over-heavy loads on the oven at any one time and balancing the modes of cooking so that usage of facilities for steaming, boiling, frying, roasting and so on all off-set each other.

Staff and equipment, whether the kitchen is working on a true partie system or not, are closely related. It is certain that to create a workable menu, the chef should have a close knowledge of the capacity of both his staff and his plant.

Promoting business with the menu

The foregoing features in menu composing constitute some of the main and practical elements with which the chef or caterer has to contend. They are on the whole matters which involve the staff and the kitchen. There is, in fact, in all these elements the simple concept of satisfying the customer. The menu balanced in all the ways that have been mentioned should reconcile the potential of the kitchen and its brigade with the factor of customer satisfaction. The good menu, however, can, and should, do much more. It should function as an appetite creator, a bait for customers, a talking point, and a fragment of publicity. It should read well, look well and have a positive power of attraction. Some of its characteristics such as printing, style and design may be beyond the responsibility of the chef but the chef and the caterer must be associated closely with the positive possibilities of the menu in promoting business.

If, for example, the menu is composed in classic style and in French, thought may be given under certain circumstances to the desirability of supplying succinct menu notes in English which would at once define the dishes and also help to create interest and appetite for them. If the menu is to be composed in English in the case of simpler hotels and non-commercial catering enterprises, then the chef and caterer must collaborate with the management in providing suitable designations which go further than 'roast beef and two veg'. Some English (perhaps more particularly American) menus have tended, perhaps, to go too far in flowery descriptions but certainly there can be nothing but good in indicating precisely the cut, origin and the method of cooking meat as in a menu item like 'Roast Shoulder of Southdown Lamb'.

In Anglicising menus it is always a vexing problem to deal with straightforward cookery processes like meunière. Many consider that it is perfectly reasonable to maintain well-known descriptive designations of this kind on a British bill of fare and find nothing incongruous in, for example, a description such as Poached Fillet of Cod Mornay. Others would insist on changing the description to Poached Fillet of Cod coated with Cheese Sauce. It is apparent that attempts to translate menu descriptions usually involve lengthening the number of words. Controversy will obviously not cease in regard to what is best and it can only be urged that within the policy determined by the individual hotelier the approach should be consistent. One rule regarding British dishes on menus should surely be that when they are distinctively British such as Scotch Broth, Lancashire Hotpot or Roast Sirloin of Beef with Yorkshire Pudding they are rendered in their own language in preference to translations into French. This is consistent with featuring specialities of other countries such as Osso Bucco, for example, in the language of their country of origin.

The literary aspect of menu writing as distinct from the technical and gastronomical aspects of its construction are important in promoting business. Like much else in the hotel and catering industry the task demands good taste, good sense and discernment if it is to be done well. It is no accident that chefs who have been good at it have been men of broad culture as well as culinary experts.

Type of menu

It is obvious that the menu as the whole basis of the kitchen operation is a subject of almost inexhaustible possibility. Hermann Senn devoted a substantial work to the subject and it is significant that his *Menu Book and Register of Dishes* was originally called in its first edition, *Practical Gastronomy*. The chef and the caterer must have recourse to works like Senn's and to Saulnier's *Repertoire de la Cuisine* and to culinary and gastronomical textbooks generally to nudge their memory and stimulate their thinking when preparing menus. There is not merely no disgrace in using such works of reference but on the contrary the skill with which an experienced chef can exploit his reference library will often be a measure of his success.

In view of the foregoing, therefore, it will be appreciated that no one work need be regarded as exhaustive on the subject of menu making for the type of menu to be composed and the special occasion for which they may be required are almost limitless. A few notes on present trends may, however, be of use.

It has to be borne in mind that menus, like meal times and cookery itself, have been subjected to constant change due to social and economic pressures. Fashions and vogues have come and gone so that probing past practices may often offer little reward other than scholarly satisfaction.

The enormous bills of fare of Regency days with many dishes listed on the menu appearing simultaneously at table are, today, of but academic interest. The long feasts of Victorian days which persisted in the Edwardian era are almost as forgotten as mediaeval banquets, though as war-time scarcities dwindle further into the background there are some moves towards larger meals with perhaps the sorbet reappearing to stimulate flagging appetites. Most progressive culinary artists with their roots in the traditions of Escoffier feel it better to look ahead rather than backwards and to concentrate on simple sequences in which there is delicacy and perfection at each stage rather than the grandiose that can easily verge on the gluttonous. The types of menu which have to be prepared will fall under the following main headings.

Breakfast

The British (and to some extent the American breakfast, is in the same tradition) resolutely continues to feature cooked items of a fairly substantial order. Before the Second World War it was commonplace for large hotels to offer fruit juices and fruits, cereals, fish, egg dishes with bacon, sausages and offals and the usual variety of breads, toasts, preserves and accompanying, appropriate beverages. Such menus are still commonplace but it is less common to find those partaking of them sampling an item from almost every course as was by no means rare in pre-war times. Even from long breakfast menus today's practice is to take a choice from fruit juice, fruits and cereal to be followed by a choice from the main fish, egg and bacon type dishes making breakfast at most, with toast and preserves following, a three-course affair. Except under certain peculiar circumstances of holiday making where a more substantial breakfast might be taken to cushion against a later picnic lunch, it is unlikely that breakfast will become any heavier.

The continental breakfast of café complete with croissants or bread rolls with butter and preserves as virtually the only solid item but with the possible addition of fruit and fruit juices is likely to command an increasing following.

In considering the origins of the British breakfast and in considering whether it is apposite today it should not be forgotten that the breakfast of cold meats and chops taken at a later hour was as much an early luncheon as a breakfast as we now know it and that changing menus once again merely reflect changing meal times linked with changing social customs.

Though today only three courses are normally taken at breakfast (e.g., (1) Fruit or Cereal, (2) Fish, Eggs or Meat with appropriate accompaniment, (3) Beverage, Breads and Preserves), the following indicates the scope of a breakfast menu.

Breakfast courses and dishes

1. FRUITS
     Fresh: Grapefruit, Melon, Juices.
     Stewed: Compôte of Figs, Prunes, Apples, Mixed Fruit, Baked Apple.
2. CEREALS
     Cold: Cornflakes, Grapenuts, Shredded Wheat, etc.
     Hot: Porridge.
     Milk Cream or Hot or Cold Milk.

3. FISH

Grilled Mackerel, Kippers, Herrings, Bloaters, Fish Cakes, Kedgeree.

Fried or meunière. Simple Sauces only, if any, such as Tomato, Butter Sauce or Mustard Sauce.

4. EGGS

Poached, Boiled, Fried, en Cocotte, sur le Plat, Scrambled and Omelettes with or without accompaniments such as Grilled Bacon (streaky or back), Tomatoes, Sausage, Mushrooms.

5. MEATS

Hot: Grilled or griddle fried Bacon, Ham or Gammon, Sausage, Lambs' Kidneys, Calves' Liver.

Accompaniments: Sauté or Fried Potatoes, Potato Fritters, Bubble and Squeak, Eggs, Poached, Boiled, Fried, en Cocotte, sur le Plat, Scrambled, Omelettes.

Cold: Ham, Tongue, Pressed Salt Beef.

Accompaniments: Potatoes, sauté, hashed, etc.

6. PRESERVES

Marmalade, Jam, Honey, Syrup.

7. DESSERT FRUITS

Apple, Apricot, Pear, Peach, Grapes, etc.

8. BEVERAGES

Tea, Coffee, Chocolate.

9. BREAD

Rolls, Croissants, Toast, Toast Melba, Brioche, etc.

Luncheon

Immediately before the Second World War, table d'hôte luncheons in large hotels were likely to offer the following courses:

1. Hors d'œuvres and/or soup.
2. Egg and/or Italian pastes.
3. Fish.
4. Entrée or a Roast Meat, Poultry or Offal.
5. Sweet.
6. Cheese.

The French (and Escoffier is on record as upholding this tradition) regarded soup as more appropriate for the evening than for luncheon and the tendency persisting from pre-war to the present day is to select an item of hors d'œuvres or a few items of hors d'œuvres variés followed by either pasta or egg or fish and with the third course as the main item. This main course is still a meat (or poultry, game or offal) course in the ordinary way.

Yet, persistent trends are noticeable in determining a new pattern for luncheon. It is increasingly common for the hors d'œuvres to be followed by a soup in place of an egg or fish or pasta course. A fashion has also arisen for the featuring of asparagus or artichoke as an introductory course rather than in its former position following the main course.

Many consider that the mild flavour of asparagus with, say, Hollandaise Sauce is perfectly appropriate to the preliminary stages of a meal. It is difficult to controvert personal preferences except where they rudely violate accepted and obvious canons and it seems likely that the modern chef will have to be prepared to compose luncheon menus briefly and imaginatively that take into account some of these present patterns as well as those of pre-war days. The note of simplicity is, moreover, evidenced in the desire of many at lunch time to drink only one wine throughout the meal and the style of menus which customers select for themselves from à la carte menus tends to mirror this single-mindness. Three lunch-time courses are common and even formal ones may not exceed four. Whereas the end of the luncheon was often the signal for the appearance of the cheese platter the practice is now widespread of sampling cheese *before* the sweet dessert. The change in position of this and other items may cause pain to the traditionalist but there is little doubt that the greatest chefs have been those who were particularly quick to note the hint of change and to exploit it to the full.

The style and pattern of luncheon is by no means as formal as dinner. There are usually fewer courses but they normally offer wider choice of dishes at each stage of the meal. For main courses at luncheon, stews, made-up dishes and simpler plats are just as appropriate as roasts and grills. Similarly, more substantial hot puddings may be featured which would be out of place at dinner-time. The following indicate the range of luncheon items:

Luncheon courses and dishes

I. COCKTAILS

Fruit or Shellfish.

Fruit: Grapefruit, Melon, Avocado Pear, Fresh Figs and Fruit Juices.

Shellfish and Other Appetisers: Oysters, Snails, Caviare, Seagull's Eggs, Potted Shrimps.

Smoked Items: Salmon, Trout, Ham (Parma, Bayonne), Salami and Sausages. Hors d'œuvres variés.

2. **SOUP**
   Clear, Velouté, Creams and Purées.

3. **FARINACEOUS**
   Macaroni, Spaghetti, Ravioli, Gnocchis.

4. **EGGS**
   Appropriately garnished eggs, sur le plat, en cocotte, mollet,
   Scrambled, Fried and Omelettes.

5. **FISH**
   Steamed, Poached, deep and shallow with simple garnish.
   Grilled, meuniére, fried.
   Cheaper Fish: Herring, Skate, etc.
   Shellfish: Hot Mussels and Scallops are as suitable as Lobsters.

6. **ENTRÉES**
   Stews, Blanquettes, Navarin, Fricassées, Hot-pot, Pies, Pud-
   dings, Oxtail, Pilaw, Goulash, Boiled and Braised Meats, Salt
   Meats, Veal Escalopes and Cutlets. Noisettes, Pork Chops and
   Cutlets. Liver, Calves' Head, Pigs' Feet, Tripe, Vienna and
   Hamburg Steaks, Sausages. Minces, Réchauffé dishes, Braised
   Game, Hare, Salmis of Game.
   Appropriately garnished with vegetables.

7. **ROASTS**
   Butcher's Meats more commonly than Poultry or Game.
   Appropriately garnished with vegetables and potatoes.

8. **GRILLS**
   Grilled Butcher's Meats and Poultry.
   Appropriately garnished with additional vegetable or grilled
   vegetables (mushroom and tomato) and fried potatoes.

9. **COLD BUFFET**
   Cold Joints, Hams, Poultry, Game, Pies, Terrines.
   Cold Fish: Salmon, Lobster, Trout, Crab, Aspic, Fish.
   Accompanied by Salads and possibly boiled or mashed potato.

10. **A CHOICE VEGETABLE DISH**
    Hot or Cold Asparagus, Globe Artichokes.

11. **SOUFFLÉ**
    Cheese, Spinach, Mushroom, etc., as an alternative to a
    separate fine vegetable.

12. **SWEET**
    Baked and Steamed Puddings, Pancakes in simple style.
    Milk Puddings.
    Fruit Desserts such as Stewed, Baked, Salad, Flans, Apple
    Dumplings, Pies, Tarts, Fritters, Trifle, Jelly, Fools, Egg
    Custards, Bavarois, Gâteaux, Savarin, Babas, Charlottes,
    Profiteroles.

Plainer Ices and coupes.

Pâtisseries.

13. CHEESES

Varied Cheese Board accompanied by celery, radish, biscuits and butter.

14. DESSERT

Fresh Fruits.

15. COFFEE

Afternoon teas

This typically British institution seldom involves menu composition. Its collection of sandwiches, scone-type items and pastries do, however, involve the chef and caterer in planning and must also affect the day's food costs and the solidity of subsequent meals.

High tea

The gourmet and the chef alike have little good to say of the high tea and there are, indeed, convincing gastronomic reasons for deploring it as a meal however firmly it may be established in the north of England and in Scotland. Many hotels and catering establishments must, however, feature this type of meal to meet customer demands. Without the refinement of the wine-accompanied dinner or supper and with the tendency for starch items to overwhelm the cooked course, chefs and caterers have devoted little attention to menu composing of high teas as a gastronomic exercise. It is, indeed, so unrewarding to the culinary craftsman and the gourmet alike that one can suggest little more than making the best of it as a social convenience in the hope that it may be developed into an early dinner or supper.

The following indicates the range of tea-time items:

Afternoon and high tea courses and dishes

SANDWICHES

Small, dainty, of well-buttered white and brown bread.

Fillings include: Egg and Cress, Tomato, Lettuce, Cucumber, pastes, and less frequently, Chicken, Smoked Salmon and even foie gras.

BREAD AND BUTTER

White, Brown, Wholemeal, Currant, Fancy and proprietary brands.

SCONES, BUNS AND GRIDDLE ITEMS

Buttered Scones, Tea-cakes, Buns, Sally Lunns, Scotch Pancakes, Doughnuts, Waffles.

TOASTED GOODS
   Toast, Tea-cakes, Scones, Crumpets, Buns, etc.

PRESERVES
   Jams, Lemon Curds, Honey, Syrup, but *not* Marmalade.

FOR HIGH TEA
   Welsh Rarebit, Buck Rarebit, Beans or Spaghetti on Toast, Eggs
   (Various) on Toast, Mushrooms on Toast.

EGGS FOR HIGH TEA
   Boiled, Poached, Fried and Omelettes.

COOKED FOOD FOR HIGH TEA
   Fried Fish, Grilled Meats, Roast or Fried Poultry, Cold Meats,
   Cold Salmon, Dressed Crab, Lobster, Salads, etc.

PASTRIES
   All varieties, afternoon tea pastries (small), Gateaux, Fruit Cake,
   etc.

DESSERTS FOR HIGH TEA
   Fruit Salads, Compotes, Mousses, Bavarois, Jellies and similar cold
   sweets.

ICES FOR HIGH TEA
   All varieties and Sundaes.

TEA
   Indian, China, Ceylon, Russian and Iced.

Dinner

As far as day-to-day eating is concerned, the mid-day luncheon in
France is as often as not the principal meal of the day, though in other
parts of the Western world where the cuisine is unmistakably French,
the evening dinner is generally regarded as the more important. In
most hotels and restaurants, therefore, dinner commands a higher price
than luncheon.

The appropriateness of hors d'œuvres or appetiser at dinner-time
has been referred to in the paragraph on luncheon. Many people will
eat and enjoy a substantial hors d'œuvres variés at any time and it is
now quite common for it to be both offered and accepted in the evening. Whilst hors d'œuvres are beginning to appear more frequently on
formal, composed dinner menus in response to customer demands, the
chef and the gourmet is still disinclined to accept the featuring of hors
d'œuvres on the dinner menu. The purist is prepared to accept one of
the finer items of single hors d'œuvres such as caviare, oyster and foie-
gras as a dinner's overture and even melon and avocado pears are
featured in this way.

, Escoffier was reputed to believe that a fine soup was the most appropriate appetiser at dinner and this is usually one of the consommés or one of the better creme or velouté soups.

A quarter of a century ago the table d'hôte menus of quite ordinary hotels would then follow with a fish course, an entrée appropriately garnished, a roast with potatoes and green salad, a sweet course, and possibly, a savoury. All chefs are aware of the types of entrées suitable for dinner as distinct from luncheon and in the menus of the classic tradition, dinner-time entrées tend to be centred on the prime small cuts like noisettes, tournedos, whilst entrées of, say, navarin style are featured only at luncheon.

The rélevés (removes) which in earlier times occupied an important place on the table, nowadays describe the larger pieces of butcher's meat or poultry which have received treatment more complex than plain roasting. A joint of veal which has been poêlé and garnished may in modern menus replace a roast at dinner (or an entrée at lunch).

The general pattern of dinner, except in so far as it was curtailed by war conditions, has altered little though there is, perhaps, a tendency to dispense with the entrée and even on rare occasions to retain the entrée but relinquish the roast. When the meal has been of great length the traditional sorbet can be introduced after the entrée and this interlude with its Russian cigarette is designed to permit the appetite to recover. Savouries, though deplored by many classicists amongst chefs are still favoured widely in Britain and there is an interesting trend towards featuring them *before* the sweet dessert instead of, as was common practice, after it.

At dinner-time there is a great inclination to feature wines and consequently the dinner menu has not been foreshortened as drastically as the luncheon for it is still envisaged as a partnership of food and wine and as an occasion in which these elements have social as well as gastronomic value. Dinner still, therefore, offers to the chef a major challenge in menu composition. Within its scope he is able still to weave interesting gastronomic patterns and the food he provides is often aided by the social importance of the occasion and the emphasis of fine wine.

The following indicates the menu range for dinner:

Dinner courses and dishes

I. COCKTAILS

        Fruit, Shellfish, but rarely fruit juices.

        Fruit: Melon Canteloupe, Fresh Figs and, less appropriately, Grapefruit.

Shellfish and other Appetisers: Caviare, Oysters, Seagulls' Eggs, Prawns, Snails, Frogs' Legs, Tunny, Sardines, Potted Shrimps, Foie-gras.

Smoked Items: Salmon, Eel, Cod Roe, Parma and Bayonne, Ham, Sprats, Trout, Salami, Breast of Goose and Turkey, Smoked Sausages.

Hors d'œuvres: At dinner-time hot appetisers served in the ante room are considered more correct than cold Hors d'œuvres variés. The latter are more appropriate for lunch.

2. SOUP

Consommés, Veloutés, Cremes, Bisques, Bortsch, Turtle Soup.

3. FISH

Poached Salmon, Turbot, Truite au bleu and other Prime fish, with appropriate garnishes.

Hot Shellfish: Lobster, Crab, Crayfish, Dublin Ray Prawns and, possibly, Scallops but not common types such as Mussels.

Sole, Trout, Salmon in meunière style.

Fried fish is not appropriate except, perhaps, Sole and possibly Whitebait.

Grilled fish is also not customary except, possibly, Lobster, Sole, Salmon.

Cold Fish: Salmon, Salmon Trout, Sole in aspic.

4. ENTRÉES

Light dishes of small cuts garnished with vegetables (are not served when a Rélevé is to follow the entrée.) They include items such as Sautés, Tournedos, Noisettes, Veal Cutlets, Vol-au-Vent, Hot Mousse.

5. RÉLEVÉS

These are larger joints requiring carving and feature Butcher's meat which would not be served as a roast on the dinner menu.

Poêlé Veal, Poêléd Saddle of Lamb, whole Fillet of Beef, Boned Sirloin, Braised Ham, Tongue, Duck and Chicken poêlé or en casserole or en cocotte.

6. SORBET

Light water ice or sherbert ice made with fine wine, Champagne or Liqueur. Russian cigarettes usually accompany the sorbet. This is a traditional course which some seek to re-introduce.

7. ROAST
> Roast Game and Poultry. Traditionally never butcher's meat, though Fillet of Beef and fine veal is now sometimes featured.
> *Salad:* Generally a fine salad from the repertoire.

8. VEGETABLE DISH
> Asparagus, Globe Artichokes, Truffles, or even sometimes Bone Marrow or a Soufflé.

9. SWEET
> *Hot:* Soufflés, Pancakes, Fritters of the finer types.
> *Cold:* Iced Soufflés, Baked Ice Cream, Bombes, Biscuits, Coupes (Melbas and the like).
> Accompanied with Petit Fours, Dipped Fruits, etc.

10. SAVOURIES
> Now sometimes served before the sweet. Savoury soufflés also featured as well as Savouries from the repertoire.

11. CHEESES
> Fine types with Celery, Radishes, Biscuits and Butter.

12. DESSERT
> Basket of fresh Fruits, Nuts and fine Raisins.

13. COFFEE

Suppers

Suppers are, perhaps, less easily definable than dinners or luncheons. Theatre suppers were often intimate little affairs after the show in which a simple assembly of courses suitable for dinner made the meal. Today's theatre suppers are often early ones preceding the entertainment. Moreover, in family dining there is a modest tendency to describe the simpler evening meal as supper irrespective of the hour of eating. The souper de réveillon which is a feature of French Yuletide festivities can be given a nice hint of formality but usually to most folk, supper implies a kind of early or late dinner of somewhat reduced scope. It often offers to the chef or menu composer an interesting exercise in the creation of a subtle as well as a simple meal.

The scope of informal supper is indicated as follows (Recherché ones are composed from repertoire items suitable also for dinner):

Supper courses and dishes

1. APPETISER COURSE
> Shellfish, Caviare, Lapwings' Eggs, Prawns, Snails, Smoked Meats (such as Parma or Bayonne Ham), Smoked Salmon, Trout and Ham.

Consommés and Consommé based Soups such as Soupe à l'Oignon and Green Turtle.

2. MAIN COURSE

Fish, Hot: Fried, Grilled (seldom Poached), even Haddock or Kippers may be appropriate.

Cold: Salmon, Salmon Trout, Lobster.

Entrées: Sautés of Tournedos, Noisettes, Cutlets, Chicken, Veal, Sweetbreads, etc., Vol-au-Vents, Kidneys, Liver and even small birds braised and poêlé.

Roasts: Are seldom served.

Grills: All kinds are appropriate for supper.

All the foregoing appropriately garnished and accompanied by vegetables.

Cold Dishes: Cold Meats, Poultry, Foie-gras, Mousse, Timbales, Terrines, etc. Accompanied by Salad, and possibly potatoes appropriately cooked.

3. DESSERT OR SAVOURY COURSE

Hot Soufflés, Pancakes or Fritters.

Iced Soufflés, Bombes, Biscuits.

Glacé, and Coupes with Petit Fours.

Savoury: Most kinds are served.

Cheese: Most varieties.

Dessert Fruits

4. COFFEE

Menus for special occasions

It cannot be within the scope of this chapter to deal at length with menus for functions and special occasions. The extent and variety is such that the chef of even the longest experience may be called upon to create a menu along lines demanding some new approach. It may be the featuring of various foods or the featuring of courses of some particular nationality or the assembling of courses to offset a particular range of wines. Whatever the function or occasion the basic aspects of menu composing remain constant and the chef who is successful in menu selection from day to day requires only the application of a little flair and finesse to rise to the occasion.

Lunch-time functions

Normal lunch dishes are featured subject to their suitability for function service; thus it is not usual to include farinaceous dishes or eggs. Some stews and savouries are avoided for similar reasons. Service as a rule is designed for speed and items featured are, therefore, commonly from the following:

1. Cocktails of fruit or shellfish, smoked items, hors d'œuvres or soups.
2. Fish from lunch selection.
3. Entrées (excluding stews and réchauffé dishes) but including simpler dinner entrées.
   Roast joints, grills or cold meats.
   Appropriate accompaniment of vegetables and potatoes or salads and potatoes.
4. Asparagus or an alternative fine vegetable may be served in season.
5. Sweet Course may include hot varieties and cold types of ices such as Bombes, Biscuit Glacé as at dinner.
6. Cheese may be offered with biscuits and celery or radishes.
7. Dessert is rarely served.
8. Coffee.

Dinner function

The chef or caterer may compose his menu from the full repertoire having service considerations and numbers in mind.

Buffet menus

Light buffets may be required for all kinds of catering including tea and supper dances. Menus should include items easily eaten with forks or even fingers. The following light buffet items are suitable for *fork* luncheons and suppers:

LIGHT BUFFET

Savoury finger toasts, to include any of the cold canapés.
Chipolata on sticks, wrapped in bacon, prune sticks, etc.
Celery branches piped with cheese spread.
Game Chips. Cheese Straws.

Patties: Chicken, Lobster, Crab, Salmon.
Sausage Rolls, Bouchées, Vol-au-Vents.

Sandwiches: Cut very small, brown or white. Smoked Salmon, Egg and Cress, Tomato, Ham, Tongue, Chicken, etc.
Mousses, Galantines, Terrines, Cut Poultry, Fish and Meats.

Sweets: Charlotte Russe, Jellies, Trifle, Bavarois, etc.
Fruit Salads or fresh raw fruits like strawberries.

Ice-creams, various flavours but not as a rule coupes.

Pastries, Gateaux, Biscuits.

Beverages: Coffee, Tea, Punch Bowl, Iced Coffee.

FULL SUPPER BUFFETS. Though full buffets are not served course by course, the items are arranged in the printed menu in appropriate groups. Items may include:

Cold Consommé.

Shellfish: Oysters, Prawns, Melon.

Smoked Salmon, Ham, Trout, Eels.

Canapés: Savoury *finger toasts.* Canapé Moscovite. Patties of Chicken, *Lobster or Salmon*, Dressed Crab. Game Chips, Chipolata, Celery stocks, Cheese Straws.

Dressed Cold Fish: Salmon, Lobster, Crab, Fillet of Sole, Turbot in Aspic.

Cold Meats: Chicken suprêmes, Mayonnaise and salads and plain cold cuts. Cold Roast Turkey, Ham decorated and jellied. Mousses and cornets, Cutlets in Aspic, Galatine, Foie-gras in Aspic.

Salads: Lettuce, Russian, various mixed and plain salads.

Sandwiches: Ham, Tongue, Chicken, Turkey, Smoked Salmon, etc.

Bridge Rolls: Egg and Cress, Pastes, etc.

Cold Sweets: Charlottes, Jelly, Trifle, Bavarois, Cream Caramel, Condés, Flans. Pastries, Gateaux.

Ices: Bombes, Biscuit Glacé, Sundaes and Petits Fours.

Beverages: Coffee, Punch, Iced Coffee and Tea.

Sometimes hot consommé or turtle soup may be served at the end of a party.

Conclusion

The art of composing menus for the formal occasion may best be perfected by studying others. To the craftsman aware of cookery methods and garnishes, the reading of a menu can be full of interest and meaning. The critical appraisal of the menus of others and particularly a study of those created by the modern masters can be stimulating as well as instructive. It is, however, worth repeating that for the special occasion, cookery skills are not enough. There is no one thing which makes a chef a man of discernment but breadth of reading, width of interest and social contact can all help towards creating the whole man as well as the practical chef. Such a man will more readily capture the importance and drama of the big occasion in culinary terms in his menu.

On ordinary days the most routine meal will gain from the planning of the cultured as well as the skilled chef. Though Brillat Savarin's aphorisms tend to have been done to death, there is one so succinct, so apt and so true, that it must be quoted in order to underscore the importance of the art of selecting dishes to compile a good meal. Savarin used five words only to express the importance of this kitchen blueprint: 'Menu mal fait, dîner perdu'. A badly composed menu is a dinner lost.

15 Food values in cooking and menu making

Chefs and others concerned in catering for hotels and restaurants may sometimes be tempted to question the necessity of concerning themselves with food values. Some of those engaged in cooking and catering in hotels often make, for example, two points regarding the acquisition of simple facts about nutrition. These points may be summarised as: (a) de-luxe restaurants offer such a wide range of top-class foods that the prospects of malnutrition are non-existent, and (b) hotels and restaurants (as distinct perhaps from the catering sections of, for example, schools and hospitals) have no compulsive powers as far as inducing their clientele to select and eat certain foods.

Such reasoning, superficial though it is, is attractive to those too lazy or too lacking in social conscience to recognise the real responsibilities borne by all those who cook and cater at whatever level.

The great chefs in all periods have been questing and inquiring folk, constantly alert to know more about the commodities they use, the best way to use them and the dietary effects they will have.

Men like Alexis Soyer, who organised soup kitchens for the poor of London and concerned himself actively with the improvement of catering for British soldiers in the Crimea, occupied himself with nutritive matters not only for those reasons which affected humbler, social groups. He knew, as do all intelligent practising chefs, that the food values of the finest raw materials may be impaired by bad cooking and incorrect methods. He knew, too, that ill-chosen bills of fare, though commonest among those with scanty means, could be reflected in bad selection by richer folk of dishes from both à la carte and table d'hôte menus. True, the chef or hotelier cannot compel the customer to choose and eat what is good for him but he can enormously influence the choice by the way in which he draws up a menu and cooks and presents the dishes featured in it.

The man of food, whether he be chef or restaurateur, is confronted with two types of dining philosophy, that, on the one hand, of eating to live and on the other living to eat. Chefs and gourmets are tremendously alive to the attractions of the table as one of the means by which civilised man heightens his appreciation of the pleasures of living. He must, nevertheless, be conscious that whatever its pleasurable aspects, eating satisfies a primary need. It is the basic feature of man's struggle for existence, for it fulfils the simple instinct to survive. The chef and the hotelier cannot, therefore, ignore the fundamental aspect of eating to maintain life and health. Their approach must be that of all rational, civilised humans that the process of nourishing the body through food and drink in a highly developed society can, and indeed should, be linked with refined enjoyment as distinct from gross indulgence. They will see that a mingling of the philosophies of eating to live and living to eat are compatible.

Nutritive knowledge

Once the culinary craftsman has brought himself to the point when he is ready and willing to interest himself in nutritive matters and to acquire a working knowledge of basic food values he may find other problems which tend to deter him.

The science of nutrition is young. Biochemists, medical men and other research workers are still discovering new facts about food and discarding or amending old ideas and theories about diet or about ways to cook. In the last quarter of a century, for example, there have been varying approaches to the problem of conserving vitamin C in cooking green vegetables. From a total prohibition of the use of bicarbonate of soda because of its adverse affect on vitamin C preservation, there was for a time a more indulgent attitude which countenanced slightly less conservative methods even to permitting the use of bicarbonate of soda if the result was to ensure that the food itself was more widely eaten and enjoyed through being more attractively dished. Even as this is being written, however, a new approach to this and kindred problems may be emerging.

The fact of the matter is that the cookery craftsman need not unduly worry about changing and developing theories in the science of nutrition once he accepts that such change and development is an integral part of the pursuit of scientific knowledge in any field. What the craftsman needs to accept and to concentrate on is that there is in existence a sufficient body of knowledge about food values to help him plan balanced menus and cook the dishes that constitute them so as to conserve their nutritive properties. In short, there is a good deal of stable knowledge about food values which is quite simple to understand and which must be learned by the efficient cook and caterer.

Those who cater for industry, schools and hospitals have so widely accepted that their functions are part of social welfare that the importance of nutrition to them is no longer questioned. Chefs and caterers in hotels and restaurants are, however, still conscious more, perhaps, of their responsibilities towards eating as a pleasurable rather than a physiologically necessary experience.

It is certainly not suggested that a hotelier should think of his restaurant as a 'calorie intake depot' nor that the chef de cuisine should consider his saucepans as test-tubes, his recipes as prescriptions and his cooks as laboratory assistants intent only on preserving vitamins. Such an approach will not best serve the cause of nutrition. Conversely, one who regards the assessment of food values as largely a matter of commonsense and care can usually achieve desirable results. If he selects fresh foods in season, offers a wide variety of dishes, ensures that food is well cooked, served when newly cooked and interests himself in flavour blends and contrasts, he will almost invariably be obeying most of the important rules of nutrition.

The nutrients

Food is composed of several different substances each of which plays a part in meeting the needs of the body and enabling it to function. These components which together comprise food are called NUTRIENTS.

Carbohydrates. These are the main sources of energy and may also be converted to fat.

Fats. Fats in the diet supply energy and may also form body-fat.

Proteins. Proteins provide substances which build and repair the body tissues. They also provide energy and excess may be converted into fat.

Minerals and vitamins. Mineral substances build and repair body tissues and regulate body processes. Vitamins are substances which regulate body processes.

Water. Water, although not strictly a nutrient, is included as it also builds body tissues and is essential for life.

Grouping food

In planning menus from the nutritive aspect a simple grouping of food in three main categories should suffice to aid the chef. These divisions are:

Body builders. This type of food, having as its main function the building and renewing the tissues of the body, comprise proteins and minerals. They are obviously of particular importance during the years of childhood, adolescence, growth, pregnancy and lactation. The main foods in this group which may be described as first-class proteins are meat (including game and poultry), fish (including shellfish), milk, cheese, eggs.

Secondary sources of body building material are pulses such as peas, beans and lentils, also cereals and nuts, and these are sometimes called second-class proteins.

Proteins are the most important substances found in living material and are the very basis of life. Protein foods are the most expensive foods and are usually the most appetising giving a feeling of satisfaction which is absent after a meal of carbohydrates. Because animal proteins

TABLE 9.

Amounts of Various Foods containing 11·7 g. Protein (i.e., one-sixth of the Daily Protein Requirement)

Item	Weight in oz	Approx. portion/measure
Meat and Fish Group		
Bacon	3·2	1½ rashers
Cod	2·6	½ portion
Cutlet	3·8	1 cutlet
Steak	3·0	1 small portion (tournedos)
Gelatine	0·3	1 tablespoon
Dairy Group		
Cheddar cheese	1·6	1¼ cube portion
Egg	3·3	1¼ eggs
Milk	12·4	1½ glasses
Cereal Group		
Bread, wholemeal	4·8	3 thick or 5 ordinary slices
Bread, white	5·1	Ditto
Spaghetti	3·8	½ cup
Oatmeal	3·4	½ cup
Rice	6·6	1 cup
Sweet biscuit	5·9	12 biscuits
Water biscuits	3·45	12 biscuits
Vegetable Group		
Cabbage	27	
Carrots	58	
Cauliflower	171	
Potato	20·5	
Fruit Group		
Apples	136	20–30 ⎫
Apricots, dried	8·5	20–24 ⎬ halves
Banana	37	10–16 ⎪
Orange	51	6–10 ⎭

especially are expensive it is important to remember that proteins obtained from both plants and animals should be mixed in the diet.

The minerals are found in the same foods as the proteins.

TABLE 10.

Percentage of Protein in Various Foods

Commodity	Protein, %
Meat Group	
Bacon	10
Beef steak	14
Gammon	14
Mutton (lean cut)	14
Pork chops	10
Dairy and Farm Group	
Cheddar cheese	25
Fresh eggs	11
Fresh milk	3·3
Fish Group	
Herring	10
Salmon	20
Sardines, canned in oil	20
Pulses	
Dried peas	25
Lentils	24
Peanuts	20
Cereals	
Flour, national	9
Oatmeal	12

Foods within this group are those which provide fuel for the work and warmth of the body. The two kinds of foods which fulfil this function are: (*a*) fats such as butter, margarine, suet and dripping, and (*b*) sugars and starches such as sugar itself, jams, syrup, honey, treacle, dried fruits and starch foods like flour, bread, oatmeal, cereals, potatoes, rice, spaghetti (and similar pastas), peas, beans and lentils. Sugars and starches constitute the food group called Carbohydrates.

Energy and heat producers

The bodily requirements of food vary according to the weight, size and age of the individual and according to the work done and the state of health so that the assessment of diets for particular categories of

TABLE 11.

Percentage of Carbohydrates in Various Foods

Commodity	Carbohydrates, %
Bread, national	51
Cornflour	86
Flour, national	74
Oatmeal	65
Rice	78
Sago	85
Tapioca	86
Peas	50
Potatoes	16
Honey	69
Jam	62
Sugar	95
Currants	57
Raisins	58

people requires expert knowledge normally outside the scope of the cook or kitchen craftsman.

It may, however, be noted that energy is required from food even when the human body is at rest for it is needed simply to keep the body living—to maintain warmth, to keep the heart beating, blood circulating and the action of breathing. The basic energy requirement for this is known as the body's basal metabolism.

Further energy from food is, of course, needed for further activity from the mild, day-to-day activities of the sedentary person to greater physical effort in work and play.

It will have been noted already that some foods fulfil more than one function and the pulses like peas and beans, whilst having a function as second-class body builders, contain an appreciable amount of heat and energy value. Food taken in by the body and capable of producing heat and energy may be converted by the body into body fat if taken in excess of requirements. In other words, if more food is taken in than is needed to perform the bodily functions of work and play and to keep it warm, there is a tendency for weight to increase because this surplus food may be converted into fat stored within the body. When food falls below the level required then conversely, the body's fat is used up as fuel for work and weight is lost.

The following list showing the weight and approximate portion size of some common foods that have 100 Calorie value may give a general indication of energy values:

TABLE 12.

100 Calorie Portions of Various Foods

	Weight in oz of edible portion	Approx. measure
Dairy Foods, Fats and Oil		
Butter	0·47	1 tablespoon
Cheese	0·86	1 in. cube
Cream	0·91	1¾ tablespoons
Egg	2·25	1 very large
Lard	0·39	⅔ tablespoon
Margarine	0·45	1 ,,
Milk, fresh	5·6	1 teacup
Olive oil	0·37	1 tablespoon
Cereal		
Bread	1·4	1 slice
Biscuit, sweet	0·7	2 small biscuits
Biscuits, cream crackers	0·95	4–5 biscuits
Cornflakes	0·95	½ cup
Cornflour	1·0	4 level tablespoons
Flour	1·0	4 ,, ,,
Macaroni	1·1	4½ tablespoons
Oatmeal	0·9	3½ ,,
Rice	1·0	4 ,,
Meat and Fish		
Bacon	0·8	1 large rasher
Cod	5·0	1 steak, ¾ in.
Herring	2·1	½ herring
Steak	1·1	¼ portion
Vegetables, Fresh		
Cabbage	13·6	½ cabbage
Carrots	16·0	5–6 carrots, medium
Lettuce	32·0	12–16
Onion	16·0	4
Potatoes	4·8	1 medium
Swedes	17·6	4 ,,
Tomatoes	25·2	10 ,,
Pulses		
Dried peas	1·2	3 tablespoons
Haricot beans	1·4	4 ,,
Fruit and Nuts		
Apples, cooking	9·9	2
Apples, eating	8·2	3 small/medium
Apricots, dried	2·0	4–5 halves
Banana	4·7	1 large
Orange	10·4	2 ,,
Peanuts	0·6	1½ tablespoons
Prunes	2·3	5

	Weight in oz of edible portion	Approx. measure
Sugar, Preserves, etc.		
Marmalade	1·4	3 tablespoons
Milk chocolate	0·7	3d. slab
Sugar	0·9	2 tablespoons
Toffee	0·77	3 ,,
Sherry	2·5	1 glass

Need for energy food will depend, as has been noted, on the type of life led. It will also depend on the size of the individual and in particular, the surface area of the body—larger folk requiring more Calories than smaller. The needs of growing children are greater than those of adults, proportionate to their size.

Daily Calorie needs

It has been calculated (H.M.S.O. *Manual of Nutrition*) that daily requirements based on varying but average activities, are as follows:

Occupation	Total daily need
Male clerk	2,220 Calories (example of sedentary occupation)
Carpenter	3,180 ,, (,, ,, moderately active job)
Blacksmith	4,260 ,, (,, ,, active workman)
Woodcutter	5,100 ,, (,, ,, very active occupation)

Mention is made below of the variable amount of food needed each day to give heat and energy and even to build tissue. Growing children and manual workers have needs which differ from those of a middle-aged clerk whose job does not involve much physical activity; and we have noted that a person's weight, size and state of health also affect their needs.

But it will have become apparent that certain general principles may be applied to broad categories of people.

The body is often likened to a machine with food as the material to replace the worn-out parts (the body builders or proteins) and the fuel (the carbohydrates and fats) to enable the machine to work and to maintain body temperature. Most people readily understand that as length is measured in feet and inches and as weights are measured in pounds and ounces, so the capacity of a fuel to give heat can be measured. The unit of measurement as far as food is concerned is the

Calorie* so that when we speak about the calorific value of foods we are referring only to the food's capacity to produce heat and energy for the body.

In the heat and energy producing group the fats have the highest Calorific value, 1 oz yielding 263 Calories, while the carbohydrates and protein both yield 116 Calories per oz.

Fat, then, is a form of 'concentrated Calories' and may be eaten to obtain much energy without overloading the stomach. Children, who are bounding with energy but have small stomachs need relatively large quantities of fat to supply their needs.

Nutritionists have not decided about the human's daily fat requirements but people generally do not find the diet palatable if it contains less than about 20%. Food would be unappetising and monotonous without this amount of fat. Fortunately adequate amounts are present in average diets. Because fats are the most slowly digested of all our foods, meals containing a good proportion of fat are the most satisfying and lasting and the most obvious disadvantage fats have is that they are nauseating if eaten in any quantity.

TABLE 13.

Percentage of Fat in Various Common Foods

Commodity	Percentage of fat
Butter	82·5
Dripping	99
Lard	99
Margarine	85
Bacon	40
Beef steak	29
Gammon	25·5
Mutton, leg	21
Pork chop	42
Herring	10
Salmon	10
Sardines, canned in oil	24
Cheese	34·5
Egg, fresh	10
Almonds	19
Brazil nuts	28
Coconut	25
Peanuts	20
Flour, national	1·5
Oatmeal	9

* Fuel value of food is measured in large Calories spelt with a capital C. This large Calorie is 1,000 times greater than the small calorie of ordinary heat measurement which latter is the amount of heat required to raise the temperature of 1 gm of water by 1°C.

Protectors which maintain health and help guard against disease

Foods of this kind are, of course, found amongst those in the two preceding groups and especially valuable are dairy foods (milk, butter, cheese), eggs, vitaminised margarine, vegetables, fruits and salads, fat fish (herrings, kippers, sardines and salmon), liver, wholemeal bread and flour and oatmeal.

These foods are valued because of their vitamin and/or mineral content. These are the elements in foods which, though present in relatively tiny amounts, perform some specially valuable function.

It is not necessary for the craftsman to have an exhaustive knowledge of all the vitamins but it is helpful for him to have an appreciation of the four principal groups and the function they especially perform.

The importance of vitamins in the diet is most dramatically revealed when they are absent or reduced to a drastically low level. Vitamin C illustrates this aspect. This vitamin which is found in fresh fruits and vegetables was inevitably lacking or inadequate on long voyages in sailing ship days when restocking with fresh foods was delayed for many months. Scurvy was almost an inevitable consequence to sailors and passengers whose diet was restricted under these circumstances. The antidote to scurvy was found to lie in citrus fruits like oranges and lemons (which contain vitamin C) even before the study and naming of vitamins really got under way. Today, in the Western world, deficiency diseases, as those illnesses are called which result from a shortage of vitamins, etc., are rare. In this country they tend to occur only amongst small and special groups like old people who live alone and tend to neglect themselves by an inability to shop for fresh foods both because of lack of means and the health and energy to get about.

We certainly do not see much in Britain of scurvy, pellagra and other deficiency diseases which afflict under-developed and poor populations in other parts of the world. There are, however, still signs that there are some who eat an insufficient quantity of the right foods in the right balance not through lack of means but through lack of knowledge. Such absence of knowledge is unfortunately a characteristic of those who use catering establishments where ill-balanced meals are composed and poor food storage, preparation and cooking methods used and in whose homes similar culinary faults are found.

The protective elements of vitamins and minerals in foods can easily be lost or reduced through faults in marketing, storage, cooking and serving. It is particularly these aspects of loss that is important for the chef to know so that he may effectively guard against them.

The four main vitamins with which the craftsman cook should

concern himself are the groups A, B, C and D. The functions that these vitamins perform in the diet may be simplified as follows:

Vitamin A

This is an element necessary for the promotion of growth and is also known to have an effect on the health and efficiency of the eyes.

Vitamin B

This is really a whole group of vitamins. Diseases resulting from a deficiency are beri-beri and pellagra, and whilst these diseases are rare, there may be evidence of the symptoms in their earlier stages when the vitamins of the group B are not adequately represented in the diet. Such symptoms may involve loss of appetite, stomach disorders and digestive difficulties and general weakness and lassitude.

Vitamin C

This vitamin is necessary to cure and prevent scurvy, a disease rare in this country. Evidence of deficiency in early stages is, however, still to be seen in a tendency to bleeding of the gums which may affect dental health. It is today thought that this vitamin is of importance also in the healing of wounds and those who are to undergo surgery are, therefore, nowadays usually given additional vitamin C.

Vitamin D

Vitamin D is also associated with growth and in particular is associated with the body's ability to absorb and make use of calcium in the growth and maintenance of bone and teeth.

Sources of vitamins

Vitamin A

This vitamin is formed in animals who produce it in their bodies by breaking down a vegetable substance called carotene. This is a yellow pigment (colouring substance) found in plants, especially the leaves.

Sometimes all the carotene taken in is converted into vitamin A but when there is a large intake not all the carotene may be converted and both the vitamin and carotene may be accumulated in the liver, blood and in the tissues and fat below the skin. Cows, for example, do not turn all the carotene they get from grass into vitamin A and consequently butter contains both carotene and vitamin A. Its colour indicates the amount of carotene it contains and which will vary according to the season and feeding of the animal. For practical purposes, therefore, we may regard foods which contain carotene as sources of vitamin A.

Sources of vitamin A are: halibut, cod and other fish liver oils. Liver of fish, poultry and animals. Fish roe, egg yolk, butter, milk, cheese, body fat of animals, heart, kidney, green, leafy vegetables, carrots and tomatoes.

Vitamin B

Yeast, yeast extract, wheat germ, wholemeal, brown bread, whole cereal are good sources of vitamins of this group. It must, of course, be remembered that there is more than one vitamin in this group, and that one or more of the vitamin Bs may be found in greater or lesser quantities in many other foods including animal foods like egg yolks, milk and meat as well as other vegetables. The foregoing list indicates only the commonest and largest sources of the vitamins of this kind in the normal Western diet.

Vitamin C

This vitamin is found in blackcurrants, citrus fruits such as oranges, lemons and grapefruit, tomatoes, uncooked vegetables, uncooked swedes and turnips, uncooked carrots, raspberries, strawberries, gooseberries, blackberries and most other fruits, including tinned fruits, green vegetables conservatively cooked, potatoes.

Sources—General

It is, of course, possible to obtain much more complete information about food sources of vitamins and the amounts normally found in the various items. Vitamins are measured in international units, a measurement which is accepted throughout the world.

Chefs and caterers should remember, however, that factual information may be misleading.

It is by no means invariably practicable to provide vitamin C in menus by selecting foods with the richest vitamin C content and an important source may be foods in which the amount is fairly small but of which we eat relatively large, and certainly, regular amounts. Potatoes are a good example of this for though they contain proportionately far less vitamin C than, for example, blackcurrants, they are for most people a much more important source than blackcurrants because of their regular appearance on the menu.

MINERALS

In addition to the protective vitamins there is another type of food constituent which, though present also in only small amounts, is extremely important to the maintenance of health. This group is made up of the minerals such as iron, calcium, iodine and so on, some of which are found only in traces. Iodine is found in dairy produce and green vegetables and, in smaller amounts, in meat and fish. Eggs, oatmeal, potatoes, carrots also contain iodine in varying amounts. Good sources of iron are wholemeal flour and meat. The absorption and utilisation by the body appears, however, to depend on other salts such as copper and manganese; just as phosphorus is associated with calcium. How these minerals are used by the body and the precise function that each performs are facts not completely known even to expert nutritionists and the craftsman cook need only concern himself with these elements in food to the extent that: (a) he should observe methods of cookery which seek to conserve them against, for example, permitting them to leach out into cooking liquors which are not to be subsequently used, or (b) to note which foods are rich in minerals such as calcium, necessary for bone and teeth formation and which need to be well represented in bills of fare for children and other special groups.

Catering for children

Children must obviously be adequately provided with body-building materials. They have a particular need for first-class protein such as milk, cheese, meat, fish and poultry.

They also need the protective elements, the vitamins to be found in fresh, green foods, citrus foods and in eggs and the fatty fish like herrings and sardines or in butter or vitaminised margarine. Finally, of course, active children leading a normal life with plenty of games and hard work and play need energy foods.

Needs of adults

Those who cater in industry or in hospitals or in institutions like colleges or hostels commonly have a good knowledge of the type of people for whom they cater and such people belong normally to one group. It is thus relatively easy to make special provision for, say, men doing heavy work on a construction job and who are fed from a canteen or hostel. Such heavy workers will need not only the basic elements of a well-balanced diet but one particularly abundant in energy-giving foods.

Those catering for a restaurant or hotel trade often know less about their clients and, therefore, have to provide menus which leave to the customer a wide element of selection.

In planning menus the chef is often aware, too, that his clientele will not eat all their meals under the same roof and he sometimes, therefore, feels that it is not realistic for him to conceive of **his** day's menus as being designed to meet ideally the day's dietary requirements of a particular person. Many menus for one meal alone in a high-class hotel are likely to contain a perfectly reasonable diet for a whole day for an average person.

It is apparent from the foregoing that foods, nutritionally speaking, have three main functions: (a) to provide warmth and energy for work and play, (b) to provide material for growth and replacement of the body, (c) to provide protection and materials to enable the body to maintain health.

It will have been seen that no single food can really fulfil all these functions (though milk and eggs come closest to this ideal) and that a good mixed diet is necessary.

It has been suggested that a basic protective daily meal plan would include a pint of milk, 1 oz of butter (or vitaminised margarine), cheese, an egg (or a portion of fat fish such as herring or sardines) and an orange or half grapefruit or uncooked salad, preferably containing watercress or tomato. How these are augmented is relatively of secondary importance though obviously wholemeal bread and potatoes are useful additions.

One needs only to think of the menus provided in quite modest inns and restaurants to realise that, if cooking and preparation are properly carried out there is little danger of the basic protective foods not being well represented and the diet being an inadequate one.

Nutritive loss in cooking

Cooking causes many physical and chemical changes in food which usually make it more acceptable to the consumer by making it more digestible and palatable and by improving its flavour. Keeping quality is also increased and if thoroughly cooked, food will be rendered 'safe' as far as bacteria are concerned.

In bad cooking, however, there may be definite nutritive losses and the food value may be decreased.

In so far as protein foods like meat, fish, poultry, eggs and milk are concerned, there is little danger of the protein being lost or its value destroyed in cooking except that unappetising presentation might lead to rejection of the dish by the eater. This is true also of fats, sugars and starches.

There is, however, some loss of the vitamins (especially C and B group) and minerals.

The danger of decreasing food value through bad marketing, poor preparatory methods, faulty cooking and incorrect service procedure are, therefore, especially related to the vitamins and to a lesser extent, the minerals.

It is, accordingly, important that the cook should have some understanding of the nature and behaviour of the important vitamins or groups of vitamins in so far as the direct exercise of his craft skills are concerned. As has been noted, the vitamins with which he should be especially occupied are A, B, C and D. Of these four, two are water soluble, that is to say, they dissolve in water or fluids like stock of which water is the bulk component and two are fat soluble, that is they dissolve in fats like heated dripping or vegetable or mineral oils. This knowledge can help to guard against cooking faults.

The water-soluble vitamins are B and C and the fat-soluble vitamins are A and D. Of the two kinds it is the water-soluble vitamins, particularly vitamin C which tend most frequently to be lost or destroyed in cooking and they should thus receive the greatest vigilance on the part of the chef.

Vitamin C losses

The water-soluble vitamin C (because of its anti-scurvy function it is named the anti-scorbutic vitamin or ascorbic acid) is not only capable of being dissolved in water but is sensitive to certain elements present in water and even in the atmosphere itself and is destroyed by heat. Just as iron, if not protected, rusts in the presence of air and water so is vitamin C affected by storage and carriage by road as well as by the actual processes of preparation and cooking. The process of destruction in this way is, of course, hastened if the foods are cut too far in advance of requirement, thus exposing more surfaces to the atmosphere. Bruising and damaging has similar harmful consequences. Generally if chefs, their commis and their apprentices appreciate this fact of vitamin C containing foods to 'rust', as it were, and in the sense that the vitamin C content of fresh food deteriorates once gathered from the fields, then they are measurably nearer the point of dealing properly in the kitchen with food containing vitamin C.

In our ordinary menus an important source of this vitamin is greenleaf vegetables and potato. Important because, as has been noted, they are regular and substantial features at our meals. In dealing with these foods, therefore, the following points should be kept prominently in mind.

1. Select vegetables as freshly gathered as possible, that are not bruised or damaged. This means having regard to supply conditions to your market and the best days for making purchases.

2. Buy the correct amounts for quick use, avoiding storage in your vegetable store, however satisfactory its conditions.

3. Ensure that the vegetable store is clean, cool, dry, well ventilated.

4. Do not prepare vegetables too far in advance and particularly avoid the premature shredding or cutting of vegetables such as cabbage and avoid washing and soaking such vegetables once they have been cut and shredded.

5. Cook in the minimum quantity of boiling water and where possible make some culinary use of the liquor.

6. Cook as rapidly as possible. Warm temperatures aid destruction but boiling temperature is not as harmful because it halts the activity of vitamin-destroying elements.

7. Remember that bicarbonate of soda aids the destruction of the vitamin. It has, therefore, been regarded as wholly wrong to use soda in vegetable cookery. (It has, however, been suggested that if all other rules are followed, it may be permissible to use this cookery aid with discretion to achieve better colour and thus promote readier acceptance of the vegetables. Professional chefs should, however, be able to achieve good results without the use of soda.)

8. Serve as quickly as possible after cooking for hot-plate storage or bain-marie storage is particularly destructive of vitamin C. Cooking of vegetables at staggered times is, therefore, greatly to be desired not only from the point of view of achieving the freshly cooked result for flavour purposes, but also for nutritive reasons.

9. Remember that the foregoing indicates that left-over vegetables are likely to have little or no vitamin C content. It should be emphasised that all these considerations apply not only to vegetables which are to be *cooked*, but to those which are to be prepared for other purposes. They also apply to salads, for example, where prolonged soaking and preparation too far in advance are common faults. The early slicing or cutting of tomatoes and the premature preparation of grapefruit or fresh orange compotes are among the procedures particularly to be avoided.

Vitamin B losses

Vitamin B is, like C, capable of being dissolved in water but those foods which contain it and are regarded as important in our diet are not generally prepared and cooked like those vegetables, fruits and salads which provide us with vitamin C. It is from wholemeal grains that we gain much vitamin B and, therefore, food selection has importance here. Wholemeal, wholemeal bread and yeast itself are important sources of vitamins of the B complex and yeast is, therefore, greatly to be preferred as a leavening agent to some chemical-raising agents and baking sodas which have a deleterious effect upon B vitamins.

Certain meats have been listed as useful sources of vitamin B. Cookery methods where fat is used rather than water (e.g., roasting, grilling, frying) may be slightly less destructive of the vitamin or, rather, less conducive to its loss. The danger of leaching into cooking water which may subsequently be thrown away is avoided but on the other hand higher temperatures reached in fat and oil cooking methods are destructive of vitamin B.

The points to observe in so far as loss of B vitamins are concerned may, therefore, be summarised as:

1. Selection of whole grain and wholemeal breads for some part of the daily feeding.
2. Control of use of baking sodas and maximum use of yeast as leavener in risen goods.
3. Full use of liquors in which meat with B content has been cooked.

A and D losses

The two fat-soluble vitamins are regarded as fairly resistant to loss in cooking. It will be remembered that carotene may be regarded as a source of vitamin A and that there is some possibility of loss through really bad techniques such as leaving sliced carrots, for example, steeping in water.

The fat-soluble A and D vitamins will, of course, dissolve in mineral as in vegetable oil and it has been said that one of the undesirable results of using mineral oil in slimming diets as, for example, a salad dressing or cooking agent, is that it dissolves the A and D vitamin and carries it away from the body without it being absorbed. For mineral oil as distinct from animal and vegetable oil is not usable as food by the body and is passed through unassimilated. (Hence, the use of liquid paraffin, for example, as a laxative.)

Mineral loss

It can be said that the chief loss of minerals is through their being dissolved in cooking liquors which are subsequently not used. It is important, therefore, to use only the minimum amount of liquor for cooking purposes, e.g., in the boiling of vegetables and to make every effort to use it in the diet.

Conclusion

This chapter is intended to cover only the most basic information with which kitchen craftsmen should be acquainted. Chefs who wish to extend their knowledge of foods and nutrition will find that the *Manual of Nutrition* (H.M.S.O.) and *Elementary Science of Food* by E. M. Hildreth (Allman & Son) will be useful for preliminary study.

Over and above planning for nutritional sufficiency on a menu it should be remembered that it is clearly the food value of what is actually on the plate and eaten by the customer which determines how he is nourished. Foodstuffs entering the kitchen may be abundantly rich in nutrients which, as has been observed, may be so destroyed during storage, preparation and cooking that the food on the plate may no longer be nutritionally sufficient.

Finally, so far as the chef in hotels, restaurants and other commercial enterprises is concerned, it is just as important for him to understand food as the chef in social and welfare catering. The hotel or restaurant chef has, however, to apply his knowledge to a field where the customer is the ultimate composer of the menu. That one man's meat is another man's poison may be trite but it is a catering truism and whatever else he may do, the intelligent chef will seek to study and understand the tastes of his type of customer. He must endeavour to satisfy these demands and at the same time reconcile them with the demands of good nutrition.

16 Foods in season

Under this heading perishable and fresh foods are listed for each month of the year. The lists are not intended to be completely exhaustive but rather to indicate what is generally available and seasonable.

It cannot be too strongly stressed that 'seasonability' is nowadays a highly controversial culinary matter. It is probable that whatever policy had been adopted in arranging foodstuffs into their seasons in this section some clash of opinion would have been inevitable but an attempt has been made to steer a middle course.

Items which are in season in their own right in Britain are, of course, included and may be regarded as the main basis of the list, but it will be obvious that the list has been extended to include imported items (for example, tangerines) which, nevertheless, recognisably have a season so far as this country is concerned.

There is no doubt also that the traditional seasons for items like roasting chickens and turkeys have been greatly extended because of modern production techniques and there will be many who would suggest that season has virtually disappeared for these and similar items.

It is, of course, obvious that district has a great bearing on season and availability and that the north of Scotland, for example, will not always enjoy what is to hand in South Devon.

This section, then, is meant to be consulted merely as a general guide as to when foods are likely to be at their freshest, cheapest and best.

In the case of game, however, seasons are linked with breeding periods and conservation, thus stricter concepts of season still apply.

JANUARY
Fruit and Nuts

Apples	Cranberries	Oranges	Tangerines
Chestnuts	Grapes	Pears	Walnuts
Cobnuts	Medlars	Rhubarb, forced	

Vegetables

Artichokes, Globe	Celeriac	Mushrooms	Scotch Kale
Artichokes, Jerusalem	Celery	Mustard & Cress	Seakale
Asparagus	Chervil	Onions	Shallots
Beetroot	Chicory	Parsnips	Spanish Onions
Broccoli	Endive	Potatoes	Spinach
Brussels Sprouts	Horseradish	Red Cabbage	Swedes
Cabbage	Leeks	Salsify	Tarragon
Carrots	Lettuce	Savoys	Turnips
			Turnip Tops

Fish

Barbel	Eel	Lobsters	Shrimps
Bass	Flounder	Mussels	Skate
Bream	Haddock	Oysters	Smelt
Brill	Hake	Perch	Sole
Carp	Halibut	Pike	Sprats
Cod	Herring	Plaice	Sturgeon
Crab	John Dory	Prawns	Tench
Crayfish	Lemon Sole	Rock Salmon	Turbot
Dace	Ling	Scallops	Whiting

Meat and Meat Products

Beef	Mutton	Rabbit	Venison
House Lamb	Pork	Veal	

Poultry

Capons	Duck	Guinea Fowl	Pullet, roasting
Cockerel, roasting	Goose	Pigeon	Turkey

Game

Duck, wild	Partridge	Ptarmigan	Widgeon
Hare	Pheasant	Quail	Woodcock
Hazel Hen	Pintail	Snipe	Venison
Leveret	Plover	Teal	

FEBRUARY

Fruit and Nuts

Apples	Grapes	Oranges	Rhubarb, forced
Chestnuts	Medlars	Oranges, Seville	Tangerines
Cobnuts	Melon	Pears	Walnuts

Vegetables

Artichokes, Globe	Celery	Leeks	Seakale
Artichokes, Jerusalem	Chervil	Lettuce	Spanish Onions
Beetroot	Chicory	Mushrooms	Spinach
Broccoli	Cress	Mustard & Cress	Spring Onions
Brussels Sprouts	Cucumber	Onions	Swedes
Cabbage	Endive	Parsnips	Turnips
Carrots	Greens	Potatoes	Turnip Tops
Cauliflowers	Horseradish	Salsify	Watercress
Celeriac	Kale	Savoys	

Fish

Barbel	Eel	Mussels	Skate
Bream	Flounder	Oysters	Smelt
Brill	Haddock	Perch	Sprats
Carp	Hake	Pike	Sole
Cockles	Herring	Plaice	Sturgeon
Cod	John Dory	Rock Salmon	Tench
Crayfish	Lemon Sole	Salmon	Trout
Dabs	Ling	Scallop	Whitebait
Dace	Lobster	Shrimps	Whiting

Meat, etc.

Beef	Mutton	Rabbit
House Lamb	Pork	Veal

Poultry

Capons	Duck	Pigeon	Pullet, roasting
Cockerel, roasting	Guinea Fowl	Poussin	Turkey

Game

Duck, wild	Partridge	Ptarmigan	Teal
Hare	Pheasant	Quail	Widgeon
Hazel Hen	Pintail	Snipe	Woodcock
Leveret	Plover		

MARCH

Fruit and Nuts

Apples	Oranges, Seville
Melon	Rhubarb
Oranges	

Vegetables

Artichokes, Globe	Celeriac	Mushrooms	Savoys
Asparagus	Celery	Mustard & Cress	Scotch Kale
Beetroot	Chervil	Onion, Salad	Seakale
Broccoli	Chicory	and Spring	Spanish Onions
Brussels Sprouts	Cucumber	Onions	Spinach
Cabbage greens	Endive	Parsnips	Spring Onions
Cabbage, Spring	Kale	Potatoes, new	Turnips
Carrots	Leeks	Radishes	Watercress
Cauliflowers	Lettuce	Salsify	

Fish

Bream	Haddock	Perch	Skate
Brill	Herring	Pike	Smelt
Carp	John Dory	Plaice	Sole
Cockles	Lemon Sole	Prawns	Sturgeon
Cod	Ling	Rock Salmon	Tench
Conger Eel	Lobster	Salmon	Trout
Dabs	Mussels	Scallops	Turbot
Flounder	Oysters	Shrimps	Whitebait
			Whiting

Meat, etc.

Beef	House Lamb	Pork	Veal
Foie-gras	Mutton	Rabbit	

Poultry

Capons	Gosling	Poussin
Duck	Pigeon	

Game

Duck, wild	Ortolan	Pintail	Snipe
Hare	Partridge	Plover	Teal
Hazel Hen	Pigeon, wild	Ptarmigan	Widgeon
			Woodcock

APRIL

Fruit and Nuts

Apples	Oranges
Grapes	Rhubarb
Gooseberries, green	Rhubarb, forced

Vegetables

Artichokes, Globe	Chervil	Mustard & Cress	Scotch Kale
Asparagus	Cucumber	Onions, Salad	Sorrel
Beans, forced	Endive	or Spring	Spanish Onions
Beetroot	Greens	Parsnips	Spinach
Broccoli	Horseradish	Potatoes, new	Spring Onions
Cabbage, Spring	Leeks	Radishes	Swedes
Carrots, new	Lettuce	Salsify	Tomatoes
Cauliflowers	Marrow, forced	Savoys	Turnips
Celery	Mushrooms	Seakale	Watercress

Fish

Brill	John Dory	Pike	Skate
Carp	Mackerel	Plaice	Smelts
Cockles	Mullet	Prawns	Sole
Cod	Lemon Sole	Rock Salmon	Tench
Crab	Ling	Salmon	Trout
Dabs	Lobster	Salmon Trout	Turbot
Eel	Oysters	Scallops	Whitebait
Flounder	Perch	Shrimps	Whiting

Meat, etc.

Beef	Pork
Grass Lamb	Veal
Mutton	

Poultry

Duck	Pigeon
Duckling	Poussin
Gosling	Spring Chicken

Game

Hare	Ortolan	Pigeon, wild	Ptarmigan
Hazel Hen	Partridge	Plover's eggs	Quail
			Woodcock

MAY

Fruit and Nuts

Apples	Gooseberries,	Melon	Rhubarb
Cherries	green	Oranges	Rhubarb, forced
Currants, French	Grapes		

Vegetables

Asparagus	Chervil	Mustard & Cress	Spring Onions
Beans, forced	Flageolet	Peas	Swedes
Broccoli	Horseradish	Potatoes, new	Tomatoes
Cabbage, Spring	Leeks	Radishes	Turnips, new
Carrots, new	Lettuce	Seakale	Watercress
Cauliflowers	Marrow, forced	Sorrel	
Cucumber	Mushrooms	Spinach	

Fish

Bass	Eel	Mullet	Shrimps
Brill	Flounder	Perch	Skate
Carp	Gurnets	Pike	Smelts
Cod	Halibut	Plaice	Sole
Crabs	John Dory	Prawns	Tench
Crawfish	Ling	Rock Salmon	Trout
Dabs	Lobsters	Salmon	Turbot
Dace	Mackerel	Salmon Trout	Whitebait
			Whiting

Meat, etc.

Beef	Mutton	Venison
Grass Lamb	Veal	

Poultry

Duck	Gosling	Poussin
Duckling	Pigeon	Spring Chicken

Game

Hare	Plovers' eggs	Quail	Woodcock
Hazel Hen	Ptarmigan	Pigeon, wild	Venison

JUNE

Fruit and Nuts

Apricots	Currants, French	Oranges
Cherries	Gooseberries	Peaches
Currants, red, black	Grapes	Rhubarb
and white	Nectarines	Strawberries

Vegetables

Asparagus	Chives	Mushrooms	Spinach
Beans	Cauliflowers	Mustard & Cress	Spring Onions
Broad Beans	Cucumber	Onions	Tomatoes
Beetroot	Flageolet	Peas	Turnips, new
Broccoli	Horseradish	Potatoes, new	Watercress
Cabbage, Spring	Lettuce	Radishes	
Carrots, new	Marrow, forced	Sorrel	

Fish

Bass	Flounder	Mullet	Shrimps
Carp	Gurnets	Perch	Skate
Cod	Haddock	Pike	Sole
Crab	Halibut	Plaice	Tench
Dabs	John Dory	Prawns	Trout
Dace	Ling	Rock Salmon	Turbot
Crawfish	Lobsters	Salmon	Whitebait
Eel	Mackerel	Salmon Trout	Whiting

Meat, etc.

Beef	Mutton	Venison
Grass Lamb	Veal	

Poultry

Duck	Gosling	Poussin
Duckling	Pigeon	Spring Chicken

Game

Hazel Hen	Pigeon, wild	Venison
Ortolan	Quail	Woodcock

JULY

Fruit and Nuts

Apricots	Currants, red	Loganberries	Rhubarb
Cherries	Gooseberries	Melon	Raspberries
Currants, black	Grapes	Nectarines	Strawberries
Currants, French	Greengages	Plums	

Vegetables

Artichokes	Cabbages	Lettuce	Radishes
Asparagus	Carrots	Marrow	Scarlet runners
Broad Beans	Cauliflowers	Mushrooms	Sorrel
French Beans	Cucumber	Mustard & Cress	Spinach
Kidney Beans	Flageolets	Onions	Tomatoes
Runner Beans	Horseradish	Peas	Turnips
Beetroot	Leeks	Red Cabbage	Watercress

Fish

Barbel	Eel	Lobster	Salmon
Bass	Flounder	Mackerel	Salmon trout
Carp	Gurnets	Mullet, grey	Shrimps
Cod	Haddock	and red	Skate
Crab	Hake	Perch	Sole
Crawfish	Halibut	Pike	Tench
Crayfish	Herring	Plaice	Trout
Dabs	John Dory	Prawns	Turbot
Dace	Ling	Rock Salmon	Whitebait
			Whiting

Meat, etc.

Beef	Mutton	Venison
Grass Lamb	Veal	

Poultry

Duck	Gosling	Pigeon
Duckling	Guinea Fowl	Pullet, roasting

Game

Hazel Hen	Pigeon, wild	Venison
Ortolan	Quail	Woodcock

AUGUST

Fruit and Nuts

Apples	Currants, red	Loganberries	Pears
Apricots	Filberts	Melon	Plums
Cherries	Grapes	Mulberries	Raspberries
Cherries, Canadian	Gooseberries	Nectarines	Strawberries
Currant, black	Greengages	Peaches	

Vegetables

Artichokes	Carrots	Marrow	Scarlet runners
Broad Beans	Cauliflowers	Mushrooms	Sorrel
French Beans	Corn, Indian	Mustard & Cress	Spinach
Kidney Beans	Cucumber	Onions	Tomatoes
Runner Beans	Endive	Peas	Turnips
Beetroot	Lettuce	Potatoes, new	Watercress
Cabbages	Maize	Radishes	

Fish

Barbel	Haddock	Mussels	Sole
Bass	Hake	Perch	Sturgeon
Brill	Halibut	Pike	Tench
Carp	Herring	Plaice	Trout
Cod	John Dory	Prawns	Turbot
Crab	Lobster	Shrimps	Whitebait
Crayfish	Mackerel	Salmon	Whiting
Dab	Mullet, grey	Salmon trout	
Eel	and red	Skate	
Flounder			

Meat, etc.

Beef	Veal
Mutton	Venison

Poultry

Cockerel, roasting	Duckling	Guinea Fowl	Pullet, roasting
Duck	Gosling	Pigeon	

Game

Blackcock	Grouse	Landrail	Quail
Capercailzie	Hare	Ortolan	Venison
Duck, wild	Hazel Hen	Pigeon, wild	Woodcock

SEPTEMBER

Fruit and Nuts

Apples	Cherries	Medlars	Pear
Apricots	Cobnuts	Melons	Plums
Barberries	Damsons	Mulberries	Quince
Blackberries	Filberts	Nectarines	Pumpkin
Currants, red, white and black	Greengages	Peach	Walnut

Vegetables

Artichokes	Cauliflowers	Lettuce	Radishes
Broad Beans	Celery	Marrow	Savoys
Kidney Beans	Chervil	Mushrooms	Scarlet Runners
Runner Beans	Corn, Indian	Mustard & Cress	Sorrel
Beetroot	Cucumber	Onions	Spinach
Broccoli	Endive	Parsnip	Swedes
Brussels Sprouts	Green Peas	Potatoes	Tomatoes
Cabbages	Horseradish	Pumpkin	Turnips
Carrots	Leeks	Red Cabbage	Watercress

Fish

Barbel	Dab	Mackerel	Salmon trout
Bass	Eel	Mullet, red and	Shrimps
Bloaters	Flounder	grey	Skate
Bream	Haddock	Mussels	Sole
Brill	Hake	Oysters	Sturgeon
Carp	Halibut	Perch	Tench
Cod	Herring	Pike	Trout
Crab	John Dory	Plaice	Whitebait
Crayfish	Lobster	Prawns	Whiting
		Salmon	

Meat, etc.

Beef	Rabbit	Veal
Mutton	Pork	Venison

Poultry

Cockerel, roasting	Duckling	Goose	Pigeon
Duck	Gosling	Guinea Fowl	Pullet, roasting
			Turkey

Game

Blackcock	Hare	Partridge	Venison
Capercailzie	Hazel Hen	Pintail	Woodcock
Duck, wild	Landrail	Pigeon, wild	
Grouse	Leveret	Quail	

OCTOBER

Fruit and Nuts

Apples	Damsons	Melon	Pomegranate
Barberries	Filberts	Nectarines	Pumpkin
Blackberries	Grapes	Peach	Quince
Cobnuts	Medlars	Pear	Walnut

Vegetables

Artichokes	Celeriac	Leeks	Red Cabbage
Artichokes, Jerusalem	Celery	Lettuce	Savoys
Beans, runner	Chervil	Marrow	Swedes
Beetroot	Chicory	Mushrooms	Spinach
Broccoli	Corn, Green	Mustard & Cress	Tomatoes
Brussels Sprouts	Cucumbers	Onions	Turnips
Cabbages	Endive	Pumpkin	Watercress
Carrots	Greens	Parsnip	
Cauliflowers	Horseradish	Radishes	

Fish

Barbel	Flounder	Mullet, grey	Salmon trout
Bream	Gudgeon	and red	Scallops
Brill	Haddock	Mussels	Skate
Carp	Hake	Oysters	Smelt
Cod	Halibut	Perch	Sole
Crabs	Herring	Pike	Sturgeon
Crayfish	John Dory	Plaice	Tench
Dab	Lemon Sole	Prawns	Turbot
Eel	Lobsters	Salmon	Whiting

Meat, etc.

Beef	Pork	Veal
Foie-gras	Rabbit	Venison

Poultry

Cockerel, roasting	Goose	Pigeon	Turkey
Duck	Guinea Fowl	Pullet, roasting	

Game

Blackcock	Hazel Hen	Pheasant	Venison
Capercailzie	Lark	Plover	Widgeon
Duck, wild	Leveret	Quail	Woodcock
Grouse	Partridge	Snipe	
Hare	Pintail	Teal	

NOVEMBER

Fruit and Nuts

Apples	Cobnuts	Melon	Pomegranates
Barberries	Cranberries	Oranges	Quince
Chestnuts	Grapes	Pear	Tangerines
			Walnuts

Vegetables

Artichokes, Jerusalem	Celery	Leeks	Red Cabbage
Beetroot	Chicory	Lettuce	Savoys
Broccoli	Corn, Green	Mushrooms	Shallots
Brussels Sprouts	Corn, Indian	Mustard & Cress	Spanish Onions
Cabbages	Cucumber	Onions	Spinach
Carrots	Endive	Parsnips	Swedes
Cauliflowers	Greens	Potatoes	Tomatoes
Celeriac	Horseradish	Radishes	Turnips
			Watercress

Fish

Barbel	Eel	Mussels	Sprat
Bream	Flounder	Oysters	Sole
Brill	Gudgeon	Perch	Sturgeon
Carp	Haddock	Pike	Tench
Cod	Halibut	Plaice	Turbot
Crab	Herring	Scallops	Whiting
Crayfish	John Dory	Skate	
Dab	Lemon Sole	Smelt	

Meat, etc.

Beef	Mutton	Rabbit	Venison
Foie-gras	Pork	Veal	

Poultry

Cockerel, roasting	Goose	Pullet, roasting
Duck	Guinea Fowl	Turkey

Game

Blackcock	Hazel Hen	Pintail	Venison
Capercailzie	Lark	Plover	Widgeon
Duck, wild	Leveret	Quail	Woodcock
Grouse	Partridge	Snipe	
Hare	Pheasant	Teal	

DECEMBER

Fruit and Nuts

Apples	Cranberries	Oranges	Tangerines
Chestnuts	Grapes	Pears	Walnuts
Cobnuts	Melon	Rhubarb, forced	

Vegetables

Artichokes, Jerusalem	Chervil	Mushrooms	Shallots
Beetroot	Chicory	Mustard & Cress	Spanish Onions
Broccoli	Corn, Green	Onions	Spinach
Brussels Sprouts	Endive	Parsnips	Swedes
Cabbages	Kale	Potatoes	Tomatoes
Carrots	Horseradish	Red Cabbage	Turnips
Cauliflowers	Leeks	Salsify	Watercress
Celeriac	Lettuce	Savoys	
Celery	Maize	Seakale	

Fish

Barbel	Eel	Lobsters	Shrimps
Bream	Flounder	Mussels	Skate
Brill	Gudgeon	Oysters	Smelt
Carp	Haddock	Perch	Sole
Cod	Halibut	Pike	Sprats
Crabs	Herring	Plaice	Sturgeon
Crayfish	John Dory	Rock Salmon	Tench
Dace	Lemon Sole	Scallops	Turbot
			Whiting

Meat, etc.

Beef	Mutton	Rabbit	Venison
House Lamb	Pork	Veal	

Poultry

Cockerel, roasting	Goose	Pullet, roasting
Duck	Guinea Fowl	Turkey

Game

Blackcock	Lark	Plover	Venison
Duck, wild	Leveret	Ptarmigan	Widgeon
Grouse	Partridge	Quail	Woodcock
Hare	Pheasant	Snipe	
Hazel Hen	Pintail	Teal	

17 Buying

Responsibilities for the buying of both perishable goods and commodities for the dry stores vary considerably in the catering industry according to the type and size of the establishment. In large hotels and hotel and restaurant groups buying is a highly specialised function and duties may be narrowed down to the purchase at the meat market of meat alone. Fish buying and vegetable and fruit buying may be similarly handled by a specialist buyer. In other establishments the duties of a buyer may be spread over a wider range of commodities.

There is, in any case, an increasing tendency for buying to be taken out of the hands of the chef and given to an executive detached from day-to-day kitchen work.

It goes without saying that the prime requisite in buying for the hotel and catering establishment is complete personal integrity and a concept of the duty as being one which means getting the best bargain in terms of quality and price that is compatible with the establishment's catering policy.

Buying should certainly not be a matter of 'automatic' re-ordering on the basis of past experience by repetition of customary orders. It should rather follow thoughtful estimating based also on intelligent forecasting, prevailing prices, stocks held and other relative factors.

It may well be that today the chef and, indeed, the catering officer or catering manager may not, therefore, have sole responsibility for purchasing goods and nominating suppliers. There are, however, many instances particularly in smaller kitchens where cooking and catering are of necessity combined with purchasing. In any event the chef will invariably be a person carrying major responsibility for the acceptance of goods delivered and it is obvious that he must have a sound knowledge of the raw materials and commodities that he and his staff are to use. His technical advice is likely to be required under any buying arrangement.

The materials used in this type of catering appropriate to the largest hotel involves an important range of commodities. On the one hand are the perishable items like meat, game, fish and poultry which involve a knowledge of meat cuts and joints used in the hotel trade as well as those used in the retail meat trade; on the other hand is a range of fruit and vegetables which include those more exotic than are commonly found in the average retail green-grocers' and fruiterers' shops.

In addition to perishables, provisions and grocery items again range far wider than the average retail grocer's shop.

Large reference volumes have been written on one or two main categories of food alone and there can be no question of either perishable items or dry goods receiving encyclopaedic treatment in this chapter. The purpose of this section is rather to indicate the main features concerning the chef or caterer in regard to buying and to suggest how he may increase his knowledge through appropriate use of reference sources and books as well as from his own experience.

Meat

It has been suggested that one of the reasons for the superiority of French cusine was the need to enhance poor quality meat. Few people, particularly those who appreciate French veal, would today wholly accept this rather naïve belief but there can be no doubt that meat plays a dominant role in the cookery of France itself, in French cookery in Britain and other parts of the Western world and in native British cookery. An ability to judge meat, therefore, and subsequently to dissect it appropriately is an important feature of kitchen management.

It may be observed that meat of all kinds is subject to inspection at abattoirs and ports of entry and there is, nowadays, little need to be concerned with emaciated carcasses or those showing real signs of disease. It may be useful for him, however, to have for reference a work such as *The Food Inspector's Encyclopaedia* (published by Ballière, Tindall and Cox), but he would undoubtedly call for the proper officer of the Local Authority if the question of meat condemnation arose. It is far more important for the chef to recognise readily the various cuts and to judge primeness with accuracy.

If meat cannot be obtained wholesale and has to be bought from a retailer, the chef or caterer should seek the most favourable arrangements and must not overlook the advantage to the meat purveyor of preparing hotel or catering orders known in advance as against spasmodic counter sales.

The caterer buys meat for resale and may expect discount (say 10% on normal retail prices) or other special terms.

Beef

In buying beef the chef has traditionally looked for marbling, that is to say, the appearance of particles of fat in the lean section of the meat. Possibly, as a result of the cult of slimming, the housewife has somewhat reacted against this tradition and the domestic purchaser has stimulated a greater demand for a leaner type of meat. Nevertheless, marbling remains an important feature of good beef. Additionally, good-quality beef should have bright, firm and fine-grained lean meat and its fat should be white rather than yellow, though this latter is affected by the breed and is certainly not as inflexible a rule as the others. Light-coloured meat with the appearance of oozing is indicative of toughness and darker shades with drier though still damp texture is usually evidence of meat having been well-hung and will not be avoided by the chef. It is generally considered that beef in quarters or large wholesale cuts should be matured for at least ten days in a temperature between 38°F–42°F before it is dissected.

Scotch breeds of beef such as the Aberdeen-Angus and Beef Short-horn have been specially reared with an eye to the table and are rightly esteemed. Home-killed Scotch beef is, therefore, a food item which should be exploited to the maximum. It should not be overlooked, however, that imported breeds raised from similar strains can give excellent results. Signs of quality are similar whatever the place of origin.

Dissection of meat varies a good deal in Britain according to the custom of the retail meat trade in a given area. Larger establishments purchase beef by sides or quarters and this enables hotels to use traditional French cuts suitable for high-class restaurant work and for catering establishments of more modest pretensions to exploit the side or quarter more economically than when it has been dissected for retailers' profit. It is not practical to give all the various variations in cuts of meat, therefore, which may be encountered in butchery but the following are the principal cuts together with an indication of their approximate weight:

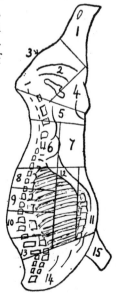

1	Shin
2	Topside
3	Silverside
4	Thick flank
5	Rump
6	Sirloin
7	Thin flank
8	Wing ribs
9	Fore ribs
10	Middle ribs
11	Brisket
12	Flat ribs
13	Chuck ribs
14	Neck
15	Shank

72 Side of Beef (Inside Cuts)

	Uses	Average weight in lb from a side of beef approx. 250 lb
BEEF *CUTS* (English and French)		
1. Shin (Jambe)	Gravy, Stock, Stewing	14–15
2. Topside (Tranche Tendre)	Roast, Braising, Carbonade, Paupiette	19–20
3. Silverside (Cite à la Noix)	Salting, Boiling	20–22
4. Thick Flank (Tranche Grasse)	General Purpose. Braising, Stewing, Pies	20–22
5. Rump (Culotte), including head fillet	Grill, Roast, Braising	20–25
6. Sirloin (Aloyau)	Roast, Grill, including Fillet (filet) and Contrefilet	16–18
7. Thin Flank (Bavette d'Aloyau)	Stewing, Pie	12–16
8. Wing Ribs (Côte d'Aloyau)	Roast, Braising	10–12
9. Fore Ribs (Côte Première)	Roast	18–20
10. Middle Ribs (Côte Decouverte)	Roast, Pot Roast	18–20
11. Brisket (Poitrine)	Stewing, Salting, Mince (Sausage Meat)	20–25
12. Flat Ribs (Plat Décotes Decouverte)	Boiling, Mince, Sausage	15–18
13. Chuck Ribs (Côte de Collier)	Pot Roast, Stew, Pie	18–20
14. Neck (Collier)	Stew, Mince	16–18
15. Shank (Jarret de Devant)	Gravy, Stock, Stewing	10–12
BEEF *OFFAL* (which, except for Kidney, are not included when buying a side or quarter)		
Heart (Cœur)	Stuffing, Braising, Bake	5½
Tail (Queue)	Soups, Stewing, Braising	2–3
Kidney (Rognon)	Soups, Sauté, Pie, Pudding	1½
Brain (Cervelle)	Boiling, Fried, Hors d'œuvres	
Tongue (Langue)	Boiling, Braising, Pickling	6
Tripe (Tripes)	Boiling, Stewing, Sauté	
Liver (Foie)	Frying, Sauté, Stewing, Braising, Terrine, Pâté	5–7
Sweetbread (Ris)	Frying, Stewing, Sauté	

Lamb or mutton

Seasonal variations in lamb and mutton buying are less important than formerly because of chilling and cold storage. Nevertheless, the fact that home-killed lamb is at its best in springtime (April and May) should not be overlooked. Mutton, on the other hand, is available and makes good eating all the year round.

Native lamb and mutton, particularly Southdown, is highly esteemed but imported meat, especially from New Zealand, reaches high standards.

The appearance of good lamb is pink rather than red with fine graining in the lean. The fat should not only be creamy coloured but have a clear, crisp appearance. Mutton will have, by virtue of its coming from an older animal, darker red meat with white and waxier fat. The cuts of lamb and mutton with their approximate weights are as follows:

1 Leg
2 Chump
3 Saddle
4 Best end
5 Shoulder
6 Breast
7 Neck, Scrag end

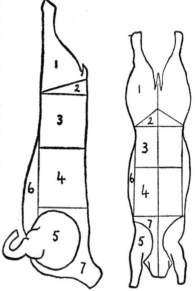

73 Carcase of Lamb or Mutton

	Uses	Approx. average weight in lb	
		Lamb: Carcass, 38 lb approx.	Mutton: 50 lb approx.
LAMB AND MUTTON *CUTS*			
1. Leg (Gigot)	Roast, Boiling (Mutton)	4–5 each	7–8 each
2. Chump*	(Chops) Grilling, Roast	1½–2	3½–4½
3. Saddle (Salle)†	Roast, Grill (in Chops), Noisettes	5–6	7–8
4. Best end (Carré)	Roast Grilling (Cutlets)	4–5	6½–7½
5. Shoulder (Epaule)	Roast, Stuffed, Braised, Poêlé	3–4 each	4½–5½ each
6. Breast (Poitrine)	Stew, Epigrammes, Bone, Stuff	4–5	6½–7½
7. Neck, Scrag end (Cou, Collier)	Stewing, Navarin	3–4	4½–5½
LAMB *OFFAL* (which, kidneys excepted, are not included when buying a carcass)			
Liver (Foie)	Fried, Sauté, Stewed, Braised, Terrine, Pâte	¾–1	2–3
Kidney (Rognon)	Sauté, Stewed, Grilled	6 oz–8 oz	8 oz–10 oz
Head (Tête)	Boiled	3	4–5

* Unless required for chops, the chump is either left on the leg to give a long leg for roasting or left on the saddle (especially when the latter is to be carved in the restaurant).

† Split down the middle the saddle makes two loins.

Veal

Native veal is available all the year round and is not as seasonal as lamb. It is, however, regarded as at its best in the summer months. In Britain, emphasis has been on the raising of herds of beef cattle and veal has not in the past reached such a high standard as beef and lamb and though there are signs of greater concentration on veal production, keen buyers for quality tend to look for Continental, particularly Dutch, veal.

The lean part of veal should be clear, pale pink with the fat firm and pinky white. Any evidence of softness or moistness in fat means staleness and is to be avoided. Further positive signs of quality is kidney well covered with fat and bright blue veins in the shoulder. The joints of veal with their approximate weights and uses are as follows:

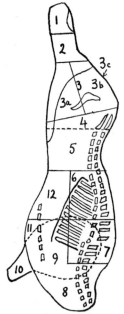

1	Shank
2	Knuckle
3	Leg
3a	Thick flank
3b	Cushion
3c	Under cushion
4	Rump
5	Loin
6	Best end
7	Low cutlets
8	Neck
9	Shoulder
10	Knuckle
11	Breast
12	Tendons

74　Side of Veal (Inside Cuts)

	Uses	Approx. average weight in lb: from carcass of fed veal approx. 170 lb
VEAL *CUTS*		
1. Shank (Crosse)	Stock and Jelly	⎱ 4–6
2. Knuckle (Jarret Derrière)	Osso Bucco, Sauté	⎰
3. Leg (Cuisse)	Roast, Braise, Escalopes, Sauté	30–35
3a. Thick Flank (Noix Patissière)	Roast, Escalopes	
3b. Cushion (Noix de Veau)	Roast, Escalopes, Fricandeau	Parts of leg
3c. Under Cushion (Sous Noix)	Roast, Escalopes	
4. Rump (Cul Deveau)	Escalopes, Roast	
5. Loin (Longe) (two comprising a saddle)	Roast, Chops	16–18
6. Best End (Carré)	Roast, Cutlets	12–14
7. Low Cutlets (Côtelettes Decouvertes)	Stewing	12
8. Neck (Collet)	Stewing	
9. Shoulder (Epaule)	Roast, Stuffed, braised, stew	15 each
10. Knuckle (Jarret Devant)	Osso Bucco, Sauté	3–4 each
11. Breast (Poitrine)	Stewing, Bone and Stuff, Galantine	8–10 each
12. Tendons (Tendrons)	Blanquettes, Goulash	Part of breast

	Uses	Approx. average weight in lb
VEAL *OFFAL*		
Head	Boiling, Frying, Hors d'œuvres	10
Tongue (Langue)	Boiled, Stewed, Cold, Salad	$1\frac{1}{2}$–2
Liver (Foie)	Sauté, grilled, Brochette, Terrine	3–4
Brain (Cervelle)	Boiled, Sauté, Ravigote	$\frac{3}{4}$–1
Kidney (Rognon)	Grilled, Fried, Sauté	8 oz–10 oz each
Heart (Cœur)	Braising, Stuffing	$\frac{3}{4}$
Feet (Pieds)	Boiling	6 (a set)
Sweetbreads (Ris de Veau)	Braising, Frying	$1\frac{1}{2}$

Pork

Pork at one time was a highly seasonal animal and was rigorously excluded from the menu in months with an 'R' in them. The importation of pork from other countries and the use of freezing and refrigerated storage has made the seasonal aspect less rigid but it is not one which will be entirely ignored by the buyer or menu maker.

Pork as distinct from bacon pig should, though young and well fed, be small rather than excessively fat. The lean meat should be pink, pale rather than bright, of firm and fine-grained texture making it resilient to the touch. The skin should be thin and the underlying fat white, firm and fine grained.

Whilst a cut surface should appear slightly moist any excessive exudation of moisture is an unfavourable sign. In older animals, flesh is coarser, darker and of drier appearance.

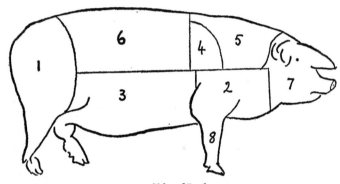

75   Side of Pork

1	Leg	4	Bladebone	7	Head
2	Hand and Spring	5	Spare Rib	8	Trotters
3	Belly	6	Loin		

	Uses	Approx. average weight in lb: from side of pork weighing approx. 60 lb
PORK *CUTS* (English and French)		
1. Leg (Cuissot)	Roast, Boiling (Salt)	14¼
2. Hand and Spring (Epaule)	Boiling, Roast (excluding knuckle)	6½
3. Belly (Poitrine)	Pickling, Boiling, Rillette	10
4. Bladebone ⎫ (Basse-Côte) 5. Spare Rib ⎬	Roast, Braising, Pickling	8¾ ⎫ 17½ 8¾ ⎭
6. Loin (Longe)	Roast, Chops (Grill and Fry)	15
PORK *OFFAL*		
Liver (Foie)	Terrine, Pâté	2–3
Head (Tête)	Brawn	5½

Bacon

Bacon is prepared from pigs older and better developed than those used for pork. The type of cure will affect purchasing considerations and green (unsmoked) bacon differs obviously from smoked. General signs of quality are smooth, thin, flexible rind, good pink colour of lean meat with firm, clean-looking fat, tinged with pink from the brining process but not showing any yellow marks. Bone taint may be encountered in bacon and should be sought by inserting a skewer deeply into the flesh adjoining the bones.

Useful information for caterers to help in buying, portioning and costing may be obtained from the Bacon Information Council, Brook House, Park Lane, London, W.1. Details of grades and types and even of cooking loss are available.

1 Forehock
2 Collar
3 Thick Streaky
4 Thin Streaky
5 Back and Ribs
6 Long Loin
7 Gammon
8 Corner Gammon

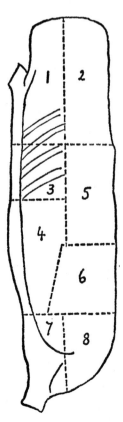

76 Side of Bacon

Bacon Cuts	Uses	Weight (lb)	Approx. number of average size rashers: from average side total weight = 55 lb
1. Fore Hock	Boil, Grill	9	} 64 × 2 oz rashers
2. Collar	Boil, Grill	8	
3. Thick Streaky	Grill, Griddle, Fry	9½	155 × 1 oz rashers
4. Thin Streaky			
5. Back and Ribs	Grill, Griddle, Fry	15	160 × 1½ oz rashers
6. Long Loin			
7. Gammon	Boiling and Grilling	13½	
8. Corner Gammon			

Poultry and game

The development of the 'broiler' industry and the prevalence of chilled and frozen poultry, bred to standard size, has obviated at some levels of catering the need for traditional types of judgment in selecting birds. The trend towards marketing standard and reliable products is likely to continue yet there will be occasions when even the most modest type of catering will need to know something of the points of quality in poultry selection. Under the designation of poultry are, of course, included all domestic birds specifically reared for eating or for their eggs; e.g., chickens, ducks, geese, turkey, pigeon and guinea fowl.

Fowls

The skin of a fowl should be smooth and its breast bone soft and flexible. Manipulating the front part of the breast bone between the fingers to test its pliability is perhaps the most reliable method of testing the youth and tenderness of a chicken. A hard, unyielding breast bone is a certain indication of an old and tough bird.

The colour of a fowl is not necessarily a mark of quality. Surreys, which are much esteemed, have a pleasing, light appearance but many buyers favour dark-skinned birds as likely to have a better flavour.

Other signs of youth are small spurs, combs and wattle with abundant small, shiny scales over legs which should be flexible and smooth in appearance. The skin should be supple as well as smooth to the touch. Naturally, plumpness should be looked for.

Signs of age are general coarseness of appearance, particularly coarse scales on the feet, rough skin and long hairs. There are times when an old fowl will be required for stockpot and similar purposes but whatever the age of a bird it should be fresh and in good condition.

General points, irrespective of age, to look for are:

Good appearance of the eyes (particularly avoid those with sunken eyes).
Unblemished skin of regular colour, avoiding birds of patchy and discoloured appearance.

Finally, of course, sense of smell must be relied on for indication of fresh condition and a bird should smell wholesome and clean. Poultry should be hung for a day at least but must not be allowed to develop a 'gamey' flavour.

Duck

Ducks make the finest eating when they are about ten weeks old and when they may still be properly described as ducklings. The season for them is springtime persisting to mid-summer. Birds of lesser quality or birds that have been frozen are, of course, available all the year round. In Britain the Aylesbury breed is particularly esteemed.

Signs of youth and quality are:

Good yellow colour of feet and bills. Softness is also sought in the upper bill which should be easily penetrated with the fingers and the feet should be flexible. As in domestic birds, generally, the vent should be well formed and firm.

Geese

Geese are in season all the year round, though there is a tendency to bring them to market for Michaelmas and Christmas eating. Similar points should be looked for as in selecting duck.

Turkey

Though at one time the season for turkey did not extend beyond October–March, with real demand concentrated in December and January, the birds tend to be increasingly used all the year round. Breeding and processing for marketing has been developed with this in view. The better, full-grown birds weigh between 8 and 12 lb and hens are regarded as more delicately flavoured than cocks, though some chefs consider cock birds are superior as far as tenderness goes. Larger birds, i.e., those over 14 lb, are usually selected for catering for reasons of economy. The cock bird is recognised by the development of the head. Turkeys should betray signs of quality similar to fowls in so far as good odour, plumpness and cleanness of appearance are concerned. Particular points to look for are smoothness and good, black colour of legs and soft white skin.

Guinea fowl

Guinea fowl are considered to be in season from early spring to early summer and they begin to appear on menus as early as February. There is a tendency for the birds to be tough and dry and, because of their relative scarcity, the caterer can seldom exercise much choice other than acceptance or rejection. Birds should weigh 2¾ lb or over if they are to be satisfactory for roasting. Though much darker hued than chickens, they may be tested for youth by softness of flesh and pliability of bone in similar fashion.

Pigeons

Pigeons are bought for the table from early spring to autumn (March to October). Wood pigeons are distinguished from domestic ones by their larger size. Signs of youth are light pink colour of the claws, plumpness of the breast and the general softness to the touch of the flesh which is of light reddish colour.

Game

Game is not confined to birds but embraces flesh foods other than fish which are brought to the table as a result of hunting or sport as distinct from domestic rearing or herding.

General considerations in choosing game birds

There are a large number of game birds and it is not proposed to deal with those other than are commonly brought to table. Some general considerations have, however, wide application in selecting game birds. Points of quality and youth to be looked for are easy breaking or penetration of the beak with a finger, smoothness and suppleness of legs and toes, ease of removal of spurs, shortness of wing quill feathers.

Specific points peculiar to common game birds are:

Grouse. Clear appearance of flesh which should be slightly pink, short quills and general freshness (though grouse may be hung to 'gamey' flavour in accordance with customer requirements, it is generally considered best eaten freshly shot rather than 'high').

Partridge. Of the two types of partridge, the grey variety is regarded as a bird to be eaten young, when the feet should be of good yellow colour and the whole appearance of the flesh smooth, soft and plump. Red-legged partridge are eaten when mature and signs of age are not, therefore, so important.

OTHER GAME

Venison. The meat, though dark in colour, should be of clean appearance and accompanying fat should be abundant, bright and clear. It is normally hung for a considerable period in a cool, well-ventilated larder or cellar; up to three weeks, in fact, is quite common when decomposition has rendered the meat tender and 'gamey' flavoured. Modern taste is inclined to favour, however, roe deer eaten comparatively fresh rather than red deer eaten 'high'.

Hares and Rabbits. Hares are brought to the table towards the end of summer up to early spring and young hares (leverets) have tender ears and claws which tear easily. Long claws and tough ears are signs of age. Young, plump hares about eight months old make the best eating but, of course, older animals are perfectly suitable for jugging, terrines, etc.

Rabbit. Much rabbit eaten has been bred for eating or for its fur and is not strictly speaking game. Wild rabbit generally betrays itself in eating by having a herby flavour according to the pasture on which they have fed. In young rabbits the ears are tender and easily torn and the lower part of the jaw will crack readily when pressed between the fingers. The flesh is much whiter than that of the hare and the fat should be clean and white.

Fish buying

The caterer will usually seek to buy fish direct from the Fish Market but if this cannot be arranged, a hotel or catering establishment would, as in the case of meat, look for a trading arrangement with a retail fishmonger and a discount of 10% on retail price would be a suitable one.

There is more than one way of classifying fish. Nutritionists, for example, as well as caterers are concerned with the difference between white and oily fish. There is a grouping of fish in fresh-water or sea-water categories and there is the shellfish or crustacean group. In buying, perhaps, it may be convenient to consider sea-fish in three main classes:

Flat Fish, Round Fish and Shellfish.

In the *flat-fish* group are those fish like brill, halibut, John Dory, plaice, sole, skate.

Round fish, comprising both white fish and oily fish varieties, include cod, haddock, whiting, herring, mackerel, salmon and the like.

The *shellfish* group include crabs, lobsters, prawns, shrimps and may be extended to take in oysters, mussels and similar types.

With the exception of herring, all sea fishes are gutted before sale and this may be done at sea or at the docks prior to marketing.

Because of the many varieties of fish it is desirable to summarise the general points indicative of general freshness and quality that should be looked for in buying. The following are of importance:

1. There should be a complete absence of any unpleasant smell.
2. The eyes should be bright, clear, transparent and convex. That is to say, they should not have a dulled, sunken appearance.
3. The fish should have its full natural colour without fading. (In plaice, for example, the reddish spots should be clearly present.)
4. The gills, similarly, should be of good colour and firm to the touch.
5. Flesh generally should be firm and resilient and should not remain depressed when touched by the finger.

The foregoing signs are, of course, all concerned with the fact that fish is a food which quickly decomposes after death and out of the sea. Such decomposition can be prevented by storage at low temperature but after marketing the purchaser must exercise great vigilance. Signs of decomposition are the converse of the positive signs of freshness and are signalled by:

1. Dull, sunken and greyish-coloured eyes.
2. Blood turning brown in colour.
3. Flesh softening and becoming easily separated from the bone.
4. The natural, moist texture imparted by the mucous becoming thick and sticky.
5. Scales becoming detached readily.

As will have been noted from the *Food in Season Calendar*, pp. 246, et seq., fish, because of breeding, migratory habits and other factors, are in some cases seasonal, and the chef and caterer will look for the time when they are most plentiful and, therefore, at their cheapest and best.

Shellfish and Crustaceans

Some types of shellfish may cause trouble to diners who have allergies. Shellfish also tend to be prone to infection in the case, for example, of contamination by typhoid germs as a result of sewage discharging near oyster beds. Particular vigilance is required, therefore, in selecting shellfish through reliable purveyors and caterers should be aware of the facilities that exist through health authorities for ensuring thorough cleansing and absence of contamination prior to sale.

Oysters. Though foreign oysters may be obtainable all the year round, there is a close season for native varieties and they are only eaten when there is an 'R' in the month. During the rest of the year spawning takes place and the oysters are indigestible and of poor taste and body. Natives such as Whitstables are considered to be in prime condition between four and five years old, though foreign oysters such as Portuguese when re-laid in British coastal waters come to maturity earlier. The smallest natives should not be less than $2\frac{1}{2}$ in. in diameter and primes should be between $3-4\frac{1}{2}$ in. in diameter.

Look for tightly closed shells or, in the case of those slightly open, immediate closure on handling. Open-shelled oysters should otherwise be rejected as dead. In opening, the shell of a fresh oyster should noticeably close upon the knife and the more strongly this closure is, so much the better indication of a sound oyster.

Mussels. Mussels, though in season from July to April, are at their best from August to November. They are generally considered more prone to typhoid bacillus carrying than even oysters or cockles but fortunately can be cleansed from contamination by being placed in clean water for a period of not less than four days.

Look for tightly closed mussels and avoid those that gape or, when bagged, rattle when the bag is shaken.

Lobsters. Lobsters are obtainable all the year but are most abundant and best in the summer. They must be alive when purchased and to test their freshness, pull back the tail which should close smartly.

Crabs. Crabs are similarly obtainable all the year but are most abundant in spring and early summer when they are at their best. Unlike lobsters they should be killed before boiling otherwise they tend to cast their claws. Avoid crabs that are discoloured and are of a faded appearance. Stickiness of claws at the joints is also a danger sign.

OTHER SHELLFISH

Similar considerations apply to prawns, shrimps and other shellfish, many of which in modern marketing are, however, purchased ready cooked and possibly quick frozen.

Vegetables and fruit

In the purchase of all commodities it is important to become familiar with the customary units of weight or measurement at which they can be most favourably bought. In the case of vegetables there are few difficulties regarding hundredweight sacks of potatoes, for example, but 'heads' of celery and 'bunches' of leeks are much more variable units and this is one of the reasons why personal supervision of purchasing is desirable.

The following have no statutory backing but are weights generally accepted in London markets for packs of home-grown produce:

Fruit		*lb*
Apples	Bushel	40
	Half-box	20
Blackberries	Chip	2
Cherries	Handle/Strike/Chip	12
	Half-bushel	24
Currants	Chip	6 or 12
	Half-bushel	24–28
Damsons	Half-box	24–28
	Bushel	50–56
Gooseberries	Chip	12
	Half-bushel	24
Pears	Bushel	40
	Half-box	20
Plums	Chip	12
	Half-bushel	28
	Bushel	56
Raspberries	Punnet	1
	Chip	2
Strawberries	Punnet	1
	Chip	2 or 4

Vegetables		*lb*
Beans, French Runner	Chip	5
	Box	28–32
Beetroot	Half-bag	56
Brussels Sprouts	Net	20
	Half-bag	28
Brussels Tops	Half-bag	30–36
Cabbage	Half-bag	30–36
	Box	36–40
	Mat	56
Carrots	Half-bag	56
Leeks	Crate	20–24
Mushrooms	Chip	4-6-12
Onions	Half-bag	56
Parsnips	Half-bag	56
Peas	Half-bag	56
Potatoes	Bag	112
Savoys	Bag	30–36
Spinach	Crate	14
Swedes	Half-bag	56
Tomatoes	Chip/Box	12
Turnips	Half-bag	56

Much has been said, too, of the wilted lettuce reserved for 'telephone' customers. Reliable greengrocers who value their connection with the chef or caterer will not stoop to petty deceptions but there obviously remains great advantage in personal selection of fresh commodities which quickly go out of condition and which may be offered in rather indeterminate units of measurement.

Despite the general benefits of wholesale terms there are, of course, some drawbacks in buying at market. Personal purchasing, particularly, consumes time which might be used for other purposes. There is also the possibility of having to make bulk purchases too large for practical purposes. Sometimes also minor price advantages are dissipated in additional transport and porterage charges or in charges for containers. The service that can be given by a local market gardener should not, therefore, be overlooked.

It is the type of establishment, the magnitude of the business done, the best use of staff time which must be considered when determining vegetable and fruit purchasing policy.

The progressive chef and caterer will familiarise himself not only with the broad seasons as indicated in this Manual's Food Calendar, p. 246, but will also make himself acquainted with the various varieties and strains and their appropriate uses. In addition to the normal fruits and vegetables, the chef and caterer will require more exotic and less usual types and will also seek the herbs necessary for sauce making and other culinary purposes. He must acquire knowledge to recognise and identify all these and in smaller towns may find it necessary to deal through one supplier who can be kept up to the mark and, indeed, brought under instruction in regard to rarer products. To extend his knowledge the chef will not hesitate to make use of gardening and horticultural manuals and even purchase guides produced with the housewife in mind (such as *My Green Grocer says*, by Alec Black, Faber & Faber).

Some of the general points that the chef or caterer must insist upon in buying both fruit and vegetables are:

1. Absence of yellow and discolouring leaves on greenstuffs.
2. Rejection of withered commodities.
3. Clean produce without excessive accompanying soil.
4. Soundness and ripeness in fruit but no over-ripeness, browning or over-soft consistency.
5. Sound, fresh smell must always be associated with all the produce of the greengrocer.

Convenience foods

It is now recognised that in many types of catering, new problems, especially those of increased labour costs, may be countered by the greater use of food products packed in ready-to-use form.

Buying must take into account the advantage of eliminating preparatory processes in, for example, garde manger and vegetable room.
The buyer should study the relationship of 'convenience' foods to the
food-service operation for this involves not only purchasing foodstuffs
but, also, in effect, the provision of service to chefs and caterers of
'prefabrication' or 'pre-preparation'.

Basically, most 'convenience' or 'ready-to-use' food products constitute what the chef himself would cause to be prepared in his own
kitchen. Because foods are processed at some previous time and in a
distant locality preservation is often required. This is usually quick-
freezing, dehydration or canning; with freeze-drying offering some
hopes for the future and irradiation still an uncertain possibility.

Canned products in various forms have long been accepted in the
kitchen and it is in the newer fields of quick-freezing and dehydration
that the greatest advances have been made in recent years.

Most of the main groups of foods are available today in 'ready-to-
use' form with the following being the most widely handled:

> Soups and soup bases
> Fish and fish products
> Vegetables and fruit
> Potatoes
> Meat and meat products
> Poultry and poultry products
> Pre-mixes for bakery and confectionery purposes
> Sweets and puddings
> Puddings, pie fillings
> Ready-to-bake pastry and pastry products
> Sauce bases
> Frozen desserts, including ice-cream
> Completely cooked quick-frozen prepared foods

How a buyer will incorporate these into kitchen routines will depend
on the nature of the catering establishment and the facilities, staff and
equipment available. Basically, however, the aim must always be to
eliminate from the kitchen all work which can more advantageously
be carried out under factory conditions where modern manufacturing
techniques can be employed so long as the standards of cuisine do not
suffer. To determine the relevant advantages, the chef de cuisine or
caterer when buying must examine operating problems and decide
whether they can be eased or overcome bearing in mind the following:

(*a*) *Labour.* The cost and the availability of kitchen labour must be assessed.

(*b*) *Time.* The speed of preparation must be considered in relation to service standards.

(*c*) *Quality and variety.* The possibility of achieving higher quality food standards must be examined as well as providing foods not otherwise available. (Absence of foods may be due to lack of skill or time or to the effects of season or locality.)

(*d*) *Space.* That lesser storage and handling space is needed when using processed foods is a consideration to be borne in mind.

(*e*) *Convenience.* The smoothness of the kitchen operation may be eased as may working conditions. Greater flexibility may be possible.

(*f*) *Hygiene.* 'Ready-to-use' foods have most, if not all, of their waste matter removed. Elimination of such refuse before food reaches the kitchen reduces food handling and avoids or eases waste disposal problems.

(*g*) *Cost.* Frequently, cost is the deciding factor. Whilst the saving of labour is usually the most apparent economy, the ability to control food quality, yield, portion size and waste are aspects which enable the caterer to regulate final operating costs more and more accurately.

Canned food

Whilst seeking to obtain all benefits from wholesale prices in substantial orders it is always important to avoid tying up capital unnecessarily in the form of food stocks. Remember that normal trading terms involve one month's credit and it is prudent to exploit this credit fully by arranging delivery of supplies at the beginning of the month. It is certainly desirable to buy those items normally consumed quickly such as canned fruits, juices, vegetables and meats in amounts no larger than one month's supply.

Differences in quality, cost and quantity between cans of similar size can be so great as to prevent any real comparison when buying. The buyer should make test purchases drain off liquid and weigh and portion the contents to estimate the real cost per weight, and serving. The Canned Foods Advisory Bureau, 17 Wigmore Street, London, W.1, exist to promote the reputation of good canned food and drink and can give useful help and information. The following guide to can sizes is based largely on information from that source:

Approx. nett weight	Commodity	Approx. no. of servings
5 oz	Baked Beans, Peas	1
8 oz	Fruit Salad, Meat Pudding, Baked Beans, Spaghetti, Vegetables, Fruit	2
10 oz	Baked Beans, Soups, Vegetables, Meats, Pilchards	2–3
14 oz	Fruit, Vegetables	3
1 lb	Vegetables, Fruit, Meat, Soup, Pilchards, Milk, Cream Fruit, Jellies, Sweet and Meat Puddings, Tongue, Galantines	4
1¼ lb	Fruit, Fruit Salads and Vegetables, Fruit and Vegetable Juices	4
1¾ lb	Fruit and Vegetables	5–6
3 lb	Meat Rolls	Catering pack (12 × 4 oz portions or 16 × 3 oz portions)
6¾ lb	Fruit, Vegetables and Tongue	Catering pack

Grocery

Familiarity with the range of grocery requires a vast knowledge on the part of the food purchaser. Few would attempt to carry all this knowledge in their heads and the wise chef will not hesitate to make full use of a reliable guide such as *Law's Grocers' Manual* (Wm. Clowes and Sons) which not only gives succinct information about a substantial range of commodities, but also indicates grades, types of pack and quality marks which are difficult to memorise but which are important to the buyer.

In addition to using a sound work of reference of this kind, much valuable information can be obtained from bodies such as the Canned Foods Advisory Bureau, already mentioned, The Ceylon Tea Bureau, 22 Lower Regent St, London, W.1, The Milk Marketing Board and similar organisations. Though designed to give a service to the ordinary consumer, chefs and caterers would do well to follow the reports of the Consumer Advisory Council (*Shoppers' Guide*) issued to its Associate Members, British Standards Institute, Orchard House, Oxford Street, London, W.1, and the reports of the Consumers Association Limited (*Which*), 333 High Holborn, London, W.C.1. Naturally these consumer associations deal with many products and only occasionally touch upon food, but study of this reasoned approach to buying is of undoubted use.

Whilst the food buyer must remain vigilant, critical and alert, it would be a great mistake for any chef or caterer to seek to have any-thing other than good relations with suppliers. What is of over-riding importance is to select dealers of sound reputation and from whom one can expect reliable goods and fair service. Skilled meat purveyors, properly trained grocers, experienced vintners, have not only the knowledge of their calling but are just as likely to have as high pro-fessional concepts as conscientious caterers. To seek to develop an atmo-sphere of mutual confidence and trust with sound merchants does not imply a naïve reliance on someone else's judgment, but it can certainly help in securing the good supplier's expert skill and assistance to aug-ment that of the caterer/buyer.

Few men in the catering industry, even after a life-time of dealing with its goods, would pretend to encyclopaedic knowledge of food commodities. The best buyers are often those of training and long experience but whose expertise is leavened with an awareness that their own judgment may sometimes require the help of a second opinion.

18   Kitchen records and control

There is little doubt that the majority of those who in the past have taken up the vocation of chef de cuisine have, initially at least, shown little taste for 'figure' work. Not only chefs but even catering officers and catering managers with the traditional background of practical kitchen training have often tended to be less than enthusiastic about their paper work. This is, perhaps, less true of the new generation who have received appropriate grounding, for many courses for chefs now cover calculations and simple records and accounts.

It is important to define the limited scope of this chapter at the outset because accounting, control and recording procedures for hotels, restaurants and catering establishments as a whole can be vast and complicated matters and have been the subject of complete textbooks. The purpose of this section of the Manual is in the main to deal only with those simple records and aspects of control which may be considered an integral part of the work of staff within the food stores and the kitchen.

Whilst other departments of the hotel and catering establishment such as, in particular, the control office, have a link with the kitchen which is of extreme importance, do not come under the control of the chef de cuisine nor the caterer and hence are largely excluded from present consideration. In the same way the overall financial and cost policy is a matter for determination by top management as distinct from departmental management and such larger issues need not be considered in detail here.

Records and control as far as the kitchen is concerned are designed for intensely practical purposes. Just as the board of directors and the top management of an enterprise must regard the keeping of accounts as a most practical activity sensitively registering their business progress and helping to control and adjust it, so must the chef and caterer attach similar importance to the records, albeit simple ones, which are necessary within their department.

It cannot be too strongly stressed how varied may be control and accounting arrangements in and for kitchens and catering operations. It is certainly not possible to deal with all possible permutations of paper work favoured under different systems; but variations of style and forms have invariably the same ends in view. In many large and small operations control measures through goods receiving office, stores, etc., are taken by the controller independently of the kitchen. Nevertheless, the chef and his staff must play their part properly within the system used.

Purpose of paper work

The importance of kitchen records can best be gauged when their purpose is clearly understood. The purpose of record keeping in food stores and kitchens may be summarised:

1. To ensure that incoming goods are in accordance with what has actually been ordered, both as regards quantity and quality.
2. To record the receipt of such goods in order to ensure their safe custody.
3. To control the movement of goods both: (*a*) from the stores to those sections requisitioning them, and (*b*) from the kitchen to the restaurant.
4. To enable a comparison to be made between the cost of goods consumed (food cost) and the corresponding figure of food sales.
5. To prevent as far as is possible losses through deterioration, carelessness and pilfering.

In considering the foregoing it may be remembered that an increase in the size of a business or catering operation tends to result in less personal supervision by the proprietor or manager, hence the need for more elaborate documentation.

It is naturally important that any recording system is fully supported by close supervision and adequate practical measures of control. The most elaborate system of bin cards, for example, in a commodity store will be rendered useless if the store is not properly secured and is left unlocked and unattended.

The staff engaged on keeping kitchen records varies according to the size and scope of the establishment. The chef or caterer may in smaller establishments do much for himself whereas in the larger ones he will be aided by kitchen clerks.

Recording receipts and issues

The following may, however, be regarded as the usual basic steps in keeping a record of goods received and issued.

1. *Ordering goods.* It is desirable to order from suppliers on a printed, serially numbered, triplicate order form. The top copy is for the tradesman, a second goes to the stores to authorise subsequent reception of goods and to provide for checks of weight and quantities on

arrival, and the third is usually sent to control or accounts office for comparison with the suppliers' invoice (when that arrives) to ensure that payment is made only for goods actually ordered and received.

Ordering of goods by telephone is, of course, quite usual and, indeed, is often inevitable. The order form is then sent as a confirmation of the 'phoned order and to avoid any possible misunderstanding with the supplier.

Specimen Order Form
[Name and Address of Establishment]
ORDER FORM

Serial Number:........................   Date: ....

To: (Name of Supplier)

Please supply on (insert date delivery required) the following:

Description	Quantity	£	s.	d.

Signed:...
Chef de Cuisine
or Authorised Deputy

Note: The quantity column is always provided; a money column is often useful.

2. *Receipt of goods.* It is essential that on receipt the goods are checked against the second copy of the order form and the suppliers' delivery note; and this check includes check weighing and counting of a thorough nature. It has been stressed that scales should be conveniently placed near the goods entrance and check weighing should take place at least on a 'sampling' basis. The original orders for goods and delivery notes accompanying goods must all be appropriately filed and will remain as vouchers supporting the entry of goods received.

Most suppliers send duplicate delivery notes; one of which is signed by the recipient and returned to the supplier as proof of delivery, the other being kept by the recipient of the goods.

Normally, invoices are entered for summarising daily as and when they are received and the summary may be made by the storekeeper or is passed to the storekeeper by the goods entrance clerk. Both invoices and delivery notes are usually passed on to the control or accounts office for filing. The invoices are, of course, entered in the stores records whether the latter be bin cards or books.

INVOICES SUMMARY							
Date	Supplier	Invoice Serial No.	£	s.	d.	Order No.	Remarks

3. *Stock keeping.* The goods taken into the various stores may be controlled either through the medium of independent bin cards or tally cards for each item. Where bin cards are used they are attached to the appropriate bin, shelf, drawer, etc., and their use necessitates a neat and orderly arrangement of the goods in the stores. Consequently, the bin-card system requires adequate storage space. Bin cards must be written up at the time goods are issued or received. Alternatively, similar records may be kept in a stock book arranged on a loose-leaf system in a manner which might be compared with bin cards bound together. While bin cards are commonly used for cellar control, in the average food store, often of restricted size, loose-leaf stock cards are often preferred. Instead of cards a stock book ruled in columns may be used but this is suitable only for simple kitchen operations with a limited range of commodities. Whatever the type of stock record kept, however, goods received must be promptly entered.

BIN CARD

Commodity:

Date	Receipt or issue voucher no.	Received	Issued	Balance

4. *Issue of goods to kitchen.* It is important that no unauthorised issues be made from the stores. A simple internal requisition or chit system is desirable. Main issues should take place early in the day though obviously unanticipated issues may have to be made from time to time as the need arises. These issues should, therefore, only be made against a signed note or chit from a chef de partie or sous chef (or the caterer and his authorised deputy). Goods issued must be promptly entered as issues on bin cards or in the stock book and the requisition chits filed in the stores remain as vouchers supporting the issue.

Where bin cards are maintained and entries are made as and when goods are issued or received, the bin card should of necessity at any given time show the running (current) balance. Where stock cards are used, the balancing of the individual cards may be done at the end of each day.

Generally, both bin cards and stock cards are concerned with and show quantities only. Calculating the value of receipts and issues is as a rule done in the control or accounts office. The chef's (or store-keeper's) first duty is to account for the quantities entrusted to him.

Stock-taking

Stock-taking must take place at regular intervals and, undoubtedly, the control department will also arrange stock-taking checks at various times.

Specimen Internal Requisition Form (Duplicate Pad)
                                    Serial No.: 43881

[Name of Establishment]
INTERNAL REQUISITION

From Section:............. (e.g., Saucier)   Date:..................

Please Supply:

Item	Quantity required

Signed..
Section...............................

It will be apparent that the foodstuffs and commodities used in a kitchen are so numerous that there is great danger of a recording system becoming enormously cumbersome by having to make provision for a multitude of entries. It is, therefore, not only permissible but desirable to group items in a logical and orderly manner both for stock-keeping purposes and also for physical storage on the shelves and bins. Such arrangements may not obviate the necessity for recording individual items but it will certainly aid simplicity if there are clearly defined groups such as fruit dried, fruit tinned, spices, preserves, etc.

Stock-taking will help reveal losses from the store due to pilfering, deterioration or negligence. It is only necessary to compare the total value of issues from the stores with the value of the goods received adjusted for commencing and final stocks. In other words, the value of issues should be equal to the commencing stock plus stores received less final stock.

In large establishments it is common for managements to require control of costly items even after actual issue to the kitchen as in the case of the more expensive perishable foodstuffs handled in the larder (or subsidiary butcher's or fishmonger's 'shops') and cold rooms. The purpose is not only to guard against losses through the kitchen but also through service channels. Commodities to be kept checked in this way will be specified by the management (through Control Department) and a kitchen clerk will maintain a weekly or monthly record on a form along the following lines. Weekly sheets are to be preferred for the sooner the losses are discovered the better.

CONTROL SHEET (LARDER)

Week:......................

Item*	Weight or measure		Day of the Week							Totals	Balance
			Su.	M.	Tu.	W.	Th.	F.	St.		
Lobster	Each	Received	—	12	—	17	—	—	—	29	
	,,	Issued	—	4	5	3	4	—	—	16	13
Sole	lb	Received	—	—	—	—	40	24	—	64	
		Issued	—	—	—	—	16	20	22	58	6
		[contd. for each item required]									

* Fish, Poultry, Game, Fruit, etc.

If these basic records of goods received, taken into stores and sub-sequently issued, are kept accurately then it is possible for remaining kitchen records and calculations to be done outside the kitchen depart-ment. In certain operations the policy of management may be to con-fine kitchen recording to such limits and with control from above being applied in terms of a ceiling of expenditure. Certainly, it is this aspect of commodity control or safeguarding of stock which is of over-riding importance but it must be supported by control of food when it is cooked for issue to the restaurant. It will, therefore, be necessary to consider the kind of simple method used at the kitchen servery in dealing with the requisitions from waiters or other staff for cooked food.

Portioning

Although the cutting or dividing by other means of foodstuffs into equal-sized profitable portions involves practical skills, it also depends on cost calculations. Portion sizes may be determined by management or it may be left to the chef to estimate in accordance with the requirement of his kitchen percentage. In either event kitchen staff should be guided by a list or chart indicating the portion sizes for main commodities for service à la carte, table d'hôte and banqueting—and for the various meals, luncheon, dinner, breakfast and tea.

Whilst food costing may be part of managerial policy, it is certainly the task of the chef to keep control of portion size and weight and to maintain records of them in accordance with that policy.

Issuing meals to the restaurant

In an hotel or restaurant conducted on the partie system, a kitchen clerk known as the aboyeur is stationed at the servery counter throughout the meal service period. On receipt of waiters' checks (bons) he announces in a loud voice (it must be heard above the kitchen clatter) the requirements of the order in traditional kitchen French.

Often he stamps the time of receiving the order on the check and usually has a board fitted with hooks or pins matching the tables or waiters' stations to which the orders relate.

It is obvious that apart from clerical skills (which he may have to employ for duties outside service times) he must have considerable knowledge of the cookery repertoire, some knowledge of methods and, particularly, time taken in preparing and cooking in order to act as intermediary between the restaurant staff and the chefs in smoothing over disputes, remedying errors and making correct and properly timed demands on the various parties. This can be a taxing task during a busy time (coup de feu).

Apart from the actual words for food and garnishes some of the common terms used by the aboyeur or heard in response includes:

Ça marche	(literally: that proceeds, i.e., the order is being done)
Faites marcher	(begin to send up)
Preparez	(prepare)
Envoyez	(send)
à la main	(in hand)
Ça presse	(urgent)
à suivre	(to follow)
Soigné	(with care)

The orders of the aboyeur, therefore, normally consist of:

(a) The designation of the chef de partie or partie addressed, thus: pâtissier, rôtisseur, etc.

(*b*) The numbers of portions required, for example, one (une).

(*c*) Name of the item, e.g., cutlet (côtelette).

(*d*) Style of cooking, say, grilled (grillée).

(*e*) Garnishes, dressing or sauce, say, plain (nature).

The orders are addressed to the partie or parties concerned and typical ones would be:

Saucier, faites marcher deux tournedos Rossini. Poissonier, preparez les quatre filets de sole Dugléré du No. 12. Saucier, envoyez les deux noisettes du jour.

The parties must acknowledge the orders and responses include 'entendu' (heard or understood), 'compris' (understood), 'bon' (good), 'bon, j'ai compris', etc.

When an order has been completed and removed from the hotplate by the waiter, the aboyeur removes the check from its hook and places it through a slit into a locked box. This, at the end of the service, goes to the control office where the key is kept for control procedure. The kitchen clerk is not involved in that function but must ensure that the box remains secured and is safely conveyed to the office.

Clerical and record work in the kitchen is thus first concerned:

(*a*) With the receipt of the raw materials for cooking and preparation and subsequently controlling issues to the kitchen.

(*b*) With the issue of the prepared dishes over the service counter to the waiting staff and, ultimately, to the customer.

Charges and prices

The kitchen's clerical system is not directly concerned with charges made to guests or customers. In an hotel, for example, a Day Book is maintained which provides an analysis of meals served from the general checking system operated. From the kitchen's records of the food actually issued, at its purchase price, is obtained the total food cost for items used to provide meals actually served. The hotel or catering establishment's accounting department can then calculate the percentage or loss on the kitchen operation.

Percentage and performance

From his earliest days in the kitchen, the chef hears a good deal about 'percentage' and 'food cost'. The reason he does so is because the knowledge of how the cost of food is related to the catering operation is necessary to the management in controlling the operation and in helping to disclose deficiencies of purchase, or storage, and losses through other forms of waste or pilferage. The chef is, in fact, concerned directly with costs rather than profits; for although he is expected to work to a pre-determined percentage of kitchen profit, the percentage is determined by management. It depends on the prices charged and the general policy of the establishment.

There are, naturally, other elements of cost which the management must take into account besides the food cost and in several sections of this Manual the importance of the cost of labour in determining selling prices and as affecting food purchase has been stressed. Additional overheads like fuel, rent, office sundries must be included by the management when ascertaining total costs. Readers will do well to give further study to all these aspects of costing. *An Approach to Food Costing*, by Richard Kotas (Practical Press), is recommended as an introduction to this important subject.

In the kitchen, however, the kitchen profit has traditionally been simplified as the difference between the food cost alone and the selling price. Percentage in the kitchen implies, therefore, gross profit expressed as a percentage of the selling price. In hotels, restaurants and many other types of catering establishments, the chef or caterer is fed back his performance figures from the controller or a 'front of the house' office.

The chef or caterer may rely on the accountant's department or a similar office for ultimate calculations of percentage and profitability for which records from the restaurant and floors, for example, are required as well as from the kitchen; but he must often remain personally responsible for much of the conscientious and accurate record keeping within the kitchen, at the service counter and in the stores. He may, and in large kitchens does, use kitchen clerks to aid him, but he must not regard such activity as alien and merely 'clerkly' but as an integral and practical part of the kitchen operation he controls.

19 Training the chef : apprenticeship

Before turning to today's methods of training chefs in Britain, it may be helpful to consider further the general system of commis and apprentices which was, and to a considerable extent still is, fundamental to the French system of chef training and kitchen organisation along partie lines.

In the French tradition during the years between the two world wars a boy who contemplated a career as a first-class cuisinier, rising at least to the status of chef de partie or higher, entered the kitchens at fourteen years of age or thereabouts. His apprenticeship was often the subject of a formal brevet d'apprentissage drawn up within a scheme approved by the Societé Culinaire de France. Half a century ago, indeed, a French boy seriously intended for this career of chef would have had a fee paid to his employer for his indenture. In France, cookery apprenticeship was regarded as seriously as we in Britain might regard becoming an articled clerk to a solicitor.

It is, however, interesting to note that concern on the continent of Europe for good cookery and food service led to the establishment of hotel schools and training centres some years before they began to be fully developed in this country. Yet today in Britain, as well as on the Continent, an apprenticeship system is again coming to be more fully recognised as likely to be the most fruitful source of supply in quality and quantity of skilled chefs de partie.

Pre-war 'house' apprenticeship

In the United Kingdom before the last war, 'house apprenticeship' along French traditional lines was the main method of training for the kitchen. Although no fees were usually paid, wages were nominal. Apprenticeship consisted of four or five years' service in the kitchen divided between different parties varying from three to nine months in each. An apprentice might, for example, spend up to nine months each under the chef saucier, chef garde manger and chef pâtissier. The remaining months might be divided into equal periods with the remaining chefs de partie.

The commis

After training as an apprentice under different chefs de partie, the next three or four years was followed by similar varied training on all the parties, but with greater responsibilities, as a commis cook. The IVme commis, for example, who, with others, might have been attached to the chef poissonnier for some months as commis poissonnier would eventually find promotion to 'IIIme, or IIme commis rôtisseur' either in that kitchen or elsewhere. He could then seek to advance along his own lines.

Learning continued with widening opportunities of gaining experience; for the commis in the French system was graded and on first making 'the grade' of commis he was 'IIIme, or IVme commis' according to the size of the partie and establishment. Subsequently, according to his ability, determination and possibly some luck, he progressed to 2nd or 1st commis and the threshold of 'chefdom'.

But the Ier commis was already an important man on his partie. If he entered the kitchens at fourteen to fifteen years he was at twenty-one to twenty-three years the right-hand man to his chef de partie. If this partie was a major one such as the sauce, the Ier commis as second in command had formidable duties and responsibilities as deputy to one of the most important and best-paid chefs. When the chef saucier was away, the premier commis was often in fact chef saucier, and as such, directly responsible to the sous chef or, in a smaller kitchen, to the chef de cuisine.

Advancement to chef

The object of this traditional apprenticeship system was to develop the best possible chef in every partie. From these a few men with good general experience and understanding of the different 'parties' gained promotion to sous chef and ultimately, perhaps, to chef de cuisine.

Today's trends

Most chefs de cuisine are well aware of this traditional concept of training and the old method of arranging it.

Like caterers and hotel managers, chefs de cuisine are frequently consulted by youngsters and their parents about career prospects in the kitchen and about training so that it is equally important that they are familiar, too, with modern adaptations of this system.

The chef de cuisine like any other good, top executive must have an up-to-date knowledge and appreciation of training and career prospects and career building for these reasons:

1. He will, as has been noted, be asked for his advice.
2. He will need to help in attracting and recruiting the right kind of newcomer.
3. He, himself, will need to make some contribution to training in one or more of the following ways:

   (a) By himself arranging 'on the job' training of apprentices and by encouraging his senior staff to assist in training by both 'on the job' means and as part-time teachers.

   (b) Arrangements for the release of apprentices to attend part-time classes.

   (c) Possible participation in voluntary work on committees in the developing of existing and new training schemes.

4. Because of his professional responsibility to the craft of cookery as a whole in addition to his duties to his own employer.

Objectives of chef training

Before dealing with the other forms which training takes today, it is opportune to consider some of the objectives of training.

First and foremost, of course, all forms of culinary training should be designed to produce good standards of kitchen craftsmanship and most forms of training are designed to produce craftsmen cooks or chefs who will adopt cookery as a career and remain in it. The qualifying word 'most' is used because there does exist basic catering training in which cookery is simply an important component. Such basic catering training is designed to deal broadly with young entrants who are attracted to the hotel and catering industry but who are not yet fully committed to specialisation in, for example, cookery within it.

But in addition to the main objective of producing craft skills and a craftsman, properly planned training is also itself an aid to staff recruitment and can be so considered by the executive chef who will recognise it as an important brick in the building of cookery craft prestige.

Advantages of training

In short, training is intended to produce more efficient kitchen craftsmen. Trained staff using correct methods are of better quality and are capable of higher output. They more readily understand instructions (such as the use of appliances, safety regulations and the like) and need less time to learn. Trained staff are not only better at their work, however, they are usually happier because of increased satisfaction in the job. Their morale and enthusiasm is kept high by their self-confidence and this helps ensure good and regular attendance and a lower rate of staff turnover.

Certificates and credentials

Subsidiary objectives of training but of vital importance to those undertaking the training are the certificates, indentures and other credentials which are to be achieved by study, experience and examinations. Thus it is important for the chef to know the kind of credentials which are, today, becoming nationally recognised and which have two important functions:

1. They give ready indication to employers of minimum standards of knowledge and skill.
2. They are an incentive to young and older employees alike to take training to improve themselves to gain these status-raising awards.

Amongst the important credentials sought by those training for cookery today are:

1. The completion of the N.J.A.C. cookery apprenticeship indentures. (Similar considerations apply to the Hospital Cooks Apprenticeship Scheme.)
2. The completion of three-year cookery training scheme (part time in kitchen, part time in school).
3. The gaining of City and Guilds of London Institute certificates in cookery and catering as a result of full-time and part-time study. These certificates include:

    (*a*) Preliminary Trade Cookery (Subject 147).
    (*b*) Catering Trades Basic Training Course (Subject 150).
    (*c*) Cookery for Hotel and Catering Establishments (Subject 151).
    (*d*) Advanced Cookery for Hotels and Restaurants (Subject 152).

4. The gaining of certificates and Diplomas in cookery awarded by reputable hotel schools and technical colleges.

Information about those centres which specialise in the cookery training of chefs may be obtained from the Training Officer, The Hotel and Catering Institute, 24 Portman Square, London, W.1.

National apprenticeship

A national apprenticeship scheme for cooks was the first scheme to follow the creation of a National Joint Apprenticeship Council in

March, 1952, so that it is still a relatively new departure for the craft of chef. In most other fields of activity and in other industries where manual skills supported by intelligence are of importance, apprenticeship has proved highly successful. Moreover, the concept of apprenticeship in the hotel and catering industry is a familiar one for as has been noted the 'house' schemes to train chefs have existed for comfortably more than half a century. The growth of the national apprenticeship scheme does, therefore, offer great promise in the solving of the problem of recruiting, training and retaining permanent skilled kitchen workers. It accordingly deserves the support and interest of all existing chefs de cuisine.

An important feature of the national joint apprenticeship scheme is concurrent part-time attendance at hotel schools or technical colleges, and though this may sometimes present problems to the chef de cuisine and to the employer, the solving of these problems of release for classes is strongly in the interest of the employer and the executive chef when viewed on the long-term basis and therefore merits sympathetic and, indeed, enthusiastic co-operation.

National apprenticeship in operation

A Council was created on 31st March, 1952, with the objects of establishing National Apprenticeship schemes for potential craftsmen in the Hotel and Catering Industry. Composed of representatives from both the employers' side of the industry and from the trade unions' side, it also includes representatives of technical education, and assessors from government departments. Its official title is the National Joint Apprenticeship Council of the Hotel and Catering Industry.

The initial target of the Council has been the creation of a satisfactory scheme for the training of craftsmen cooks, other schemes may well be put in hand for other departments of hotel-keeping and catering.

Advantages for employers

From the employers' angle, a well-organised scheme, carrying a national hallmark, attracts and *retains* the right type of young person to ensure that the future of the industry is not jeopardised by shortage of highly trained craftsmen and leaders. The recruitment of juvenile labour is simplified, and the retention of the young worker is more firmly assured to the employer for a given number of years.

During the period of apprenticeship, the employer can generally be assured that the young worker will be interested in his job; that he will make a serious study of his chosen work; and that he will be increasingly valuable and useful to his employer.

Employers and their chefs de cuisine, in addition, have the advantage of knowing that their establishment has been officially approved as being of a sufficiently high standard to enable young persons to be trained to the nationally recognised level.

Advantages for young persons

For the young person, apprenticeship under the national scheme offers security of employment for the period of indentures; a guarantee of systematic training on a progressive plan, both in employment and in hotel school or technical college; the opportunity of earning nationally recognised certificates which will qualify him for progressively more important positions; and the assurance that his approval as a registered apprentice has placed a hallmark upon his potential capacity as a future craftsman of the industry.

Participation

Those who desire to partake in the scheme should contact The Secretary, N.J.A.C., 24 Portman Square, London, W.1, for further information and the address of their local Apprenticeship Committee. Regional Hon. Secretaries are frequently in possession of the names of young persons desirous of taking up indentures and can give employers introductions to the local Youth Employment Officer as well as the Regional Hon. Secretary. Boys and girls who desire to enter apprenticeship, and who are not in touch with an employer, should consult their local Youth Employment Officer first, with a request that the Regional Hon. Secretary should be approached if necessary.

Apprenticeship may start from the statutory school-leaving age, but older applicants as, for example, under the Late Entry provisions below, may be considered.

Late entry

Where a potential apprentice has attended a full-time course of catering education at a hotel school, technical institution or other approved educational establishment, and is certified to have attained a standard approved by the Council, a reduction in the apprenticeship period equivalent to the period of such course, or two years, whichever is the less, may be granted by the Council at their discretion.

The Council is prepared to consider a reduction of not more than two years in cases where the potential apprentice has followed a full-time course of academic education since the statutory school-leaving age, but any reduction made in such cases is within the Council's discretion.

Practical training within industry and further education

Apprentices must be trained to the agreed standards of the Council set forth in their Recommended Scheme of Training, and employers participating are required to agree to observe these standards. It is, moreover, an essential condition of the scheme that apprentices shall be released without loss of pay or loss of time off for one day, or two half-days, each week, or for an equivalent continuous period during each year of the apprenticeship, for training in trade cookery and related subjects at a hotel school, technical institution or other educational establishment approved for this purpose, and that the apprentice diligently and regularly attends such training.

Indenture

All apprentices are indentured in a form approved by the Council. An apprentice may be transferred to another establishment, when it is considered desirable in the interests of the apprentice, subject to the express consent of the employer, the parent or legal guardian, and the apprentice.

Where, for any reason, an employer ceases to carry on his business, the apprenticeship agreement may be transferred to another employer by the Council. Apprentices must satisfy a registered medical practitioner, appointed and paid by the employer, as to their fitness to undertake the apprenticeship.

National Cookery Apprenticeship Regulations

The purpose of the scheme is to provide for the recruitment and systematic training of young workers, either male or female, as cooks. The period of apprenticeship is normally five years, terminating at the twenty-first birthday. In special circumstances the Council may allow termination after the twenty-first birthday.

Rates of pay, hours of work and conditions of employment, provision of working clothes and annual holidays must not be less favourable than conditions under any order made by the Ministry of Labour and National Service pursuant to proposals sent to him by the appropriate Wages Council.

The first six months of the period of apprenticeship is a probationary period, during which any party to the apprenticeship agreement may determine the indenture, in accordance with provisions determined by the Council.

Applications for approval

Employers desiring to register an apprentice have to complete in duplicate a form provided by the Council and these are normally obtainable from, and returnable to, the Honorary Secretary to the Regional Committee.

Employers who have not previously applied for registration of apprentices are also required to forward to the Committee a request for approval of their establishment. Such request may be in the form of a letter and employers may apply for approval of their establishments before engaging, or intending to engage, an apprentice.

The Committee endorse the application for approval of apprenticeship, or for approval of establishment, as the case may be, with their recommendation, or otherwise, and forward to the Council for decision.

The Council consider applications forwarded by the Committee and notify their decisions on applications to the Committee *and to the employer*.

Specimen

C	INDEX NUMBER

THE NATIONAL JOINT APPRENTICESHIP COUNCIL OF THE HOTEL AND CATERING INDUSTRY

FORM OF APPLICATION FOR APPRENTICESHIP

(To be completed in *duplicate* as shown)

Section A. **To be completed on behalf of the Apprentice.**

1. Apprentice's Surname (in block capitals) ....
2. Apprentice's first names (in full) ....
3. Apprentice's address ....
4. Full names and address of Parent or Legal Guardian ....
   ....
5. Apprentice: (*a*) Date of Birth ....
   (*b*) Name and type of School attended ....
   ....
   (*c*) Date of leaving School ....
   (*d*) Name of Technical Institution attended (if any) ....
   ....

(e) Nature of course taken at Technical Institution and dates....

....

....

(f) Date present employment started..................................

6. Previous Employment (if any):

(a) Name and address of Employer(s)..................................

....

....

(b) Nature of Employment ....

....

(c) Dates of Employment..

7. (a) Name of Technical Institution now being attended:

....

State here: (i) Day or Evening Classes or both................

(ii) Type of Course...

(b) If classes not being attended, give the name of the Technical Institution which it is proposed should be attended.................................

8. Employer's Name...

9. Employer's Address ....

10. Signature of Employer.................................... 11. Date.............

12. Signature of Apprentice .... 13. Date.............

14. Signature of Parent or Legal Guardian .... 15. Date.............

....

Section B. **To be completed by Employer only.**

16. Name and Address of the Establishment where the apprenticeship will be carried out:

....

....

17. State number of staff in Kitchen, **excluding the apprentice whom it is desired to register**, showing classification of duties:—

....

....

....

....

....

....

....

....

....

Total No. Kitchen Staff..................

18. State total number of above Cooks considered capable of giving training........

....

19. State total number of apprentices already accepted for registration under the National Scheme (excluding that now applied for).................................

20. Signature of Employer.. 21. Date........................

NOTE.—This form on completion should be sent (*in duplicate*) to the National Joint Apprenticeship Council of the Hotel and Catering Industry, 24 Portman Square, London, W.1, or to the Secretary of the.. Regional/Area Apprenticeship Committee at ....

....

Section C.   To be left blank by Employer and Apprentice.

Report by................................Regional Committee of the N.J.A.C.

22. This application is/is not recommended for approval.

23. If not recommended for approval state reasons................................

....

24. Signed................................Chairman ....Regional
................................Secretary.   Apprenticeship Committee

This part of Form should be completed (*in duplicate*) by the Regional Committee of the N.J.A.C. and *both* copies sent to the National Joint Apprenticeship Council of the Hotel and Catering Industry, at 24 Portman Square, London, W.1.

REGISTRATION PARTICULARS

Section D.   For N.J.A.C. Headquarters use only.

25. Considered by Council........................(date).   Approved/Not Approved.

26. Apprenticeship commenced..(date).

27. Apprenticeship to terminate..(date).

28. Registered ....(date).

29. Signed........................ *Secretary*, National Joint Apprenticeship Council.

Registration, issue and return of indentures

Indentures, in the form approved by the Council, are sent by the Secretary of the Council direct to employers for signature and sealing by all the parties to the agreement.

The signed and sealed indentures are then returned by the employer to the Council for registration, together with:

(*a*) The fee laid down by the Council.
(*b*) A copy of the apprentice's birth certificate.
(*c*) The medical certificate.

The Council register the indentures, endorse the registration particulars upon the documents and return both copies of the registered indentures to the employer, with a card for the apprentice to retain, certifying his registration.

Specimen

The National Joint Apprenticeship
of
The Hotel and Catering Industry

APPRENTICESHIP INDENTURE FOR COOKS

This Apprenticeship Indenture

made the.................day of..19.......

BETWEEN ....

of...

(hereinafter called the 'Employer') of the first part;

....

of...

(hereinafter called the 'Guardian') of the second part; and

....

of...

(hereinafter called the 'Apprentice') of the third part;

Witnesseth as follows:—That is to say

    1. The Employer hereby covenants with the Guardian and the Apprentice

        (*a*) to accept the Apprentice as his apprentice for a term of...............years from and after the...............day of.............................nineteen hundred and.................................which is the commencement of this Indenture notwithstanding the date hereof declaring that the first six months of the said period of years shall be in the nature of a trial period at any time during which it shall be in the option of either party to terminate this Indenture.

        (*b*) to teach and instruct the Apprentice to the best of his knowledge and ability or cause him to be taught the business and trade of a Cook and all things relating thereto, according to agreed standards decided upon by the National Joint Apprenticeship Council.

        (*c*) to release the Apprentice without loss of pay for one day or two half days each week or for an equivalent continuous period during each year of apprenticeship for training at a Technical College or other educational establishment accepted for this purpose by the National Joint Apprenticeship Council; where daytime courses are not available to grant reasonable facilities and time to enable the Apprentice to attend evening classes.

    2. The Guardian and the Apprentice hereby jointly and severally covenant with the Employer that

        The Apprentice will during the period of service:—

        (*a*) Obey the lawful orders of the Employer or his representative;

        (*b*) Promote to the best of his ability the interests of his employer; and

        (*c*) Not absent himself from the Employer's service without leave.

3. **The Apprentice** shall not during the said term of Apprenticeship reveal the secrets of the Employer's business.

4. **The Apprentice** shall attend regularly the approved course of instruction referred to in clause 1 (*c*) hereof.

5. **If** the Employer shall during the period of Apprenticeship die or have a Receiving Order in Bankruptcy made against him or become permanently incapacitated or cease to carry on his said business or if the Employer be a Company and a resolution shall be passed or an order made for the winding up except for the purpose of reconstruction or amalgamation only then he or his personal representatives or the Official Receiver Trustee or Liquidator shall use their best endeavours to procure the assignment of this Indenture to some other Employer approved by the Guardian and the National Joint Apprenticeship Council.

6. **If** the Apprentice shall during the said period of apprenticeship be in wholetime service under the National Service Act 1948 or any amendment or reenactment thereof for the time being in force the said period of apprenticeship shall at the option of the Apprentice be extended by such a period (not exceeding the period of such wholetime service) as the parties hereto shall agree or failing agreement shall be determined in accordance with the provisions of clause 5 hereof. Time spent in an appropriate unit in the Forces in his trade capacity shall likewise be taken into consideration in determining the length of the period necessary to complete the Apprenticeship.

7. **If** the Apprentice shall at any time during the said term be wilfully disobedient to lawful orders or commands of the said Employer or be slothful or negligent or shall otherwise grossly misbehave himself towards the Employer then it shall be lawful to cancel this Indenture and discharge the said Apprentice.

8. **Any** matter in dispute between the parties concerning the instruction and training of the Apprentice shall in the first place be referred to the Area Committee of the National Joint Apprenticeship Council which, in turn, shall refer to the National Apprenticeship Council any case of difficulty which cannot be resolved locally and the decision of the Council shall be final and binding on all parties.

9. **It** is also hereby mutually agreed and declared between the parties that the conditions set out in the Schedule hereto initialed for identification by the signatories to this Indenture shall form part of this Indenture and shall be valid and effective as if they had been incorporated herein.

10. This **Indenture** shall be registered with the National Joint Apprenticeship Council.

In Witness hereto the said parties have hereunto set their hands and seals the day and year first before written.

Signed Sealed and Delivered ⎫
by the above-named ⎬ .... (*Employer*)
in the presence of:— ⎭

Witness...

Signed Sealed and Delivered ⎫
by the above-named   ⎬ .... (*Guardian*)
in the presence of:—   ⎭

Witness...

Signed Sealed and Delivered
by the above-named   .... (*Apprentice*)
in the presence of:—

Witness...

CERTIFICATE OF SERVICE

WE HEREBY CERTIFY that the above-mentioned Apprentice well and faithfully served his Apprenticeship in accordance with the foregoing Indenture.

Date...   ....
                                                    Employer.

                                        ....
                                        Chairman, National Joint Apprenticeship Council.

SCHEDULE OF CONDITIONS RELATING TO THE APPRENTICESHIP INDENTURE FOR COOKS

This Indenture applies both to boys and girls.

1. Evidence of Age and Medical Examination

Every applicant for Apprenticeship must produce his or her birth certificate or other evidence of age. He shall also be required to satisfy a Registered Medical Practitioner, appointed and paid by the Employer, of his fitness to undertake the apprenticeship.

2. Recognition of full-time attendance at approved Technical Classes

The term of apprenticeship may, by prior approval of the National Joint Apprenticeship Council, be reduced by a period not greater than two years in respect of an equivalent (or longer) period of attendance at a full-time course of approved instruction at a Technical College or other appropriate educational establishment.

3. Provision of Knives

The Apprentice shall supply his own knives in accordance with the Employer's standard of requirements.

4. Rates of Pay
Hours of Work and Conditions of Employment
Provision of Working Clothes
Annual Holidays

The above shall be not less favourable than condition under any Order made by the Minister of Labour and National Service pursuant to proposals sent to him by the appropriate Wages Board.

ASSIGNMENT

IT IS HEREBY AGREED AND DECLARED that with the consent of the Employer the Guardian the Apprentice and the National Joint Apprenticeship Council as from the................day of.....................19...... all obligations of the Employer under the foregoing Apprenticeship Indenture (hereinafter referred to as 'the first Employer') shall be undertaken and performed by...

of..

and that as from the said date the first Employer shall be absolved from all further obligation whatsoever.

Signed Sealed and Delivered
by
In the presence of:—
}.. SEAL
(First Employer)

Signed Sealed and Delivered
by
In the presence of:—
}.. SEAL
(Guardian)

Signed Sealed and Delivered
by
In the presence of:—
}.. SEAL
(Apprentice)

Signed Sealed and Delivered
by
In the presence of:—
}.. SEAL
(Second Employer)

Transfer approved by the
National Joint Apprenticeship Council...
Chairman.

REGISTRATION

This Indenture was registered by the National Joint Apprenticeship Council of the Hotel and Catering Industry on the date shewn below.   Secretary
Date of Registration: Registered Number:

Vocational training

The apprentice is required regularly and diligently to attend the technical institution selected for him for vocational training and attendance for vocational training is regarded as paid employment.

The employer should inquire of the Local Education Authority as to whether he can be furnished with periodical confidential reports on the apprentice's attendance and progress.

Transfers

Where it is deemed expedient that an apprentice should be transferred from one employer to another, either to further his training, or on compassionate grounds, an application has to be submitted to the Committee for recommendation, or otherwise, for approval by the Council, with written consents to the transfer signed by:

(a) The apprentice.
(b) The apprentice's parent or legal guardian.
(c) The first employer.
(d) The second employer.

When, and not before, the transfer is approved by the Council, the appropriate clauses in the indenture are signed, and sealed if necessary, by the first three parties, and the apprentice transferred to the second employer, who signs and seals, if necessary, the transfer clause, and forwards both copies of the indenture deed, together with the apprentice's registration card, to the Council, for registration and return.

Cessation

During the first six months of employment, or during the period between application for registration and signature of indentures, whichever is the longer, the engagement may be determined by the apprentice, the parent or legal guardian, or the employer on giving seven days' notice in writing.

After this period apprenticeship may only be determined by mutual consent. Where it is deemed expedient that such determination shall occur, then employers must forward to the Council consent to such determination from:

(a) The apprentice.
(b) The parent or legal guardian.
(c) The employer.

Such consent has to be in writing, signed by the person giving it, and witnessed. If the employer is a company, the consent must also be sealed with the Common Seal of the Company as provided in the Articles of Association.

Further information about national apprenticeship may be obtained from the Secretary to the Council at: 24 Portman Square, London, W.1.

Recommended scheme of training for apprentice cooks

The following outline has been drawn up and approved by the National Joint Apprenticeship Council for the Hotel and Catering Industries and its purpose is to provide a guide to employers and their chefs de cuisine as to the broad lines upon which apprentices should be trained within industry, bearing in mind the complementary training to be given within appropriate educational institutions.

It is the responsibility of the employer (and the chef de cuisine acting for him) to organise the apprentice's training within industry on planned, progressive lines and to take a general interest in the apprentice throughout the period of training. To support the recommended general lines of training within industry, employers and chefs should:

(*a*) Encourage apprentices to keep notebooks.

(*b*) Make available to apprentices current trade journals and technical papers.

(*c*) Advise apprentices on suitable textbooks.

The National Joint Apprenticeship Council ask employers to maintain appropriate progress records of each apprentice.

SPECIMEN TIMETABLE (FIVE YEARS)

For Training within the Hotel or Other Catering Establishments

It is appreciated that the following timetable will vary according to the type of establishment taking apprentices. There is not necessarily any fixed sequence of departmental training, and it is realised that, in accordance with circumstances, the order given below may have to be varied.

In certain establishments, the work of some departments may be combined; for example, butchery, fish and poultry falling within the larder period.

1. Butchery preparation   *two months*
2. Fish preparation   *two months*
3. Poultry and Game preparation   *two months*
4. Larder   *nine months*
5. Soup Corner   *six months*
6. Roast and Grill Corner   *four months*
7. Vegetables; Eggs and Farinaceous Cookery   *six months*
8. Fish Corner   *eight months*
9. Sauce Corner   *nine months*
10. Pastry   *nine months*
11. Relief Cook   *last three months of apprenticeship.*

SUGGESTED OUTLINE OF KITCHEN TRAINING

Within the Hotel or other Catering Establishment

Section (i) General. The following points should be borne in mind in every section of kitchen training:

1. Correct use of knives and other small utensils.
   Care, maintenance and proper use of knives, sharpeners, picks, openers, etc.

2. Underlying principles of cookery.
   (*a*) By this it is meant that the fundamental processes of cookery must be classified and developed in the training as distinct operations. (*b*) Preservation of food values.

3. All equipment and apparatus.
   (*a*) Principles of and method of working. (*b*) Maintenance and cleaning. (*c*) Scullery work. (*d*) Clothing.

4. Kitchen organisation.
   (*a*) Routine and plan of work. (*b*) Rosters. (*c*) Hygiene. (*d*) Stillroom work. (*d*) Avoidance of waste.

5. Compilation of menus.
   (*a*) Quantities for covers ordered. (*b*) Costs. (*c*) Balance—colour, variety, flavours, garnish, season, etc.

6. Culinary adjuncts. Origin, derivation and use.

7. Principles of good services.
   (*a*) Relationship between kitchen and room staff. (*b*) Check system for ordering. (*c*) Methods of service.

8. General.
   (*a*) Culinary vocabulary. (*b*) Quantities, methods, times, yields, temperatures, garnishes, in relation to all recipes and processes, should be given.

Section (ii) By Stages

1. Butchery preparation.
   (*a*) The various types of meat. Storage, quality, uses and weights of various cuts and preparation for kitchen. (*b*) Source and preparation of offals. (*c*) Production and use of by-products. (*d*) Pickling of meat. (*e*) Sausage manufacture.

2. Fish preparation.
   (*a*) The various types of fish. Storage, quality, uses and weights of various cuts and preparation for kitchen. (*b*) Preparation and

filleting (where appropriate) of all fish, including shellfish. (*c*) Smoking and brining of fish.

3. Poultry and Game preparation.

(*a*) The various types of poultry and game, including hare and rabbit; storage, quality, seasons, uses. (*b*) Preparation (cleaning and trussing) for the kitchen.

4. Larder.

Preparation and service of: (*a*) Hors d'œuvres and appetisers. (*b*) Mayonnaise and vinaigrette sauce groups. (*c*) Salads of all types. (*c*) Cold buffet work. (*e*) Sandwiches. (*f*) Appropriate dishes, including pies, for the kitchen.

5. Soup Corner.

Methods of preparation of: (*a*) The various stocks used for soups (meat, fish, poultry, game). (*b*) Clear soups, broths, purées, veloutés, cream soups, special soups (including chilled). (*c*) Garnishes for clear and thick soups, with their accompaniments and service.

6. Roast and Grill Corner.

Methods, preparation, service of and recipes for:

(*a*) All roast meat joints and garnishes. (*b*) All roast game and poultry dishes and garnishes. (*c*) Deep frying. All fritters. (*d*) All grills and garnishes. (*e*) All savouries and canapés. (*f*) Carving.

7. Vegetables; Eggs and Farinaceous Cookery.

Preparation, cooking and service of: (*a*) All root vegetables. (*b*) All green vegetables. (*c*) The mushroom family. (For these three, also attention to seasons, quality, storage, etc.) (*d*) Pulses. (*e*) Potato variations. (*f*) Frozen vegetables. (*g*) Various types of egg dishes. (*h*) Farinaceous products.

8. Fish Corner.

(*a*) Preparation, cooking and service of fish of all types, including shellfish where applicable, using the following methods: poaching, frying, baking, grilling, steaming, meunière, court-bouillon. (*b*) Appropriate sauces and garnishes.

9. Sauce Corner.

(*a*) Various types of roux and their preparation. (*b*) Preparation and cooking of espagnole, demi-glace, velouté jus lié, meat glaze. (*c*) Other basic sauces and derivatives. (*d*) All types of entrées and their preparation and cooking, with particular attention to the culinary processes involved.

10. Pastry.

Preparation, cooking and services of: (*a*) Various types of pastry. (*b*) Sponges, cakes, yeast mixtures. (*c*) Various types of pudding mixtures. (*d*) Hot and cold sauces. (*e*) Hot and cold sweets. (*f*) Compôtes and fruit dishes. (*g*) Various types of ices. (*h*) Soufflées. (*i*) Dessert fruits, including season and quality. (*j*) Elementary sugar work to include decoration. (*k*) Special pastry dishes.

11. Relief Cook.

This is the period of general revision, prior to completion of the apprenticeship.

Complementary training in technical institutions

Complementary training by part-time attendance at hotel schools or technical institutions with hotel and catering departments is an integral part of the apprenticeship training scheme. The Local Authority, through its education offices, can give full information about courses available in each district. Complementary training must normally be taken within the area of the Local Authority but if, for reason, say, of low demand for such training, it is not available in the immediate locality information about alternatives will be given. Employers (and their chefs de cuisine) are urged to familiarise themselves with the training provided by the educational institutions concerned, and to take an interest in the apprentices' studies.

The hotel and catering industry, nationally, has adopted the following syllabuses of the City and Guilds of London Institute in Basic Training in Cookery.

The *Recommended Training* for an apprentice registered by the Council is that he shall take Course No. 147, followed by Course No. 151.

Preliminary Trade Cookery (City and Guilds of London Institute, Course No. 147)

This course provides a good all-round training in the fundamental subjects of the kitchen, including cookery, commodities, kitchen organisation, simple calculations, hygiene and the use and care of kitchen equipment. Cookery provides over half of the time in the course.

This course is of particular value to the new entrant, in that it not only gives him training in the basic principles of cookery, but also, through the related subjects included, makes him aware of the theoretical basis to all that he does in the kitchen. The course is normally spread over two years of day-release teaching.

Cookery for Hotels and Catering Establishments (City and Guilds of London Institute, Course No. 151)

This course covers a general knowledge of methods of cookery, and the related subjects, comparable to the contents of Course No. 147, but taught at a more advanced level, including the presentation and service of complete meals. The standard of practical work in this course is high.

The course is intended to provide for the needs of cooks in hotels and catering establishments. The course may be spread over one or two years.

Subsequent training

The Apprenticeship Council is aware that from time to time particularly gifted apprentices may be able to complete the above training in sufficient time to allow them to take at the end of their apprenticeship the City and Guilds of London Institute, Course No. 152 (Advanced Cookery for Hotels and Restaurants), but in general they recommend that an apprentice who completes Course No. 151 proceeds at hotel school or technical college to a special course leading to Course No. 152, which he can take after the completion of apprenticeship.

Hospital cook apprenticeship

A similar scheme of national apprenticeship exists in the specialised field of hospital cookery. Details of this training are available from: National Joint Apprenticeship Committee for Cooks in Hospitals, 14 Russell Square, London, W.C.1.

Three-year training scheme

Whilst nationally approved apprenticeship seems to many to offer the best prospects of ultimately providing kitchen experts who will stay permanently in the kitchen to follow a career, there are other forms of training in cookery. 'House' apprentices and trainees may still be found despite the greater effectiveness and prestige of a national system and there is also a nationally approved alternative to full cookery apprenticeship, a three-year scheme.

Importantly, hotel schools and technical colleges now take a great part both in complementing apprenticeship training and (particularly in the case of older entrants on part-time courses) offering an efficient alternative to it. In this section these other training methods are outlined.

A three-year training scheme for cooks in hotels and catering establishments on apprenticeship lines has been evolved largely as a result of the demands of those hoteliers and restaurateurs with smaller establishments who could not offer training facilities suitable for the full five-year apprenticeship scheme and were, in any case, unlikely to be able to offer employment of the kind most likely to attract employees trained to these higher levels.

It has to be recognised, therefore, that the scheme's target is inevitably somewhat more modest than that possible under the full five-year apprenticeship arrangement. Those who embark on the shorter training may subsequently take additional steps to ensure their future advancement but it would seem that the scheme itself provides training sufficient only for work in smaller and more modest establishments.

Further details of this scheme, which has similarity (in its more limited way) to the five-year apprenticeship scheme, may be obtained from the Secretary, 24 Portman Square, London, W.1.

Hotel school and technical college training

Training at technical colleges and hotel schools is of two kinds. On the one hand full-time training which is primarily designed for those leaving school and, on the other hand, part-time training for those already engaged in cookery or in some other activity in the hotel and catering industry.

Full-time training

There are, of course, obvious advantages in full-time training. It is not within the scope of this Manual to deal with educational principle in detail but there is no doubt that those who can take the two two-year courses for chefs which exist at some of the full-time training centres are able to acquire a strong foundation of craft knowledge and skill relatively quickly and conveniently. They also benefit considerably from the general atmosphere and approach to work within a technical institution.

Though not always followed by apprenticeship, full-time craft training in hotel school or technical college is an excellent (indeed, the ideal) start and, as has been noted, the National Apprenticeship Scheme for Cooks recognises such training fully by reducing the length of apprenticeship by the number of years spent in full-time training. Details of colleges offering full-time training in cookery can be obtained from: The Training Officer, The Hotel and Catering Institute, 24 Portman Square, London, W.1.

Part-time training

Concurrent attendance at a technical institution is, as has been noted, an integral part of the national apprenticeship schemes and of the three-year training scheme for cooks. There are, however, in the United Kingdom, over 150 centres where part-time training is available for those already engaged as ordinary employees in the hotel and catering industry. Very many of these centres regard the provision of part-time training in cookery as one of the most important activities within their hotel and catering departments.

Proficiency pay

A powerful inducement to take part-time training is, of course, the fact that some sections of the hotel and catering industry already reward those who gain certain nationally recognised qualifications (mainly the City and Guilds of London certificates 147, 150, 151) by additional proficiency pay. A substantial number of such certificates are gained each year by those attending part-time courses at technical institutions.

The City and Guilds certificates in Cookery and Catering have already been briefly described earlier in this section and in the case of those who seek to gain them by part-time study, further information regarding facilities available locally may be obtained from the offices of the local education authorities or from the Training Officer of the Hotel and Catering Industry, 24 Portman Square, London, W.1.

Part-time courses for City and Guilds cookery certificates usually involve two attendances a week for three hours per attendance. Evening classes are frequently held between the hours of 6 and 9 p.m., but it is to be hoped that there will be an increasing demand for part-time classes during the day as a result of greater support and encouragement by employers, and chefs de cuisine and other executives in the hotel and catering industry and a growing readiness on their part to afford the necessary facilities and encouragement for staff to attend.

Part-time courses usually extend over two full academic years or sessions and begin normally at the opening of the academic year in September and close in the June or July of the following calendar year. The academic year or session is broken by vacations and commonly consists of three terms of approximately twelve weeks per term.

The widespread availability of part-time training may be considered as one of the factors which will enable the craft or profession of cookery to receive new blood and reinforcement. Chefs de cuisine should, of course, guard and maintain their craft standards and be particularly

zealous in cherishing apprenticeship as an important means of qualifying. They should not, however, deny to ambitious employees in
humbler roles in the kitchen (or other departments of the hotel) the
right to improve themselves with a view to gaining chef status through
less conventional means and aided by part-time study and training.

Continental training and experience abroad

Continental hotel schooling

Before the last war many young hotel executives sought training in
continental hotel schools for the good reason that they offered a facility
which was not then available in this country. Training in French,
Swiss and other schools was not, however, sought to the same extent
by those seeking specialised training as chefs. This may be due to the
fact that before the war the one institution in the United Kingdom
offering full-time training along hotel lines stipulated a low age of
entry; thus appearing to indicate that it was concerned with the training
of craftsmen rather than potential executives. This school, The Westminster Technical College Hotel School, earned (and still enjoys) a
first-class reputation for the training of chefs and there was consequently little inducement for aspiring kitchen craftsmen to go overseas
for basic craft schooling.

Today the position is even better for not only are there increased
facilities in Britain for training as chefs in technical institutions but the
emergence of first-class hotel schools for the training of potential
executives has obviated the need even for the managerial prospect to
enter continental hotel schools.

Foreign experience

The advantages of hotel and restaurant experience abroad (and its
attractions for the young travel-minded recruit) remain strong. The
opportunity to see other countries, other techniques and standards and
to become adventurous in food as in other matters still cause young
men with kitchen ambitions to go abroad during the early years of
their training.

In some cases this is a result of arrangements made by hotel schools
in Britain with their counterparts abroad. (The Scottish Hotel School,
for example, has in recent years made exchange arrangements for hotel
work during the long summer vacation in association with hotel
schools in France and Sweden.) Under these arrangements students
work in seasonal hotels during their holidays to augment training they
get during their course of study.

B.H.R.A. exchange scheme

By far the most important and usual way for young kitchen employees to go abroad is, however, through the exchange scheme operated in this country under the auspices of the British Hotels and Restaurants Association. Further information regarding foreign exchanges may be obtained from the association's headquarters at 88 Brook Street, London, W.1.

It is, perhaps, worth stressing that the facilities for gaining training and experience both in hotel schools and in hotel and catering establishments in this country are such as to attract large numbers of continentals each year. In other words, this is very much a two-way traffic at the present time in which there is no question of trainees from this country requiring to go abroad because of lack of opportunity to learn and train here but simply that many countries realise that they have much to learn from each other and reciprocate on a free and equal basis.

It should certainly not be necessary today to advise any youngster initially to enter an hotel school abroad for first-class training of that kind is available here. On the other hand it can be wholeheartedly recommended that following such training or other apprenticeship early in a career, experience in kitchens abroad should be gained (and fortunately can be quite easily gained) by our young chefs and would-be chefs.

The training position summarised

In this section there has been a backward glance at the traditional concept of apprentice training in the 'French' manner, the 'house' apprenticeship and a review of the modern well-planned National Apprenticeship scheme which is supported by enlightened employers, employees (through their trade unions), the government (through the Ministry of Labour) and employees themselves through trade union representation. There are always those who tend to be nostalgic regarding past times and past methods and it often seems to the older generation that the 'masters' and methods of their youth were more giant-like than those of the present.

In evoking a memory of the older systems of training, tribute has been rightly paid to the high concepts of craftsmanship and disciplined work that it involved. There is no doubt, however, that some of the old-time 'on-the-job' training methods were extremely onerous. A vivid but unsympathetic picture of conditions in the early part of the century in both French and English hotel kitchens is, for example, given by Pierre Hamp in his biographical work *Kitchen Prelude* (Constable).

That the art of cookery seems to be emerging from the doldrums in this country would appear to be due almost entirely to the effort being made to break new ground in training through the improved National Apprenticeship schemes, the high level of facilities at hotel schools and technical colleges and the constant efforts to attract the better type of youngster into professional kitchens.

Training, therefore, is at the very root of improved food and service in this country and it should be the prime concern of the up-to-date, efficient and far-sighted chef de cuisine to be well-informed about facilities, qualifications to be gained and other aspects of national and local training programmes. Chefs, as other departmental executives must, however, be mindful that training is not something to be left to the hotel schools and technical colleges alone, nor even to those hotel and catering establishments participating (because of their size and standard) in the bigger apprenticeship schemes. They should, rather, regard it as a matter of partnership involving every qualified chef and every good kitchen.

Executive chefs as well as employers will also be wise to remember that training alone is not a sufficient inducement always to attract the right type of ambitious young entrant and that the way in which the recruit is received into the kitchens and the career prospects in material and non-material terms are of vital importance. Good working conditions, opportunity for promotion and reasonable welfare amenities are important in themselves. Because, too, these factors contribute strongly to craft prestige they will further encourage recruitment to the kitchens. What is more they will persuade those recruited to continue training in their chosen craft of cookery and to remain in that field of work.

Employment, bureaux and chef societies

Since the war and until quite recently the wages of chefs as of other categories of employees in the hotel and catering industry were controlled by statutory regulations under the Catering Wages Act, 1943. In 1959 this Act was repealed and the Wages Boards which had been set up under it were converted into Wages Councils. These Councils which vary in their composition according to the section of the industry, operate in a manner similar to the former Wages Boards and in effect determine wages and conditions of employment much as if the old Act still operated. Details regarding current statutory requirements governing pay and conditions may be obtained in literature published by Her Majesty's Stationery Office (particularly *Terms and Conditions of Employment Act,* 1959).

In fact, for chefs in hotels and restaurants (and, indeed, in some other sections of the catering industry) wages regulations are largely indicative of minimum rates of pay because, since the war, good chefs and good cooks have been at a premium and employers generally offer much more attractive wages than the minimum laid down under the regulations.

Because there has been a shortage of skilled and experienced kitchen craftsmen, employment bureaux have, during the past decade or so, tended to be of more use to employers than to chefs de parties and cooks. Nevertheless, prevailing rates of pay, conditions of employment and the means by which employment may be secured or changed are matters with which employees, particularly those who aspire to assume responsibilities should become acquainted.

Hotel and Catering Trades Employment Exchange

The hotel and catering industry is regarded as unique in several respects but there is one in which it is indisputably different. It is the only industry for which the Ministry of Labour has set up a specialist employment exchange. The Hotel and Catering Trades Employment Exchange was established at Denmark Street, London, W.C.1, in 1930 for the specialised work of placing into employment hotel and catering employees from managerial level to less skilled categories. Though situated in London, 'Denmark Street' is responsible for its specialised work throughout southern England, the Midlands and part of Wales. In the north of England, Leece Street Employment Exchange, Liverpool, has a hotel section which is able to maintain contact with Denmark Street and in Glasgow the hotel section of the Central Employment Exchange is also able to draw on the specialist knowledge of the London office.

The Denmark Street Employment Exchange caters for all categories of employees from the age of eighteen and above in hotels and restaurants, licensed houses, industrial catering establishments, and has three main departments in order to give maximum service to employers and employees alike. It should be realised, for example, that the appointments department responsible for senior grades of staff handles a vast number of important posts of managers, *chefs de cuisine* and heads of departments such as housekeepers, head receptionists as well as hotel office and administrative staff. The women's department and the men's department naturally deal with many types of hotels and restaurants and catering employees but provide a particularly useful service as far as the cuisine is concerned in dealing not only with cooks but with semi-skilled and less skilled kitchen assistants of various kinds.

Not only can the Ministry of Labour, through its specialist office in Denmark Street and the hotel sections of employment exchanges in the principal cities, help in routine staffing matters but (and this is particularly true of Denmark Street) give most useful advice in personnel matters based on specialist experience and study over many years, including the seasonal availability of labour and employment conditions in various parts of the country or overseas. Advice is also available regarding training and contact can be arranged with Youth Employment Officers. Welfare matters, training of the disabled and foreign labour and labour permits are all matters in which Denmark Street can help or advise.

Mention should also be made of the work of the private employment bureau for the long-established firms of repute who have specialised in work for the hotel and catering industry have given useful service over the years.

Licensed appointments bureaux

Perhaps the best known of the private agencies in London is the Alfred Marks Bureau Ltd, 8 & 9 Frith Street, Soho Square, W.1. This bureau was founded in 1919 by the late Alfred Marks (whose family still conduct the business today) with the aim of offering a complete service of staff, kitchen and otherwise to the hotel and catering industry.

The bureau met an obvious need and was, therefore, almost immediately successful. It developed steadily in size and importance to become, in the 1930s, what was claimed to be the 'largest specialised organisation of its kind in the world'.

The service of staff which the bureau sets out to provide is completely comprehensive. As far as the kitchens are concerned the service ranges from the provision of unskilled kitchen porters to arranging the appointments of chefs de cuisine of major West-End hotels. Additionally, an overseas department is operated by the bureau and deals constantly with vacancies for chefs and chefs de parties from such places as British West Indies, U.S.A., Canada, South Africa, Australia, India, North Africa, Middle East, West Africa, etc. Overseas employers almost invariably leave the selection of chef or other personnel they require in the hands of the bureau.

Another agency which has specialised in and developed strongly a service in catering staff is the Burnett Bureau Ltd, 77 Dean Street, Oxford Street, London, W.1.

The advertisements of others may also be found in the Situations Vacant and Wanted columns of the weekly trade paper, *The Caterer and Hotelkeeper*. The classified advertisement sections of other trade papers and the daily press (the *Daily Telegraph* has a specialised section for hotels and catering staff) are also useful sources of information about appointments.

The operation of private employment agencies is subjected to statutory safeguards and in London, for example, they are required to be licensed each year by the London County Council. The L.C.C. satisfy themselves that bureaux are conducted in a proper manner. In making use of privately owned employment agencies both chefs and employers should, of course, make sure that they clearly understand the terms (particularly relating to fees) on which the service is provided. Fees have tended to alter according to the laws of supply and demand. In the days when kitchen staff was much more freely available it was invariably a service for which the employee had to pay but today some agencies are prepared to make no charge to trained or scarce staff but will gain their remuneration from the employer whose need is greatest.

There are some who are cynical about the fee aspect in relation to job finding and staff placement but certainly in the case of the larger and better-known bureaux a useful, worthwhile and ethical service is provided which assists both employers and employees alike. Both sides will, however, do well to approach with caution lesser-known agencies and 'consultants'.

Culinary and other associations

One of the useful functions of chef associations and trade associations is to assist in the matter of securing appropriate employment for their members or aiding members to find suitable staff.

Before the Second World War there were a number of culinary and catering associations serving the interests of cooks of different nationalities. The Swiss and Italian chefs, for example, were organised for social and other purposes in London. Since the war and with the diminution in the numbers of foreign chefs employed in Britain there has been a corresponding decrease in activity of this kind.

The Association Culinaire Française

The sole remaining chef society with a distinctively foreign flavour is the long-established Association Culinaire Française which represents the old French, culinary tradition in London. The Association has, however, in recent years, begun to admit chefs not of French origin. The headquarters of the Association is at 99a Charing Cross Road, London, W.C.2.

Conseil Culinaire Français de Grand Bretagne

The council was formed in 1952 as a result of an idea put forward by M. Henri Malet to the Association Culinaire Française with a view to recognising culinary craftsmen of all nations. M. A. Avignon was the first President and many distinguished names were in the first committee of the Council.

International Society of Chefs de Cuisine and Association of Cooks in Great Britain

This society has been developed from the former International Academy of Chefs de Cuisine which was founded by Jean Conil at the end of the last war. It is registered under the Friendly Societies Act and its aims might be summarised as the advancement of cookery and promoting the interests of chefs irrespective of nationality. Its main contributions in recent years to the advancement of cookery have been in organising and participating in cookery competitions.

The Cookery and Food Association

This association reached the peak of its power and influence as far as chefs and cooks were concerned in the time of Charles Herman Senn and when it was known as the Universal Food and Cookery Association. In those days the Association was strongly supported by chefs themselves and under the leadership of men like Senn and later Ivan Kriens, accomplished pioneer work in the establishment of training and professional standing for men of the kitchen. The Association was, in fact, largely responsible for the founding of the first Hotel School in Great Britain, that at Westminster Technical Institution. In recent years it has again expanded in membership and still plays a lively part in the Salon Culinaire Internationale de Londres for which purpose the Association originally came into being. It has, however, become more generally interested in catering and does not appear to be so clearly identified with chefs and cooks as such. The Association has an appointments bureau.

The Hotel and Catering Institute

The Institute is not, of course, a Trade Association but a professional body of qualified hoteliers and caterers. Prior to the introduction of its examination scheme it admitted chefs into various degrees of membership. Today, however, kitchen specialists would require to study hotel-keeping or catering more widely if they were to secure membership by examination.

The Institute has, however, done a great deal to promote culinary training and many chefs who are anxious to have recognition of their professional standing are hopeful that the possibility of offering specialist membership for leading staff in the cuisine (as in other departments of hotel and restaurant and catering activity) may ultimately be reconsidered.

Other associations

Many other catering associations exist which are actively concerned with specialist fields such as hospitals, industrial and institutional catering and to which in certain cases chefs and cooks or former chefs and cooks may belong.* There are not, however, any other associations in which kitchen staff as such take the dominant part.

It would seem to be the case that the leaders of the culinary profession have not, as yet, fully responded to the challenge which the growth and development of catering in this country has brought. Perhaps, because of the tradition of grouping societies by nationality or because

---

* Such associations include: Hospital Caterers Association (Hon. Sec., H. E. Taylor, 115 The Strand, W.C.2); Industrial Catering Association, 53–54 King William St., London, E.C.2; National Caterers Federation, 156 Camden High St, London, N.W.1; Catering Managers Association of Great Britain (Hon. Sec., Miss A. McMichen, Ruchill Hospital, Glasgow, N.W.).

of the absence of individual enthusiasts like Senn, the development of one supreme chef association in which culinary interests are absolutely dominant has lagged behind the progress made by the Hotel and Catering Institute, for example, and by other major trade and personnel organisations.

It would seem that there is still room for an association with simple membership qualifications such as the completion of National Apprenticeship, completion of approved training at a hotel school, the holding of City and Guilds Certificates in trade cookery (to the exclusion of those with broader catering interests) so that cooks and cookery can become a more closely knit unity with a more effective voice and influence. Where such measures have been essayed (in, for example, the Cookery and Food Association a few years ago) there has been an immediate response but there are still not sufficient signs of resolute leadership to harness the aspirations and hopes of trained kitchen staff.

Glossary of Kitchen Terms

NOTE: The following list of words and terms is not intended to be exhaustive but is regarded as constituting a basic technical vocabulary as used in the professional kitchen or as encountered in professional cookery books of the past and present. It should be regarded merely as interpreting some commonly encountered technical jargon. It has consequently not been complicated by the addition of grammatical, etymological or phonetic information. It may be assumed that the words are French (or of French origin) unless otherwise stated.

A

ABAISSE. A piece of paste rolled to required size ready for use

ABAISSER. To roll (pastry)

ABATS. Offal such as liver, heart, tripe, etc.

ABATTIS (DE VOLAILLE). Trimmings (of poultry, winglets, giblets)

ABOYEUR. The kitchen clerk who calls the orders from the hotplate

ABRICOT. Apricot

AGITER. To stir

AIGREFIN. Haddock

AIGRETTES. Cheese Fritters

AIGUILLE À BRIDER. Larding needle

AIGUILLETTES. Meat, fish or poultry cut into fine strips

AIL. Garlic

AJOUTER. To add (an ingredient when cooking)

AILERONS. Chicken Suprêmes to which the wingbone is left attached, also commonly used for winglets of chicken

AIRELLE ROUGE. Cranberry

AGNEAU. Lamb

À LA. In the style, e.g., à la Française, in the French manner

À LA CARTE. Literally 'from the card', the menu which lists the entire resources of the kitchen and from which the customer can compose his own menu as distinct from the set, 'table d'hôte' meal

ALOSE. Shad

ALLUMETTES. Strips cut to match size (commonly for potatoes)

ALOYAU. Sirloin of beef

ALYCOT. A dish of giblets and liver (speciality of south-west France)

AMALGAMER. To mix together several ingredients

AMEAUX. Puff pastry incorporating eggs

AMOURETTES. Pieces of marrow from the spinal bone of ox or calf

ANCHOIS. Anchovy

ANCHOIADE. Anchovy flavoured fish dish

ANDOUILLE. A type of pork chitterling sausage

ANDOUILLETTE. Similar, but usually smaller than andouille

ANGÉLIQUE. Angelica

ANGLAIS (À L'). (1) English style, plainly cooked, e.g., boiled, deep-fried, plainly roasted. (2) Egg and breadcrumbing for deep frying. (3) Eggs, oil and seasoning beaten together

ANGUILLE. Eel

ANIMELLES. Lamb's fry

ANIS. Aniseed

ANNONCER. To announce (to call out orders)

APPAREIL. A mixture of various ingredients assembled to prepare a dish. Hence, the appareil à soufflé (ingredients and materials for soufflé making), etc.

APPLIQUER. To apply

APPROCHER. To truss the limbs of poultry and game close to the body

AROMATES. Sweet-smelling herbs, spices and flavourings

ARRÊTER. To stop (in cooking by, for example, adding cold water)

ARROSER. To sprinkle or baste

ARTICHAUT. Globe artichoke

ASPIC. A gelatine or calves' feet preparation for dressing cold dishes

ASPERGE. Asparagus

ASSAISONNER. To season

ATTERAUX (DE RIS DE VEAU). Roundels (of sweetbreads)

ASSIETTE. Plate or dish

ASSIETTE ANGLAISE. Dish of assorted cold meats

AUBERGINE. Egg plant

AU BLEU. Terms used to describe mode of cooking fish (especially trout) when live, in a plain court-bouillon (q.v.)

AU FOUR. Literally 'in the oven', hence baked (e.g., pommes au four—baked jacket potatoes)

B

BABA. A light sponge cake leavened with yeast, usually containing currants and normally served soaked in rum flavoured syrup

BABEURRE. Buttermilk

BAIN-MARIE. A double saucepan for slow cooking and when direct boiling is to be avoided. Also a container for boiling water in which smaller pans and their contents are kept hot

BALLOTINE. Meat, usually chicken or larger game birds, boned and stuffed

BANDE. Paste cut into narrow length, thus Bande aux Fruits (a narrow type of flan)

BAQUET. Bucket, usually a mould of finger biscuits, almond paste, etc., to present a preparation (for example, Chantilly cream) of the pâtissier

BAR. Bass

BAR RAYÉ. Rock salmon

BARBEAU. Barbel

BARBUE. Brill

BARDER. To cover (usually game birds) with slices of pork, back fat or fat bacon

BARDES (DE LARDE). Thin slices of back fat or bacon cut to required size for covering game birds prior to roasting

BARDETTE. A dish of stuffed cabbage

BARON. Of mutton or lamb, the saddle with legs attached; of beef, double sirloin

BARQUETTE. A small boat-shaped piece of pastry, etc.

BASILIC. Basil

BATON. Stick (commonly denotes small stick garnish)

BATTERIE DE CUISINE. Kitchen equipment (see Chapter 13 for further list of terms)

BAVAROIS. 'Bavarian Cream', a dessert made principally with egg, gelatine cream

BAVETTE. Thin flank of beef

BÉCASSE. Woodcock

BÉCASSINE. Snipe

BÉCHAMEL. The basic savoury milk sauce, a white sauce, one of the foundation sauces

BEIGNET. A Fritter

BETTERAVE. Beetroot

BEURRÉE. Buttered, basted or sprinkled with butter

BEURRE MANIÉ. Butter worked to a blend with flour and used for thickening sauces

BIEN CUIT. Well or thoroughly cooked

BIFTECK. Steak

BISCOTTE. Rusk

BISQUE. A type of thickened soup normally made from shellfish, e.g., Bisque d'Homard (lobster soup)

BLANC. Water thickened with flour and water paste and acidulated with lemon juice (used to cook vegetables such as Jerusalem artichokes to keep them white)

BLANCHAILLE. Whitebait

BLANC D'ŒUF. White of egg

BLANCHIR. To blanch (meat, vegetables, etc.) by immersing in cold water, bringing to boil, draining and 'refreshing' by re-immersion in cold water

BLANQUETTE. A white stew of white meat such as veal and being made from cubes of meat trimmed free of bone

BLEU. Blue (when applied to grilled meat such as steak, very underdone)

BLINIS. Yeast-leavened flour, water and egg paste, cooked pancake style and served hot with caviar

BŒUF. Beef

BOMBES. Originally bomb-shaped ices now commonly made in shell-shaped mould

BOMBAY DUCK. Dried, salt fish, served with curries

BORDURE. Border, usually decorative, e.g., a bordure of pommes Duchesse

BOUCHÉES. Small puff pastry patty cases usually stuffed with chopped poultry, fish or meat dressed in sauce

BOUDIN, BLANC. White sausage

BOUDIN, NOIR. Blood sausage or black pudding

BOULANGER. Baker

BOUQUET GARNI. Faggot of herbs. A small bundle of kitchen herbs such as bay leaf, thyme, parsley tied within strips of celery or leek

BOUILLIR, BOUILLI. To boil, boiled

BOUILLON. Clear meat stock or soup

BOUILLABAISSE. A fish stew, a speciality of the Marseilles region

BOURGEOISE. Dish prepared in 'bourgeois' style, methods originating from French family cookery

BOURGOGNE. Burgundy (wine)

BOUTONS (DE BRUXELLES). Buttons (of Brussels), poetic menu term for Brussels sprouts

BRAISER. To braise, i.e., cook slowly in closed vessel

BRAISIÈRE. Braising dish

BRANDADE. Dish of cod (salted) with garlic and oil

BRÈME. Bream

BRIDER. To truss (poultry, etc.) with needle and string, see also trousser

BRIOCHE. Yeast-leavened sponge

BROCHE. Spit, hence à la broche, meaning roasted by traditional spit means. The term 'broche' is also sometimes used to indicate the clear gravy of the roast dish

BROCHETTE. Skewer (hence à la brochette, cooked on a skewer)

BRUNOISE. A garnish (usually vegetables) cut into fine dice

BRUT. Coarse

BRUXELLOISE, À LA. In the Brussels style

C

CABILLAUD. Codfish

CAILLE. Quail

CANAPÉS. Pieces of toasted or fried bread or pastry garnished and served as appetisers, hors d'œuvres or snacks

CANARD. Duck

CANARD SAUVAGE. Wild duck

CANDIR. To candy (fruit for candied fruit)

CANETON. Duckling (male)

CANTALOUP. Melon

CARAMEL. Last stage in cooking sugar when it reaches brown shade

CARAMELISER. To caramelise, i.e., to cook sugar until it is coloured

CARBONNADE. Stewed or braised meat. Commonly steak cooked with beer

CARCASSE. Carcase (poultry) without its meat, also bony structure of shellfish

CARMINE. Red colouring

CAROLINE. Small appetisers made from choux paste and savoury filling

CARPE. Carp

CARRÉ. Best end of lamb (or veal), i.e., the small 'square' (hence the name) joint cut from the best end and consisting only of joined cutlets trimmed of chine bone

CARRELET. Flounder

CARTOUCHE. A greased round of paper for covering meat dishes during cooking

CASSEROLE. Fireproof dish, hence the name of dishes cooked in casseroles

CASSIS. Blackcurrant (and blackcurrant liqueur)

CASSISSINE. Blackcurrant-flavoured jelly

CASSOLETTES. Small casseroles for individual portions, thus hot savouries (hors d'œuvres) of small, round casserole shape

CASSOULET. Type of braised dish featuring haricot beans often with pork, mutton or goose

CÉLERI. Celery

CÉLERI RAVE. Celeriac or celery root. A turnip-like rooted celery

CÈPE. Edible fungus, a kind of yellowish flap mushroom

CERFEUIL. Chervil

CERISE. Cherry

CERNER. To make incisions lightly on raw puff paste

CERVALAS. Saveloy-type sausage

CERVELLE. Brain

CHAMPIGNON. Mushroom

CHANTERELLES. Mushrooms (Cantharellus variety)

CHANTILLY. Cream whipped with a little sugar

CHAUDFROID. Cooked food served cold, usually coated with cold sauce

CAYENNE. A very hot, red pepper

CHAPELURE. Fine breadcrumbs made by crushing oven-dried slices of bread

CHAPON. Capon (castrated cockerel); also used to describe bread crust, rubbed with garlic and boiled in soup

CHARCUTIER. Pork butcher and sausage maker, hence *charcuterie* (pork butcher's shop)

CHARTREUSE. Moulds made of Bavarois-type mixtures and garnished and decorated

CHÂTEAUBRIAND. Double steak cut from the 'head' or thick end of the beef fillet or undercut

CHEFS. See Chapters 4, 5 and 6 for definitions of the various chefs

CHEMISER. To line a mould with a thin layer of a substance such as jelly, aspic or ice cream

CHEVREUIL. Venison

CHICORÉE. Endive

CHIFFONADE. Lettuce or sorrel cut into thin ribbons cooked in butter for a soup or sauce garnish

CHINOIS. (1) A conical strainer (literally Chinese, apparently from shape of strainer resembling Chinese coolie hat). (2) A type of small preserved orange

CHIPOLATA. A type of small sausage

CHOUCROÛTE. Sauerkraut, cabbage pickled by special process involving fermentation

CHOU-FLEUR. Cauliflower

CHOU. Cabbage, but also a type of pastry made with eggs used for éclairs, profiteroles, etc.

CHOU-FRISÉ. Curly Kale

CHOUX DE BRUXELLES. Brussels Sprouts

CHOU DE MER. Seakale

CIVET. A brown stew of jugged hare or other game

CISELER. To slice finely (particularly lettuce, sorrel)

CLARIFIER. To clarify or clear liquids, e.g., consommé with minced raw beef and egg white

CLOUTER. To pierce meat or poultry with small holes and insert pieces of bacon, truffle, etc., hence oignon clouté—onion stuck with cloves

COCOTTE. A small ovenproof glazed dish

CŒUR. Heart, hence cœur de laitue, etc., heart of lettuce

COLIN. Coal fish

COLLER. To thicken a sauce

COLLET. Neck of veal

COMMIS. An assistant, hence commis chef—assistant chef

COMPÔTE. Stewed fruit (also, less frequently, other stews)

CONCASSER. To chop roughly (commonly tomatoes)

CONCOMBRE. Cucumber

CONDENSER. To condense, to reduce, e.g., by boiling and evaporating

CONFIR. To preserve by coating in sugar (e.g., confits of almonds or fruits)

CONFIT D'OIE. Goose cured, cooked and preserved in its own rendered fat

CONFITURE. Jam

CONGRE. Conger Eel

CONTISER. The process of making incisions at regular intervals for the insertion of truffle, garlic or other material

CONTRE-FILET. That part of the boned sirloin which faces the fillet or undercut

COQ (AU VIN). Cock (cooked in wine)

COQ DE BRUYÈRE. Blackcock

COQ DES BOIS. Capercailzie

COQUELET. Cockerel

COQUILLE. A shell, usually a scallop shell, hence a dish cooked and served in a shell

COQUILLE ST JAQUES. A scallop

CORBEILLE. Basket

CORDÉ. Rubbery condition of pastry when worked too much and too quickly and gluten has been developed

CORDON. Literally ribbon. Usually refers to a thread of sauce poured round dish

CORDON BLEU. A title used to describe a woman cook of skill

CORSER. To flavour and enrich

CÔTE. A side cut of meat. A piece of meat with the ribs attached, thus Côte de bœuf

CÔTE D'ALOYAU. Wing ribs of beef

CÔTELETTE. Cutlet

COTIGNAC. Quince Jelly

COULIBIAC (DE SAUMON). A method of cooking salmon in brioche paste

COULIS. Cullis. The result of reducing meat and fish liquors usually thickened
and garnished with strips of the meat or fish concerned

CÔTE COUVERTE. Fore-rib of beef

CÔTE DÉCOUVERTE. Middle rib cut of beef

CÔTE DU COLLIER. Chuck ribs

COUPEAUX. Parings

COUPER. To cut

COUPES. Bowls (individual) for serving ices

COURGE. Marrow

COURGETTE. Young marrow

COURT-BOUILLON. A light stock of water, vinegar or wine, herbs and seasoning
for poaching fish

CRABE. Crab

CRÈME. Cream

CRÈME PÂTISSIER. A custard-like filling cream

CRÈPES. Pancakes

CRÉPINE. Part of pig's intestines (pig's caul) used as casing for sausage and force-
meat

CREPINETTES. Individual portions of meat, chicken or pork enveloped in crépine

CRÊTES DE COQ. Cocks' combs—used as a garnish

CREVER. To par-cook rice

CREVETTE (ROSE). Prawn

CREVETTE (GRISE). Shrimp

CROISSANTS. Crescent-shaped bread rolls

CROMESQUIS. (Kromeski), a type of deep-fried croquette

CROQUETTE. Minced or pounded foodstuffs, e.g., potato (or blends of foodstuffs,
e.g., ham and chicken) moulded, egg and crumbed and deep fried

CROÛTE AU POT. A beef broth, popular in France, garnished with vegetables and
dried crusts

CROUSTADES. Pastry crust, dishes topped with pastry crust

CROÛTES. Fried bread used for dishing small roast game birds, tournedos, etc.

CROÛTONS. (1) Fried pieces of bread of various sizes and shapes served as
accompaniments to soups, principally purées such as pea soup. (2) Also used
to denote pieces of aspic cut into small pieces for garnishing

CRU. Raw

CUIRE. To cook

CUIT. Cooked

CUISINIER. A cook

CUISSON. (1) The natural juices of meat or natural cooking liquor exuded as a
result of cooking. (2) Cooking time

CUISSE (AND CUISSOT). The leg or haunch of veal, beef, etc.

CULOTTE. Rump of beef

D

DARNE. A slice. Usually a thick middle cut of large fish such as salmon

DARIOLES. Small moulds of baba mould shape

D'ARTOIS. Puff pastry with ham (or occasionally savoury) filling

DAUBE (DE BŒUF). A form of braise (of beef)

DAUBIÈRE. Earthenware cooking vessel for the cooking of daubes

DÉBARASSER. To clear away

DÉBRIDER. To remove trussing string after cooking

DÉBRIS. Remains, trimmings, pickings

DÉCORER. To decorate

DÉCOUPER. To cut (pastry and cake edges)

DÉGLACER. To dilute (with wine, stock, etc.) the pan residue after cooking

DEGORGER. To seep in fresh water to remove impurities

DÉGRAISSER. To remove the grease from stews, stocks, sauces, etc.

DÉLICES. Menu term to describe fine pieces of fish or meat without bone, i.e., a
      picturesque term for fillets

DEMI-GLACE. Half glaze. Brown sauce

DEMI-TASSE. A small cup (literally a 'half' cup)

DÉPILER. To remove hairs and bristles (by scalding)

DÉPOUILLER. To remove scum from surface of liquid during cooking

DÉS. Dice

DESOSSER. To bone or fillet

DESPUMATE. To boil out sauce

DESSECHER. To dry

DIABLOTINS. Small pieces of Gnocchi or croutons sprinkled with grated cheese
      and browned

DINDE. Turkey

DINDONNEAU. Young Turkey

DORADE. John Dory

DORER. To gild. (1) To brush with egg wash or milk before baking. (2) To
      colour by frying or brushing with fat and placing under salamander

DRESSER. To dress (a dish for service)

DUXELLE. Chopped shallots and mushrooms cooked in butter

E

ÉBARBER. To beard shellfish, e.g., to remove the dark edge from oysters

ÉBOUILLANTER (OR ÉCHAUDER). To plunge food into boiling water to facilitate
      peeling

ÉCARLATE (À L'). Red (or scarlet) jelly napped over salted, cooked meat such as
      ox tongue

ÉCHALOTTE. Shallot

ÉCREVISSE. Crayfish

ÉCUMER. To remove scum from the surface of a stock

ÉCLAIRS. Choux pastry baked in thick fingers, filled with cream or crème
      patissier and covered with chocolate or icing

ÉMINCER. To mince, to cut as finely as possible

ÉGOUTTER. To drain, strain off liquid

ÉMONDER. To strip off useless branches

EMPATER. To cover with a paste

EN. In, served in

EN PAPILLOTE. In paper. Mode of cooking (particularly fish) in greased paper

ENROBER. To cover (with sauce)

EN TASSE. In cup

ENTIER. Whole

ENTRÉE. A principal course of meat or offal preceding the roast at luncheon or dinner

ENTRECÔTE. Steak cut from the contrefilet of beef

ENTRECÔTE MINUTE. Very thin entrecôte steak flattened for quick cooking

ENTREMETS. Sweets, also (now less commonly) dressed vegetables, egg dishes, savouries

ENTREMÉTIER. Cook who deals with vegetables and egg dishes

ENVELOPER. To wrap

ÉPAULE. Shoulder

ÉPERLAN. Smelt

ÉPLUCHER. To peel, trim and core fruit and vegetables

ÉPLUCHURES. Trimmings (commonly of truffles, mushrooms and tomatoes)

ÉPIGRAMME (D'AGNEAU). A portion of lamb consisting of a cutlet and a piece of breast cut to cutlet shape and size, cooked, egg and crumbed and sautéd

ÉPIGRAMME (DE PERDREAU). A portion of partridge involving suprêmes without bone and cutlets made from minced leg meat

ÉPINARDS. Spinach

ÉPOUDRER. To dust (with sugar or flour)

ESCALOPE. A collop or slice

ESCALOPER. To cut or form into small scallop shapes

ESCARGOT. Edible snail

ESPAGNOLE. Basic brown sauce

ESTOUFFADE. Brown meat stock

ESTURGEON. Sturgeon

ESTRAGON. Tarragon

ÉTUVER. To cook slowly under cover with minimum of added liquor

EXPRIMER. To express. To squeeze out

F

FAGOT. Faggot (of herbs), bouquet garni

FAIRE LEVER. To cause to rise (e.g., leaven with yeast)

FAIRE REVENIR. To par-fry and brown meat or vegetables without cooking through

FAIRE SUER. To sweat, to cook in butter without colouring

FAISAN. Pheasant

FAISANDÉ. 'High' or 'gamey', i.e., game allowed to decompose

FARCE. Stuffing or force-meat

FARCIR (FARCI). To stuff (stuffed)

FARINER. To dust or to coat with flour

FAUX-FILET. Sirloin boned out and with fillet removed (as contrefilet)

FÉCULE. Potato or starch flour used for thickening gravies, etc.

FENOUIL. Fennel

FEUILLETAGE. Puff pastry

FÈVE DES MARAIS. Broad bean

FILET. (1) Fillet. The most delicate cut of meat, poultry, etc., or the flesh of fish removed from bone. (2) A thread, referring to the thread of jus (rich gravy) or oil added to a dish normally at the last moment, thus filet de jus, filet d'huile

FILET MIGNON. Fillet from the saddle of lamb or mutton

FINES HERBES. Finely chopped tarragon, chervil, chives, parsley mixed together

FLAMBER. (1) To flame, i.e., to finish cooking by soaking the food in a spirit such as brandy and igniting. (2) To pass a bird through the flame to singe off hair, etc.

FLAN. Open Tart

FLANCHET. Beef skirt

FLÉTAN. Halibut

FLEURONS. Small fancy puff pastry shapes (usually crescent shaped)

FLUTE. Long, thin roll of crisp French bread of flute shape

FOIE. Liver

FOIE GRAS. Fat liver from specially reared geese

FONCER. To line the bottom of a cooking dish with bacon, etc., or the bottom of a mould with paste

FONDANT. (1) A kind of icing sugar. (2) In melting state

FONDS (DE CUISINE). (1) Basic stocks or essences. (2) Bottoms such as artichoke bottoms

FONDUE. (1) A cheese dish (Swiss) of melted Gruyère cheese. (2) Softened mashed state of vegetables after prolonged cooking

FONTAINE. The well or hole made in the dry flour, etc., before adding liquid to make pastry

FOUET DE PÂTISSERIE. Whisk of thin metal used in the pastry department for whipping cream, etc.

FOUETTER. To whip or whisk

FOURRER. To fill or to coat with sugar and cream

FRAISE. Strawberry

FRAMBOISE. Raspberry

FRANGIPANE. A custard-like pastrycook's cream

FRAPPÉ. Iced

FRAPPER. To ice

FRÉMIR. To simmer so gently that the cooking is barely visible

FRÉMISSEMENT. Beginning to boil

FRIAND. Gourmet

FRIANDS. Pies or pastries

FRIANDISES. Dainty items of food, particularly sweet. Petits fours (q.v.)

FRICANDEAU. Cushion or fillet of veal braised until very tender

FRICASSÉ. A white stew of white meats such as veal or chicken differing from a blanquette in that bone may be present with the meat

FRIRE. To fry

FRIT. Fried

FRITURE. (1) Deep frying pan. (2) A dish of fried whitebait

FUMER (FUMÉ). To smoke. (Smoked)

FUMET. Concentrated stock or essence particularly used of concentrated fish stock

G

GALANTINES. A preparation of stuffed chicken and veal in the form of a large roll usually glazed with chaudfroid sauce and decorated

GALETTES. Flat, pastry rolls

GARDE MANGER. The larder

GARBURE. A thick soup of vegetables

GARNIR (GARNI). To garnish (garnished)

GARNITURE. The garnish or surrounding dressing of a dish

GÂTEAU. A decorated cake

GAUFRE. A light sponge biscuit

GAUFRETTE. Wafer biscuit served with ices and other sweet dishes

GELÉE. Jelly

GELINOTTE. Hazel hen

GENOISE. A paste of sugar, eggs, butter and flour usually baked about $1\frac{3}{4}$ in. thick

GITE À LA NOIX. Silverside of beef

GIGOT. Leg (of lamb or mutton)

GLACE. Frozen or glazed

GLACE DE POISSON. Fish glaze or extract, made by reducing stock or fumet to the consistency of syrup

GLACE DE VIANDE. Meat glaze or extract, usually made by reducing meat stock to a dark, thick semi-liquid

GLACER. (1) To freeze or chill. (2) To glaze or cook in such a way as to acquire a rich, shiny surface. (a) For meats and poultry, by perpetually basting with own liquor. (b) For vegetables, by cooking until liquor is absorbed and a shiny coating remains. (c) By colouring under salamander or hot oven. (d) Painting hot or cold dishes with concentrated glazes or coating with aspic. (e) Sweets glazed with icing, fruit and sugar purées, etc.

GNOCCHI. Paste (usually of semolina or flour) of walnut size

GRATIN. Browned surface of foods formed by cooking in hot oven or under salamander

GRILLER (GRILLÉ). To grill (grilled)

GOUJON. Gudgeon, hence goujons and goujonettes de sole (or other fish) denoting that the sole (or other fish) has been cut into small strips (roughly of gudgeon size)

GRATINER. To brown a dish sprinkled with breadcrumbs and/or grated cheese under a salamander or in the oven

GROSEILLE. Currant

GROSEILLE À MAQUEREAU. Gooseberry

GROSEILLE VERTE. Gooseberry (Green)

GROS SEL. Freezing salt, coarse salt

GROS (f. GROSSE). Fat (Large)

H

HACHER. To chop finely

HACHIS. Mince, e.g., hachis de bœuf, minced beef

HARENG. Herring

HARICOT BLANC. Bean

HARICOT VERT. French bean

HATELET. A skewer, particularly a decorative silver skewer used in mounting buffet pieces

HOMARD. Lobster

HORS D'ŒUVRES. The first course or appetiser course usually in the form of a variety of cold, piquant dishes

HUITRE. Oyster

I

INCISER. To score, to make incisions on, for example, the skin or rind of joints, Fish, etc.

INFUSION. Infusion made by pouring boiling water on aromatic vegetable substances such as tea, mint, etc.

J

JAMBE. Leg (uncooked), shank

JARDINIÈRE. A garnish of mixed vegetables cut into small rectangular shapes

JARRET (DE VEAU). Knuckle or shin (of veal)

JAUNE D'ŒUF. Yolk of egg

JETER. To throw or spin sugar

JULIENNE. Garnish (of meat, vegetables, etc.) cut into fine strips

JUS. Gravy

JUS LIÉ. Thickened gravy

K

KACHE (DE SARRASIN). A preparation of cooked buckwheat paste cut into pieces and fried for use as soup garnish

KACHE (DE SEMOULE). A preparation of cooked semolina used in making coulibiac of salmon

KALTSCHALE. A wine and fruit cup including, *inter alia*, peaches, raspberries, red and white currants, white wine (infused with cinnamon) and champagne

KILKIS. Norwegian anchovies sold ready for serving

KROMESKI. A type of meat croquette

L

LAITANCE. Soft herring roe

LAITUE. Lettuce

LAMPROIE. Lamprey

LANGOUSTE. Crayfish

LANGUE. Tongue

LAPIN. Rabbit

LARD. Bacon or salt, fat pork

LARDER. To lard, i.e., to thread strips of fat with a larding needle into lean meat

LARDONS. Strips of pork back fat or bacon used for larding. Also used generally for small pieces of bacon

LAURIER. Bayleaf

LEVRAUT. Leveret, young hare

LIAISON. A thickening or binding agent, commonly egg yolk and cream or butter to thicken soups and sauces

LIÉ. Slightly thickened

LIER. To thicken (usually with fécule or egg)

LIÈVRE. Hare

LIMANDE. Dab, Lemon sole

LIT. Bed

M

MACEDOINE. Diced, mixed fruits or vegetables

MACERER. To macerate, to leave in prolonged contact such as soaking of fruit in liquors

MADELEINE. Small cake similar to queen cake baked in a small, scallop shell-shaped mould

MAIGRE. Lean (repas maigre—Lenten meal (without meat))

MAINTENON. A preparation of Béchamel sauce, eggs and soubise used to stuff dishes à la Maintenon

MAIS. Maize, sweet corn

MAÎTRE D'HOTEL. Restaurant manager

MANIÉ (BEURRE MANIÉ). Manipulated (butter worked to a cream with a spatula, with flour added if for thickening)

MANIER. To manipulate, particularly to work butter with a spatula

MAQUEREAU. Mackerel

MARINADE. Blend of liquids and flavourings used in marinating

MARINER. To marinate, to steep meat or game to become tender or flavoured in, for example, seasoned and flavoured oil, wine or vinegar

MARMITE. Earthenware stockpot

MARMITE, LA PETITE. A type of consommé cooked and served in a small earthenware pot

MARQUER. To set aside or earmark foodstuffs with their adjunct in readiness for cooking

MARRON. Chestnut

MASQUER. To coat or mask with sauce, jelly, etc.

MATIGNON. A preparation of carrot, onion, celery and thyme, bayleaf and ham cooked in butter and deglacéd with Madeira. Used for flavouring joints and birds in similar way to mirepoix

MEDAILLONS. Round, medal-shaped pieces of, for example, meat or meat preparation

MELANGER. To mix two or more ingredients together

MENTHE. Mint

MERLAN. Whiting

MERLUCHE. Hake

MEUNIÈRE. A method of cooking in which the article is dredged in flour and shallow fried in butter

MIGNONETTE. Whole peppercorns roughly ground

MIJOTER. To simmer very slowly

MILIEU. Middle (hence milieu d'aloyau, middle cut of sirloin)

MIREPOIX. A flavouring base to soups and sauces made by shallow-frying cubed ham or bacon scraps, vegetables and herbs

MIS EN PLACE. The kitchen expression for being prepared or to describe things properly in readiness for cooking and service

MITONNER. To steep and boil slowly for a long time

MODELER. To model (in paste, sugar, etc.)

MOELLE. Marrow from a beef shin bone

MOLLET. Soft boiled egg

MONDER. To clean, particularly in the sense of stripping off husk or skin from almonds, grain, etc.

MONDÉ. Stripped-off husk, envelope or skin

MONTER. The beating of cream, egg whites, etc.

MONTER AU BEURRE. To enrich a sauce or reduction by dropping in small pieces of butter and tossing to blend

MORTIFIER. To hang game, meat, etc., to become tender and flavoursome

MORUE. Salt cod

MOUILLER. To add liquid or moisten with stock as necessary for cooking

MOULE. Mussel

MOULIN. Mill. Commonly to denote pepper grinder

MOUSSERON. A type of mushroom

MOUSSELINE. (1) Smaller-sized mousse-type preparation, usually individual-sized portions and commonly served hot. (2) A sauce (hollandaise blended with cream)

MOUSSE. Literally froth or foam, hence sweet or savoury dish of that character prepared in moulds for service for several covers

MOUTON. Mutton

MULET. Mullet, grey

MUR. Ripe

MÛRE. Blackberry

N

NAPPÉ. A stage reached in the cooking of sugar or sugar preparations, the large thread stage

NAPPER. To coat with sauce, aspic, etc.

NAVARIN. A type of brown, lamb stew

NAVET. Turnip

NAVET SUÉDOIS. Swede

NOISETTE. Nut, or in reference to meat, a boneless delicate portion such as a cutlet trimmed of bone and excess fat.

NOIX DE VEAU. A cushion of veal, a cut from the rump

NOUGAT. A sugar confection containing nuts and often glacé cherries

NOQUES (AU PARMESAN). Light, nut-sized preparation of egg, butter and flour, nutmeg flavoured. They are poached and served with grated Parmesan cheese and beurre noisette

NOUILLES. Noodles

NYMPHES À L'AURORE. Escoffier's poetic designation for frogs' legs served cold, coated with pink chaudfroid sauce

O

OIE. Goose

OIGNON. Onion

OIGNON CLOUTÉ. Onion studded with cloves

OIGNON NOUVEAU. Spring Onion

OISON. Green Goose

OSEILLE. Sorrel

P

PAILLES. Straws (hence pommes pailles, deep fried straw potatoes)

PAILLETTES. Cheese straws

PAIN RASSIS. Stale bread

PALMETTES. Palm-shaped puff pastry pieces

PANADA. A binding agent, usually an extremely thick roux-made white sauce

PANAIS. Parsnip

PANER, PANÉ. To coat with breadcrumbs, breadcrumbed

PANIER. Basket, particularly the pulled sugar basket

PANNEQUETS. Pancakes

PANURE. As chapelure (q.v.) fine crumbs from oven-dried breads

PAPILLOTES. Paper case, en papillote—cooking in paper wrapping

PAPRIKA. Red, but mild, Hungarian pepper

PARER. To prepare (vegetables), to trim (meat, etc.), to remove irregularities of shape or waste matter

PARFUMER. To impart bouquet by addition of aromatic herbs, etc.

PARTIR. To brown meat over intense heat before oven-cooking

PARURES. Parings or trimmings either cooked or raw

PASSER. To pass, to sieve or to strain

PASSER (PASSER AU TAMIS). To strain through a sieve

PASSER À L'ÉTAMINE. To pass through tammy cloth

PASSER À L'ŒUF. To dip in egg (prior to crumbing)

PASTILLAGE. Confectionery pastes of sugar and gum used in modelling

PÂTE. Paste or pastry

PAUPIETTES. Thin flattened slices of meat, fish, etc., rolled and stuffed

PAYSANNE. A garnish of mixed vegetables of small, triangular-shaped slices

PÊCHE. Peach

PÉLAMIDE. Pilchard

PELER (AU MORTIER). To pound (in a mortar)

PERCHE. Perch

PERDREAU. Partridge

PERSIL. Parsley

PERSIL HACHÉ. Chopped parsley

PERSILLÉ. Sprinkled with chopped parsley (hence pommes persillées—boiled parsley potatoes)

PETITS FOURS. Small sweetmeats, tiny, glazed cakes, biscuits, dipped fruits, etc., accompanying the dessert course

PETITS POIS. Peas

PIÉCE MONTÉE. Food item (normally pâtisserie) mounted in architectural style

PIED. Foot

PIEDS DE BŒUF. Cowheels

PIEDS DE PORC. Trotters

PILAW, PILAFF. Rice cooked in stock and flavoured with onion, etc., and garnished

PIMENT. Capsicum

PINCER. (1) To adhere, in the case of a joint, to the roasting tin through the browned, escaped meat juices. Hence this term is also sometimes used to describe the colouring of meat under the salamander or in the oven before adding moisture to the dish. (2) To pinch pastry together to join and/or decorate it

PINTADE. Guinea fowl

PIQUER. To insert small pieces of fat or fat bacon into lean meat, etc., with a special needle

PLAQUE À ROTIR. Roasting tray

PLAT. Plate or dish

PLAT DE CUISSE. Silverside of beef

PLAT DRESSÉ. Dressed or decorated dish

PLAT DU JOUR. Dish of the day (speciality of the day)

PLAT À SAUTER. Sauté pan (see sauter)

PLIE. Plaice

PLIER. To fold

PLONGEUR. Scullery man

PLUCHE. Leaf or shred, particularly of chervil in soup garnish

PLUCHER. To peel

PLUVIER. Plover

POCHER. To poach, etc., to cook in liquid, simmering but not boiling

POÊLER. A method of oven-cooking similar to braising or pot roasting

POÊLONS À SUCRE. Sugar boiler

POINTE. (1) Tip (of a knife or of asparagus). (2) Tiny quantity, particularly of strong aromats such as cayenne or garlic

POIRE. Pear

POIREAU. Leek

POITRINE. Breast, hence also brisket

POIVRADE. Flavoured with pepper

POIVRE. Pepper

POMME. Apple. Also used in menus and in kitchen as short for pomme de terre

POMME DE TERRE. Potato

POJARSKI. A minced cutlet of veal reassembled on the cutlet bone

PORC. Pork

POTIRON. Pumpkin

POULARDE, POULARDINE. Young, fat chicken

POULE. Hen

POULET. Young chicken

POULET D'INDE. Young turkey

POUSSIN. Young, immature chicken

POTAGE. Soup

PRALINÉ. Toasted almonds in caramelised sugar, flavouring with toasted almonds

PRÉ-SALÉ. Refers to lamb or mutton raised in French sea-coast areas and deemed of high quality

PRINTANIER. Garnish of mixed spring vegetables cut to various shapes and sizes

PROFITEROLES. Choux paste usually in small or medium small shapes. When tiny used in soup garnish, when larger filled with cream and covered with chocolate (or chocolate sauce) as dessert

PRUNE. Plum

PRUNE DE DAMES. Damson

PURÉE. Mashed or sieved vegetables, fruit, etc.

Q

QUARTIER. Quarter. To divide or cut into quarters

QUARTIER D'AGNEAU, DE MOUTON. A quarter of lamb or mutton

QUENELLES. Small spoon-fashioned mousses of fish or flesh

QUEUE. Tail

QUICHE LORRAINE. Savoury flan of egg, ham and cheese

R

RABLE (DE LIÈVRE). Saddle (of hare)

RADIS. Radish

RAFFINADE. Refined sugar

RAFFINER, RAFFINÉ. To refine, refined

RAFRAÎCHIR. To refresh, commonly by plunging into cold water or surrounding with ice

RAIDER. To soften, to pass meat through heated butter. To stiffen and seal it without colouring

RAIFORT. Horseradish

RAIE. Skate

RAGOÛT. A type of savoury stew

RAMEQUIN. A tartlet of cheese and also a type of case for serving savouries, etc.

RAVIER. Literally radish dish, but used to denote hors d'œuvre dish

RAVIOLIS. A form of Italian paste, small diamond or square-shaped pieces with savoury stuffing

RÉCHAUFFER. To reheat

RÉCHAUFFÉ. Reheated

RECTIFIER. To correct (seasoning, shape, etc.)

RECHERCHÉ. Out of the ordinary, uncommonly fine

REDUCTION. The result of reducing

REDUIRE. To reduce. Stocks, sauces, etc., are reduced by evaporating caused by rapid boiling

REINE (OR POULET REINE). Chicken

REINE-CLAUDE. Greengage

RELEVÉ. The remove course, a course at dinner usually of large joints of butcher's meat

RENVERSER. To turn out

REPÈRE. Flour and water paste used for sealing cocotte lids in cooking dishes such as tripes à la mode de Caen

REVENIR. To fry quickly to colour

RILLETTES. Pâté of pork, potted pork

RIS. Sweetbreads

RISSOLER. To toss in hot fat to give brown colour

RIZOTTO. Italian dish of rice flavoured with tomato, cheese, etc.

ROBE. Dress, thus 'en robe', literally 'in dress' or to denote in jacket—jacket potatoes, or items covered in pastry

REPAS MAIGRE. Literally 'meagre meal' indicating one served during Lent or on other fast days

ROGNON. Kidney

ROGNONNADE (DE VEAU). Saddle (of veal) complete with kidneys

ROGNURES. Trimmings

ROMAINE. Cos lettuce

ROQUEFORT. A 'blue' French cheese, made from sheeps' milk

RÔTIR, RÔTI. To roast, roasted (the roast course on a menu)

RÔTISSEUR. Roast cook

ROUELLE. A round slice, e.g., when carrots, lemons are cut across or round slice of beef or veal (a cut from the silverside)

ROUGER. To redden

ROUGET. Red mullet

ROUX. Thickening agent made by stirring flour into melted butter or other fat

ROYALE. A kind of unsweetened or savoury custard cut into various shapes and used as a garnish

RUSSE. Stew pan

S

SABAYON. French version of Zabaglione (q.v.)

SAIGNANT. Underdone

SAISIR. To seal (meat) surfaces by fierce cooking

SAINT PIERRE. John Dory

SALAMANDRE. Salamander (a top-fired grill or glazer)

SALÉ. Salted

SALMIS. A type of game stew

SALMISIER. To pickle meat in brine

SALPICON. A mixture of various ingredients usually diced poultry or game or ham or tongue and mushrooms in sauce

SANGLER. To freeze by surrounding vessel with ice and freezing salt

SARCELLE. Teal

SAUCER. To sauce, to cover with sauce

SAUMON. Salmon

SAUGE. Sage

SAUMURE. Pickling liquor

SAUCISSES. Sausages

SAUCISSON. Cooked sausage

SAUERKRAUT. As choucroute (q.v.)

SAUTER. Literally to jump. In cooking by tossing in hot fat in a sauté pan

SAUTEUSE. Shallow pan with sloping sides. Vegetable stew pan

SAUTOIR. Another name for sauteuse

SAVARIN. Light yeast sponge (as baba mixture without currants). Usually baked in ring mould

SAVARIN MOULD. A circular ring- or crown-shaped mould

SEL. Salt

SELLE. Saddle (selle d'agneau—saddle of lamb)

SOIGNÉ. Highly finished, well done, prepared with care

SORBET. A water ice served towards the end of long and important dinners to stimulate appetite

SOUBISE. A thick sauce preparation of onions stewed in butter

SOUCHET. A fish stew resembling a fish soup with solid garnish

SOUFFLÉ. A light sponge confection either sweet or savoury owing its risen form to egg

SPATULE. Spatula, a flat spoon or knife

SUER. To sweat by cooking slowly in fat without colouring so that the juices are liberated

SUPRÊME. (1) The best part or fillet of meat, game or poultry or fish, e.g., the wing and breast of chicken with bone removed. (2) Used to describe a fine, white sauce made from cream. Cream and egg thickened chicken fumet

T

TABLE D'HÔTE. Literally the host's table, implying the set menu for the day, a meal of a given number of courses of limited choice at a fixed price

TAMISER. To sieve, to tammy

TAMPON. A bed of rice or vegetables on which meat, etc., is placed

TANCHE. Tench

TASSE. Cup, hence *en tasse*—served in a cup

TARTINE. Slice of bread

TÊTE (DE VEAU). Head (calf's head)

TENDRE DE TRANCHE. Topside of beef

TERRINE. Earthenware cooking vessel and hence designation of pâté cooked in a terrine

THON. Tunny fish

TIMBALE. A deep, straight-sided circular dish or mould (thimble shaped but, varying in size)

TOMATÉ. Flavoured with tomato or tomato purée

TOMBER. Literally to fall. Sometimes used to denote reducing and also tossing in an open pan

TOMBER À GLACÉ. Reduce to a glaze

TOPINAMBOUR. Jerusalem artichoke

TOURNÉ. Turned, e.g., when sauce, soup or stock has soured or when mayonnaise or hollandaise separates out in cooking

TOURNER. To turn, to shape vegetables with a knife. Also to turn sour

TOURNEDOS. A small steak consisting of a fairly thick, neat round slice from the tail or thin end of a beef fillet, grilled or sautéd and served as an entrée

TORREFIER. To scorch, to toast

TRANCHE. A slice

TRANCHER. To carve or slice

TRANCHEUR. Carver

TRANCHE DU CIMIER (DE BŒUF). Aitchbone of beef

TRANCHE GRASSE. Thick flank cut of beef

TRAVAILLER. To work, to manipulate or knead

TRITURER. As travailler, i.e., to work or knead, to reduce to powder or small pieces

TREMPER. To place foodstuffs in sauce, cream paste, etc. To steep or soak in liquid. To plunge blanched, fried potatoes into hot fat immediately before serving

TRONCON. A small, thick slice, usually applied to fish

TROUSSER. To truss (see also brider)

TRUFFE. Truffle, a delicate black fungus which grows underground

TRUITE. Trout

TRUITE SAUMONÉE. Salmon trout

TRUMEAU. Silverside of beef

TURBAN. Dishes moulded into turban shape, usually fillets of fish, poultry or game

TURBOTIÈRE. Turbot kettle

V

VANDOISE. Dace

VANNER. To blend by stirring with a spoon or spatula to ensure smoothness and prevent formation of surface skin

VARNISER. To varnish. Brush pastry with egg wash, milk, etc., to give shine when baked

VEAU. Veal

VELOUTÉ. Literally 'Velvet'—but used to denote smooth, thick-textured white soup or sauce

VESIGA. A preparation of dried sturgeon spine marrow

VERS DE CUISSON. Not quite cooked

VENAISON. Venison

VIDER. Disembowel, clean by gutting poultry, fish, etc.

VIENNOISE, À LA. In Viennese style

VOILER (VOILÉ). To veil (veiled), for example, with spun sugar

VOLAILLE. Chicken

VOL AU VENT. Puff pastry case

W

WATERZOI. A type of fish stew, usually fresh-water fish such as carp, eel, perch, pike, etc.

Z

ZABAGLIONE (ITALIAN). Sabayon (French). Italian dessert of wine-flavoured egg whisked over bain-marie

ZAMPINO. Italian charcutier's product of stuffed leg of pork

ZESTE. Zest, the outer rind of lemon or other citrus fruit

Index

The numerals in **bold** type refer to the *figure numbers* of the illustrations.